The Philosophy of Perception

Publications of the Austrian Ludwig Wittgenstein Society
New Series

―

Volume 26

The Philosophy of Perception

Proceedings of the 40th International Wittgenstein Symposium

Edited by
Christoph Limbeck-Lilienau and Friedrich Stadler

DE GRUYTER

ISBN 978-3-11-076348-5
e-ISBN (PDF) 978-3-11-065792-0
e-ISBN (EPUB) 978-3-11-065446-2
ISSN 2191-8449

Bibliographic information published by the Deutsche Nationalbibliothek
The Deutsche Nationalbibliothek lists this publication in the Deutsche Nationalbibliografie; detailed bibliographic data are available on the Internet at http://dnb.dnb.de.

© 2021 Walter de Gruyter GmbH, Berlin/Boston
This volume is text- and page-identical with the hardback published in 2019.
Printing and binding: CPI books GmbH, Leck

www.degruyter.com

Content

Editorial — IX

1 Objectivity and Realism

Tyler Burge
Perception: Ground of Empirical Objectivity — 3

Howard Robinson
Objectivity: How is it Possible? — 23

Olivier Massin
Realism's Kick — 39

Michael Schmitz
The Good, The Bad, and The Naïve — 57

2 Content and Intentionality

Michael Tye
How to Think About the Representational Content of Visual Experience — 77

Marcello Oreste Fiocco
Structure, Intentionality and the Given — 95

Guillaume Fréchette
Brentano on Perception and Illusion — 119

Sofia Miguens
The Problem with J. Searle's Idea That 'all Seeing is Seeing-as' (or What Wittgenstein *did not* Mean With the Duck-Rabbit) — 135

3 Perception, Cognition and Images

Uriah Kriegel
The Perception/Cognition Divide: One More Time, With Feeling —— 149

Pierre Jacob
Why Verbal Understanding is Unlikely to be an Extended Form of Perception —— 171

Mark Eli Kalderon
Sound and Image —— 189

4 The Cognitive Penetrability of Perception

Berit "Brit" Brogaard
Bias-Driven Attention, Cognitive Penetration and Epistemic Downgrading —— 199

Athanassios Raftopoulos
Pre-Cueing, Early Vision, and Cognitive Penetrability —— 217

Ophelia Deroy
Predictions do not Entail Cognitive Penetration: "Racial" Biases in Predictive Models of Perception —— 235

5 Epistemology of Perception

Charles Travis
Boundless —— 251

Johannes Roessler
The Manifest and the Philosophical Image of Perceptual Knowledge —— 275

Philipp Berghofer & Harald A. Wiltsche
The Co-Presentational Character of Perception —— 303

Frédérique de Vignemont
Knowledge Without Observation: Body Image or Body Schema? —— 323

6 Perception and the Sciences

Romana K. Schuler
Scheinbewegungen. Wahrnehmung zwischen Wissensgeschichte und Gegenwartskunst —— 337

Ulrich Arnswald
Zur Analogie von Wittgensteins Konzept des Aspektwechsels und der wissenschaftlichen Metapher als Vehikel der Innovation —— 357

7 Wittgenstein

David G. Stern
The Structure of *Tractatus* and the *Tractatus* Numbering System —— 377

Hans Sluga
Wittgensteins Welt —— 399

Index of Names —— 417

Editorial

This volume contains most of the invited papers delivered at the 40th International Wittgenstein Symposium in Kirchberg/W. in Lower Austria, August 6-12, 2017. It took place under the title "The Philosophy of Perception and Observation". The intention of the symposium was to give a general overview of the newest topics in the philosophy of perception. It also included as usual papers on Wittgenstein, more or less related to the conference topic. This is not surprising, when we realize the lifelong dealing of Wittgenstein with the problem of perceiving and seeing-as – from a grammatical and psychological perspective. We all perceive the world with our senses and are processing this information from the external world. Most of us have already faced the following problem: did I see this accurately or was I deceived? What did I see exactly and what is the content of my perceptual experience? What did I see and what is a cognitive addition to my perceptual experience, through attention, memory or concepts? Already Wittgenstein raised similar questions, as in the well known passage from the *Philosophical Investigations*, (193 f.):

> I contemplate a face, and then suddenly notice its likeness to another. I see that it has not changed; and yet I see it differently. I call this experience 'noticing an aspect [...]'. And I must distinguish between 'continuous seeing' of an aspect and the 'dawning' of an aspect [...]. I see two pictures, with the duck-rabbit surrounded by rabbits in one, by ducks in the other. I do not notice that they are the same. Does it *follow* from this that I *see* something different in the two cases?

The aim of the symposium was to reflect the state of the art in the field of the philosophy of perception. In the last decade, the philosophy of perception underwent a strong expansion and revival. This was not only driven by results of scientific disciplines like the neuroscience and psychology and a stronger integration of the philosophy of perception with these sciences. It was also driven by a growing integration of the philosophy of perception with other subdisciplines of philosophy, like epistemology or metaphysics. The growing importance of the philosophy of attention, memory and imagination also yielded fruitful overlaps with the philosophy of perception. The sections of the conference aimed to reflect these new developments. The program sections of the conference focused on „Perception and Intentionality", "Perception and Concepts", "Epistemology of Perception", „Perception and the Cognitive Sciences" and „Theories and Observation". As it is a tradition, the conference also included a general section on Wittgenstein, more or less connected to issues on perception. Additionally, we had scheduled a special workshop on „Brentano and the Myth of the Given" on the occasion of Brentano's centennial, which was also celebrated with a big conference in Prague and Vienna in June 2017 (thanks go to the organizers of that workshop Johannes Brandl and Guillaume Fréchette).

In recent years the debate between intentionalism and a relational view of perception, as well as the debate about different forms of direct realism, had been in the center of attention in the field. This is partially reflected in the first two sections of the volume. The first section focuses on the role of perception as a source of objectivity, as well as on different versions of perceptual realism. The second section includes papers on different views of intentionality and perceptual content, but connects also this debate to its historical origin in Brentano´s conception of intentionality. Special attention of the volume (and the conference) is dedicated the uncertain distinction between perception and cognition: Can we find a clear-cut difference between cognitive and perceptual processes? How is verbal understanding connected to our perceptual capacities? This is the topic of the third section. Connected to these questions is the ongoing debate about the cognitive penetration of perception, which is the focus of the fourth section discussing the penetrability thesis as well as its epistemological and social implications. The epistemology of perception has been particularly enriched by the recent developments in the philosophy of perception. A section is dedicated to the questions related to the justificatory role of perception and the consequences this role may entail for our conception of the nature, object and content of perception (section 5). After a section on perception and its connection to the sciences (section 6), a final section covers general issues in the philosophy of Wittgenstein, focusing especially on the *Tractatus*. These were some of the central questions addressed by the most renowned philosophers in this field at the 40th International Wittgenstein Symposium and documented in this volume. We hope that the present volume will further contribute to the flourishing of the field.

The success story of the Wittgenstein Symposium of the Austrian Ludwig Wittgenstein Society had begun already in 1976. On the occasion of the 40th symposium there was an official public celebration in front of the community building of Kirchberg with the presentation of a brochure as a documentation of these symposia incl. personal reminiscences and reports, which is accessible in the website of the Wittgenstein Society.[1]

We want to thank all invited speakers, among them 11 plenary speakers, and the authors of the conference pre-proceedings and of the present proceedings, obviously a set of the most renowned scholars in this field. Already in 2017 we

---

[1] https://www.alws.at/past-symposia-and-summer-schools/

have published the pre-proceedings, including 95 submitted papers.[2] Our thanks go also to David Stern and Hans Sluga, who were the lecturers of the summer school 2017, organized by Volker Munz and dedicated to "Meaning, Mind, and Action: Wittgenstein's Lectures, Cambridge, 1930-33".

Concluding thanks go the staff of the Wittgenstein Society in Kirchberg directed by Margret Kronaus, together with Christiane Kuntner, in addition for the special service (editorial work, graphic design) provided by Sascha Windholz, to Brigitte Fuchs, the representative of our host as director of the beautiful Elementary School in Kirchberg/W., and to director Johannes Pepelnik on behalf of the supporting bank (Raiffeisenbank). Each symposium could not take place without the support and collaboration of the mayors of the Wittgenstein communities, above all Willibald Fuchs (Kirchberg/W.), as well as Johannes Hennerfeind (Trattenbach), Karl Mayerhofer (Otterthal), supported by the former mayor and honorary member of the Wittgenstein Society Ernst Schabauer. Last but not least we are grateful to the Province of Lower Austria governed by Johanna Mikl-Leitner, as the funding institution of the annual symposia, especially via the Science and Research Unit in St. Pölten, headed by Martina Höllbacher. In the long run also this volume as number 26 of the series *Publications of the Austrian Wittgenstein Society. New Series* is the result of a good cooperation with our publisher De Gruyter, represented by Christoph Schirmer, to whom we are grateful for a professional and friendly cooperation. We are also very thankful to Josef Pircher for the text editing of the present volume.

Vienna/Kirchberg, May 2019
                        Christoph Limbeck-Lilienau and Friedrich Stadler

---

[2] Christoph Limbeck-Lilienau and Friedrich Stadler (eds.) *The Philosophy of Perception and Observation. Contributions to the 40th International Wittgenstein Symposium*, Vol. XXV, Austrian Ludwig Wittgenstein Society, 2017, ISSN 1022-3398.

1 Objectivity and Realism

Tyler Burge
Perception: Ground of Empirical Objectivity

Abstract: Several types of objectivity are surveyed. The role of perception as a type of empirical objectivity, and as a source for more sophisticated types of objectivity that it itself does not realize, is discussed. Perceptual representation is distinguished from the sort of representation explained in terms of information theory. Perceiving is also distinguished from sensing. Some threads in the history of philosophy that have taken perception not to be a type or source of objectivity are discussed and criticized. Often inevitable limitations on the types of objectivity that perception can embody have been misconstrued as marks of subjectivity. Often perception has been mis-characterized in the interests of one or another philosophical ideology. The irony of this history is that the ultimate basis for the objectivity of the empirical sciences has commonly been miscast in the philosophical tradition.

Keywords: Perception, objectivity, perceptual constancy, representation

My topic is the objectivity of perception. I begin by surveying various kinds of objectivity. Then I discuss how perception realizes some of these kinds. Finally, I consider some limitations of perception. I try to explain why these limitations should not be taken to undermine the kinds of objectivity that perception in fact has. For the empirical sciences, perception is the ground and *sine qua non* of all other types of objectivity, even the types that perception cannot itself measure up to.

First, a brief survey of kinds of objectivity.[1]

The largest division is that between subject-matter types and representation-of-subject- matter types. The broadest, least restrictive example of a subject-matter type is the objectivity of all that is real, or all that exists, or all that has being. The contrast is with the purported, unreal "objects" of fantasy and delusion. Since such "objects" have no being, there is no genuine contrast class for the objective in this broadest sense.

Some subject-matter types of objectivity are more restrictive than the objectivity of everything that is. For example, it is common to count mind-independent

---

[1] Most of what follows on types of objectivity is drawn from my *Origins of Objectivity* (Oxford University Press, 2010), chapter 2.

aspects of the world as objective – and contrast them with mind-dependent aspects. Here and throughout, I exclude the mind of any deity from consideration. Mud, atoms, stars, and trees are mind-independent, hence objective on this categorization. Pains, beliefs, desires, and theories are non-objective on this categorization. In a sense, not all trees are mind-independent. Many are planned and planted.

To avoid this piece of awkwardness, let us take 'mind-independence' to mean 'constitutive mind-independence' – independence of mind for being the sort of thing it is. It is not a constitutive aspect of a tree that it be planned. Even with this restriction, quite a lot of things turn out to be mind-dependent, besides mental items themselves. Hammers are constitutively mind-dependent. What it is to be a hammer involves having some function or use, presumably for some being with a mind. Animals such as cats have minds constitutively. Something would not be a cat if it lacked a natural capacity for perception. On many views, colors are constitutively mind-dependent. For example, if colors are secondary qualities – dispositions in objects to produce certain sensations in a class of individuals –, then colors are constitutively mind-dependent. The constitutively-mind-independent type of subject-matter objectivity counts quite a lot of things non-objective: hammers, cats, nations, and perhaps colors. Such consequences are rarely recognized when people put forward notions of objectivity in terms of mind-independence.

A subject-matter type of objectivity that is more restrictive than the whole-real-world type and less restrictive than the constitutively-mind-independent type is the objectivity of things that are not themselves representational perspectives or states of consciousness. This type would include hammers, cats, colors, and nations as in themselves objective, but exclude beliefs, perceptions, pains, theories, and statutes.

I have cited three subject-matter types of objectivity. All are to be distinguished from representation-of-subject-matter types. Most uses of the term 'objective' apply to certain types of representation of a subject matter, rather than to subject matters themselves.

I divide representation-of-subject-matter types of objectivity into two large sub-classes – vertical types and horizontal types. The intuitive idea is that vertical types are characterized by a relatively direct representational relation to a subject matter. Horizontal types, by contrast, are characterized by types of representation or relations among representations.

The vertical relations to a subject matter are all aspects of or contributors to veridicality. Such relations as being true of, or accurate of, a subject matter are aspects of veridicality. Referring to a subject matter is a contributor to veridicality. Being *veridical* – that is, being either accurate or true – is itself a vertical relation to a subject matter, by virtue of its dependence on these sorts of relations.

Different types of subject matters differentiate among types of vertical representation-of- subject-matter objectivity. For example, being true of a real subject matter, being true of a subject matter that is constitutively mind-independent, and being true of a subject matter that consists of things that are not themselves representational perspectives or states of consciousness are different types of vertical representation-of-subject-matter objectivity.

A stricter type of vertical objectivity is representation of laws or of certain structural invariances. This type loomed large in Kant's work and is central to modern physics.

The horizontal types of representation-of-subject-matter objectivity are a more varied lot. An example of horizontal objectivity is following a procedure that yields representations in a way that is independent of the whims of any particular individual. Following a set procedure in civil law counts as objective in this sense. Perhaps the central procedural type of objectivity in the history of philosophy, again emphasized by Kant, is representation that follows rational procedures, according to some canon or other.

A closely related family of types of objectivity comprises representation in impersonal terms, representation that is independent of first- or second-person pronouns, representation that is independent of demonstratives or indexicals, representation that is independent of individual attitudes or training. These are types of the objectivity of impersonality. Many specifications of laws have striven to be impersonal in some of these ways. The horizontal types can overlap.

A final type of horizontal objectivity is representation that accords with representation by others. Often the others are taken to follow some procedure – such as being rational or being scientific. The intersubjective versions of horizontal objectivity present straightforward contrasts with the subjectivity of idiosyncracy and the subjectivity of privacy.

Some broad points can be made about relations among the horizontal and vertical representation-of-subject-matter types of objectivity. Although many have championed inter- subjectivity as a central type of objectivity, philosophers have wisely tended to qualify intersubjectivity by placing some condition on the subjects to assure that intersubjectivity is not that of agreement among crazies. Kant took intersubjective objectivity to occur among subjects that follow rational or scientific procedures. Frege associated the communicable with law.

There is, of course, evidence that over the long run, a kind of efficiency, sometimes even group rationality, emerges from the aggregate actions of the group. These are instances of the so-called wisdom of crowds.[2] I believe that if rationality, as opposed to efficiency or evolutionary success, is at issue, the individuals in a group must have basic rational competencies. Genuine rationality is not an aggregate upshot of efficient behavior of non-rational individuals.

The large point that I want to emphasize is that taking *vertical* representation-of-subject- matter types of objectivity to be constitutively more basic than horizontal ones is fundamental to a realist view of the world. Peirce defined truth as what rational procedures would lead to in the limit. Kant took following rational and/or scientific procedures to be what objective validity consists in – at least from what he called the transcendental point of view. These are idealist strategies. What I take to be the correct view is that rationality is to be understood partly in terms of being conducive to truth, given certain limitations of information and competence. Good scientific method should be understood partly in terms of truth or approximate truth. It must be method that can be expected to lead toward true or approximately true scientific theory. Statements of laws are often very far from being exactly and literally true, although such statements can serve many useful purposes. But representations of laws are ultimately to be judged by whether they describe, to some approximation, real lawful patterns in the world.

Of course, science must idealize. Few of our methods lead to precise truths. We are constantly finding limitations in our methods and both limitations and imprecision in our theories. But ultimately our procedures are evaluated by how well they describe reality.

Understanding reality in an illuminating way is the basic aim of science. Being veridical is the fundamental idealization that guides our conceptions of rational and scientific procedures.

So horizontal types of objectivity are to be understood as serving vertical types, given a realist attitude toward science and metaphysics. The primary norm for vertical types of objectivity is to be veridical-true or accurate. Veridicality is fidelity to subject matter. So the subject-matter types of objectivity provide the primary basis for assessing the objectivity of vertical representation-of-subject matter types. And as noted, the objectivity of horizontal representation-of-subject-matter types functions to serve vertical types. So subject-matter objectivity – essentially, what *is* – is in this sense fundamental.

There is a further sense in which the subject-matter types of objectivity are fundamental with respect to representation-of-subject-matter types. The contents

---

[2] F. Galton, 'The Wisdom of Crowds', *Nature* 75 (1907), 450–451, http://galton.orf/essays/1900-1911/galton-1907-vox-populi.pdf; G. Gigerenzer and W. Gaissmeier, 'Heuristic Decision Making', *Annual Review of Psychology* 62 (2011), 451-482.

of representations and representational states, at least for empirically based representations, are determined to be what they are through interaction with their subject matters. The subject matters of such representations are partial determiners of the natures of our representations.[3] One can think, metaphorically, of the world's stamping itself – primarily through causal interactions – into the very contents of our representations.

I turn from these vertiginously general reflections to more specific points. I focus on ways in which perception is objective and on the role of *its* objectivity in the objectivity of more sophisticated types of representation.

To understand the role of perception in this welter of types of objectivity, it is crucial to distinguish perceiving from non-perceptual sensing. Sensing is an extremely broad phenomenon. Plants are *sensitive* to light and respond to it. I say that they do not *sense* anything, because they do not act and sensing serves action. Still, they are sensitive to the environment. Even laying aside the distinction between sensing and being sensitive, numerous organisms sense their environment without perceiving it. Bacteria sense light and swim away from it. Rotifers sense food through their cilia. Ticks sense warmth and crawl toward it.

No science explains these instances of sensing in terms of states that have conditions for being accurate. Sensing is causally based, statistically significant interaction with the environment that has a function for the organism. Relevant functions here are biological functions and functions associated with action. Fulfilling such functions are broadly, and in many cases richly, *practical* successes. We can speak of the accuracy of such sensing. But we are thereby describing nothing more than fulfillment of a practical function. In fulfilling a biological function, an organism or state contributes to fitness for survival long enough to mate. In fulfilling a function of an action – in reaching the action's target –, an organism commonly contributes to such fitness. Fulfilling such functions is not being accurate or inaccurate. Talk of these sensory states as being accurate or inaccurate is metaphorical.

An organism has perception only when it has states that are accurate or inaccurate, where having accuracy conditions is a real, non-metaphorical feature of the states' natures. Finding that having accuracy conditions is a feature of a state's nature is discovering that strong causal explanations appeal to states with accuracy conditions. In such cases accuracy is not merely a matter of biological functional success. Such success is constitutively a practical matter – being useful for survival long enough to reproduce, including fulfilling or contributing to

---

[3] This point is a form of anti-individualism. For more on this matter, see my *Foundations of Mind* (Oxford: Oxford University Press, 2007), essays 4–10, and *Origins of Objectivity, op. cit.* chapter 3.

fulfilling biological functions of action and reaction for the animal or animal species. Accuracy in perception or belief is not constitutively a practical matter. A perceptual state can be accurate but practically deleterious, or practically useful but inaccurate.[4]

The term 'representation' is often used, even in science, in two importantly different ways. One way applies to all sensing, perceptual or not. The other way applies to a distinctively psychological capacity. This latter is the type of representation that underlies the main types of representation-of-subject-matter objectivity, vertical and horizontal.

To understand the former type of representation, one must first understand the basic idea of Shannon information theory, a theory of statistical correlation. State X provides (Shannon) information about state Y if X and Y are statistically correlated to some relevant degree.

Providing information is a symmetrical relation.[5] Clearly, providing information in this sense is not in any way equivalent to the sort of representation that we evaluate for veridicality.

Shannon information is a component element in applications of the term 'representation' that require meeting more conditions than providing information. These applications have been useful in understanding animal behavior. The conditions for state kind X's *informationally registering* state kind Y are (a) that state kinds X and Y are statistically correlated (provide information with respect to one another) to some significant degree; (b) that instances of Y commonly cause instances of state X; and (c) that such causal correlation is functional. Whereas the shadow cast by the sun off a rock statistically correlates with the direction of the sun and is caused by the sun's rays' hitting the rock from that direction, the causal correlation has no function. So there is no information registration. By contrast, a bacterium's sensing the light and a plant's sensitivity to

---

4 Similarly, of course, for a belief. Action that involves representation is a more complex matter. An agent's making his/her/its representation of the action's target veridical by acting in such a way as to satisfy the representation of the target is indeed both a representational success and a practical success. But there are always richer, more basic, practical norms and functions for each action, and richer, more basic types of practical success. These norms and functions are not fulfilled simply by the action's meeting whatever target it has. I believe that representational success in conation does not reduce to any of these richer types of practical success. Nor do these richer types reduce to conative representational success—acting so as to meet one's set (represented) target. These are, however, matters beyond the scope of this article.
5 C. Shannon, 'A Mathematical Theory of Communication', *Bell System Technical Journal* 27 (1948), 379-423; M. Mansuripur, *Introduction to Information Theory* (New York: Prentice Hall, 1987).

the light are not only caused by and statistically correlated with the light; this causal correlation is also functional. It is present in the world because it tends to enable bacteria to survive long enough to reproduce.[6] Thus it is said that the bacterium's sensory state represents light. It does so, but only in that it informationally registers light.

This information-registration use of the word 'representation' can seem to come close to being cognate with the use of 'representation' that figured in our discussion of objectivity. But it is not the same use. The distinction is marked in the explanatory practice of relevant sciences. No scientific theory of the sensing of food by a rotifer characterizes the sensory states in terms of their conditions for accuracy. The causal account is purely in physiological terms, or in terms of how aspects of proximal stimulation are weighted in such a way as to cause certain behavior.

The functional account is purely in terms of how the causal sensitivity to aspects of the environment contributes to the organism's biological success. Scientists sometimes attribute accurate perception to such organisms as rotifers – indeed to trees, because of their sensitivity to light. This is meta-patter, often with an advertising purpose. It is not straight-out science. No such patter figures in literal scientific explanation. Invocation of states with veridicality conditions is not needed or illuminating in causal explanations or functional explanations of a rotifer's behavior.

By contrast, there is a science of perceptual psychology whose primary aim is to explain the formation of accurate and illusory states. The science invokes such states in its causal explanations. It takes some causes and some effects as having conditions for accuracy as aspects of their natures – or as marking the kinds of states that figure in those explanations. Having conditions for veridicality (for accuracy or truth) is the hallmark of a representational state. So scientific practice and theory distinguish non-perceptual sensing from sensory perception. Non-perceptual sensing is a form of information registration, but not representation in the traditional sense. Sensory perception is not only information registration. It is a type of representation that has veridicality conditions, as an aspect of the causal-explanation-grounding natures of sensory perceptual states. Such

---

6 The notion of function explicated in this sentence is a slight simplification of what has become a standard notion of function in evolutionary biology. See L. Wright, 'Functions', *The Philosophical Review* 82 (1973), 139-168. The notion of function that I use in other contexts is broader. It includes representational functions, for example, as well as biological functions. However, in understanding information registration, the notion of biological function suffices.

states can be assessed, quite literally, for vertical objectivity with respect to a subject matter.

What underlies this difference in types of scientific explanation? The broad answer is that perceptual states are products of perceptual constancies, whereas mere non-perceptual sensory states – or mere informational registrational states – are not. A perceptual constancy is, roughly, a capacity to perceptually represent the same environmental property or relation *as* that property or relation, despite significant variation in proximal stimulation. For example, a perceptual state that represents a surface as a certain shade of green can, within limits, represent the surface as being that shade of green, despite significant variation in illumination of the surface (say, variation between white and red illumination). Difference in illumination has a huge effect on proximal stimulation. A system with color constancy can filter out differences in illumination and respond to the surface reflectance – roughly, the color – itself. Similarly a perceptual state that represents a surface as circular can do so whether the surface appears head-on or at a considerable slant. Again, representation as of a given environmental property succeeds despite significant variation in proximal stimulation. Sensory states in rotifers and snails show no such perceptual constancies.

Within a given perceptual system, in the formation of perceptual states, there is always some change-over from the immediate effects of proximal stimulation – which are non-perceptual, sensory, information-registrational states – to perceptual states. It can be a delicate matter to specify when such change-over occurs, and to motivate such specification. One must allow for vagueness in specifying a boundary. Still, the practice of the science does show fairly consistent agreement on what states are perceptual representations of the environment and what states are either immediate registrations of the proximal stimulus or subsequent filtered registrations of patterns in the proximal stimulus. The non-perceptual registrational states provide more information about the initial proximal stimulus array than about the environment. They remain merely informational-registration states. Perceptual systems, however, at some stages of processing, generate perceptual states that are embedded in perceptual constancies, and that are capable of being accurate or inaccurate, as an aspect of the basic kinds of states that they are.

Detailed accounts of why the science draws these distinctions in specific cases are complex and beyond the scope of this paper. But there are at least two key differences.

One is that perceptual contancies tend to fit a perceptual state to attributes in the distal environment. Invariances in sensory registration do not. They fit a state only to more or less abstract aspects of the proximal stimulation (for vision, the light array just as it strikes the retina – the retinal image). The pre-perceptual registrations fit well with features in the retinal image, but poorly with the counterpart attributes in the physical environment, even when instances of those attributes are distal causes of features of retinal image.

For example, the registration of a contour in the retinal image (the array of light just as it strikes the retinal receptors) fits that contour very well. But although it in fact came from a specific contour in the distal physical environment, it is in itself consistent with a nearly infinite number of possible contours that could have produced that very same retinal image contour, all differing in their shape, length, and exact orientation in three-dimensional space. At the stages of processing in which a retinal image contour is being merely information-registered, nothing distinguishes the contour in the distal environment that is the actual cause from the nearly infinite array of other possible environmental contours that are consistent with that contour in the retinal image. At later stages of processing, states are produced that present the orientation, shape, and length of a contour in three-dimensional space. The science assumes that visual perception represents entities in the distal environment, not entities in the retinal image. Those are the entities that make a perception accurate or not. So the science distinguishes perceptual representation of three-dimensional contours (say, of branches in the distal environment) from sensory registration of two-dimensional contours in the retinal image. The latter registration is not taken by the science to be accurate or inaccurate.

Of course, even the non-perceptual information registrations function to aid action and reaction to aspects of the distal environment. Functional explanation of information registrations very frequently connects non-perceptual sensory states to aspects of the distal environment. But until science postulates relevance to the distal environment in its specification of sensory kinds embedded in the science's causal explanations, there is no postulation of perceptual states. Such specifications occur when sensory systems show perceptual constancies.

A secondary difference between pre-perceptual and perceptual sensory states concerns the role of perception in action. In animals that have perception in a given modality, pre-perceptual registrations that lead up to perceptual representations do not have the systematic role in action that perceptual representations do. Of course, if one stopped a perceptual process before it got to a perception, an animal would have to act on the information it had. But a systematic account of action by animals that have perception will normally take action to be guided by perception, not by those pre-perceptual registrations. A detailed account of the role of perception in action can help distinguish constancies or invariances among sensory registrations that are not perceptual from invariances that are part of genuinely perceptual constancies in the same modality.

Since perception is the most primitive type of representational state, the most primitive type of state whose nature admits evaluation for veridicality, perception is the most primitive state that can be counted objective. Accurate perceptions have vertical, representation-of-subject-matter objectivity. Since information registration is not, in itself, a type of representation that marks mentality, information registration cannot, in itself, qualify as either subjective or objective in any representation-of-subject-matter sense.

The vertical objectivity of perception is narrower than that of veridicality with respect to any subject matter that is real. Our conscious sensations are real. The classical British empiricists took objects of perception to be our own conscious sensations. Perceptual psychology firmly rejects this position. The entities that perception represents are entities in the subject's body or in the physical environment. These entities are either constitutively mind-independent, or at least not themselves representational perspectives. Perception is vertically objective inasmuch as it veridically represents entities that are not themselves representational or otherwise mental.[7]

Perceptual constancies, as understood in perceptual psychology, comprise the key phenomenon that, at the most primitive level, distinguishes representation that can be literally evaluated for accuracy from information registration that cannot be. Being embedded in a perceptual constancy is, I think, a necessary and sufficient condition for an accurate perceptual state to have this vertical, representation-of-subject-matter type of objectivity. It should be noted that perceptual constancies exhibit a primitive form of horizontal objectivity. They are capacities to represent a given attribute or particular on different occasions despite substantial differences in proximal stimulation. Substantial differences in proximal stimulation correlate with substantial differences in representational perspective. Embedded in perceptual capacities is, necessarily I think, an ability to cut through local, idiosyncratic aspects of a proximal stimulus situation to center on aspects of a distal stimulus that remain constant across perspectives. Thus there are antecedents to structurally invariant and impersonal types of horizontal objectivity in the perceptual constancies. Since most perceptual constancies track

---

[7] I think that although we consciously sense our pains, we do not strictly perceive them. Our awareness of the felt quality of pain does not exhibit perceptual constancies. We may, however, perceptually attribute bodily locations to them.

lawlike patterns that are constant across variations in perspective on the patterns, the perceptual constancies even bear an implicit relation to types of objectivity that represent laws.

Of course, perceptions do not represent laws. Constitutively, they function to represent particulars, that are in fact localized in space and time. Obviously, perceptions do not count as objective on the conception that takes objectivity to be veridical representation of law. They are not in themselves science.

The history of philosophy has undergone a run of philosophical claims to the effect that perception is not objective, full stop. Threads in Descartes suggest that he thought that perception is fundamentally misleading regarding the real nature of the world. Leibniz took ordinary perception to be confused and indistinct. Sometimes, in both cases, ordinary perception seems to be portrayed as a hindrance rather than a help to science. Perception needed to be corrected and transcended by a natural philosophy that amounted to a metaphysics. As mentioned, the British empiricists assimilated perception to awareness of one's own sensations – a paradigmatically subjective enterprise. They made this mistake because they wanted to take perception as a foundation for knowledge that could resist scepticism and because they thought that the only way to resist scepticism was to postulate an infallible foundation. Of course, perception is not infallible. So there was no place in their account for genuine perception.

Kant is sometimes cited as holding that representation of laws is the only true type of objectivity, thus excluding perception from the realm of the objective. Frege is sometimes taken to locate objectivity purely in laws and structures, again excluding any representation that is as particular-bound as perception is.

These construals of Kant and Frege are, I think, mistaken. Kant was the father of several modern uses of the term 'objective'. He certainly regarded representation of laws and necessities as a paradigmatically important type of objectivity, for scientific cognition. But he clearly and explicitly counted empirical intuition – ordinary perception – as objectively valid and objectively real.[8] Kant denied objectivity to sensation, not to perception. Similarly, Frege contrasted structural objectivity only with incommunicable "intuitions" (misinterpreting Kant). He

---

[8] I. Kant, *Critique of Pure Reason*, P. Guyer and A. Wood trans. (Cambridge: Cambridge University Press, 1998), B376–377. Kant's uses of the term 'empirical intuition' ('*empirische Anschaung*') correspond reasonably well with modern uses of the term 'perception' (that is, 'sensory perception').

counted singular thoughts based on perception as synthetic aposteriori truths, thus as vertically objective.[9]

There are, however, major threads in both traditional rationalism and traditional empiricism that do suggest, quite amazingly, that perception is not a source of objectivity. It is true that relevant authors often suggest only that perception is not a source of some favored type of objectivity, which science clearly does aspire to and that perception clearly does not attain.

But there is the thread in the rationalist tradition that perception is actually a hindrance to understanding the world, as opposed to navigating it. And there is the thread in the empiricist tradition that "perception" – or what the tradition substitutes into the role of perception – is in itself subjective, in not getting beyond the contents of the perceiver's own mind.

Although most of us are beyond being tempted by the traditional Empiricist view of perception as primarily a connection to our own sensations or ideas, it is hard to understate what a pernicious effect this view has had on the history of philosophy. The view gives an account of knowledge that leaves genuine perception completely out of the picture. The view starts with *sensa* and urges inferring things about the physical world from such *sensa*.

By contrast, perception represents the physical world directly – not by way of representing anything other than the physical world. Perceptual representations – that is, instances of specific types of perceptual states — are formed through complex, largely automatic processing that is, of course, fallible. Such processing is not the sort of propositional, intellectual inference postulated by traditional models of reasoning and knowledge. Ironically, there is no place in the Empiricist view for genuine perception.

This omission shows up not only in Locke, Berkeley, and Hume. It infects the work of Russell, Moore, early Carnap, Quine, mid-career Sellars, and Davidson. For many of these philosophers, genuine representation – capable of veridicality – begins with propositional attitudes. It begins with beliefs and other states on which propositional reasoning can operate. These philosophers maintained this benighted position because they lacked a clear-sighted view of perception. And they rightly regarded mere sensing, or sensation, as something that cannot be

---

9 G. Frege, *Foundations of Arithmetic*, J. Austin trans. (Evanston, Illinois: Northwestern University Press, 1968), sections 3, 12, 26. For discussion of this matter, see my 'Frege on Apriority', in P. Boghossian and C. Peacocke eds., *New Directions on the A Priori* (Oxford University Press, 2000); reprinted in my *Truth Thought Reason; Essays on Frege* (Oxford: Oxford University Press, 2005).

evaluated for veridicality. As a consequence, they postulated a direct transition from sensations to empirical beliefs, leaving out perception altogether.

Helmholtz, the father of modern perceptual psychology, did not make these mistakes. He distinguished non-perceptual sensing from perception, and saw in perceptual constancies a structural element that could support the idea that perception is objective. But he was so concerned to distinguish sensing from perceiving that he insisted that perceiving is a mere manipulation of signs. The obvious iconic aspects of perception, for which there is now massive empirical evidence, were largely ignored, at least in Helmholtz's official glosses on perception.[10]

Pylyshyn is a modern day follower in this regard.[11] Picture and map-like aspects of perception, grounded in isomorphisms between neural populations and the spatial world, beginning with the two-dimensional proximal stimulus array, are the basis for the format of spatial representation in vision and touch.[12] Helmholtz's determination to avoid the mistake of the Empiricists – the mistake of assimilating perception to sensation – led to an overly abstract view of perception.

Paradoxically, traditional Rationalists are less guilty than traditional Empricists of distorting what perception is. However, they tended to underplay perception's role in science because they thought that Aristotelian common sense, based on perception, yielded a distorted view of the world of fundamental physics. I think that they were right in having some inkling of the enormous gulf between the world that perception and common sense give us, on one hand, and the world that fundamental physics gives us, on the other. But up through Leibniz, traditional rationalists tended to overrate how far they could get in understanding the world through armchair metaphysical reasoning and to underrate how central perception is to arriving at a scientific understanding of the world.

Newton and Kant were the first to recognize the basic, if unsharp, distinction between science and metaphysics. Their drawing this distinction was revolutionary. Leibniz's complaints about Newton's *Principia* and Hegel's, Schelling's, Bradley's, Royce's post-Kantian idealist metaphysics, unconstrained by science, show that the distinction that Newton and Kant insisted upon did not go down easily. However, gradually but decisively, their conception of natural science as an experimental, observation-grounded enterprise has long since won the day.

The Rationalists' concerns about perception are, however, not all wayward. Those concerns are, I think, worth addressing from our current perspective. That

---

10 H. von Helmholtz, *Handbuch der Physiologischen Optik* (Leipzig: Voss, 1867).
11 Z. Pylyshyn, *Seeing and Visualizing* (Cambridge, Mass.: MIT Press, 2003).
12 T. Burge, 'Iconic Representation: Maps, Pictures, and Perception', in S. Wuppuluri and F. Doria eds. *The Map and the Territory* (Cham, Switzerland: Springer, 2018).

perspective has the advantage of a powerful science of perception, a meta-understanding of science that is largely free from armchair metaphysics, and a consequent recognition that perception is the necessary starting point for natural science.

One limiting fact about perception is that each perceptual system evolved to serve the needs of specific types of animals. Dolphins and bats use echolocation to locate objects. Spiders can locate and even identify specific shapes that are associated with prey, predators, and mates, by feeling the ripple effects of movement in their webs. Dogs and dolphins have hearing ranges that are different from ours. Many fish use tactile perception of water currents, whereas others use electrical signals, to locate prey. We lack these capacities, but have a versatile and acute visual system. Even with respect to vision, we are not pre-eminent among terrestrial animals in all respects. Hawks can see with more acuity at greater distances than we can.

A common lightheaded response to these facts has been to suggest that this dependence on the perceptual equipment of one's species makes perception non-objective. The response is lightheaded inasmuch as it sets an impossible ideal for the objectivity of perception. Perception is inevitably from a finite, limited perspective. It cannot represent all features of the world. We are limited receptacles. When the world stamps its features into our representation, it cannot do so in all detail. One should not confuse selectivity with subjectivity. Our perceptual intake is inevitably selective. It is selective because it was selected for through long interaction with the environment. It does not follow that it is not objective within its species-dependent domains.

There are, of course, important types of objectivity that perception cannot realize – the objectivity of representation of laws or structures *per se*, the objectivity of demonstrative- and indexical-free representation, and so on. What it can provide is the objectivity of approximately veridical representation of certain constitutively mind-independent or perspective-independent aspects of the world. Approximately accurate perceptual representation grounds more general, even law-like, representation. Perception also grounds the empirical objectivity of intersubjectivity. Perceptual systems and perceptual representations are broadly similar within species. In fact, our visual system is broadly similar to the visual systems of nearly all mammals. Given that we humans have similar perceptual systems and are able to conceptualize our perceptions and express such conceptualizations in language, and given that we are often in a position to recognize and correct each others' perceptual mistakes, we have a common basis for communicating results of observations and for checking one another's reports against independent perceptions of similar environmental conditions.

Moreover, the aspects of the physical environment that perceptual systems were selected to represent include some of the most fundamental features of the world. Most perceptual systems are dominantly focused on spatial and temporal aspects of the world. Every animal must deal with distance and direction, size and shape, motion and duration, cycles and intervals.

Perceptual representation of such attributes is crude and certainly does not hint at the deeper fine-structure of space-time. Perception provides only ego-centric, indexically-based, local, highly macro maps of space and time. These do not have the perspective-independent objectivity that physics strives for. What perception does provide is approximately accurate representation within its domain. Mammalian vision has turned out to be rich enough to provide the basis for a science that goes vastly beyond what perception provides.

Although we got to our science primarily through vision, we can plausibly speculate that other species might use other types of signals – auditory or electrical signals for example – to come to scientific results regarding space-time that are similar to our own. If the signals were rich enough and the non-human scientists were intelligent enough, I see no bar to their acquiring comparable science by non-visual means.

The point about not confusing selectivity with subjectivity applies not only at the level of differences among species, but also at the level of differences among individual perceivers.

There have been recurrent rejections, even within science, of expert observation as a ground for objective scientific representation.[13] One ground for such strange resistance is that expert observation is not common enough to be objective. Certainly, if a single individual made uncheckable observations, they would be useless for science. But experts' observations can be shared, because expertise can be taught. As a nearly general rule, experts do not differ from non-experts in that they utilize fundamentally different ranges of perceptual attributives. They and their perceptual systems utilize shape, size, color, texture, motion, body, face attributives – as do the perceptual systems of non-experts. Rather, experts notice and remember things that non-experts do not notice or remember. And their perception may be sharper and more differentiated, on key cues, through applications of attention. This sort of selectivity expands the range of useable information provided by perception, rather than contracts it.

Another limitation of perception is its imperfect acuity. This is the limitation that Leibniz focused on. Leibniz' concern has been echoed, for example by Eddington and by Sellars, with recurrent reminders about how our lack of perfect

---

[13] L. Daston and P. Galison, *Objectivity* (New York: Zone Books, 2007).

acuity produces a different image of the world than the image produced by basic physics. Sometimes this line is accompanied with an ontological bias. It is said that physical bodies that we see appear to be solid, but actually they are groups of particles with large stretches of space between them. They are not solid at all. Or we see some surfaces as smooth, but microscopically all surfaces are jagged landscapes of fast- moving particles. So we do not see the world as it is.

This line hinges on assuming that the representations of solidity and smoothness when applied to macro bodies are to be understood as micro-physics might understand them.

Perceptual attributives for solidity and smoothness have approximately veridical applications in the macro domain. These applications are not pre-empted by the micro-physical. A macro surface is smooth on a scale that distinguishes it from surfaces with macro-large peaks and valleys. The spatial patterns and spatial contrasts that vision distinguishes are real. They just should not be expected to ground immediate insight into scales of the world that are too small, or too large, for the limited acuity of vision. Limited acuity is another form of selectivity. Selectivity is not the subjectivity of non-veridical representation.

Of course, a pervasive limitation of perception is that it is subject to error. Error really is contrary to the most primitive type of objective representation: veridical representation. Perception cannot realize the ideal of traditional empiricism–infallibility. In fact, perception is subject to *brute* error – error that occurs despite no misuse of perception and no malfunction in operations of the perceptual system. This limitation is an inevitable result of the causal dependence of perception on distal antecedents. Perceptual states are formed on the basis of proximal stimulation. If a system is given a certain proximal stimulus, then assuming that the antecedent and concurrent states of the psychology are held constant, and bracketing noise, it will produce a specific perceptual representation. The same proximal stimuli can be produced by different distal stimuli. When the distal stimulus is non-standard – not the type of stimulus that gave the perceptual state its representational content –, the system will produce a misperception. Susceptibility to brute error is an inevitable fact of life for any perceptual system.

Noise is another, indeed pervasive, source of error. Noise results from interferences in perceptual processing that derive from the imperfections of any physical system. In fact, for scalar properties – such as distance, size, shape, speed, and color, as distinguished from yes-no properties – such as ordinal depth –, *most* perceptions are slightly inaccurate. But within ranges of normal operation, mammalian visual systems are close to being as optimal with respect to accuracy as physical limitations, such as noise and imperfect resolution, allow.

Susceptibility to error should not be overrated as a limitation on the sorts of objectivity that perception can provide. Many errors in observation are not strictly perceptual errors. They are errors of bias or of over-interpreting what perception provides. The attributives employed in perception form a relatively limited range. Visual perception in humans, for example, has attributives for shapes and other spatial properties or relations, textures, colors, lightness, motion, body, faces, and probably a few other generic types of attributives, including perhaps some functional attributes like *prey*.

Perceivers can learn to group various bodies by their shapes or characteristic motions. Such groupings utilize more specific attributives – attributives for bodies with specific characteristic shapes and motions. The shapes or motions can be those that trees, cars, toothbrushes, aardvarks, or even X-Ray machines typically have. Of course, it does not follow that perceptual attributives have contents like tree, car, toothbrush, aardvark, or X-Ray machine. Perception lacks the resources to distinguish natural kinds from bodies with the characteristic shapes, colors, and motions that certain natural kinds have (such as bodies with the shape, color, and motion of tigers). Perception cannot respond to many types of artifactual function – like the functions of X-Ray machines. Perception tends to concern itself with surfaces, bodies, shapes, spatial relations, temporal relations, colors, textures, motions, and so on. But it can group so as to apply attributives that are approximately extensionally equivalent with such attributives as those listed just above.

There is some evidence, still disputed, that human visual perception has attributives whose content attributes being a causal event, and being an action. The list will probably be extended on empirical grounds. But it will remain limited in comparison to the range of concepts that language and science provide us.

Most of the kinds, properties, and relations that we think about are not attributed in perception. Many errors of observation involve over-interpreting what perception in fact yields.

On the basis of these perceptual attributions, the errors connect perceived properties erroneously with properties that are not strictly perceptually indicated or attributed. For example, one might correctly perceive a body as having a specific shape (that is in fact typical of X-ray machines) and mistakenly take the body to be an X-ray machine. Obviously, such errors are not the fault of perception. They are errors of inference or in other transitions between perception and thought.

Similarly, errors that derive from expecting perception to provide veridical information beyond its natural domain of application are not perceptual errors.

Human visual perception does not yield accurate information about ordinal depth of surfaces beyond about 200 or 300 yards.

Similarly, visual perception is not fitted to yield accurate representation of the movement or size of distant heavenly bodies. The view, held before early modern astronomy, that the stars are fixed and relatively small derived, I think, from an inference, not a misperception. Given lack of normal cues to the distance and size of a perceived object, the perceptual system is likely to go non-committal about distance and size. Traditional errors about the distance and size of heavenly bodies probably stemmed from inference, not from perception itself.

The familiar errors of bias are again rarely the fault of perception itself, though such errors can affect perceptual attention and hence perceptual groupings. Much work in social psychology that is supposed to show that bias commonly affects perception itself rests on poor methodology and will not stand. Of course, errors that derive from malfunctions – errors caused by cataracts or lesions, for example – do not reflect on perception *per se*.

The main failure in perception to achieve approximate accuracy is brute error. Although there is nothing intrinsic to perception that guarantees that it is even reliable, much less infallible, our actual perceptual systems – specifically our visual system – are, as noted, amazingly approximately accurate, within their proper domain of operation. An important area of research in perceptual psychology has grown up in the last ten or fifteen years that develops this point with great rigor. The idea of the research is to state a function of a given perceptual task, for example, to correctly estimate the speed and direction of visible motion at relatively close distances. Then, known natural limitations of acuity and noise in the system are factored in. A normative optimality theorem is then proved. The theorem states the theoretical limit of accuracy, given such natural limitations. Finally, human visual performance is experimentally compared, in ordinary conditions, to the limit of optimal performance. In cases studied so far, human visual performance is near optimal. One can expect similar results for other species.[14] Neither accuracy nor reliable accuracy is selected for *per se* in evolution.

---

14 C. Blakemore, 'The Range and Scope of Binocular Depth Discrimination in Man', *Journal of Physiology* 211 (1970), 599–622; W. Geisler, J. Perry, B. Super, and D. Gallogly, 'Edge Co-occurrence in Natural Images Predicts Contour Grouping Performance', *Vision Research* 41 (2001), 711–724; D. D'Antona, J. Perry, and W. Geisler, 'Humans Make Efficient Use of Natural Image Statistics', *Journal of Vision* 13 (2013), 1–13; J. Burge and W. Geisler, 'Optimal Disparity Estimation in Natural Stereo Images', *Journal of Vision* 14 (2014), 1–18; S. Gepshtein and I. Tyukin, 'Optimal Measurement of Visual Motion Across Spatial and Temporal Scales', in M. Favorskaya and L. Jain eds., *Computer Vision in Advanced Control Systems Using Conventional and Intelligent Paradigms* (Berlin: Springer-Verlag, 2014).

But reliable approximate accuracy is useful enough for fitness enough of the time that it is a characteristic of many perception-action packages that *have* been selected for. Our visual systems have had a long time to become the near optimal organs of representation that they have become. The non- perceptual sensory systems from which our perceptual systems evolved used that time well.

My conclusion is so simple that it should not have needed stating. Perhaps you will think that it really *did not* need stating. Despite the risk of having wasted your time, I hope that you think this. Here is the conclusion anyway. Perception is a primitive but powerful source of certain types of objectivity – pre-eminently, approximately veridical representation of a fairly large but restricted range of environmental subject matter. Perception's providing this type of objectivity undergirds, in empirical science, the achievement of types of objectivity that perception itself can never achieve. It is a striking fact about the history of philosophy that perception has been ignored or denigrated. It has not consistently been recognized and honored as a basis for our achieving objectivity in understanding and explaining the world. I trust that it will occupy such a place more securely in the future.

References

Blakemore, C. (1970): 'The Range and Scope of Binocular Depth Discrimination in Man'. In: *Journal of Physiology* 211, pp. 599–622.
Burge, J. and Geisler, W. (2014): 'Optimal Disparity Estimation in Natural Stereo Images'. In: *Journal of Vision* 14, pp. 1–18.
Burge, T. (2000): 'Frege on Apriority'. In P. Boghossian and C. Peacocke (Eds.): *New Directions on the A Priori*. Oxford: Oxford University Press.
Burge, T. (2005): *Truth Thought Reason; Essays on Frege*. Oxford: Oxford University Press.
Burge, T. (2007): *Foundations of Mind*. Oxford: Oxford University Press.
Burge, T. (2010): *Origins of Objectivity*. Oxford University Press.
Burge, T. (2008): 'Iconic Representation: Maps, Pictures, and Perception'. In S. Wuppuluri and F. Doria (Eds.): *The Map and the Territory*. Cham: Springer.
D'Antona, D.; Perry, J. and Geisler, W. (2013): 'Humans Make Efficient Use of Natural Image Statistics'. In: *Journal of Vision* 13, pp. 1–13.
Daston, L. and Galison, P. (2007): *Objectivity*. New York: Zone Books.
Frege, G. (1968): *Foundations of Arithmetic*. J. Austin trans. Evanston, Illinois: Northwestern University Press.
Galton, F. (1907): 'The Wisdom of Crowds'. In: *Nature* 75, pp. 450–451, http://galton.orf/essays/1900-1911/galton-1907-vox-populi.pdf
Geisler, W.; Perry, J.; Super, B. and Gallogly, D. (2001): 'Edge Co- occurrence in Natural Images Predicts Contour Grouping Performance'. In: *Vision Research* 41, pp. 711–724.

Gepshtein S. and Tyukin, I. (2014): 'Optimal Measurement of Visual Motion Across Spatial and Temporal Scales'. In: M. Favorskaya and L. Jain (Eds.): *Computer Vision in Advanced Control Systems Using Conventional and Intelligent Paradigms.* Berlin: Springer-Verlag.

Gigerenzer, G. and Gaissmeier, W. (2011): 'Heuristic Decision Making'. In: *Annual Review of Psychology* 62, pp. 451–482.

Helmholtz, H. von (1867): *Handbuch der Physiologischen Optik.* Leipzig: Voss.

Kant, I. (1998): *Critique of Pure Reason.* P. Guyer and A. Wood trans. Cambridge: Cambridge University Press.

Mansuripur, M. (1987): *Introduction to Information Theory.* New York: Prentice Hall.

Pylyshyn, Z. (2003): *Seeing and Visualizing.* Cambridge, Mass.: MIT Press.

Shannon, C. (1948): 'A Mathematical Theory of Communication'. In: *Bell System Technical Journal* 27, pp. 379–423.

Wright, L. (1973): 'Functions'. In: *The Philosophical Review* 82, pp. 139–168.

Howard Robinson
Objectivity: How is it Possible?

Abstract: What gives perception objective reference to the external world? The direct realist says that it is our direct conscious contact with the world. The traditional empiricist, following Hume, says that it is the structure and ordering of our experience that makes us take it as objective. Burge explains it entirely in terms of sub-personal or pre-conscious processes, denying that phenomenology or conscious experience plays any essential role. I discuss Burge's arguments in detail and try to show that, from a philosophical point of view, at least, it is not possible to ignore the relevance of phenomenology to objectivity, and that Hume was on the right track.

Keywords: Objectivity, Burge, Hume, phenomenology, externalism

1 Introduction

It seems reasonable to assume that our notion of an objective, public world, which exists independently of us, must somehow be derived from our perceptual experience. For what else tells us about the world outside of us? But what is it about experience that delivers to us the idea of an objective world.

There seem to me to be three accounts of this. Two of them are defended at length in the literature. The third has been mentioned, but hardly taken up in a serious way. I believe that it is this last account that is correct.

The first account is found amongst a group of direct realists – who are also disjunctivists. Their claim is that it is only by being directly in contact with the physical world in normal perception that we can have a conception of such a world: if experience were in some way internal, then we could never even conceive of an external reality. John McDowell (1986), Bill Brewer (2011) and John Campbell (2014) are paradigms of this group.

The second theory is that objectivity comes from the dependence of our concepts on the existence of a causal connection between events internal to the individual and the external world. Tyler Burge will be my stalking horse for this theory.

One way of understanding the difference between these theories is that the former theory holds that connection with the world is essentially phenomenological; the second makes it essentially causal-semantic; the phenomenology plays either a minor role or no role at all.

The third theory is that our conception of objectivity comes from the way our experience is organized: what David Hume called the *coherence and consistency* of our experience. I defended this theory in Robinson (2013), it was taken up in Farkas (2013) and Cassam (2014) It is elegantly defended in Ayer (1963), but, as with most classical empiricist insights, it is wilfully ignored in much of contemporary debate.

I discussed and rejected the direct realist option in Robinson (2013) and I will say no more about it here. My target here is Burge's causal semantic account of objectivity, though I shall end up by sketching the Humean alternative.

2 The Causal-Semantic Account of Objectivity: How it Differs From the Direct Realist Account

Tyler Burge summarizes his view as follows.

> The objectivity of perceptual states is formed partly through patterns of non-representational causal relations to a mind-independent environment, and partly by subindividual objectifying operations in sensory systems that distill the environmental from the sensory effects of proximal stimulation. Both of these sources of objectivity are blind. The patterns of causal relations are part of blind nature impacting the lives of simple organisms and of the blind primitive agency of organisms on nature. The objectification is not an exercise of individual agency. The developmental, phylogenetic, psychological, and constitutive sources of objectivity in perception lie below the level of individual representation, control, awareness, or responsibility.
>
> ...Individuals do not construct objective perception from subjective representation or consciousness. (Burge 2010: 547)

It is important that the source of objectivity is very primitive and sub-personal, but it shares features with both the direct realist theory I cited above and the Humean theory which we will briefly discuss next. It shares with the former insistence on the role of the 'mind independent environment' which is 'distilled' from the 'sensory effects of proximal stimulation'. In other words, by virtue of such phenomena as perceptual constancy, it is the distal cause, not the proximal cause that comes through as the object of perception. On the other hand, Burge agrees – unknowingly I think – with Hume that it is the *patterns* of the stimuli that enable the perceiver to take them as objective, not the mere fact of their externality. Where he differs from both the other theories is that 'subjective representation or consciousness' play no role; the grounds of objectivity are to be found in creatures too primitive to be conscious, and, even in our case, operate at a sub-personal level.

I shall discuss later whether what Burge says need be controversial for those who hold a different theory, or whether the causal mechanisms he describes are only the background to the problem philosophers are usually discussing. First let us consider why he rejects the naïve or direct realist approach.

Burge dismisses naïve realism because he has no patience with the disjunctivism that necessarily accompanies it.

> Disjunctivism is implausible. Not only common sense but ...scientific knowledge...support this initial evaluation...
> Disjunctivism entails that token distal differences, in the causal chain leading to perceptual states, that make no relevant difference to proximal stimulation, or to other causal processes that provide input to our perceptual system, or to antecedent psychological states, determine differences in perceptual state types...This view is not only undermined by scientific knowledge. It controverts well-entrenched views about the form of causal explanation in psychology. (Burge 2005: 27)

Burge, consequently, is some kind of a common factor theorist. It might be thought that he, therefore, has two options. He might attribute to this common factor an intrinsic intentionality by which it represents, or purports to represent, the external world. Or he might be a traditional representative realist, like Locke or Mackie. In fact he explicitly rejects both these positions, on the grounds that the internal common factor, which he identifies with the basic phenomenology, is inadequate to explain the intentionality of perception.

> ...attempts to individuate perceptual states in *purely* phenomenological terms fail to provide any insight into the intentionality of perceptual states. Either they help themselves to representational power associated with our phenomenology, without explaining that power, or they offer a feature, phenomenology-with-representational-content-bracketed, that does nothing to explain representational power. (Burge 2005: 20–21)

This rejection is not surprising, because both the positions he is here rejecting are *individualistic*: they both allow perceptual experience to be conceptually independent of the external world, and, as Burge implies in the last quotation, he believes that individualistic theories fail to explain how representation works. But *prima facie* Burge is in a position which leaves him some explaining to do. Common factor theorists are normally or naturally representationalists of a sort that seems to require an internalist approach to perceptual experience. That is why perceptual externalists tend to be disjunctivists.

It is interesting to follow those respects in which Burge goes along with internalism (or, as Burge prefers to say, individualism) in the nature of experience, and those respects in which he rejects it, and to see whether he manages to reconcile these two tendencies.

Burge does not deny that something rather like a brain in a vat – which possessed a central nervous system like ours – could have a phenomenology like ours, but does deny that this would constitute an adequate basis for its having perceptual-type experience. Thus, when arguing against Brian Loar's 'brain in a vat' scenario, he considers the following possibility.

> Suppose that we...imagine a system that is molecule for molecule homologous to our brains, but came together as a cosmic accident. I have little confidence about how to imagine such a being from the inside or outside. At least in its first moments, it would seem to lack most of the cognitive and perceptual systems that I have. I am inclined to think that it would have similar qualitative, phenomenal "feels", since I conjecture that certain qualitative aspects of the mind depend purely on the underlying chemistry. But at least until it has interacted with its world, I do not think that it has any "outer-directed" intentionality. I think that it does not even have a visual system until it has interacted with its world.
> One can be easily confused in phenomenal exercises. One can imagine that things would "look" just the same to the homologous accident. Such an imagining would be corrupt. The notion of "look" already depends on presumptions of perceptual and conceptual content that I believe are illegitimately imported into the envatted accident. The processes in this thing at first lack meaning and function. At most the individual would have similar phenomenal features. (Burge 2003: 444)

Thus Burge distinguishes between the phenomenological component in perceptual experience, and the representational. To put it in the common jargon, he distinguishes between phenomenology and *content*, and denies that there could be the latter without there being, paradigmatically, a genuine causal relation to the appropriate feature in the external world.

The issue is to consider whether Burge manages to reconcile internalism about phenomenology with externalism about perceptual experience. To approach this we need to consider at least two issues.

(i) Does Burge manage to reconcile his claim that science does not allow distal causes to have an unmediated influence on our mental states with their externalist role in influencing 'how things look'?

(ii) What positive arguments does Burge have for his externalism in perception?

3 Burge on Distal Causes and the Experience of 'how things look'

At the outset, I presented the following quotation from Burge.

> Disjunctivism entails that token distal differences, in the causal chain leading to perceptual states, that make no relevant difference to proximal stimulation, or to other causal processes that provide input to our perceptual system, or to antecedent psychological states, determine differences in perceptual state types...This view is not only undermined by scientific knowledge. It controverts well-entrenched views about the form of causal explanation in psychology. (Burge 2005: 27)

Later, I quoted what he said when discussing the spontaneous 'brain in a vat' case.

> One can be easily confused in phenomenal exercises. One can imagine that things would "look" just the same to the homologous accident. Such an imagining would be corrupt. The notion of "look" already depends on presumptions of perceptual and conceptual content that I believe are illegitimately imported into the envatted content. The processes in this thing at first lack meaning and function. At most the individual would have similar phenomenal features. (Burge 2003: 444)

These two quotations seem, at the very least, to be in tension. It is difficult to see how he squares the latter with the scientific realism he castigates the disjunctivist for ignoring. It is natural to take *how things look* to be something experiential, so if things look differently, or fail to look at all, then it is experientially different for the subject. But Burge says that how things look depends on distal factors – what has been the standard, typical or appropriate external cause – whereas in the first quotation he says that the idea that distal causes that make no difference to proximate stimuli should influence the perceptual state goes against science and psychology. Burge is working with a distinction between 'phenomenal features', sometimes called 'phenomenology', and 'how things look', which is part of normal perception. (But notice that Burge says that distal causes cannot directly influence the *perceptual* state, not just the phenomenal contents.) *Ex hypothesi*, the brain in a vat has the same proximal states as the normal subject, but Burge wants to claim that whether these give rise to proper perceptual 'looks' depends on their having, directly or indirectly, the right aetiology.

Burge might be thought to have the following way out of the problem. It might be argued that he is not a simple common factor theorist, in the following way. A straightforward common factor theorist would claim that the perceptual experience as a whole depended, for its phenomenology, entirely on the brain. This is what Burge appears to be affirming in the quotation from (Burge 2005: 27) above. But he appears to believe that less central factors do affect the phenomenology a phenomenologically indiscernible hallucination, produced by direct stimulation of central areas of the brain, rather than through visual pathways, might not even count as a perceptual state.

His reason for this is that for a genuine perceptual duplication, it must be the case 'that relevant afferent and efferent internal processes that provide input to the perceptual system are the same.' (Burge 2005: 25) This means that we must imagine the BIV as being more than a brain – more like a total nervous system. I cannot see that this makes any difference: imagine the whole nervous system in a vat and the stimulation provided by the evil scientist to be peripheral or central, as required. This *may* not infringe the 'same proximate cause, same immediate effect' principle, provided that the extended process in the nervous system can be regarded as a complex proximate cause of the experience. But this does not help with the present problem, for it only extends the *internal* states that are relevant; it does nothing to accommodate the role of distal causes.

The reason why 'looks' depend on the right aetiology is because how things look depends on intentionality, which is a semantic phenomenon. This might seem to force one to conclude that, for Burge, how things look is not a matter of phenomenology, experience, or 'how it is for the subject' at all, but of a more abstract, purely conceptual, feature of the experience. It is simply that a certain experience only 'counts as' being as of an external object if it has a certain aetiology, though this makes no difference at all to how it seems to the subject. Apart from being massively counterintuitive, it would also be a perverse use of 'looks', which is a 'how it is for the subject' term, if anything is. It would also go against the general 'common sense' tone of Burge's exposition of his own theory.

It is worth noting what seems to me to be a particularly blatant case of trying to have it both ways. When discussing a 'Twin Earth' type of case in which the same internal states are associated with different distal stimuli, called '*O*' and '*C*', he says of the counterfactual – *C* – case

> They regularly obtain information about instances of *C*; and we may imagine that their physical movements and discriminative abilities are quite different from the ones they have in the actual circumstances. *Only the protagonist's body, non-intentionally and individualistically specified, need remain the same.* (Burge 1986/2007: 204; italics added)

How can the agent's *physical movements* be different if his internal physical states are all the same? His *behaviour* might (somewhat tendentiously and misleadingly, in my view) be differently characterized, but the sheer movements cannot differ if his internal states are the same and the external world is, as in a Twin Earth, only indiscriminably different. It is again unclear how Burge can hold the internal fixed and really alter the mental, externalistically conceived.

Burge has, therefore, failed to make a plausible case for excluding the phenomenology from *how the world looks* and, therefore, from the core account of perception.

4 Burge's Positive Arguments for his Externalism in Perception

The problem for Burge is to explain what it is that generates the externalism, given his rejection of direct realism. In the case of the direct realists, the ground for externalism is clear: external objects themselves constitute the phenomenal contents of experience. This is how they interpret the so-called transparency of perceptual experience. Burge has replaced this direct entrapment of the external world into experience by something that looks much more like an ordinary causal relation, hence he needs to explain how his theory comes to be externalist. The following quotation is typical.

> [...] what makes representational states what they are – indeed, an aspect of their natures – is that they set veridicality conditions, which when fulfilled are true or accurate...[I]n setting veridicality conditions, which can be fulfilled by conditions in the physical environment, representational states bear systematic, non-accidental representational relations to the environment. It is not accidental that a thought as of aluminium bears a non-accidental relation to aluminium. And this sort of non-accidental relation is massively systematic...This system of non-accidental connections between the natures of psychological states and non-psychological environmental attributes can be in place only if there are specific systematic, non-representational, typically causal, relations between environmental entities and psychological states. These relations ground constitutive explication of both the representational relation and psychological states' representations of environmental entities *as being* ways that they are. (Burge 2010: 80–81)

The problem for Burge is how he can show that this dependence is *constitutive* and not merely *causal*, given his common factor theory and the ban on distal influence without mediation.

Burge's main argument is, I think, to be found in (Burge 1986/2007: 198–207). I shall initially represent the argument as follows.
(1) The same internal states – dispositions, phenomenology etc – can represent different external things in different worlds or scenarios.
(2) A perceptual state is a perception *of* what it represents.
Therefore (3) Perception is (in part, at least) externally constituted.

I want to contrast this line of thought with the one I would attribute to the classical representationalist or Humean. In order to express that I need to adapt an expression of Sellars's, namely the *Manifest World* (MW). MW is the world of common sense and of the naïve realist. Colours are essentially as they seem, shape, space and time are as they seem. This contrasts with the *Scientific Image* of the world, which lacks secondary qualities and in which, if Russell is right space and time are nothing like the way they seem: the scientific world and the manifest world share a formalizable structure capturable in mathematics and that is all. One can hold to the contrast between the manifest and the scientific without accepting Russell's extreme position: one could follow Locke in thinking that there was qualitative resemblance on the primary quality level. With this jargon in place, the un-Burgean argument goes as follows.

(4) The MW as we perceive it is a projection of our qualia.

(5) Qualia are internal/individualistic.

Therefore (6) Our perception of the MW is individualistic.

As I do not think that the validity of this latter argument is in dispute, and as Burge is an internalist about qualia and phenomenology, and so would accept (5), the disagreement must concern (4). It is in fact (4) and (1) that are in conflict, for if the-world-as-we-perceive-it is a projection of qualia, it cannot be systematically true that the same qualia could represent different features of a MW. We seem to be on familiar ground. This is the same territory as the claim that, if you see grass the way I see fire-engines, then your red qualia represent green. This would be the Burgean option. The alternative view is that we represent the MW as being significantly different, though we would never realize this. I think that the second option is compulsory, if one accepts that there is a MW at all, as I think we must.

Why does Burge accept (1)? In Burge's own exposition of the line of argument I have given to him, his first premise is

> (7) I begin with the premise that our perceptual experience represents or is about objects, properties and relations that are *objective*. That is to say, their nature (or essential character) is independent of any one person's actions, dispositions, or mental phenomena. An obvious consequence is that individuals are capable of having perceptual representations that are misperceptions or hallucinations…To put this consequences with some gesture of precision: for any given person at any given time, there is no necessary function from all of that person's abilities, actions and representations up to that time and the nature of those entities that that person interacts with… (Burge 1986/2007: 198–199)

From this premise Burge concludes as follows.

> My first premise [which is (7) in my reconstruction] gives us this much. The objectivity of the objects of perception entails that there is always a possible gap between the proximal

effects of those objects on an individual's mind or body...and the nature of the objects themselves...The same proximal effects, representations, thought, and activity could in certain instances derive from different objective entities. (Burge 1986/2007: 204)

He combines this gloss on (7) with his second premise, which is equivalent to (2). This is that perceptual representations '*specify* particular objective types of objects, properties or relations *as such*'. From (7), glossed as in the quoted passage, and the idea that representations are essentially of objective external features, he concludes that the same proximal effects could represent different entities – that is, (1) in my exposition of the argument.

Burge's transition of thought is that the objectivity of things that we perceive allows for the possibility of error and that this generalizes in a 'Twin Earth' kind of way to the possibility that the same internal representation could systematically represent different things. This transition might be challenged in two quite different ways. First, it is not obvious that the same basic dispositions to bodily movement could fit different primary quality features. (Bennett's contrast between colour blindness or spectrum inversion, which can pass unnoticed, and size or shape blindness, which would be radically disruptive, is relevant here (Bennett 1971). You cannot map the body movement appropriate to getting through a large rectangular door onto climbing through a small round porthole. So, too, is the passage I remarked on at the end of the previous section, where Burge seems to think that the same internal state could give rise to different bodily movements.) Second, and more salient from my point of view, is the fact that Burge's theory seems to omit the manifest world altogether. On Burge's theory, how the world looks is a function of what it is objectively like, not of the nature of the qualia it gives rise to. Just as contrasting qualia could equally represent green, so it is not the qualitative nature of our visual or tactile shape qualia that condition our common sense conception of space, but what space is actually like, for that is what determines, according to Burge, how the world spatially looks – for remember that

> Qualitative or phenomenological features of perceptual states do not *in themselves* bear any explanatory relation to the environmental properties that perceptual states represent. (Burge 2010: 76)

It is as if Burge is combining a radical Russellian view that the world may share no qualitative components with our subjective experience, with a kind of direct realism according to which we perceive it as being the way it actually is. In defending his second premise, that perceptual representations '*specify* particular objective types of objects, properties or relations *as such*', he has to insist that

> Perceptual representations do not all have the contents like those of 'whatever normally causes this sort of perceptual representation' – or 'whatever normally has this sort of perceptual appearance', where the description denoted some objective property. (Burge 1986/2007: 199)

Such expressions would be appropriate on Russell's theory for denoting the properties in the scientific image of the world. Burge seems to think that our perception, through our semantics, captures these properties directly, although they cannot be thought of as mirroring the qualitative nature of our subjective experience. By contrast, the manifest world draws its qualitative content from the phenomenal content of experience. According to Burge, a world of experience cannot be constructed in this way, so the manifest world is lost. There are only phenomenal contents, which cannot constitute anything even seemingly objective, and the world of objective – presumably scientific – fact, which perception represents. This is blatantly not how experience is.

5 Empirical Evidence and a More Plausible Possible Interpretation

The argument taken from 'Cartesian error and the objectivity of perception' discussed in the last section, does, I believe, commit Burge to the extreme position reached by the end of the section. This is because, according to that argument, and to his attack on the idea that there could be similarity between phenomenal content and objective properties, the content of individualistic states cannot contribute content to what they represent. Nevertheless, one might adopt a weaker position, according to which qualia can be projected as qualities of the manifest world, but only if they paradigmatically stand in the right causal relation to the features of the external world they are perceived as being. This strategy would deprive Burge of the argument discussed in the previous section, because that depended on there being an absolute divide between what qualia are like and what the objective properties they represent are like. So what argument could be provided for this more moderate position, especially given the availability of the Humean alternative?

Something that Burge thinks is very important to externalism and which might be used to defend the moderate position is the fact that the proximal causes of our experiences underdetermine the content of the experiences themselves, and it is the distal cause that fixes the content. He cites cases such as colour constancy as examples of this. His conclusion is that our processing systems have biases towards interpreting proximate stimuli in certain ways. Merely for shorthand, I will express this idea by saying that the *object concept* is hardwired – that is, we are naturally disposed to interpret the proximate stimuli in the way that makes them informative about the external world of stable objects. It is not obvious, however, why this innate bias should support externalism, but Burge does think that it does, especially in relation to perception. The sentence immediately following the quotation from (Burge 2005: 25) above is

> Reflection on the role of biasing principles in determining perceptual kinds yields a detailed elaboration of empirical aspects of anti-individualism. Such reflection indicates how perceptual anti-individualism informs and is made specific through empirical explanation.

It is by no means obvious why the fact that we are, thanks to evolution or design, hard-wired to jump to certain conclusions on the basis of strictly inadequate evidence, supports externalism. It could not, in fact, have happened without external causes, but it is essential to Burge's position – as he repeatedly acknowledges – to distinguish between

(i) It is a *causal* truth (if, no doubt, a very important one) that we *would* not and *causally could not* have had the representations of crucial external features of the world if we had not lived in an environment with those features.

And

(ii) It is a *conceptual* truth that we *could* not have had representations of crucial external features of the world if we had not lived in an environment with those features.

(i) will not suffice to justify externalism. Its claim is only about causal processes, so there is no reason why an Evil Scientist or Demon could not have mimicked the effects that the external features in fact produce in our nervous systems. Burge, therefore, needs (ii) – which is, roughly, (i) with a necessity operator in front of it – and, though he insists on the 'constitutive' nature of the dependence, it is not easy to find arguments that justify a more-than-causal dependence, once the general argument discussed in the last section is dismissed.

The message is that the internal states would not be, or count as, representations of the external features of which they are representations, if it were not for the 'non-accidental' and 'massively systematic' causal system into which they fit. A first reaction to this claim might be that this view of what constitutes something as a representation might be plausible within some kind of functionalist framework, for then the causal relations are what makes something into a representation. But Burge is emphatically not a functionalist or reductionist of any sort. In particular, he is not a reductionist about the phenomenology of perception, so why cannot the phenomenology carry the burden of representation? We have seen in the above discussion that his treatment of the role of phenomenology is inadequate. Moreover, important causal truths are 'non-accidental' and can be (and, in this case, are) 'massively systematic', so these constraints do not support the more-than-causal interpretation.

6 Innateness of "the Object Concept" as an Alternative to Externalism

It is important to distinguish (i) and (ii) from a further principle, which one might call *the Kantian principle*. Burge's discussion of underdetermination, if correct (and I do not wish to dispute it here) shows that the concept of the stable external world cannot simply be constructed from the patterning of the proximate stimuli alone. We might put this succinctly by saying the *object concept* must be hardwired. This claim is parallel to the rejection of the phenomenalist reduction of physical object concepts into terms that do not mention objects. This would justify what I have called *the Kantian principle.*

(iii) If we are to represent the external world at all, the idea that perceptual experience is *of* external things must be built into the representations themselves – it cannot be constructed or derived – and so they must be innately interpreted in the light of the object concept.

It is not unusual for Burge to talk as if he were equating internalism with nonintentionality, but there is no problem for a Kantian to be an internalist, for the resources for making the Kantian interpretation of experience are hard-wired and, hence, internal. So (iii) of itself does not justify (ii).

Burge, I think, is caught between two opposites, in two ways. First, as we have seen above, he wants both to explain how perception acquires its representational function, rather in the way a functionalist needs to give an explanation, and at the same time to accept a non-reductive, intuitive view of the phenomenology. I will argue in the next section that the latter removes any need for the former explanation, once one has taken Hume on board. But second, and more important, Burge wants to combine his anti-disjunctivist belief in a 'common factor' with externalism, even though the common factor is something internal. He rejects disjunctivism because he thinks that science demands the Proximality Principle, which requires that the same kind of proximal cause produces the same kind of effect. (This is discussed elsewhere, for example in Robinson 1994 and 2013) McDowell (1986) has convincingly shown that simply adding an external causal connection to an inner state does not, of itself, make that inner state into an *experience* as of something external. The external causal connection would somehow have to transform the experience itself – affect the phenomenology – but Burge neither seems to claim this (maintaining a firm distinction between phenomenology and representational content) nor to provide the materials on which such an explanation might be based.

7 Constancy and Coherence: the Humean Account of Objectivity

Neither the direct realist account, nor the causal semantic one are at all plausible. How does the Humean account fare?

The two contemporary theories completely ignore the most important classical account of how we come to take most of our data as external, namely David Hume's.

Hume's account of how our conception of the world is built up from our experience of sensible qualities is to be found in 'On scepticism with regard to the senses' in Part I of the *Treatise*.

Hume argues that 'the opinion of the continu'd existence of body depends on the COHERENCE and CONSTANCY of certain impressions...' (1964: 195). In other words, given that the ordering of the sensible qualities is such as it is, then there is no other way of making sense of these patterns other than to take them as being of enduring, external physical objects. Whether this process be a rationally defensible one – an implicit argument to the best explanation, for example – or brute irrational habit and association, is another matter. We can state the principle as follows:

> Given the natural rationalizing dispositions of the human mind, (Hume's 'tendencies of the mind') the presentation of sensible qualities in the kind of ordering in which they are presented, is both a necessary and sufficient condition for their being taken as being experiences of a physical world.

Despite the title of the chapter in which Hume introduces this account, one does not have to be either a phenomenalist or a Humean sceptic to think that this is essentially a true account of how we come to take most of our experiences as objective. Hume's scepticism and phenomenalism rest, not on his account of how we form our conception of the objective world, but on his sceptical approach to causation and explanation.

That such an ordering in experience is necessary for objectivity can be seen by considering the problems facing the naïve realist theory. The naïve realists argue that, if we did not perceive the external world directly, we could have no conception of such an external or objective world. In McDowell's striking phrase, all would be 'darkness within'. But that direct contact with the external world is not enough to ground a conception of it, can be seen by considering the following case.

Suppose a normally blind person very occasionally had a direct realist perception of the external world, but that these experiences were too fragmentary for him to connect them with his normal tactile and other perception of the world. As far as he was concerned, they would just be odd sensations that he had. The fact that the content is actually external would make no difference without the presence of the appropriate structure and order. So ordering within experience seems necessary for that experience to be taken as objective. It is tempting, too, to regard it as pragmatically sufficient. How could a creature of roughly human construction and intelligence have experiences ordered in the way ours are, without coming to interpret them as being of a physical world? We cannot imagine any other way of rationalizing – rendering manageable and projectable – our experience, taken qualitatively, than the physical interpretation we give to it.

It is, I think, worth emphasizing that no consideration at all is given in the contemporary debate about our grasp on the notion of objectivity to the broadly Humean approach, despite its massive intuitive plausibility. The burden seems to me to be on the anti-Humean to prove that order of the right kind could not be sufficient to suggest externality, especially as it is clearly necessary, which, on the direct realist account, it ought not to be.

I said at the start of the discussion of Burge that he shared with the Humean a belief in the essential role of patterns in the way we are stimulated. 'Patterns' and 'constancy and coherence' signify essentially the same thing. But for Burge this coherence is not a feature of conscious experience and for Hume it is. What is the significance of this apparent disagreement? I think both parties (and perhaps everyone, including the naïve realists) could agree about the following.

(a) If it had not been for the kinds of mechanisms that Burge describes in primitive creatures and those subpersonal mechanisms we possess as an evolutionary result of them, then our conscious experience (if there were any at all) would not manifest Hume's coherence and constancy.
(b) If one wished to build a robot that 'perceived' and interacted with its environment, it would need to embody a structure of the kind Burge describes.

I said in my formulation of the Humean theory that it followed '(g)iven the natural rationalizing dispositions of the human mind, (Hume's 'tendencies of the mind')' that appropriate ordering of experience would give rise to our conception of an external world. Burge's theory merely fills in some of the details about the genesis and grounding of those 'tendencies' and 'dispositions'. Let us suppose that the mechanisms Burge postulates exist, but that they happen not to give rise to a Humean constant and coherent conscious experience. Could we, then, as conscious beings, have a conception of an objective world? I do not see how.

Given the existence of the right kind of coherence and consistency in the phenomena, there is no issue of how our experience manages to represent the world. In a sense, the situation is just the opposite: the world of common experience – the manifest image world or the world of naïve realism – is a creature of our phenomenology. What it is like to see red, and what red is (naively) like, what it is like to see, head on, a square patch and what squareness is visually like, these are two sides of the same coin. It could not be further from the truth to say, as Burge does above, that

> Qualitative or phenomenological features of perceptual states do not *in themselves* bear any explanatory relation to the environmental properties that perceptual states represent. (Burge 2010: 76)

Beyond the issue of 'the right kind of ordering', I do not see why there should be any problem about how representation gets into perceptual experience. To suggest that there is a problem here is to ignore the difference between what one might call the iconic representation in perception and the digital or conventional representation in thought and language.

8 Conclusion

I argued in Robinson (2013) that direct realism, without 'coherence and constancy' could not deliver objectivity. I have argued above that sub-personal structure alone cannot give it either. The Humean criterion is the only one to give objectivity for conscious beings, even if it depends causally on mechanisms of the sort Burge delineates.

References

Ayer, Alfred (1963): "Privacy", in his *Concept of a Person and Other Essays*. London: Macmillan, pp. 52–81.
Bennett, J. (1971): *Locke, Berkeley, Hume*. Oxford: Clarendon Press.
Brewer, Bill (2011): *Perception and its Objects*. Oxford: Oxford University Press.
Burge, Tyler (1986): "Cartesian error and the objectivity of perception". In: *Subject, Thought and Content*, Petit, Peter and McDowell, John (Eds.). Oxford: Clarendon Press, pp. 117–36.
Burge, Tyler (2003): "Tyler Burge replies". In: *Reflections and Replies: essays on the philosophy of Tyler Burge*, Hahn, Martin and Ramberg, Bjorn (Eds.). Cambridge: MIT Press, pp. 289–470.
Burge, Tyler (2005): "Disjunctivism and perceptual psychology". In: *Philosophical Topics* 33, pp. 1–78.
Burge, Tyler (2007): *Foundations of Mind*. Oxford: Oxford University Press.
Burge, Tyler (2010): *The Origins of Objectivity*. Oxford: Oxford University Press.
Campbell, John (2014): *Berkeley's Puzzle: What Does Experience Teach Us?* Oxford: Oxford University Press. Co-authored with Quassim Cassam.
Cassam, Quassim (2014): *Berkeley's Puzzle: What Does Experience Teach Us?* Oxford: Oxford University Press. Co-authored with John Campbell.
Farkas, Katalin (2013): "Constructing a World for the Senses". In: Kriegel, Uriah (Ed): *Phenomenal Intentionality*. Oxford: Oxford University Press, pp. 99–115.
Hume, David (1964): *A Treatise of Human Nature*. In: L. A. Selby-Bigge (Ed.), Oxford: Clarendon Press.
McDowell, John (1986): "Singular Thought and the Extent of Inner Space". In: Petit, Peter and McDowell, John (Eds.): *Subject, Thought and Context*, Oxford: Clarendon Press, pp. 137–168.
McDowell, John (2010): "Tyler Burge on disjunctivism". In: *Philosophical Explorations 13*, pp. 243–55.
Robinson, Howard. (1994): *Perception*. London: Routledge.
Robinson, Howard (2013): "The failure of disjunctivism to deal with 'philosophers' hallucinations". In: McPherson, Fiona and Platchias, Dimitris (Eds.): *Hallucinations* Cambridge Mass.: MIT Press, pp. 313–330.

Olivier Massin
Realism's Kick

Abstract: Samuel Johnson claimed to have refuted Berkeley by kicking a stone. It is generally thought that Johnson misses the point of Berkeley's immaterialism for a rather obvious reason: Berkeley never denied that the stone feels solid, but only that the stone could exist independently of any mind. I argue that Johnson was on the right track. On my interpretation, Johnson's idea is that because the stone feels to resist our effort, the stone seems to have causal powers. But if appearances are to be taken at face value, as Berkeley insists, then the stone has causal powers. I argue that such causal powers threaten not only Berkeley's view that only minds are active, but also, and more fundamentally, his central claim that sensible things depend on perception.

Keywords: Berkeley, effort, realism, phenomenalism, causal powers, perception

Johnson famously tried to refute Berkeley by kicking a stone:

> After we came out of the church, we stood talking for some time together of Bishop Berkeley's ingenious sophistry to prove the non-existence of matter, and that every thing in the universe is merely ideal. I observed, that though we are satisfied his doctrine is not true, it is impossible to refute it. I never shall forget the alacrity with which Johnson answered, striking his foot with mighty force against a large stone, till he rebounded from it, — "I refute it thus." (Boswell, 1826, 370)

Johnson's "refutation" is not only widely held to miss the point, it is held to do so for an obvious reason. Berkeley denies that the stone exists independently of its perception. As he stresses, this is wholly compatible with the stone feeling solid. Johnson's refutation would seem so question-begging that a sophism was named after it: argumentum ad lapidem.

I here argue that Johnson's refutation is indeed a refutation. I am not the first to attempt a rehabilitation of Johnson's kick. H. F. Hallett (1947) and D. L. Patey (1986) have already put forward extensive re-evaluations of the kick.[1] Indeed, I am sympathetic to their respective central claims. Hallett maintains that Johnson's refutation is primarily targeted at Berkeley's view that only minds are active. Patey, meanwhile, maintains that Johnson's refutation appeals to the view that the experience of resistance to our voluntary efforts presents us with the

---
[1] To whom Silver (1993) may be added.

mind-independence of its objects. While these ideas tend in the right direction, in order to refute Berkeley's immaterialism we still need to do two things:

- First, with respect to Hallett's proposal, we need to understand the connection between immaterialism and the view that only minds can produce effects in nature: why can't immaterialists agree that stones are active, so long as stones and their activity depend on their perception?
- Second, with respect to Patey's interpretation, we need to address the worry that in appealing to the resistance of the stone to our will, Johnson changes the subject: Berkeley challenges the idea that perceptual objects are existentially independent *from our perception* of them, to which Johnson seems to answer that objects are exist independently *from our will*. Such an answer, on the face of it, misses the point. Worse still, it expresses a view – namely, the will-independency of sensible things – with which Berkeley explicitly agrees.

In what follows, I hope to answer to these two concerns. First, I argue in section 1 that what Johnson seeks to establish by kicking the stone is not that the stone feels solid, but that the stone feels mind-independent. Such an experience of mind-independence may be understood as arising from ordinary perception, or as arising merely from a specific kind of experience: the experience of resistance to our effort. Next, I argue in section 2 that the idea that ordinary perception presents us with the mind-independency of its objects is untenable and unlikely to be the idea behind Johnson's kick in any case. Then, in section 3, I argue that Johnson endorses the plausible thought that, in experiencing resistance to our will, we are presented with the mind-independency of the stone. Finally, section 4 argues that relying on this form of mind-independence to refute Berkeley is not as question-begging as it might first appear. To the contrary, while independency from the will and independency from perception are indeed distinct, I argue that the kind of will-independency displayed by the stone entails its independency from perception.

1 Johnson's Refutation Reconstructed

What is immaterialism, the view that Johnson intends to rebut? Let us begin by defining *sensible things*, as Berkeley understands them:
Sensible things: the immediate objects of perception, e.g., heat, colour, extension, motion, solidity…. and collections thereof.

Do sensible things exist independently of our perception of them? Those who answer positively, such as Thomas Reid, are called direct realists. Those who answer negatively divide into two sub-camps, depending on the answer they give to a second question: is there some mind-independent unthinking substance behind those mind-dependent sensible things? Proponents of the positive answer are, with Locke (or at least on the standard interpretation) indirect realists. Those who answer 'no' embrace Berkeley's phenomenalism or immaterialism (here I shall equate the two).

Phenomenalism/immaterialism: sensible things existentially depend on our perception of them, and there is no mind-independent unthinking substance beyond them.

What, then, is Johnson's refutation of immaterialism? The common (and I think *uncharitable*) interpretation goes as follows:
P1 The stone feels solid.
C1 Some sensible things seem solid. (from P1, by existential generalization)
C2 Some sensible things are mind-independent. (from C1, allegedly)[2]

The move from C1 to C2 is, of course, unwarranted: there is no logical connection between *seeming solid* and *being mind-independent*.

The first step on the way to fixing the refutation is to modify P1. What Johnson wants to call our attention to, I suggest, is not the fact that the stone feels *solid*, but that the stone feels *mind-independent*. With this amendment, the refutation reads as follows:
P1' The stone feels mind-independent.
C1' Some sensible things seem mind-independent. (from P1, by existential generalization)
C2 Some sensible things are mind-independent. (from C1, allegedly)

Again, the move from C1' to C2 is unwarranted, but we are getting closer since the two propositions now bear on the same property: mind-independence. The premise needed in order the render the argument valid is now clear:
P1' The stone feels mind-independent.

---

[2] The 'solidity' reading of the argument was proposed early on by Kearney, in an added note to Edmund Malone, who helped Boswell to compile his biography, as well as providing extensive annotation: "Dr Johnson seems to have been imperfectly acquainted with Berkeley's doctrine; and his experiment only proves that we have the sensation of solidity, which Berkeley did not deny. He admitted that we had sensations or ideas usually called sensible qualities, one of which is solidity: he only denied the existence of matter." (Boswell 1826: 370)

C1' Some sensible things seem mind-independent. (from P1, by existential generalization)
P2 Sensible things are as they seem.
C2 Some sensible things are mind-independent. (from C1, P2)

This argument is valid (one quibble is the move from "feel" in P1 to "seem" in C1', which is, I assume, unproblematic). I believe that this is the argument that Johnson had in mind. This may sound like a bold claim. After all, Johnson's refutation is highly enthymematic: from no premise – but merely a gesture – a conclusion is drawn. Can such a terse argument really contain two premises?

Let us begin with P2. One may wonder whether appealing to such a premise is not question-begging in the context of an argument against immaterialism. After all, isn't it an obvious consequence of immaterialism that things are not as they seem? Berkeley answers negatively. P2 is in fact a strongly Berkeleyan premise. One chief motivation driving Berkeley's immaterialism is precisely to rebut the sceptics, who are defined as those who refuse to trust their senses: "I am of a vulgar cast, simple enough to believe my senses, and leave things as I find them." (Berkeley: *Three Dialogues*: 229).[3]

The main point of immaterialism – bracketing theological considerations – is to enable one to take appearances at face value. P2, therefore, is not a premise that Johnson either needs to defend or state: his opponent grants it.

This, then, leaves us with P1': the claim that the stone feels mind-independent. This is, I believe, the bone of contention – *der Stein des Anstosses* – between Johnson and Berkeley. P1' is the only premise that Johnson needs to state and defend. He does this by kicking the stone.

Now, there are two main ways of interpreting P1':
1. It is a feature of ordinary perception to present us with the mind-independency of its objects.
2. Only a very specific form of experience (viz., the experience of resistance to our will) embeds a presentation of mind-independence.

I argue in the next section that the first proposal is untenable and unlikely to be the idea behind Johnson's kick in any case.

---

[3] Pagination refers throughout to the Luce and Jessop's edition. See also *Three Dialogues* 113, 173–4, 215; *Principles* §40, §101 and Saporiti (2008) for discussion.

2 Experiencing Mind-Independence: Ordinary Perception

Before considering whether ordinary perception presents us with the mind-independency of its objects, let us take pause to distinguish clearly between two questions that we are concerned with here. Recall that we began with the question: *are* sensible things mind-independent? We are now interested in the question: do sensible things *seem* mind-independent? Call the former, *the question of the reality of appearances*, and the latter *the question of the appearance of reality*.[4] These two questions are distinct and in principle independent, unless, as we saw, one admits that sensible things are as they seem, and they seem mind-independent. In such a case, phenomenalism is refuted.

Focusing henceforth on the question of the appearance of reality, Berkeley consistently answered negatively to that question:

> [our senses] do not inform us that things exists without the mind, or unperceived. (*Principles*, §18; see also *Three Dialogues*: 201)

On this, he was followed by Hume:

> As to the independency of our perceptions on ourselves, this can never be an object of the senses. (Hume 2007: 1.4.2.)

As well as Reid:

> It is evident, that we cannot, by reasoning from our sensations, collect the existence of bodies at all. This has been proved by unanswerable arguments by the Bishop of Cloyne, and by the author of the "Treatise of Human Nature" (Reid 2000: 687)

Let us make a quick comment on Reid. It may be found surprising that Reid (a direct realist who subscribed to the mind-independence of sensible things) nevertheless rejects the view that sensible things are experienced *as* mind-independent. However, on his account, our belief in the mind-independency of perceptual objects is not grounded in our experience of their mind-independency, but in our

---

4 Siegel (2006) draws basically the same distinction between these two questions, and addresses a version of second one. She doesn't address however the question of whether or not perceptual objects seem *existentially* independent from us, but the question of whether or not they seem to *have and keep the same properties* independently of the location from which we perceive them.

very nature. Although mind-independence cannot be perceived, we cannot help believing that what we perceive exists independently from us.

Clearly, then, even direct realists were prone the reject the view that mind-independence can be perceived at the time. This stands in stark contrast with contemporary philosophers of perception, who tend to take P1' for granted:

> Mature sensible experience (in general) presents itself as [...] an *immediate* consciousness of the existence of things outside us. (Strawson 1979)
> All (or almost all) serious theories of perception agree that our perceptual experience *seems as if* it were an awareness of a mind-independent world. (Crane 2005)[5]
> Perceptual experience subjectively presents as if it puts us in touch with mind-independent objects. (Allais 2015: 53)

I side with Berkeley, Hume, and Reid. Ordinary perception, I believe, is silent with respect to the mind-independency of its objects. Why? One argument against the possibility of experiencing mind-independence is given by Hume. After having argued that the claims '*x continues to exist when unperceived*' and '*x exists independently from its perception*' entail each other, Hume continues:

> To begin with the SENSES, 'tis evident these faculties are incapable of giving rise to the notion of the continu'd existence of their objects, after they no longer appear to the senses. For that is a contradiction in terms, and supposes that the senses continue to operate, even after they have ceas'd all manner of operation. (Hume 2007: 1.4.2.)

Perceiving independence would be as hopeless as trying to see whether the light in the fridge stays on when we close the door. In order to perceive something as mind-independent we would have to perceive it when it is unperceived—a patent impossibility.

Hume's argument is, however, flawed. It relies on the assumption that the only way to perceive the mind-independence of x is to perceive x when it is not perceived. This is arguably too strong a requirement. In order to perceive x as mind-independent, we do not need to perceive it as actually existing unperceived: we only need to perceive it as *possibly* existing unperceived. That is, if, while seeing x we have the impression that x would exist even if we were not perceiving it, then we are presented with x's mind-independence. No contradiction ensues.

---

5 This so, Crane suggests, because "One's awareness of the *objects* of one's perceptual experiences does not seem to be an awareness of something which depends on experience for their existence." But this is a non-sequitur: perception might simply be mute with respect to the mind-(in)dependency of its objects, as I shall argue below.

Such an answer nevertheless raises new worries that, I believe, renders the view that mind-independency is presented in ordinary perception highly implausible. Though no more contradictory, the perception of independence now appears very demanding. It requires that, together with the perception of the object, we be presented:
1. With *counterfactual* states of affairs: we must be aware of a situation *distinct from the one we are actually in*, in which the object exists while we do not perceive it.
2. With *negative* states of affairs: we must be aware of a situation distinct from the one we are actually in, in which the object exists while we do *not* perceive it.
3. With *reflexive* states of affairs: we must be aware of a situation distinct from the one we are actually in, in which the object exists while *we* do not *perceive* it.[6]

It has been claimed in various places that modal properties or states of affairs can be perceived, that negative properties or states can be perceived, and that reflexive properties or states of affairs can be perceived. But to claim that all these three suspect kinds of properties are presented together in all perceptions is another matter. That a presentation of a counterfactual, negative, reflective states of affairs is embedded in every ordinary perception strikes as implausible. It is not the case that, looking at a ladybird, we see, on top of its shape, redness, motion, etc., its property of *possibly existing unperceived by us*.
One may reply that I am here using "perception" in too conservative a sense, and that a more liberal account of the contents of perception would capably accommodate the complexity of perceptual content. But recall that we are here assessing *Berkeley's* claim that perception cannot present us with the mind-independency of its objects. If we are to reply that perception *does* present us with the mind-independency of its objects, we need to use "perception" in the same way that he does. And he uses the term in a conservative manner: everything that is perceived is perceived directly and consists in sensory qualities. Even if there is a sense of "perception" in which the counterfactual-negative-reflexive property of "possibly existing unperceived" is systematically perceived (which I doubt), relying on that sense is irrelevant in the present context. Berkeley would retort that in his terminology we are merely claiming that mind-independence can be *inferred* or *conceived* (a view he also rejected, for different reasons).

---

6 A point rightly pressed by Hume: "Now if the senses presented our impressions as external to, and independent of, *ourselves* both the objects and ourselves must be obvious to our senses, otherwise they cou'd not be compar'd by these faculties. The difficulty, then, is how far we are ourselves the objects of our senses." (Hume 2007: 1.4.2)

But perhaps we are being led astray by the tacit assumption that mind-independence should be understood *modally*. Thus far, we have implicitly defined mind-dependence in terms of possible unperceived existence:
Modal account of mind-independence: x is mind-independent $=_{df}$ it is possible that x exists without being perceived.

But there are reasons to think that this modal account of mind-independence is mistaken. Suppose, as many believe, that God exists, that he is a necessary being, that he sees everything, that he created the world and its laws a long time ago and that he no longer intervenes in the world except for sporadic miracles. According to the modal conception of independence, the world then *existentially* depends on the perception of God: no objects are real since nothing could possibly exist without his perception.[7] But this is strongly counter-intuitive: for even if the world cannot exist without being perceived by God, it is not the case here that the world exists *because* God perceives it. Instead of being a sense-datum of God, the world appears to follow its course independently of God perceiving it.[8] Thus, the modal view of mind-independence appears to be false: possibly existing unperceived is a sufficient but not a necessary condition for existential independence. The general problem with the modal approach to existential independence, to paraphrase Fine, is that it registers only the fact that in each world where x exists, y exists, but it remains silent about the *source* of such a modal correlation. The correlation may be due to the dependent nature of x, but it may also be due to the necessary nature of y. We want to exclude the latter case. How can we do so?

As an alternative, K. Fine (1995) and J. Lowe (1998) have proposed to define existential dependence with the help of the notion of the identity (or essence) of an object. The notion of essence is taken to be modally irreducible: the essence of a thing is what makes it what it is: its real definition (Fine 1994). Every essential property is a necessary property but not every necessary property is an essential one. To take an example from Fine: it is necessary that Socrates is distinct from the Eiffel Tower, but this is not essential to him. The idea is then that x depends on y if and only if the existence of x necessarily implies the existence of y *in virtue of the identity of x*. In other words, the source of the necessary correlation must rely on the dependent object in order to avoid the conclusion that everything is

---

[7] I've adapted the God example proposed by Simons (1987: 295) to the case of perception. For more detailed criticisms of the modal conception of dependence, see Fine (1994, 1995); Lowe (1998, chap. 6); Correia, (2005). Jenkins (2005) applies this criticism to the definition of realism in terms of mind-independence.
[8] If God is passive or not almighty, the world may even end up failing to comply to his will.

dependent on necessary beings. Thus, although it is necessary that if John exists, then 2+2 = 4, John is not ontologically dependent on 2+2 being 4 because this necessity does not find its source in John's nature. This solves our problem of the all-seeing God: while it is true in this situation that the world cannot exist without being perceived by God, *this is not true in virtue of the nature of the world* –but in virtue of the nature of God. What the world is doesn't necessitate that God perceives it. Thus, we arrive at the following essential definition of independence:
Essential account of mind-independence: x is mind-independent $=_{df}$ it is not true in virtue of the nature of x that x exists only if it is perceived.

On this account, the mind-independence of x is compatible with its being necessarily perceived.[9] Furthermore, this account, one might think, paves the way for the possibility of perceiving the mind-independence of perceptual objects, since this no longer entails perceiving such objects as possibly existing unperceived.

However, such hopes are vain.[10] Yes, we have gotten rid of modal properties in the content of the alleged perception of the mind-independence of external objects: we have replaced them with essential ones, and these are arguably less problematic. Thus, those who uphold the revelation thesis about colours, for instance, find it natural to claim that visual perception presents us with the nature of colours. Note first, however, that perceiving mind-independence of some object still requires us to perceive some negative and reflexive properties of it: that of *not being essentially such that one's existence requires one's being perceived*.

Second, the replacement of modal properties by essential ones may be a merely pyrrhic victory. In order to experience that it is not in the essence of a to require b, one must be aware that *nothing* in the nature of a requires b. For this, one must experience that one is presented with the *whole* nature of a. Short of

---

9 Correia (2005) has given another definition of dependence in terms of *ground*, which avoids the reference to essences or natures while still excluding the trivial dependence on necessary beings. According to Correia, x depends on y iff "y's existing helps makes x exist." That is, one entity existentially depends on another when its existence is *explained* (in an objective sense), or *grounded* in, the existence of the other. From this, mind-independence can be defined as follows:
Foundational account of mind-independence: x is mind-independent $=_{df}$ x's existence is not grounded in x's being perceived.
The foundational account also avoids the conclusion that the world is a sense-datum of the all-seeing God, for clearly, in this example, the world does not exist because God perceived it. The differences between the essential and foundational accounts of mind-independence can be ignored for our present purpose. What matters is that in both cases mind-independence is no longer defined in terms of possible existence unperceived.
10 Notwithstanding having claimed the contrary in Massin (2011).

such complete awareness, we would not be in a position to exclude the idea that some unpresented part of *a*'s essence requires *b*. Put differently: it is not enough not to be presented with any part of *a*'s nature that requires *b*; one must, furthermore, be positively presented with the fact that *this is all there is to a's nature*. Such a totalling condition, it seems, is as elusive to perceptual awareness as counterfactual situations. The appeal to an essential account of mind-independence saves us from one difficulty only to land us in another: we have expunged modal content at the price of introducing an equally suspicious totalling content.

I conclude that Berkeley, Hume, and Reid were right to hold that perception cannot present us with the mind-independency of its objects. Does it follow that Johnson's refutation is rebutted? Only if "feel" in P1' is a perceptual verb. However, there is good reason to think that Johnson was calling our attention to a distinct sort of non-perceptual (or at least not *only* perceptual) experience. For suppose that Johnson only had in mind some ordinary tactile experience of the stone—such as feeling the pressure or solidity of the stone. What then would be the reason for kicking the stone, instead of merely pointing at it? It is hard to see. After all, it is unclear why touch should be in a better position than sight or hearing when it comes to the presentation of the mind-independency of its objects. Against the view that some sensory modalities are trust-worthier than others, Gibson (1966: 55) notices that: "To kick a stone is no better guarantee of its presence than to see it".[11] If Johnson's kick is to avoid this worry, the relevant experience that ensues from it had better be of a non-perceptual kind.

Owing to this, Johnson must be calling our attention to something other—or something more—than mere tactile experience. What is this special experience that presents us with the mind-independence of the stone? In Scheler's words:

> (1) What is the givenness of reality? What is experienced [*erlebt*], when anything whatever is experienced as real? This is the question of the phenomenology of the lived-experience of reality. (2) In what sorts of acts or modes of human behavior is the factor of reality [*Realitätsmoment*] originally given? (Scheler 1973 [1927]: 313)

---

11 Cf. Destutt de Tracy, 1801, pp. 113–4.

3 Experiencing Mind-Independence: the Feeling of Resistance

Johnson's suggested answer is, I submit: *the experience of resistance to our voluntary effort*.[12] (This, incidentally, is also the answer endorsed by Scheler). Call this the Resistance Thesis:

Resistance Thesis: the feeling of the resistance of the stone against our voluntary effort presents us with the independency of the stone from our mind.

On an historical note, one of the first explicit formulations of this thesis is to be found in the work of the French philosopher Destutt de Tracy (1803): "What ensures us of the existence of beings other than us is their resistance to our acting will". The view became very influential in many different areas and schools of thought (see Massin 2018, for a detailed list of references). Indeed, fewer than 80 years later, James (1880) writes: "There is no commoner remark than this, that resistance to our muscular effort is the only sense which makes us aware of a reality independent from ourselves." Although some anticipations of the Resistance Thesis may arguably be found in Malebranche, Hartley, and Condillac[13], it is fair to say that at the time Johnson kicked the stone, the thesis had not yet been explicitly defended. Johnson's kick, therefore, may constitute the first endorsement of the Resistance Thesis in philosophical history. (As we shall see, the Resistance Thesis is not to be conflated with the cognate view, endorsed by Berkeley, according to which sensible things, contrary to ideas of imaginations, cannot be modified at will).

What, then, is an experience of resistance? Paradigmatic experiences of resistance occur when we carry a heavy bag, when we swim against the stream, or

---

12 This is also the interpretation of Johnson's kick endorsed by Bain (1855: 377), Patey (1986), Baldwin (1995), Williams (2002, 136). Hallett defends a cognate but distinct interpretation, according to which "the essence of [Johnson's] argument is plainly the inference from his own experienced physical agency with that of the stone (with which it is the same in kind)". Although there is a lot to be said in favour of Hallett's interpretation—as we shall see—I believe that the agency of the stone is not *inferred* from the experience of our own agency, but that both are experienced together.
13 Malebranche (1991 [1687]: 40-43) argues that if resistance to our physical effort gives us reason to believe in the reality of solid bodies, then, *a fortiori*, resistance to our will should give us reason to believe in the reality of ideas.[13] Hartley (1749) introduces the genetic question of how the self distinguishes itself from the external world, hinting at the role of muscular feelings; Condillac (1997 [1754], part II, chap. V) argues that it is only when equipped with effortful touch and capacity of motion that his statue becomes aware of a world distinct from itself.

when we hold back a pram on a staircase. I shall here assume the following views (for a full defence see: Massin 2010; Massin 2018; and Massin & de Vignemont, forthcoming).

1. A body, *B*, resists an agent, *A*, iff *A* makes an effort on *B*.
2. *A* makes an effort on a body *B*=$_{df}$
   (i) *A* exerts a force F_1 on *B* in order to make it (or some of its parts) move (or stay at rest);
   (ii) *A* resistive force F_2 partly or fully counteracts the force F_1 exerted by *A*.[14]

This corresponds to the following schema:

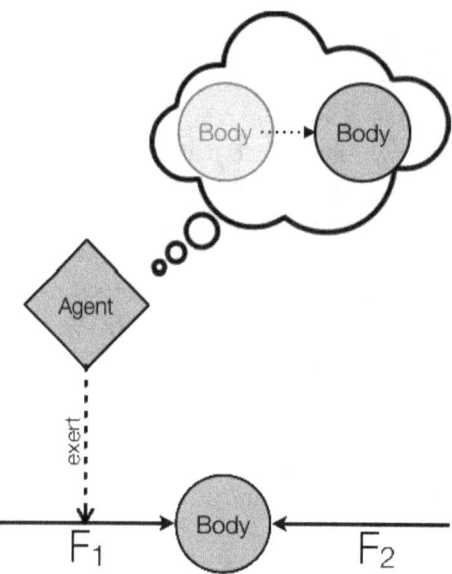

Fig. 1: The structure of an effort

When Johnson kicked the stone, he exerted a force on it (not least a "mighty" one, according to Boswell), and the stone exerted in return a resistive force, causing his foot to rebound. The relation between the two forces at stake here—the one exerted by the agent and the one exerted by the stone—is a relation of mutual

---

14 NB: fully counteracted efforts are not necessarily failures. One might make an effort to ensure that the body does not move. And partly counteracted efforts might be failures, e.g., if we wanted the body to stay where it is.

causal prevention: each force prevents the other from causing the acceleration of the stone it would have cause, had it acted alone (Massin 2017).

Now, *experiencing* resistance (or effort) is experiencing all of this: it is to experience that, in response to the force that one exerts in trying to move it, the stone exerts a resistive force. Why, then, should the experience of resistance give us a presentation of mind-independence? Simply put, if the body on which we act opposes and resists us, this suffices to show that it is not under the immediate control of our will. Unlike (many) ideas of our imagination, physical bodies do not comply with our demands without resistance (resistance that may or may not be insuperable). The behaviour of bodies is partly independent of our will.

Owing to this, P1' is vindicated: by kicking the stone, Johnson experiences its resistance to his will, which amounts to an experience of its mind-independence. From this and P2 (the anti-sceptical premise granted by Berkeley), Johnson concludes that the stone is mind-independent. Is Berkeley thereby refuted?

4 One Dialogue Between George and Samuel

George. I read your "refutation", dear Samuel. It is rather terse, but here is my best reconstruction of it: because the stone resists your will, it appears to you to exist outside of your mind. And this, you think, contradicts my immaterialism. Tell me, Samuel: did I get you right?

Samuel. Absolutely!

George. In that case, I am afraid your "refutation" does not contradict me in the least. For I have never denied that the stone exists independently from my will. Quite the contrary! This is precisely how I distinguish ideas of the senses—such as your stone—from ideas of imagination. The latter, but not the former, are dependent on our will.[15] You are equivocating, I fear, between two forms of dependency on our mind: the dependency of sensory things *on our perception*, which I defend, and the dependency of sensory things *on our will* – which, like you – I *reject*.

Samuel. You seem to me to be the one equivocating here between two senses of "independence from our will". For in the sense I have in mind, your ideas of perception do not oppose the slightest resistance to my will. The stone does.

---

15 *Three Dialogues*, 235.

George. What? If ideas of perception do not resist your will, then explain to me, pray, how you manage to see the sky green or my face square?[16]

Samuel. I happily confess that I cannot. But this inability of mine is not owing to colours *resisting* my endeavours to change them.

George. What else?

Samuel. My aboulia, George.

George. I am very sorry to hear that Samuel, I had no idea.

Samuel. This is no disease of mine, good George. It is our normal human condition with respect to colours and other sensible qualities. The source of the impossibility to modify colours at will does not lie in *their* resistance. It lies in the limits of *our* will: colour changes are not the kinds of changes that we can will.

George. And are you going to claim that pain, for which we have the strongest aversion, can never become an object of our will either? How absurd! Don't you want your pain to cease?

Samuel. Desiring, wanting...none of this is willing. I do *desire* and *want* the cessation of my pain. But I cannot *will* it. To will to modify a thing, I must be able to directly act on it. How else could this thing *resist* my will? I know how to make a stone move: I should push it, or kick it. But, unfortunately, I cannot immediately act on my pain. Hence, stones, but not pains, can resist my will.

George. So long as in both cases things fail to comply with our will, I do not see much of a difference here.

Samuel. But my point is precisely that these are two very different ways for things to fail to comply with our will. Being deaf to orders is not the same as refusing to obey them. Among the things that cannot be modified at will, some are beyond its reach, others are resistant to it. To ideas of the senses (contrary to ideas of imagination) belong the first ones—you are right. But the stone I kicked displays another kind of independence from my will: I acted on it and it resisted.

George. Perhaps Samuel, perhaps. But will you stop splitting hairs and tell me now how these fine-grained distinctions between varieties of will-independency can help you to prove the *perception*-independency of sensible things?

Samuel. We are nearly there. Note, first, that the fact that the stone resists my effort directly runs counter to two theses of yours.

George. Well! Which ones?

Samuel. What is resistance if not a force?

George. I cannot see what else it could be.

Samuel. So, if resistance can be felt and is a force, forces are neither abstractions nor occult qualities, as you claim. They are sensible things.

---

[16] *Principles*, §29; *Three Dialogues*, 196.

George. I reluctantly grant this to you. For my view that forces are abstractions is anyway incidental to my immaterialism: put forces in the same group as colours, shapes, and sounds if it befits you. Forces will, then, be sensible things depending on our perception of them. While we are here, put as many other chimeras among sensible things as you please: unless their independency from perception is itself perceived – an obvious impossibility – it will remain true that their *esse* is *percipi*.

Samuel. You underestimate, George, how much your immaterialism depends on your view about forces. To see that, consider the second claim of yours that the resistance of the stone contradicts.

George. Now! Which scholium of mine are you going to attack this time?

Samuel. The view that only minds are active. Do you still accept this?

George. I surely do! Only minds can produce effects on nature; no sensible thing, be that solidity, figure, motion...can produce any effect in another sensible thing.[17]

Samuel. But I felt the resistance of the stone, and since appearances are not deceiving, the stone has to be endowed with some causal power. The stone seems to have – and therefore actually has – the power of exerting forces against what strikes it.

George. Truth be told, I cannot make sense of the idea of a stone being active and resisting your effort. When I kick things, I feel discomfort, pain;[18] I experience the constant conjunction between the motions of my foot and that of other corporeal things, but I experience nothing like a force or resistance actively exerted by them. Sensible things are visibly inactive.[19]

Samuel. Not muscularly! Don't you feel tensions in your muscles?

George. This strikes me as a highly implausible description of what I experience, but I am ready to grant it to you as well—on one condition, however.

Samuel. What is it to be?

George. That you stop attacking my turrets, and that you finally launch your assault against my dungeon: will you tell me at last how all of this is relevant to your self-proclaimed refutation of my immaterialism, and not to you rejecting some side-theses of mine?

Samuel. Here is the problem, George. Consider the motion of my foot. This motion, you maintain, depends on its being perceived. But my foot was repelled by the stone, as you conceded. Hence its motion is also explained by the resistive

---

17 *Principle*, §61; *Three Dialogues*, 196
18 *An Essay on Motion*, §4.
19 *Principles*, §25.

force exerted by the stone. The same bounce ends up being explained twice: once by the activity of the soul, the other by the force of the stone. There is one principle of motion too many.[20]

George. Hold on, Samuel. The soul is real, but the force isn't. I granted you—reluctantly—that forces, instead of being abstractions, are sensible things; I never conceded that forces can exist unperceived!

Samuel. But I am not relying on that hypothesis, George. There are two main ways in which philosophers have tried to make sense of the notion of real being. Those who, following the Eleatic stranger of Plato's *Sophist*, said that being real is to have causal power; and those who said that to be real is to exist independently from perception. I claim that those two criteria of reality are not independent: being endowed with causal powers entails existing independently from perception.

George. How so?

Samuel. Once sensible things are acknowledged to have causal powers, they start banging against each other and have a causal life of their own. Perception becomes incidental to the explanation of their behaviour, which amounts to saying that their behaviour is independent from perception.

George. That would be true if sensible things had causal powers. But I doubt that your inference to the effect that sensible things have causal powers is correct.

Samuel. But I am drawing no inference George: that sensible things have causal powers is something we know by experience: kick a stone!

George. Ideas may seem to bang against each other to you, but as a matter of fact they don't: only minds affect ideas.

Samuel. Can ideas seem to be one way and be another?

George. Certainly not.

Samuel. So, if ideas seem to affect each other, they do.

George. That is precisely the point, Samuel: you and I disagree on appearances. Ideas, I maintain, do not seem to act on each other. Indeed, I conceded the contrary to you, and I am grateful to you for having helped me see how tightly connected my immaterialism and views about forces and activity are. But don't be too quick to shout victory. For all that you have shown is that immaterialism is false under a far-fetched description of sensory appearances.

Samuel. Far-fetched?

George. To say the least! It is not just appearances that you overloaded with kooky ideas of forces and powers: the very concept of an active body is so extravagant that only metaphysicians desperate enough to distinguish themselves from the

---

20 See Winkler (1994: 116) for a close consideration.

vulgar would endorse it. Frankly, Samuel, an obstructing being, so powerful as to oppose invincible resistance to your most resolute endeavours, so alert as to immediately react to your smallest pushes, so recalcitrant as to thwart all your attempts: what else could it be but another mind?
Samuel. A stone!

References

Allais, Lucy (2015): *Manifest Reality: Kant's Idealism and His Realism*. Oxford: Oxford University Press.
Bain, Alexander (1855): *The Senses and the Intellect*. New York: D. Appleton and Company.
Baldwin, Thomas (1995): "Objectivity, Causality, and Agency". In: *The Body and the Self*, J. L. Bermùdez, A. Marcel, N. Eilan (Eds). Cambridge (Mass.): MIT Press, pp. 107–125.
Boswell, James (1826): *The Life of Samuel Johnson*, Hester, Lynch Trale, & Edmond, Malone, William Pickering (Eds.). London, Talboys & Wheeler: Oxford.
Condillac, Etienne Bonnot de (1997): *Traité des sensations, traité sur les animaux*. Paris: Fayard.
Correia, Fabrice (2005): *Existential Dependence and Cognate Notions*. München: Philosophia Verlag.
Crane, Tim (2005): "What is the problem of perception?". In: *Synthesis Philosophica* 2 (40), pp. 237–264.
Destutt de Tracy, Antoine (1801): *Eléments d'idéologie: idéologie proprement dite*. Didot: Paris.
Destutt de Tracy, Antoine (1803): *Eléments d'idéologie: grammaire*. Didot: Paris.
Fine, Kit (1994): "Essence and modality". In: *Philosophical Perspectives* 8, pp. 1–16.
Fine, Kit (1995): "Ontological Dependence". In: *Proceedings of the Aristotelian Society* 95 (1), pp. 269–290.
Gibson, James J. (1966): *The Senses Considered as Perceptual Systems*. Oxford: Houghton Mifflin.
Hallett, H. F. (1947): "Dr. Johnson's refutation of Bishop Berkeley". In: *Mind* 56 (222), pp. 132–147.
Hume, David (2007): *A Treatise of Human Nature: A Critical Edition*. Oxford: Oxford University Press.
Hartley, David (1749): *Observations on Man, his Frame, his Duty, and his Expectations*. London: Vol. 1, London: Richardson.
James, William (1880): "The feeling of effort". In: *Anniversary Memoirs of the Boston Society of Natural History*.
Jenkins, Carrie (2005): "Realism and Independence". In: *American Philosophical Quarterly*, Volume 42, Number 3, July 2005, pp. 199–211.
Lowe, Edward Jonathan (1998): *The Possibility of Metaphysics: Substance, Identity, and Time*. Oxford: Clarendon Press.
Luce, A. A. & Jessop, T. E. (Eds.) (1948): *The Works of George Berkeley, Bishop of Cloyne*. Thomas Nelson.

Malebranche, Nicolas (1991): "Entretiens sur la métaphysique et sur la religion (1687) ". In: A. Robinet (Eds.): *Oeuvres Complètes*. Paris: Vrin.

Massin, Olivier. (2011). "Résistance et Existence". In: *Etudes de Philosophie, 9*, pp. 275–310.

Massin, Olivier (2017): "The Composition of Forces". In: *British Journal for the Philosophy of Science* 68 (3), pp. 805–846.

Massin, Olivier (2018): "Towards a Definition of Efforts". In: *Motivation Science* 3 (3), pp. 230–259.

Massin, Olivier & de Vignemont, Frédérique (forthcoming): "'Unless I put my hand into his side, I will not believe': The Epistemic Privilege of Touch". In: Dimitria Gatzia and Brit Brogaard (Eds): *The Rational Role of Perceptual Experience: Beyond Vision*. Oxford University Press.

Patey, D. L. (1986): "Johnson's Refutation of Berkeley: Kicking the Stone Again". In: *Journal of the History of Ideas*, pp. 139–145.

Reid, Thomas (2000): *An Inquiry into the Human Mind on the Principles of Common Sense*. Pennsylvania: State University Press.

Saporiti, Katia (2008): "Weshalb die Welt so ist, wie wir sie sehen : Berkeleys These der Unfehlbarkeit unserer Wahrnehmung". In: Perler, Dominik; Wild, Markus (Eds): *Sehen und Begreifen: Wahrnehmungstheorien in der frühen Neuzeit*. Berlin, New York: Walter de Gruyet, pp. 265–286.

Scheler, Max (1927): "Idealismus-Realismus". In: *Philosophischer Anzeiger* II, Bonn: Verlag Friedrich Cohen; trans. D. R. Lachterman. In: Scheler, Max (1973): *Selected Philosophical Essays*, Envanston: Northwerstern University Press.

Siegel, Susanna (2006): "Subject and object in the contents of visual experience". In: *Philosophical Review* 115 (3), pp. 355–88.

Silver, Bruce (1993): "Boswell on Johnson's refutation of Berkeley: revisiting the stone". In: *Journal of the History of Ideas* 54 (3), pp. 437–448.

Simons, Peter (1987): *Parts: A Study in Ontology*. Oxford: Oxford University Press.

Strawson, Peter F. (1979): "Perception and its objects". In: Macdonald G.F. (eds) *Perception and identity* . Palgrave: London, pp. 41–60

Williams, Bernard (2002): *Truth and Truthfulness: An Essay in Genealogy*. Princeton: Princeton University press.

Winkler, Kenneth P. (1989): *Berkeley: An Interpretation*. Oxford: Oxford University Press.

Michael Schmitz
The Good, The Bad, and The Naïve

Abstract: A perceptual realism that is naive in a good way must be naively realistic about world and mind. But contemporary self-described naive realists often have trouble acknowledging that both the good cases of successful perception and the bad cases of illusion and hallucination involve internal experiential states with intentional contents that present the world as being a certain way. They prefer to think about experience solely in relational terms because they worry that otherwise we won't be able to escape from radical skepticism. I argue that experiential relations to objects require that their subjects be in internal experiential states. But this does not mean that these states are our epistemological starting point which can be known independently of any knowledge of the external world. We do escape the epistemological predicament of radical skepticism because the good cases are primary over the bad ones. But this is not because the good cases alone provide reasons for belief, but because we do not need a reason to think we are in a good case, but do need a reason to think we are not, and such a reason must come from a good case. So bad cases can only be thought of as deviations from good cases. And we can only understand experiences as states with contents distinct from their objects and present in good and bad cases once we understand misrepresentation, that is, bad cases, and therefore only as we ascribe knowledge of the external world to ourselves.

Keywords: perception, naïve realism, intentionalism, externalism, skepticism

> Die Übereinstimmung, Harmonie, von Gedanke und Wirklichkeit liegt darin, daß, wenn ich fälschlich sage, etwas sei *rot*, es doch immerhin nicht *rot* ist. Und wenn ich jemandem das Wort "rot" im Satze "Das ist nicht rot" erklären will, ich dazu auf etwas Rotes zeige. (Wittgenstein 1984: § 429)

> Ein Wort ohne Rechtfertigung gebrauchen, heißt nicht, es zu Unrecht gebrauchen. (Wittgenstein 1984: § 289)[1]

---

[1] Elizabeth Anscombe translated these as follows: "The agreement, the harmony, of thought and reality consists in this: if I say falsely that something is *red*, then, for all that, it isn't *red*. And when I want to explain the word "red" to someone, in the sentence "That is not red", I do it by pointing to something red." and " To use a word without justification does not mean to use it without right." (Wittgenstein 1958).

https://doi.org/10.1515/9783110657920-004

1 Introduction

We directly perceptually experience objects – things, properties, states of affairs. That is, for example, I see a table, I see its white color, and I see that it is white. That I perceive these objects directly means that I do not first experience something else – ideas, sense data, or the like – directly and then the table only indirectly. But which objects I experience depends not only on the state of the world external to me, but on my subjective, internal, experiential state. It depends on how the world seems to me to be. That is, it depends on the content of my experience – how it presents the world as being – and on whether that content matches how the world really is. Usually it does. Illusion or hallucination are much rarer than one might suspect from the outsize attention philosophers have given to them, but when such misexperiences do occur, they are cases of contents without corresponding objects.

This is a naively realistic view of perception which seems like mere common sense to me, except perhaps that I used the slightly technical notion of content. Its distinctive feature on the contemporary theoretical scene is that it is naively realistic about world *and* mind. This is worth noting because the label 'naive realism' has recently been appropriated by views which seem less than naively realistic about the mind. Such views emphasize experiential relations between subject and world, but are shy about acknowledging that such relations can only obtain in virtue of a subject's inner experiential and intentionally contentful states. But why would anybody feel a tension between embracing experiential relations and experiential subjective states if – approaching things naively – it seems obvious that the former could not exist without the latter? I believe that in order to understand this and make progress on the issue of perceptual realism we need to engage in a Wittgensteinian diagnosis and therapy of the underlying concerns.

In this spirit, I will provide a very brief and schematic history and diagnosis of some of these concerns in the next section. In the third section, I will more precisely characterize the views I am criticizing as forms of "austere relationism". The fourth section will provide a blueprint of the positive view to be defended, the fifth will address some concerns about the central notion of content, and the sixth the deep epistemological worries underlying the reluctance to acknowledge experience as an inner state, before I outline the positive alternative in the final seventh section.

2 Subjectivism vs. Objectivism

At least since René Descartes, philosophy has been torn between subjectivism and objectivism. Descartes made mind the starting point of philosophy and created a chasm between mind and world. While Descartes himself believed that this chasm could still be bridged in a realistic fashion, idealism and other forms of subjectivism despaired of this task and instead tried to overcome this chasm by making world dependent on mind or constructing world out of mind. For subjectivism mind is metaphysically and epistemologically primary. For example, phenomenalists tried to construct ordinary objects out of sense data. Epistemologically, for the subjectivist ideas, sensa, sense data etc. become the immediate objects of experience and thus block direct access to the world. This also brings with it a view of our awareness of our own mental states that seems badly naive: the awareness of ideas is immediate and independent of any knowledge of the world. Experience is the epistemological starting point that supposedly can be made sense of independently of whether we actually succeed in representing the world. Consequently, this success becomes very problematic.

Subjectivism dominated philosophy for a long time, but in the 20th century philosophers increasingly felt this was intolerable. There was a strong reaction against subjectivism and objectivist viewpoints became more and more influential. For objectivism world is metaphysically and epistemologically primary. Mind is dependent on world or can be constructed out of world. For example, behaviorists construed mental states out of behavior. Moving closer to our present concerns, content externalists hold that mental content may be determined through features of the world – e.g. whether the stuff from lakes and rivers that they drink is H_2O or XYZ (Putnam 1975) – that subjects are unaware of – at least in any ordinary sense. On the content externalist view, world is partly constitutive of what subjects mean and think in the sense that *features unknown to them can determine it*. This externalism was then sometimes invoked to respond to epistemological concerns. Even if we are brains in a vat – in the scenario that updated Descartes' demon thought experiment – might not most of our beliefs still be true because our words and thoughts refer to the regular causes of our experiences (Putnam 1981)? The price for accepting this response to skepticism is that intuitively these causes – the electrical stimuli controlled by the evil neuroscientists – are rather different from what they appear to be.

Externalism is still orthodox in contemporary philosophy. But one of its most perceptive critics, Donald Davidson, already gave a compelling diagnosis of its shortcomings very early: it provides no more than a "transposed image of Cartesian skepticism" (Davidson 2001: 22). Davidson's point was that now the subject loses its grip on its own mental states. But not even our conception of the relation between these mental states and the world has really improved. The subject is still just as out of touch with the world as on the subjectivist picture. The illusion that something has improved substantially arises only because objectivism invites us to take an external, 3rd person point of view on the situation. By adopting this point of view we can see what the person really refers to or what their beliefs are really about (compare Searle 1983: 230). But this external determination is revealed as cold comfort when we take up the point of view of the subject. From the point of view of the subject, the relevant features remain unknown. The abyss between mind and world persists: only apparent progress has been made by declaring ostensibly unknown features of the world to be constitutive of mind.

3 What is "Austere Relationism"?

Against this historical background let me now characterize more closely what I think is a bad kind of naive realism, the kind of view that Susanna Schellenberg (2011) has aptly called "austere relationism". According to austere relationism, the good cases (of successful perception) and the bad cases (of illusion and hallucination) are not of the same kind, or at least not of the same *fundamental* kind. Nor do the good and the bad cases share the property of having intentional content. Austere relationism is a form of disjunctivism. Introspectively, I can only say that my current state is *either* a perceptual experience (relationally conceived), *or* an illusion or hallucination. I cannot say that there is a common factor here, namely that they all involve (non-relational) experiences with intentional content that presents the world as being a certain way. This is what makes this relationism austere.

Austere relationists certainly deny that perceptual experience is representational and has intentional content, but is their relationism so austere that it rejects experience as an internal subjective state in any sense at all? I don't want to make such an accusation lightly and I am not sure about all philosophers who have held views in this ballpark of ideas, but certain things that its proponents have said (and have not said) are hard to make sense of otherwise. For example, one frequently finds in this literature claims like that features of the external world constitute the phenomenal character of experience (e.g. Campbell 2002: 116). For example, the redness of the table constitutes the phenomenal character of an experience of redness. Since the notion of phenomenal character was explicitly introduced to capture the *what it is like* of a state, that which makes it the state of consciousness that it is, it is hard to see how this move could not be intended to replace any notion of inherent subjective properties of perceptual consciousness. Nor is it intelligible how an internal state of such consciousness could even exist while lacking any inherent phenomenal properties.

A further piece of evidence: when austere relationists do acknowledge the obvious fact that there must be internal enabling conditions for experiential relations to objects – that whether such relations obtain cannot only depend on the state of the world around the organism, but must also depend on the state of the organism itself – they only characterize these conditions in physiological terms (Fish 2009), or in terms of "cognitive processing" (Campbell 2002: 118), but not in experiential terms. But again: if we want to make sense of the experiential perceptual relation, we need an internal, subjective experiential state. When I experience the table, when I am perceptually conscious of it, it is only me that has an experience or is in a state of experience or consciousness. The table does not experience anything and is not part of my experiential state, but just its object. Only my subjective experiential state can turn my relation to it into an experiential relation.

Therefore, neither subjectivism nor objectivism can make sense of the perceptual relation. Subjectivism internalizes it as a relation between subjects and subjective items such as ideas or sense data. It therefore fails to make epistemological sense of perceptual relatedness to external objects, and it is easy to see why this must be so: if we can make sense of experience independently of any awareness of the external world, how could it ground such awareness? The only escape then is to try to construct world out of mind. Conversely, as we have seen, austere relationism cannot make sense of the experiential perceptual relation because it finds itself unable to acknowledge internal subjective experiential states, which alone can turn this relation into an experiential relation. The only escape then is to try to construct mind out of world, e.g. to claim that external objects constitute the phenomenal character of experience.

I believe that a central motivation for this and other kinds of externalism is epistemological even when these views are not expressly presented as epistemological. Putnam justified his version of content externalism mostly by appeal to semantic intuitions. But a broader motivation was surely to escape subjectivism and to bring the world (and our fellow creatures) into our theories of meaning and thought. And as we saw, Putnam soon tried to make epistemological hay out of content externalism. Similarly, a core motivation for austere relationism is certainly the idea that only experience as construed relationally could adequately ground our knowledge of the world and defeat skepticism. And properly understood, these motivations are quite valid. As I argued, the problem is just that the externalist proposals reproduce the precarious, broadly Cartesian, character of the relation between mind and world and merely invert its description. In either case, the mind appears unable to distinguish e.g. between whether this is H_2O or XYZ in its environment; whether it is experiencing a red table or merely the electrical stimulations generated by the evil neuroscientist; whether it is experiencing anything real at all, or just undergoing an illusion or hallucination. The subjectivist responds by making world dependent on mind, the objectivist by making mind dependent on world.

4 How to be a Naïve Realist About Mind and World

The blueprint for a better response, for a view that genuinely overcomes the Cartesian predicament rather than just inverting it, can be taken from the Wittgenstein quote that I used as one of the epigraphs for this paper (PI, § 429). Wittgenstein talks about thought and negation, but his point equally applies to experience and mere seeming. We can rephrase it as follows: when I undergo an illusion or hallucination of redness, the redness that is not there, that merely appears to be there, is still inextricably tied to the real redness that I experience in successful perception. I cannot explain – not even to myself – what it is that I appeared to be perceiving without pointing to a real instance of redness. (In some cases, the connection might be more indirect, but the basic point still holds.) In this way, mind and world are not married by force, as it were, from an external point of view, by making mind dependent on a feature whose presence or absence it cannot detect, but by arguing that misrepresentation can only be conceived in relation to and as a deviation from cases of successful representation. Far from opening up an unbridgeable chasm between mind and world, misrepresentation presupposes successful representation.

The notion of content is also tied into this nexus. Experiential states are internal states of the organism and their content is an inherent feature of these states. It is that feature which embodies their intentional significance, which puts us into contact with certain features of the world, but not others. Content can only be understood in relation to external objects. That is why the fact that something visually seems to be red (square) – that there is a visual content presenting redness (squareness) – can only be understood in relation to things that are really red (square). The subject can only fully distinguish content from object by understanding the bad cases of misrepresentation, by distinguishing appearance from reality, by being able to think something like: it seems visually to me to be red, but it is not really red. And again, bad cases can only be understood in relation to good ones.

This means that there is a sense in which on the view to be developed, perceptual experiential relations are prior to mere experiential states. In this regard the view is a relational account. But it's not an austere relationism because it insists that both the good and the bad cases must involve experiential subjective states with intentional content. So like several recent authors (Dorsch 2010; Schellenberg 2011; McDowell 2013) I try to find a synthesis between intentionalism and relationism (and internalism and externalism). Accordingly, this view can be called "relational intentionalism".

Let me state its main tenets as explicitly as possible. There are experiential *relations* – which can be reported by sentences such as "I experienced the monitor in front of me". But these relations obtain partly in virtue of experiential *states* of the subject – states that can be reported by sentences such as "I had an experience as of a monitor in front of me". We conceptually focus on experiential relations with factive reports, which entail representational success and on experiential states with neutral reports such as "It visually seemed to me that there was a monitor in front of me", or with counterfactive reports such as "I hallucinated a monitor in front of me". States are present in bad and good cases, relations only in good ones. Experiential states are internal and subjective states of the organism that have intentional content that determines conditions of satisfaction.

The main task of this paper will be to explain the sense in which experiential relations and good cases are primary relative to bad cases and mere experiences / states and thus to address the epistemological worries which are the main force driving austere relationism. But before I come to this, it will be useful to address some of the main misunderstandings and concerns with regard to the notion of content.

5 Some Concerns About Content

The most tempting mistake about content is to think that it is somehow 'between' mind and world, such that a subject would first refer to content and then only indirectly – if at all – to the world. To think about content in this way is to turn it into some kind of epistemic intermediary between mind and world like a sense datum. But content is not between mind and world at all. Content talk just refers to the way the experience is with regard to its intentional significance. We are not aware of content at the level of experience at all – but only of objects and of ourselves. Only at the level of reflection do we become aware of content as distinct from object. Content is subjective and what makes it the case that we are aware of certain objects but not others. For example, right now I experience the computer screen in front of me, but if the content of my experience were different, I would be aware of different objects, or none at all, even if all the external facts were the same.

Content is therefore also needed to make sense of the good cases. It is important to emphasize this, since we tend to focus on the bad cases when thinking about content, as then the absence of relevant objects makes content more conspicuous. But content is also required to make sense of the bad cases: *these can only be bad relative to conditions of satisfaction set by content*. Experience (as a state) can only misrepresent or mispresent when it presents the world as being a certain way. That is just what it means to have content. If we deny content in this sense, we make a mockery of the bad cases which are essentially cases where things seem to be a certain way which they are not. For any hallucination or illusion, for any experience, there must always be an answer to the question: how did things seem to the subject, how did it experience them as being?

For the same reason, experience cannot be "object-dependent" and content cannot be "gappy" in the way that has sometimes been suggested in the literature (e.g. Schellenberg 2011). The idea of gappy content is the idea that, for example, there is a gap or hole in the content of hallucination corresponding to the hallucinated object. But the notion of gappy content has things back to front. The gap or hole is actually in the world and can only exist relative to conditions of satisfaction set by content. Only because the experience requires the presence of an object in order to be veridical, does its absence turn it into a hallucination. If there were really a gap in content there, content would not require the presence of the object and there would be no hallucination.

The idea that some content is object-dependent is a residue of externalist objectivism. It makes mind locally dependent on world. It is certainly no accident that it does so where particular things are concerned. In the philosophical imagination, particulars have long stood out as paradigms of reality. There is a direct line from Russell's suggestion that particulars might actually be constituents of propositions to the theory of gappy content. This kind of mindset is also reflected in the importance that has often been given to the distinction between illusion and hallucination and in the closely related idea that content must be completely general and thus cannot account for reference to particulars. Before I discuss this idea, let me define a minimal notion of content.

On a minimal construal, content is first and foremost the property of internal states that sets conditions of satisfaction. Nothing can be the object of such an intentional state except by matching its content. That is, an entity could not determine itself, so to speak, to be the object of an intentional state, but could only be that relative to content. And conversely, the world can also only fail to satisfy a state because that state has content. The minimal notion is meant to formulate a bare realism about intentionality and content. But intentionalism is often rejected because a stronger notion of content is implicitly or explicitly assumed. I will now discuss some of these additional commitments often associated with intentionalism, beginning with the notion that content must be completely general or descriptive.

This understanding of content still tends to be taken for granted. It is not only manifest in the theory of gappy contents, but also in the common presupposition that content could not be irreducibly indexical – for example, in Putnam's (1975) classic argument for externalism (compare Searle 1983: ch. 8). So let us consider a twin earth scenario here. Does my experience present my computer screen and myself in completely general terms? Does it say something like "There is a screen there with certain features and it is in front of somebody with certain features", so that this descriptive content might apply just as much to my twin on twin earth as it does to me? Now, my experience of course does not really say anything, nor does it really present anything in general terms or concepts – because its content is not conceptual at all – nor even in indexical, demonstrative terms – because it is not in any way linguistic. Still it seems clear that its content is more akin to demonstrative content. It is certainly no accident that demonstrative expressions have generally been thought to more immediately latch onto perception than other expressions. Therefore I believe we can say that the content of my experience is more akin to something like "*This* screen in front of *me*...". It does not pick out anything – whatever it may be – that meets a certain description, but this particular screen in front of this particular creature. More could be said about this, but in the present context this should suffice to shift the burden of proof to those who assume that perceptual content must be general or descriptive. One can be an intentionalist about perception without being a descriptivist.

Historically, the notion of content originated in the context of thought about that-clauses, propositions, concepts and other linguistic or quasi-linguistic items, and this has often led to content being identified with propositional and conceptual content. This in turn is why some philosophers reject the application of the notion of content to perceptual experience (or, generally to 'basic minds'), because they rightly feel that it cannot be understood in language-centric terms (e.g. Hutto & Myin 2012). But I think the proper response is just to reject the language-centric notion and embrace content that is non-propositional and non-conceptual. I find it hard to understand what intentionality without content might even be, because, again, what should bring a state in intentional contact with certain objects – but not others – and how could there be a perceptual experience, where there is no answer to the question *what* was experienced, how the world seemed to its subject?

Similar remarks also apply to the austere relationist attempt to replace all talk of content with talk of the phenomenal character of experience. Even setting aside the already discussed problem that this character is supposed to be constituted by external objects, it is not clear how this attempt could succeed. The suggestion can hardly be that the phenomenal features of perceptual experience are non-representational in the sense in which e.g. mood experience is arguably non-representational, or in the sense which on some conceptions sensations are non-representational. This would seem to be inconsistent with the insistence that experience "brings our surroundings into view" (Travis 2004: 64) and can justify beliefs about it, which is absolutely central to relationism. But then in which sense is experience supposed to be non-representational – where the representational includes the presentational? Perceptual experience has all the marks of being intentional or representational: it is *about* certain features of the world, its subject is *directed* at these. It is hard to understand what the relationist is driving at here, unless we take her to reject any notion of experience as an internal state, and / or to use a notion of content that is linguistic by definition.

Having addressed some confusions about content, we are now in a position to confront the epistemological worries driving austere relationism.

6 The Epistemological Worry Driving Austere Relationism

I believe the central worry driving austere relationism might be put as follows. If we accept the distinction between experiential relations and experiential states and the claim that the states are also present in the bad cases, don't we then have to accept experience in the sense of seemings neutral between the good and the bad cases, as our epistemological starting point? And aren't we then back in the original, Cartesian subjectivist epistemological predicament: things seem to me to be a certain way, but what reason can you give me that they really ever are as they seem? We can call this the "plus predicament": what do we have to add to (non-relational) experience to defeat skepticism? From there, I think one can see the pull of insisting a) that experience is fundamentally relational, and b) that it provides us with reasons, so that we are justified in beliefs based on it – as it guarantees we are in the good case! A) here encapsulates the metaphysical aspect or version of relationism / disjunctivism, and b) its epistemological aspect or version, the idea that being in the good case puts the subject in an epistemologically privileged position. This instantiates the pattern that we already identified in the case of Putnam's content externalism. Broadly metaphysical intuitions are invoked to support an externalist thesis which then is supposed to bring an epistemological payoff. Some may try to get the supposed epistemological advantage even without the metaphysical commitment (e.g. McDowell 2013), showing that the former is really the driving force.

I now want to argue that this reasoning, while tempting, "cheerfully accepts the Cartesian premise, while trying to deny the Cartesian conclusion", as Saul Kripke (1980: 145) put it in commenting on materialist responses to the metaphysical mind-body problem. As John Searle (1992: ch. 1) has shown, the typical materialist accepts the Cartesian conceptual dualistic opposition between mind and body and thus can only avoid the Cartesian conclusion of ontological dualism by construing mind out of world, that is, body. Analogously, the relationist accepts the Cartesian epistemological opposition between mind and world, according to which experience is our epistemological starting point, from which we can raise the question whether we have knowledge of the external world. The only way then to avoid the subjectivist conclusion that we lack any such knowledge is to construe experience and / or the subject's epistemological position out of world, that is, purely relationally. But the Cartesian starting point is optional.

Before I outline an alternative, let us think about how relationism is supposed to show our epistemological situation in a better light, so that we feel warranted in rejecting skepticism. Of course, we can definitionally tie experience to the good case, but obviously that does not improve our chances of being in the good case. To put it disjunctivist style, we are still faced with the initial disjunction that we are either experiencing something, or undergoing an illusion or hallucination. Nor does thinking of experience as providing reasons help, because we are still not in a better position to know that we possess this reason. Now, it might be objected that I'm missing the point. "Look," somebody might say, "of course relationism cannot improve our chances of being in the good case. The point is just to put us at ease that it is rationally ok to move from experience to belief in the face of skepticism. And only a conception that ties experience to the good case and thinks of it as providing reasons can do this." That the point is to declare experiences to be reasons so that we feel rationally justified in moving from experience to belief highlights how relationism revolves around another broadly Cartesian notion, namely that our response to skepticism should take the form of providing a reason in support of our belief in the external world. Philosophers have suggested many such reasons, but no proposal has seemed convincing. Now the relationist suggests that experience itself could provide reasons. But, as I will now argue, perceptual experience is ill-equipped to provide reasons.

What are reasons? For present purposes, we do not need to take a stance on the extensive, though to my mind largely, if not entirely, verbal debates about whether reasons are states of affairs or mental states (or propositions). I will just insist here that whatever we say, reasons must be tied to reasoning. That is, they must either themselves be intentional attitudes (states or speech acts) that figure in reasoning, or they must stand in some relation to such attitudes such as being their object. A state of affairs such that it is raining could therefore not be a reason independently of any such relation to an intentional state. Now the point is that the move from experience to belief is not reasoning.

Experiential states do not qualify for the roles of reasons or reason-making states because they lack the appropriate propositional and logical structure, as the content of experience is pre-conceptual and non-propositional and does not contain logical operators. Intuitively it also seems clear that the move from experience to belief or assertion based on it is not reasoning. Typically, I will just look at what is in front of me and say or think, for example, that there is a monitor in front of me. No reasoning required. Sometimes I may squint my eyes and take a closer look at what it is that I am dealing with, and this may even be motivated by reasoning. Was this really a mountain lion that I saw? Are its back and sides tawny to light-cinnamon in color and its chest and underside white? Here reasoning directs my perceptual attention, but that does not make the move from experience to belief reasoning. Rational capacities are manifest in inferring bits of information and weighing them against one another in what Wilfred Sellars called the "space of reasons". Are there even mountain lions in Austria? Might one have escaped from a nearby zoo? But the move from experience to thought is different in character. We do not need a reason to enter the space of reasons; there couldn't even be such a reason because to possess it we would already have to be in that space. So experience can't provide reasons.

The notion that experience itself already involves rational capacities, as John McDowell (e.g. 2013) in particular has long claimed, so that by perceiving something we would already be in the space of reasons, is very implausible. One has to be very much in the grip of a philosophical idea to think that seeing, hearing or touching something is an exercise of rationality. The idea in question here is the idea that we need a reason to believe in the reality of the external world, and, as we saw, the only epistemological advantage the relationist construal of experience might be thought to have is that it allows us to think of experience as providing reasons by tying it to the good case. But given the implausible consequences of this idea, we should consider alternatives.

One alternative is provided by Tyler Burge. Burge (2003) gives similar arguments against the idea that experience provides reasons, but then goes on to distinguish two kinds of warrant: justification, which involves reasons and is accessible to the subject, and entitlement, for which neither is true, and which has to do with things like normal conditions and reliability. So Burge opts for epistemological externalism as against McDowell's epistemological internalism: "Epistemology must acknowledge elements of warrant that are not conceptually accessible as reasons to the warranted individual if it is to give a tenable account of perceptual belief" (Burge 2003: 529). But does the move from experience to belief really need a post hoc 3rd person justification from epistemologists, who do reason about these matters, if reasoning about normal conditions, reliability etc. does not and could not play any role for subjects making this move? And given this inaccessibility, in which sense then is entitlement really an epistemological and thus normative status? The natural view is that such a status would have to be in the space of reasons. Moreover, as Burge points out himself (Burge 2003: 537), his explication of entitlement does not address skepticism. Nor could it, since a notion of reliability under normal conditions already *presupposes* the reality and knowability of the external world. But then it seems his explication does not really address the most fundamental aspect of the move from experience to belief and the concerns of McDowell and others.

Faced then with the equally implausible alternatives of declaring experience itself and / or the move from experience to belief to be an exercise of rationality, or of dissociating epistemological status from such exercises, I suggest we try out a different perspective.

7 An Alternative Account

Let us not uncritically accept the Cartesian ideas that we can understand experience independently of any knowledge of the external world and that our response to skepticism should take the form of providing a reason for belief in that world. Regarding the first point, I propose to take a lesson from developmental psychology. Let us use actual development as an antidote, as part of a bit of Wittgensteinian therapy, against both traditional subjectivism and the objectivist, externalist overreaction to it. Let us accept the false belief test as a criterion for understanding mind and so let us take seriously the finding that experiencing world precedes understanding mind, as the false belief test is passed around four years (classical version), or around one year – if we accept the newer violation of expectation paradigms as revealing genuine belief understanding – but in any case certainly after the infant has been perceptually experiencing the world. The rationale for accepting the false belief test as a criterion for understanding mind is pretty straightforward in the light of our earlier reflections: only if a subject can make a clear distinction between how things are and how they seem, that is, between content and object, can it clearly separate mind and world.

In this way the Cartesian question is turned on its head. We can no longer take experience for granted while asking whether it ever gets the world right, but instead we have to ask how we understand mind and experience on the basis of experiencing world. The role of reasons is also turned on its head. They do not lead us from experience to the corresponding beliefs, but from beliefs to *understanding* experience and mind more generally. We start by perceptually experiencing objects as being related to us (and others) – spatially and also causally (Searle 1983). We stand in intentional and experiential relations to the world and may even have some understanding of them in our own case and that of others, but we don't yet understand that they obtain in virtue of experiential states with contents distinct from their objects. Our understanding is still very primitive – somewhat similar to the deliberate primitivism of austere relationism – and at a level prior to the differentiation of mental and bodily features (Schmitz 2015).

A proper understanding of experience and mental states more broadly begins only when we start making assertions and forming beliefs on the basis of experience and learn to resolve inter- and intraindividual conflicts between attitudes by means of reasoning. In this way, we gradually come to understand misrepresentation by separating appearance and reality, content and object. For example, I come to understand that I mistook a lynx for a mountain lion or that the lines in the Müller-Lyer illusion only seem to differ in length.

How to respond to skepticism? From this perspective, the possibility and actuality of misrepresentation can never lead to skeptical doubt, because to ascribe a misrepresentation we need a reason and such a reason can only come from what (is taken to be) a good case. For maximum clarity, let us spell out this argument as a series of steps:

1. To understand experience we need to understand misrepresentation.
2. To ascribe a misrepresentation (bad case) one needs a reason.
3. This reason can only come from (what is taken to be) a good case.

Conclusion: Bad cases presuppose good cases. Misrepresentation can only be thought of as a deviation from the normal case of successful representation.

For example, I can only ascribe the Müller-Lyer illusion to myself because I take myself to know that the lines are actually of equal length. The same kind of argument also applies to doubt. As Wittgenstein pointed out long ago, doubt also stands in need of reasons (ÜG 1984: 122), and these reasons must also come from good cases. For example, the fact that mountain lions are not native to Austria gives me a reason to doubt that I have seen one.

To use the phenomenon of misrepresentation to try to raise global skeptical doubt is therefore to misuse it. The skeptic overlooks the fact that when I ascribed a misrepresentation to myself or doubted my representational success I presupposed the representational success of what gave me reasons for the ascription or for doubt. Doubt without reasons is not genuine. Not the person who accepts the reality of the external world around her is dogmatic, but the skeptic who doubts it without reasons. This is because believing on the basis of sense experience does not require reasons, while doubting does.

I thus agree with certain relationists as well as with proponents of the factive turn in epistemology that the good cases are primary over the bad cases and that a proper account of perception should help to put skepticism to rest. But on my view the skeptic-defeating primacy of the good case does not consist in that experience only provides reasons in the good case, but in that we do *not* need reasons to think we are in the good case, but that we do to doubt that we are, or to think that we are in the bad case. That is why the bad case can only be thought as a deviation from the primary good case. The skeptical doubt is misplaced and not genuine because, first, the move from experience to belief is not an exercise of rationality and therefore in the basic case does not allow, much less require, justification. And second, once we have acquired the reasoning capacities that put us into the space of reasons, these capacities operate by weighing beliefs against one another and resolving conflicts between them, which is why rejecting, even doubting, one can only be rational on the basis of affirming others. So global skeptical doubt and the attendant demand for justification is either misguided because it is directed at something that is not an exercise of rationality and therefore cannot be questioned as such, or because the relevant exercises of rationality already presuppose that we are in good cases.

At an even more advanced level of reasoning we can also cite the fact that we have perceived something as a special kind of reason – one that specifies the source of a belief. While such reasons involve experience, it is still a "conceptual mistake" (Burge 2003: 529) to think that therefore experiences themselves are reasons: not only because reasons are propositional and for the other reasons discussed already, but also because in experience itself we are not yet aware of experience. Such reasons appeal to the reliability of sources, but any determination of reliability, whether under normal or other conditions, already presupposes the existence and knowability of the external world and therefore cannot have a foundational role in responding to skeptical doubts.

We can now explain the sense in which the experiential perceptual relation is fundamental. It is fundamental in the sense that the good case as a default is prior in the epistemological order because it does *not* need a reason. At the same time, the experiential perceptual state is fundamental in a different sense, namely ontologically / for purposes of psychological explanation. It is a more basic constituent of the world because it is present in the good as well as in the bad cases. This shows how the present proposal reconciles intentionalism and relationism, or, more broadly, internalism and externalism, and integrates elements of both into the view that I above called "relational intentionalism". This view is intentionalist in so far as experiential states with intentional contents are taken to be present in the good and bad cases, and it is internalist insofar as it accepts the obvious fact that these are states of organisms located within them. But it is also relationist. It also accepts the obvious fact that there are experiential relations to external objects, and it holds that these relations are epistemologically primary in the sense that one needs a reason to think that there merely seems to be such a relation. Since misrepresentation can thus only be thought of as a deviation from the normal case of successful representation, and understanding experience – clearly separating mind and world, subject and content – in turn requires understanding misrepresentation, the view is also externalist in the sense that experience and its content cannot be understood independently of reference to the external world. The key insight here is the Kantian insight that our understanding of mind and world are interdependent, transposed into an unmistakably realist framework. This interdependence is not to be confused with the attempt to invert our interpretation of a case where mind and world are out of touch by constructing mind out of world. Once we see that and leave behind the excesses of both subjectivism and objectivism, we can be naive realists about mind and world.[2]

---

[2] Thanks for their questions and comments go to audiences in Berkeley, Bochum, Vienna, Osnabrück and Kirchberg, and in particular to Mike Beaton, Peter Epstein, Christopher Gauker, Mikkel Gerken, Alex Kerr, Benjamin Kiesewetter, Sofia Miguens, Gabriele Mras, Christoph Pfisterer, Jesse Prinz, Paul Ritterbush, Tobias Schlicht, Bernhard Schmid, Eva Schmidt, Susanna Schellenberg, John Searle, Umrao Sethi, Paul Snowdon, Klaus Strelau, Charles Travis and Tim-

References

Burge, Tyler (2003): "Perceptual Entitlement". In: *Philosophy and Phenomenological Research* 67 (3), pp. 503–548.
Campbell, John (2002): *Reference and Consciousness*. Oxford: Clarendon Press.
Davidson, Donald (2001): *Subjective, Intersubjective, Objective*. Vol. 3. Oxford: Oxford University Press.
Dorsch, Fabian (2010): "Transparency and Imagining Seeing". In: *Philosophical Explorations*, 13 (3), pp. 173–200.
Fish, William (2009): *Perception, Hallucination, and Illusion*. Oxford: Oxford University Press.
Hutto, Daniel and Erik Myin (2012): *Radicalizing Enactivism: Basic Minds Without Content*. Cambridge, MA: The MIT Press.
Kripke, Saul (1980): *Naming and Necessity*. Cambridge, MA: Harvard University Press.
McDowell, John (2013): "Perceptual Experience: Both Relational and Contentful". In: *European Journal of Philosophy* 21 (1), pp. 144–157.
Putnam, Hilary (1975): "The meaning of 'meaning.'" In: *Minnesota Studies in the Philosophy of Science*, 7, pp. 131–193.
Putnam, Hilary (1981): *Reason, Truth and History*. Cambridge: Cambridge University Press.
Schellenberg, Susanna (2011): "Perceptual Content Defended". In: *Noûs*, 45 (4), pp. 714–750.
Schmitz, Michael (2015): "Joint Attention and Understanding Others". In: *Synthesis Philosophica*, 58, pp. 235–251.
Searle, John R. (1983): *Intentionality: An Essay in the Philosophy of Mind*. Cambridge: Cambridge University Press.
Searle, John R. (1992): *The Rediscovery of the Mind*. Cambridge, MA: The MIT Press.
Travis, Charles (2004): "The Silence of the Senses". In: *Mind* 113 (449), pp. 57–94.
Wittgenstein, Ludwig (1958): *Philosophical Investigations*. Oxford: Basil Blackwell.
Wittgenstein, Ludwig (1984): *Philosophische Untersuchungen*. Frankfurt: Suhrkamp.
Wittgenstein, Ludwig (1984): *Über Gewißheit*. Frankfurt: Suhrkamp.

---

othy Williamson. Thanks for helpful written comments to Federico Castellano and Ingvar Johansson. I want to especially thank the editor Christoph Limbeck-Lilienau for very helpful written comments and discussions and Xiaoxi Wu for moral support.

2 Content and Intentionality

Michael Tye
How to Think About the Representational Content of Visual Experience

Abstract: A number of different theses concerning the representational content of visual experience are canvassed and a new proposal is made. It is shown that the new proposal accounts satisfactorily both for hallucinatory experiences and for the justificatory role visual experiences play.

Keywords: Representational content, existential content, singular content, illusions, justification, particularity, pictures, property complex

The topic of this essay presupposes that visual experiences *have* representational content. Why should we believe that? Here are three standard reasons. First, when one encounters some object and believes it to be a certain way, it makes sense to ask, "Is it really that way?" Belief thus has accuracy conditions. Correspondingly, when one sees an object and it looks to one a certain way, again it makes sense to ask "Is it really that way?" Visual experience thus has accuracy conditions too.

Some have complained that this inference is too fast. Consider two recent examples from Wylie Breckenridge (forthcoming): walking proud and driving American. Let us not quibble over the English used in these examples. Breckenridge's point is that it makes sense to ask whether someone who walks proud really is proud or that someone who drives American is indeed American. But no one supposes that walking and driving have representational content! Rather what is going on in these cases is that 'proud' denotes a certain way of walking, the way proud people typically walk and 'American' denotes a certain way of driving, the way Americans typically drive. This being so, if I walk proud, I may be proud but I may also not be. Similarly, in the case of driving American. So too for 'looks', according to Breckenridge. Thus, the claim that visual experience is representational has not been established.

This is a big topic. I agree with Breckenridge that after 'looks' the qualifier sometimes functions in this way, as a comparative definite description. But it does not always do so. Take the color term, 'red', for example. Here a case can be made that the modifier just refers directly to the color red (Tye forthcoming). So, the proposed analogy with walking proud and driving American fails, and no reason remains, at least for some instances of looking F, to question the analogy with belief. Much more can be said here but let me turn to a second consideration.

For a range of ways of looking (though not all), when something looks a certain way, bent, for example, or red, and it isn't that way, we all agree that there is a visual illusion. In an illusion, the visual system misfires and we experience the seen object as having properties it lacks.[1] In experiencing the seen object as having properties it lacks, we visually misrepresent it. Or so it seems very natural to hold.[2] But if there is misrepresentation, there is representational content.

A third consideration derives from the evidential role visual experiences play. Visual experiences justify perceptual beliefs. They provide reasons for those beliefs. How can visual experiences do that if they lack any representational content?

Reflections along one or more of the above lines have led many philosophers to hold that visual experiences generally have representational content (either accurate or inaccurate), that it is part of the nature of visual experience to be representational. These two claims, as I shall show later, are not equivalent but for the moment I shall let this pass and turn to the question of the logical category of the content of visual experiences: do visual experiences have an existential content, a singular content, in some cases a gappy content or is their content to be categorized in some other way?

1 The Existential Thesis

The existential thesis is the thesis that visual experiences have only existential representational contents. Martin Davies puts the thesis this way:

> ... we can take perceptual content to be existentially quantified content. A visual experience may present the world as containing object of a certain size and shape, in a certain direction, at a certain distance from the subject. (Davies 1992: 26)

Davies here mentions only a very circumscribed list of properties, but it is no essential part of the existential thesis that the relevant properties be so restricted.

An apparently killer objection to this view is that it gets the wrong result for the case in which a yellow cube straight ahead is hidden from my view by a mirror in front of me at an angle of forty five degrees while a blue cube on the right is

---

[1] Nothing like this goes on with walking or driving, I might add. There is no corresponding misfiring.
[2] This is not the only possibility, however. For alternative views, see Brewer 2008, Martin 2006. For more here, see section 10 below.

reflecting light back into the mirror and is so illuminated that it looks yellow to me.

On the existential view, my experience represents that there is a yellow cube ahead, and there is a yellow cube straight ahead. So, my experience is accurate. But I don't see that cube. I see the cube on the right and it is neither yellow nor straight ahead. My visual experience, thus, should be classified as inaccurate.

John Searle (1983) has a clever reply to this objection: make the existential content more complicated. My experience should be taken to represent that there is a yellow cube ahead that stands in such-and-such a causal/contextual relation to *this very experience*, where the relevant causal/contextual relation is the one needed for seeing the relevant cube. Now my experience does have an inaccurate representational content.

This proposal encounters several difficulties, some more pressing than others. First, the proposal that experiences, in part, refer to themselves is not easy to swallow; for intuitively, if I see a tomato, say, my experience is not about <u>itself</u> in addition to the tomato. Secondly, the proposal makes the content much too complicated. After all, very small children undergo visual experiences. This objection can be handled easily enough if it is admitted that visual experiences, or at least some visual experiences, have nonconceptual contents. But there is a further related objection here. Consider, a police radar gun, R, which is trained on my car. R's reading represents the speed of my car via a certain causal relation which R's reading bears to my car. It is the existence of this relation which determines that R is then representing the speed of my car and not that of the Tesla of the chairman of my department. But the relation itself is surely not part of the content of R's reading. The reading does not 'say' that my car bears the appropriate relation to that very reading (or that there is a car that does so). Why should we treat visual experience any differently?

Searle's response to this objection is to deny that the two cases are parallel. In his view, it is plausible to suppose that the seen object is represented *as* seen in the visual experience. And this makes the experience case different from the radar gun one. But this seems wrong to me. The seen object is certainly represented as having a certain color, shape, relative position, and other such apparently external qualities. Why hold that it goes further than this, that visual experience, by its nature, represents seen objects as seen by their viewers? The answer, it seems to me, is that without this stipulation, the existential thesis is refuted. That doesn't seem good enough, especially if we can provide a simpler account that doesn't involve such ad hoc stipulations.

Thirdly, the proposal does not do full justice to the thought that the cube I see looks to me other than it is. Take the earlier set up. I see the cube on the right and I experience it as yellow and in front of me. This is possible only if the cube I see is itself a component of the content of my experience.

One possible reply here is to say that in seeing the cube on the right, I am caused to undergo a visual experience. Since this visual experience represents that there is a cube I am seeing that is yellow and ahead, it is inaccurate. So, I misperceive the cube on the right. It looks yellow and ahead and it isn't.

This, I accept, is a possible response but there are prima facie insuperable difficulties created by more complex examples. Suppose I see two cubes, A and B. I am wearing both color inverting and spatially displacing lenses. A is red and on my right but it looks green and on my left. B is green and on my left but it looks red and on my right.

Take the case of A. My experience misrepresents it. A looks green to me (and on my left). It isn't. How is this to be handled on the existential thesis? A causes in the right way a visual experience in me that represents … what, on the existential content thesis? Not that there is a cube I am seeing that is green and on my left. This proposal makes the content accurate. Not that there is a cube I am seeing that is green and to the left of a red cube. Again, we have an accurate content. I see no way to handle this objection and the conclusion I draw is that the existential thesis is in deep trouble.

2 The Singular Content Thesis

The singular content thesis is the thesis that the seen object enters into the representational content, which is itself a singular proposition made up (minimally) of the seen object and the properties that object appears to have. This works well for veridical perception and illusions. But what about hallucinations?

One solution to the problem presented by hallucinatory experiences is to make the content gappy in these cases. But what exactly is a gappy content? If we think of the singular content (in the simplest case) as an ordered pair of the seen object and property experienced, then it seems we should suppose by analogy that the gappy content is an ordered pair of a gap and property. But this is unintelligible. There cannot be a pair with only one member. Of course, we could introduce the empty set here to fill the gap as a surrogate for the seen object in normal cases. But then we will have to say that in hallucinations subjects see the empty set! This is absurd. Unfortunately, without an empty set, there isn't any truth-evaluable (accuracy-evaluable) content left.³ I shall return to this point a little later in connection with a related proposal.

3 The Possible Worlds Thesis

An alternative is to think of the content in possible worlds terms. Specifically, we might let the content be the set of possible worlds at which the actual seen object has the property it looks to have (in the case that there is a seen object). Thus, if $\underline{a}$ is the seen object and F the property it looks to have, the relevant set of worlds is the set at which a is F. This gives simple accuracy conditions for veridical and illusory cases (where a looks F to person, P, $\underline{P}$'s visual experience is accurate at the actual world just in case the actual world belongs to the set of possible worlds at which a is F) and it preserves a kind of singularity via the specification of worlds in terms of object a.⁴

What about the case of hallucination? Here there is apparent singularity without a real object. The subject hallucinates something and she can introduce a name for the object she takes to be present (going only on the basis of her experience). Let the name be 'a' and the apparent property F. Then, as above, the content is the set of possible worlds at which a is F. Since 'a' is an empty name, it is empty at all possible worlds. So, the set of possible worlds is the empty set. The hallucinatory experience accordingly gets to be counted as inaccurate or false.

There is a price paid for this success. Phenomenally different hallucinatory experiences now have the same representational content. So, phenomenal character no longer supervenes on representational content. This threatens representationalism about phenomenal character (Tye 1995). It also makes content an 'idle wheel'.

A partial solution to this problem is to restate the supervenience thesis as a thesis linking phenomenal character with the properties represented. Truth-evaluable or accuracy-evaluable content now drops out as phenomenally irrelevant. But this being so, why should we keep (truth-evaluable or accuracy- evaluable) content *at all* in the hallucinatory case? Why not simply say that hallucinatory experiences are not accurate without their being inaccurate? They are neither accurate nor inaccurate. The question to which we are now led is: how should we

---

3 I ignore here so-called 'objectual' or de re hallucinations.
4 See here Sainsbury and Tye 2012. Veridical hallucination is impossible on this view.

think of visual experiences so that this doesn't just seem an ad hoc way of rescuing the representational view of experience? I turn next to an instrument model for visual experiences as a possible way to answer this question.

4 The Instrument Model of Visual Experience

In my garage, there is a fuel gauge lying on a bench. The fuel gauge, as it lies there, does not represent the level of gas in any particular gas tank. It simply has marks on it that represent various fuel levels. Once it is connected to a car in the right way, it represents the fuel level in the car's tank via its causal connection with that tank. And it can do so accurately or inaccurately. Without being hooked up, no question of accuracy arises.[5]

The proposal to be considered is that we use this as a model for how visual experiences represent. Let us suppose, then, that visual experiences have features (not themselves introspectible, on my view[6]) that represent external properties. We may then hold that where there is a seen object, a given visual experience represents it as having the represented properties via the appropriate causal/contextual connection between the experience and the seen object. In the case of hallucination, there are properties represented but no question of accuracy arises, since the relevant causal/contextual relation is missing.

It may be wondered whether it is part of commonsense that hallucinatory experiences are inaccurate. I think not. Hallucinatory experiences are unsuccessful experiences. They aim to make contact with the world but they fail. So, they are not accurate. But equally they are not inaccurate either. They are not candidates for accuracy.

What about veridical hallucinations? What if I hallucinate a blue ball bouncing before me, say, and, as it happens, there is such a ball? This, I suggest, is like the case of the speedometer sitting disconnected on the front seat of my car with the pointer momentarily registering '30' (due to the car hitting a large bump and the pointer flipping to that number on the gauge) while the car happens to be going 30 mph. Is my speedometer here fortuitously accurate? No, for it is not con-

---

[5] Can't there be an inaccurate or faulty gauge that is not hooked up? Yes, of course. But in calling such a gauge "inaccurate", all we mean is that if it were hooked up, it would not accurately represent the fuel level of the relevant vehicle.
[6] I endorse the thesis of transparency with respect to the properties of which one is aware when one introspects a visual experience. See here my 2014.

nected to my car. And without any connection, why pick this car to evaluate accuracy? Is it inaccurate? No, for the same reason. Still the speed it represents happens to match the speed of my car. Correspondingly, my hallucinatory visual experience is not veridical since it is not accurate (nor is it inaccurate). But the properties it represents happen to match the properties the ball possesses. Generalizing, veridical hallucinations are literally impossible.

The thesis that emerges here has it that visual experiences represent properties and do so essentially (in something like the manner of instruments). However, only some, not all, visual experiences have accuracy-evaluable representational contents. Thus, having an accuracy-evaluable content is not essential to a visual experience.

So far so good. But a large problem looms, a variant on a problem Frank Jackson raised for the account adverbial theorists give of after-image experiences. Jackson called the original problem "the many property problem" (1977) and the problem I have in mind here also involves many properties.

Suppose I hallucinate a red square to the left of a green triangle. This is a different experience from that of hallucinating a green square to the left of a red triangle. In both cases, the same properties (and relations) are represented. However, intuitively, the experiences are representationally different. They are also phenomenally different. What it is like to experience the one is different from what it is like to experience the other.

The upshot, I suggest, is that typical instruments are just too simple to serve as a good model for visual experiences. They represent only single gradable properties: temperature, speed, etc. and determinates of them. Visual experiences are representationally much more complex.

What model would capture better this complexity? Let us consider next the case of pictures.

5 The Pictorial Model of Visual Experience

Consider the real-world scene shown below of a triangle and a square, as seen from a particular point of view. Call the triangle '*A*' and the square '*B*'.

Fig. 1

Suppose you tell me to create a realistic picture of this actual scene, from that point of view. Here is my picture:

Fig. 2

My picture is not a good one. It does not accurately depict the real, actual world scene. Why not? Well, it gets *B* wrong. We can put the situation representationally this way: overall, the picture represents *A* and *B* as jointly instantiating a certain *property complex* that they don't instantiate, that of being a black triangle to the left of a black parallelogram. But suppose this picture is something I create on my own without it being a picture of any particular real, actual scene. Then no question of accuracy or inaccuracy arises, even if there is a black triangle to the left of a black parallelogram so that the property complex is instantiated.[7]

Why? My answer is that it is a bit like the instrument case though more complicated. As far as accuracy conditions go, a picture represents with respect to the objects pictured that they instantiate a given property complex. This is why, where the picture is not a picture of any real objects, no question of accuracy conditions arises. But when there are pictured objects, there is singular content and with singular content, there are accuracy conditions.

My proposal, then, is that visual experiences represent in something like the way that pictures do. This proposal fits with some claims that have been made by well-known cognitive psychologists about both vision and imagery.[8] It also fits

---

[7] For more on property complexes, see Johnston 2004.
[8] See, for example, Stephen Kosslyn 1994, 1995.

nicely with the representational richness of visual experiences. Their richness is like the richness of pictures. Of course, there are important differences between pictures and visual experiences. My picture above, for example, is black in part: my visual experience is not. But what matters here is that visual experiences have features that represent colors and other visible properties (features that are not themselves colors, for example) and parts that represent things pictured and also that they have a general representational structure similar in important ways to that of pictures.[9]

Thus, if we return to the version of the many property problem for hallucinatory experiences, what we can now say is that when I hallucinate a red square to the left of a green triangle, my experience has parts jointly instantiating a complex of features representing the property complex of being a red square to the left of a green triangle. A different property complex is represented when I hallucinate a green square to the left of a red triangle. So, the two experiences are representationally different.

How should we state the accuracy conditions, then, for a visual experience of (as of) a red square to the left of a green triangle? Corresponding to the picture case, we should say that the experience is accurate just in case the seen objects together instantiate the relevant property complex.[10] So, in the hallucinatory case, where there are no seen objects, there is neither accuracy nor inaccuracy.

6 The Issue of Particularity in Visual Experience

Obviously, where there is a seen object, at least as far as the content goes, particularity can be accommodated via the object's entering into the content. But what about the hallucinatory case? It is often said that there is particularity here, that it is for one as if one were seeing a particular thing. How exactly is this claim to be understood?

---

[9] How this similarity is to be cashed out further is a complex issue. It seems plausible to hold that the most basic visual experience parts represent just noticeable object parts (patches of surface) lying on different lines of sight in the field of view so that greater distances among represented parts of experienced objects are represented via greater numbers of basic experience parts. For more here, see ibid; also Tye 1991.

[10] The claim that the seen objects together instantiate the relevant property complex is to be understood in the same sort of way as the claim that John and Jill together lifted the piano or the claim that the children jointly stood in a circle.

One thesis is that in hallucinating, it seems to one that one is seeing a particular thing. But this is obviously too strong. After all, mind blind creatures can hallucinate. Another thesis is that in hallucinating, it seems to one that a particular thing is present. But on the face of it, this thesis requires that one have the concept of particularity and this again seems too strong. A third thesis is that in hallucinating, for some value of 'F', one experiences *an F*. This strikes me as reasonable; and it is compatible with the view I am proposing.

Consider the case of a picture being a picture of *an F* even if there is no particular F being pictured. This is achieved via the picture having a part (a blob of paint) with a feature pictorially representing the property of being F. In this way, the picture has a pictorial singular mode of presentation, as we might put it, even though there is no particular object pictured. Similarly, a hallucinatory visual experience of an F has a part with a feature representing the property of being F. In the more complicated cases of hallucinating several objects, there are several parts, relations between which, and properties of, represent experienced relations and properties. And this is another way in which the case of visual experience is more complicated than the simple instrument case. Take, for example, the case of a speedometer. Even when the speedometer is hooked up, there is no *part* of it representing a particular vehicle (simply a pointer and numbers on the dial for various speeds). But, as just noted, with a visual experience, there may be multiple objects experienced and multiple parts representing them.

A further way of taking the particularity thesis that, in hallucinating, it is as if one is seeing a particular thing, is that the phenomenal character of one's experience, in hallucinating, is the same as (or indistinguishable from) that of seeing a particular thing. This claim is compatible with the proposed view too; for experiences representing the same property complexes can occur in both veridical and hallucinatory cases and with representational identity at this level comes phenomenal identity (I claim).

7 Comparison with P. F. Strawson on "the King of France"

Even though I am proposing a pictorial model, I think it is worth comparing briefly some of the claims I have made with P.F. Strawson's view of sentences using definite descriptions in his debate with Bertrand Russell.

Strawson (1950) held that "The present king of France is bald" is neither true nor false. The sentence is meaningful, nonetheless. The same sentence, used in a different context, e.g., in the seventeenth century, would have said something true or false, but not as uttered today. A token of the sentence has a part that is a token of a description, "the present king of France", parts of which linguistically represent features, being a king, ruling France, etc. By producing that token today, the speaker has produced an ostensibly referring expression that has misfired. It doesn't refer.

Correspondingly, I claim that hallucinatory experiences are neither accurate nor inaccurate. **If** we type experiences by their phenomenal character, experiences occurring in hallucinations can occur elsewhere in contexts in which they are evaluable for accuracy, namely when something is seen. I underline 'if' here since not all wish to type experiences in this way. But assuming we do so type them, hallucinatory experiences, on my view, have quasi-pictorial, singular modes of presentation even though there are no objects just as Strawson's sentence has a descriptive, singular mode of presentation without an answering object.

8 A Quasi-Linguistic Alternative: De Re Conceptual Modes

Having mentioned P.F. Strawson and a linguistic example, let me turn briefly next to an alternative quasi-linguistic or conceptual model of visual experience, specifically, as we might think of it, a demonstrative sentence model. Here is the idea, which is proposed by Susanna Schellenburg in several articles (2012, 2016).

Experiences use de re demonstrative modes of presentation and de re predicative modes. These modes are ways of thinking of a sort used in discriminating and singling out. In hallucinations, there is no truth-evaluable content. Rather in hallucinations, the modes have holes in them where the seen entities go in the veridical case — the seen manifest object(s) and the property instance(s).

I reject this view. First, demonstrative modes need not be used *in* experience. Suppose I hallucinate Pegasus, for example. If thought is involved in the experience, can't I just think of Pegasus as Pegasus here? I can then *go on* to say that I experienced *that* horse prancing before me and in so doing use a demonstrative, but I need employ a demonstrative simply in undergoing the experience.[11] Sec-

---

11 Some people think that demonstratives are involved in names (Burge, for example) — that Pegasus, for example. Those who take this view won't be moved by this objection.

ondly, as many have argued (myself included), some visual experiences are non-conceptual through and through. This is not permissible on the above view. Thirdly, in hallucinations, there are no property instances. So, all that is available are the conceptual modes, in principle accessible to someone without phenomenal states (a zombie). What, then, accounts for the sensory richness of hallucinatory phenomenology? Fourth, and more generally, how is the incredible richness of visual experience to be handled? It is very hard to see how a simple demonstrative-predicative model can capture this

9 Un-instantiated Properties

In hallucinations, on my view, un-instantiated property complexes are represented, and relatedly (as with some pictures) locally un-instantiated properties are represented too. Some philosophers find this puzzling. I do not. Think about the case of a malfunctioning thermometer. The thermometer represents that the temperature is N degrees Fahrenheit even though, as it happens, nothing is at N degrees. Is that so strange? A state can have the function of indicating feature F and thereby represent F (Dretske 1995) even if all F things are destroyed and nothing has F.

Consider also the case of Mary's uninformed cousin, who has been locked in a black and white room since birth (Tye forthcoming b). Suppose she is released from her room and made to hallucinate a red patch, an orange patch and a green patch. Thereby, she comes to know that red is more similar to orange than to green on the basis of her visual experience. This is a case of primary fact awareness. She does not come to know that red is more similar to orange than to green by knowing some other fact.

How can she come to know this fact unless she is aware of the colors, red, orange and green even though she is hallucinating? But if she is visually aware of these colors, and visual experience is representational, the natural view is that Mary's cousin undergoes a visual experience that represents them.[12]

---

12 A parallel: seeing an object is undergoing a visual experience that is about (represents) it.

10 The Justificatory Role of Visual Experiences

Sitting now at my desk, as I look out the window, I undergo a rich and varied visual experience. I see, or at least I seem to see, a silver car, a courtyard with red and white flowers, a willow tree with its branches hanging low. On the basis of my visual experience, I believe that these things are before me in my field of view. My visual experience provides a *reason* for my belief. How does it do that? How does my visual experience *justify* my belief?

A natural thought is that my visual experience must have a content that stands in the appropriate evidential relation to the content of my belief. The experiential content must entail the belief content or, more modestly, in a relevant restricted range of possible worlds in which the experiential content is true, the belief content must be true. This suggestion immediately encounters problems, however. For one thing, the mere fact that the experiential content stands in an entailment relation to the belief content or some weaker relation that is suitably truth-preserving does nothing to show that the experience justifies the belief. If I fear that carbon dioxide levels in the atmosphere are dangerously high and you believe what I fear, the content of my fear entails the content of your belief, but my fear certainly doesn't justify your belief.

Furthermore, if I am now having a remarkably vivid hallucination of a car, a courtyard and a willow tree, my experience, even though non-veridical, still justifies my belief that these things are present in front of me. How can this be, if, as I have argued, hallucinatory experiences lack truth-evaluable content?

Some say that hallucinatory experiences do *not* justify beliefs via their contents since evidence can consist only of known propositions and hallucinatory experiences have false contents (Williamson 2000). This has the consequence that if, unknown to me, I am hallucinating, my visual experience being caused by an Evil Demon intent on deceiving me, my perceptual belief that there is a tomato in front of me, say, is not arrived at on the basis of the same evidence as it is in the case that I am genuinely seeing a tomato. In the good case, I know *far* more than in the bad case with the Evil Demon, and so, on the above conception of evidence, I will be much more reasonable in believing what I do.

This view goes against the intuition that in both cases, I have exactly the same evidence. Perhaps this intuition can be given up. But surely, it cannot be denied that in the bad case, in forming my belief, I am not being unreasonable, *period*. After all, it is not as if I am irrationally believing that a certain horse will win a race, since it is wearing my favorite number or believing that the earth is flat, since the soles of my shoes are. Furthermore, in the bad case, as in the good one, I have no reason whatsoever to think that my experience is *not* veridical. How, then, can my belief be *entirely* without justification?

One response that can be made to this point by those who hold that evidence consists in known propositions is to say that in the above bad case, as in the good one, I do know that it *appears* to me that there is a tomato before me. *This* is my evidence for my belief. Having such evidence, I am not being entirely unreasonable in believing what I do in the bad case, even if I am not *as* reasonable as in the good case.

The obvious problem with this response is that if evidence consists in known propositions, I may lack the relevant evidence; for in a given scenario I may form no belief using the concept APPEAR, believing only that there is such-and-such a thing in front of me, and having no such belief, I do not know that it appears to me that so-and-so is the case. A related problem is that a young child who altogether lacks psychological concepts, and thus is in no position to form *any* beliefs as to how things *appear*, many nonetheless be justified in believing that the dog is wagging its tail, say, on the basis of her experience.

A third difficulty is that intuitively if there is a fact that justifies a given visual experience, it is not part of the relevant fact that I am having a visual experience. Take, for example, the case in which I am seeing a real tomato on a table. What justifies my belief that there is a tomato on the table? What is my evidence here? Surely, the relevant fact is the fact that there is a red, round bulgy shape on a smooth, brown surface (or something similar). In this case, intuitively, it is the *content* of my experience that matters. It is not the fact that I am having a *visual experience* with that content. The visual experience is the vehicle of certain information; and the vehicle itself is not part and parcel of what justifies my belief.

So, what is the solution to the problem of justification for perceptual beliefs? As a way of bringing out my answer, recall Descartes, Hume and others speaking of the *testimony* of the senses. Descartes famously noted that the testimony may turn out to be radically mistaken. And evidently things are not always what they seem. Consider the Muller-Lyer diagram:

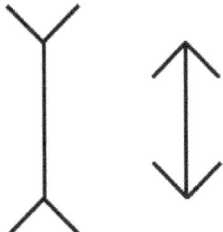

Fig. 3

The lines look to be different lengths even though they are not. Take also the Titchener circles. The inner circles certainly look different sizes.

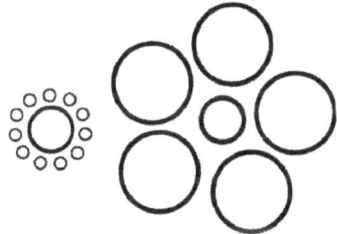

Fig. 4

What these illusions remind us is that the senses don't *merely* testify. They *command*. Or rather the visual experiences they generate command. My visual experience, as I view the Muller Lyer diagram, commands me to believe that the lines are of different lengths. Of course, I know better. So, I do not follow the command. But I feel it *compelling* me to believe. Going only on how things look, I find myself *under pressure* to accept that the lines are of different lengths. In general, I cannot help but believe that things are as they appear. I am under pressure to so believe. Why? What accounts for this pressure? Answer: visual experiences issue commands -- commands to us to so believe.

In the basic case, our visual experiences command us to believe that the property complexes they represent are tokened by the objects in the field of view. We generally obey these commands because they come from an authority we know to be reliable. We are justified in forming the perceptual beliefs we do on the basis of our visual experiences because our experiences command us to form those beliefs (or beliefs that straightforwardly entail those beliefs) and we know that, in obeying those commands, we are obeying an authority that we have no reason to question in the relevant cases.

On this view, visual experiences have imperative contents in addition to the representational features adumbrated earlier.[13]

11 Objections and Clarifications

<u>Objection 1</u>: very young children have visual experiences but they lack the concepts needed to obey the commands their visual experiences supposedly issue. They lack the concept BELIEF, for example, and so they can't obey any command to believe anything.

<u>Reply</u>: the fact that young children lack the concepts to grasp the commands their experiences issue and thus cannot obey them does not show that the experiences do not issue commands. A Russian person I know to be authoritative might issue a command in Russian that I do not follow because I don't understand it. Still, the command was issued.

Here is a related point. Visual experiences, in authoritatively issuing the relevant commands to believe, *provide* reasons to form those beliefs. But their subjects need not *have* the reasons so provided. And they won't have those reasons if they can't even grasp the commands being issued.[14]

<u>Objection 2</u>: if nothing is seen – the subject is hallucinating – then there is no genuine, contentful belief that *those* things have *that* (where *that* is the complex of properties the visual experience represents and *those* things are the objects seen) and so the subject's experience cannot issue a command to form such a belief.

<u>Reply a)</u>: the experience can still issue a command to form a belief that those things have that. It's just that the relevant belief has no truth-evaluable content. The immediate difficulty with this reply (other than its counter-intuitively giving

---

[13] Is having an imperative content an essential property of visual experiences? Probably not. Take the case of after-images or phosphenes. But typically visual experiences have such a property.

[14] An example: The fact that John has a heart condition provides a reason for believing that he will die early. But that need not be a reason he himself has to believe that he will die early. Perhaps he has never been to a doctor and is unaware of his heart condition.

up the view that beliefs essentially have truth-evaluable contents) is in explaining how the existential perceptual belief that there is an *F*, formed on the basis of experience, is justified. It cannot be via the belief that *those have that*, where that = *F-ness*, for the latter belief has no content, on the above view, if one is hallucinating.[15]

Reply b): there is such a contentful belief as the belief that *those* objects have *that* in the above case. It exercises the concepts THOSE OBJECTS and THAT, where the former is a plural demonstrative concept without a referent. The experience issues a command to hold this false belief. Of course, we need a story about the content of such a belief; I have offered such a story elsewhere.[16]

Objection 3: imperative contents do not fit in well with a naturalistic perspective. How could a state have an imperative content that is not *conventionally* assigned to it?

Reply: consider my saying "Shut the door!". In uttering this sentence, I issue a command. The function of my remark is to bring about a certain state of affairs, that of the door's being shut. This is a case of conventional function. But there are also functions in nature. The function of the heart is to pump blood, for example. And this clearly is not a matter of conventional assignment. The heart has a certain job to do, and it has that job whether you or I or any humans are aware of it. Visual experiences have jobs to do too. Their function is to bring about certain states of affairs. For example, if an object I see looks blue, my visual experience represents the color blue and it issues a command to believe of the seen object that it has that color. The latter is achieved via my experience having the natural function of bringing about the state of affairs of believing of the seen object that it is blue.

So, that's how to think about the representational content of visual experience. Many questions remain, of course. For example, do *any* visual experiences have a wholly nonconceptual content? What kinds of properties can enter into the contents of visual experience? Can natural kind properties enter, for example? Interesting as these questions are, they are topics for another occasion.

---

15 One possible response here I'll just mention is to broaden the command issued so that it includes forming the belief that the property complex is instantiated as well as the belief already noted.
16 In Sainsbury and Tye 2012. It is not applicable to visual experiences.

References

Breckenridge, Wylie (forthcoming): *Visual Experience: A Semantic Approach*, Oxford: Oxford University Press.
Brewer, Bill (2008): "How to Account for Illusion". In: *Disjunctivism: Perception, Action, Knowledge*, A. Haddock & F. Macpherson (eds.), Oxford: Oxford University Press.
Davies, Martin (1992): "Perceptual Content and Local Supervenience". In: *Proceedings of the Aristotelian Society*, 92, pp. 21–45.
Dretske, Fred (1995): *Naturalizing the Mind*, Cambridge, Mass.: the MIT Press.
Jackson, Frank (1977): *Perception*, Cambridge, Mass.: Cambridge University Press.
Johnston, Mark (2004): "The Obscure Object of Hallucination". In: *Philosophical Studies*, 120, pp. 113–183.
Kosslyn, Stephen (1994): *Image and Brain: The Resolution of the Imagery Debate*, Cambridge, MA: MIT Press.
Kosslyn, S.; Thompson, W.; Kim, I.; Alpert, N. (1995): "Topographic representations of mental images in primary visual cortex". In: *Nature*, 378 (6556), pp. 496–498.
Martin, Michael G.F. (2006): "On Being Alienated". In: *Perceptual Experience*, T. S. Gendler & J. Hawthorne (eds.), Oxford: Oxford University Press.
Sainsbury, Mark and Tye, Michael (2012): *Seven Puzzles of Thought (and How to Solve Them)*, Oxford: Oxford University Press.
Schellenberg, Susanna (2012): "Perceptual Content Defended". In: *Nous*, 45, pp. 714–750.
Schellenberg, Susanna (2016): "Perceptual Particularity". In: *Philosophy and Phenomenological Research*, 93, pp. 25–54.
Searle, John (1983): *Intentionality*, Cambridge, Mass.: Cambridge University Press.
Strawson, Peter F. (1950): "On Referring". In: *Mind*, 59, pp. 320–344.
Tye, Michael (1991): *The Imagery Debate*, Bradford Books, MIT Press.
Tye, Michael (1995): *Ten Problems of Consciousness*, Bradford Books, MIT Press.
Tye, Michael (2014): "Transparency, Qualia Realism, and Representationalism". In: *Philosophical Studies*, 170, pp. 39–57.
Tye, Michael (forthcoming a): "There is no phenomenal sense of 'looks' (nor any epistemic or comparative one)", forthcoming in a collection of essays in honor of Brian Loar, edited by Arthur Sullivan.
Tye, Michael (forthcoming b): "What Uninformed Mary Can Teach Us", forthcoming in a collection on Mary edited by Sam Coleman.
Williamson, Timothy (2000): *Knowledge and its Limits*, Oxford: Oxford University Press.

Marcello Oreste Fiocco
Structure, Intentionality and the Given

Abstract: The given is the state of a mind in its primary engagement with the world. A satisfactory epistemology—one, it turns out, that is foundationalist and includes a naïve realist view of perception—requires a certain account of the given. Moreover, knowledge based on the given requires both a particular view of the world itself and a heterodox account of judgment. These admittedly controversial claims are supported by basic ontological considerations. I begin, then, with two contradictory views of the world per se and the structure one experiences. I draw out the consequences of these two views for what intentionality is. The two views yield incompatible accounts of the given. The definitive spontaneity of the one account, and passivity of the other, can be understood in terms of the structure (or lack thereof) in the given. In defense of the claim that a structured given is not an apt epistemic basis, I examine an attempt to found an epistemology on such an account in light of the so-called myth of the given. I maintain that the given, if it is to provide some justification for taking the world to be a particular way, must be unstructured. To support this, I first discuss a significant problem with traditional foundationalism. I then argue that a satisfactory (foundationalist) epistemology requires the rejection of the orthodox propositional view of judgment in favor of a non-propositional, reistic view.

Keywords: Ontology, intentionality, acquaintance, naïve realism, myth of the given, foundationalism

Introduction

The most basic epistemological issues, the ones that determine the scope of epistemic inquiry and the answers to the questions therein, turn on the primary engagement between a mind and the world, the all-inclusive totality encompassing one. What a mind is, then, and what the world per se is are questions that are not central merely to the philosophy of mind and to metaphysics, respectively, but crucial to a thoroughgoing epistemology. I maintain that the answer to the question of what the world is—and, hence, how it comes to be *structured*—illuminates what a mind is and how to understand *intentionality*, the capacity of a mind to engage the world. Such an understanding provides insight into the *given*, the state of a mind in its primary engagement with the world.

https://doi.org/10.1515/9783110657920-006

There is much controversy regarding the given. The controversy arises from considering whether such states are apt to serve as the basis of one's knowledge. I argue that on one view of the world, any instance of the given is itself *epistemically idle*, providing no justification for taking the world to be one way rather than another. This view of the world requires a certain spontaneity, an active contribution, on the part of a mind engaging the world. Such spontaneity renders the given conditional, making ineluctable the question of whether the world in fact meets the condition inherent to that state. This conditionality not only undermines the epistemic efficacy of any instance of the given, but is, on this view of the world, inconsistent with the very project of epistemology. The only way to avoid the conditionality is by accepting the opposing view of the world. The given can serve as an epistemic foundation on this view, for it allows utter passivity and, hence, a revealing directness, in the engagement between a mind and the world. The foundationalism this yields, with its naïve realism regarding perception, seems to be the only tenable approach to epistemology.

I begin with some very general ontological considerations pertaining to the world and the things it comprises. These indicate two contradictory views of the structure one experiences and, thus, of the world per se. I draw out the consequences of these two views for what intentionality is. The two views yield incompatible accounts of the given, differing with respect to how active a mind must be in order to engage the world. The definitive spontaneity of the one account, and passivity of the other, can be understood in terms of the structure (or lack thereof) in the given. In defense of the claim that a structured—and thereby conditional—given is not an apt epistemic basis, I examine an attempt to found an epistemology on such an account in light of the so-called *myth of the given* (in this connection, I consider the work of John McDowell). A satisfactory epistemology requires the given to be unstructured and so unconditional. To support this claim, I first discuss a significant problem with traditional foundationalism (in this connection, I consider the work of Laurence BonJour). I then argue that a satisfactory epistemology requires the rejection of the orthodox view of judgment, of what it is to adopt a view regarding how the world (or part thereof) is, in favor of the sort of non-propositional, reistic view propounded by Franz Brentano. Therefore, knowledge based on the given requires both a particular view of the world and a heterodox account of judgment. In conclusion, I present some of the upshots of these ontological-cum-epistemological considerations for recent debates concerning perception.

1 Structure and the World

The world is the all-encompassing totality that surrounds one. It is, I hazard, indubitable that the world is differentiated. To this extent, it comprises distinct things. This last claim should not be controversial. I intend 'thing' here to be understood with the utmost generality, so that any being: any quality, universal or particular; any substance, universal or particular—indeed any entity of any category whatsoever—is equally a thing.

One experiences the world as structured, as an array of fairly determinate things behaving in fairly regular ways. This determinacy of and regularity among things arises from constraints on them. Some thing is constrained and, hence, limited to be a quality and so can qualify some other thing in a distinctive way; something else is, perhaps, constrained to be a particular substance of a certain kind and so has certain qualities and capacities to interact with other things in set ways. The world is structured, then, in virtue of primordial constraints on things. One of the most important questions in philosophical inquiry, because so much turns on it, is what the source of these constraints is. There are traditionally two opposing accounts of this source.

On one, each thing is constrained in itself. What it is to be at all is to be constrained, and so to exist is to contribute to this all-encompassing totality in circumscribed ways. The structure in the world is a corollary of the things that exist: there are things and because each is constrained in itself, each is fairly determinate and each is limited to interacting with other things in fairly regular ways. Since, on this account, to exist is to be constrained, at least some of the constraints intrinsic to a thing are definitive of it, in that it would not be the very thing it is were it not constrained in those ways. Each thing, therefore, is in this sense *natured*.[1] Consequently, a good deal of the structure in the world is necessary, for it arises from the very things there are and, given that these exist and must be certain ways, so too must the structure to which they give rise. This account of the source of structure yields, then, *a broadly Aristotelian view of the world*, one on which it is rife with (necessary) order, comprising things constrained by what they themselves are and that, in turn, impose further constraints on those things with which they interact.

---

1 One might think it more natural to say that *each thing has a nature* (or *an essence*). I avoid this locution for it suggests misleadingly that a nature or essence is itself a thing: a thing to be had by another. There are no natures, no essences—though each thing is *natured*, that is, certain ways *essentially*.

On the other account of the source of the constraints on things, constraints are not concomitant with existence. Rather, they are imposed on things by some privileged thing (or sort of thing). There are, then, entities that are in no way limited in how they are or what they do; such things defy further characterization. The structure in the world arises from the interaction of some privileged thing(s) and these others. Insofar as the former must (somehow) be as it is, the structure it imposes is necessary. Still, the things necessarily constrained to be how they are and do as they do are in themselves wholly unconstrained. The most familiar and influential versions of this sort of account are ones on which the privileged thing is that which enables experience of the world in the first place. It is, then, a mind that is the ultimate source of the structure in the world. Thus, this account yields *a broadly* Humean *or* Kantian view of the world, one on which it is ordered, but only by means of the workings of a mind.

These two views of the world rest on distinct accounts of the source of constraints in—or on—things. Hence, the two views and accounts depend on different notions of a thing in general: one on which each thing is constrained in itself, the other on which a thing can exist without constraint (to be constrained only by another). I doubt the coherence of the latter notion and, hence, the view of the world based on it. This view includes things that are wholly unconstrained. Such a thing need not be any way at all, so it need not even be wholly unconstrained. If it need not be wholly unconstrained, then it could be constrained. Yet if it could be constrained, there are some limitations on its being—it is, however, supposed to have none. This seems to me to be inconsistent. Nevertheless, I grant the feasibility of this view for the sake of argument. My primary purpose here is to reveal the epistemological consequences of these ontological underpinnings.

2 Structure and Intentionality

A mind is a thing, one that enables experience of the world. It does so in virtue of its capacity to present the things in the world. This capacity enables a mind to relate to things in a unique way, namely, so as to allow consideration. Call this capacity, the definitive feature of a mind, *intentionality*. The two opposing accounts of the source of the constraints on things and, hence, of the structure in the world—with their different notions of a thing in general—have consequences for how exactly intentionality permits a mind to relate to things. Not surprisingly, then, the two accounts are epistemologically pregnant.

2.1 Intentionality in a World of Intrinsically Constrained Things

Assume the Aristotelian view of the world is correct. The world comprises ever so many natured things, each constrained by its very existence. Each thing, then, *must* be certain ways simply because it exists. Natured things interact constrainedly with others. Structure is just a corollary of these things and their interactions. Among the things in the world are minds. This claim is incontrovertible. It is beyond dispute, in this context of philosophical inquiry, that something, literally some *thing*, presents the world (or part thereof) so as to allow consideration and thereby permit inquiry. A mind, like any other thing, is constrained in its being. A mind is, perhaps, nothing more than a thing with this capacity to present others, that is, a thing with intentionality.

It seems that intentionality is a capacity, like certain others (e.g., the capacity to be heated and to give heat, the capacity to be shaped and to give shape), that can be realized both passively and actively. It is obvious that in some cases a mind can be directed actively toward some thing(s); in other cases, though, it seems a mind can come to be engaged without such active direction.[2] So a mind can *actively present* the world, being directed so as to relate to something to the exclusion of others. It can also *passively present* the world, as when another thing simply impresses itself upon a mind thereby coming to be related to it. *Acquaintance*, a relational mental state of direct presentation, wherein a mind is presented with a thing in itself, just as it is independently of any relation, can be understood in terms of this passive realization of intentionality. The directness of acquaintance consists in its passivity: a mind need not make any contribution—it need not be any certain way—in order to become acquainted with a thing. *Sensibility* (or *sensation*) is a faculty that depends on the passive realization of intentionality and is a variety of acquaintance. In particular, sensibility is the power to be passively engaged, through one's various senses, by things in one's relatively nearby spatial environment. (*Intuition* is, perhaps, another faculty that depends on the passive realization of intentionality and is a distinct variety of acquaintance; to wit, the power to be passively engaged by things not in space.)

The passivity of intentionality is important below. Note that there is nothing objectionable about such passivity on the view of the world and structure being supposed here. The world comprises natured things, things that are (and must be) certain ways just in existing. Such things are available to present themselves

---

2 In Fiocco 2015, I argue that a mind *must* have the capacity to interact passively with things.

as they are to a thing whose definitive feature is the capacity to present and, hence, engage with others.

2.2 Intentionality in a World of Imposed Constraints

Now assume that the Humean-Kantian view of the world is correct. There is structure in the world – it is indeed ordered – but this structure is imposed on it by some mind(s). Thus, the structure arises ultimately from the engagement between a mind and the world. A mind is simply a thing that presents the world. There are different ways, on this view, of characterizing the world with which the mind engages and somehow presents. The world is supposed to be, independent of minds, without constraints. It is, then, perhaps, an amorphous lump of potentiality, containing in itself no things (and so no sorts of things). Or perhaps it is a welter of things, every possible one, overlapping chaotically, each interacting with any other in any which way. From this potency or this pandemonium, via the efforts of a mind, structure emerges.

Structure emerges in different ways depending on how the world itself is supposed to be. Structure requires some more or less determinate things. If, in the first instance, there is to be any determinate thing at all, a mind, with its intentionality, must either construct a thing from mere potency or else circumscribe uniquely something from the ontological turmoil. In either case, intentionality must supply some condition—*that some thing is so-and-so*—that is met, by potency or turmoil, to yield a determinate thing. Thus, in order for there to be structure at all, the mind must be active, making some contribution; in this sense, it must be *spontaneous*. If the world per se is a lump of potentiality, the condition provided by this spontaneity is what constrains that potential to yield a particular, actual thing. If the world per se is a welter of things, this condition constrains a unique thing from ever so many overlapping similar ones.

Therefore, on the Humean-Kantian view, regardless of how the world itself is unconstrained, intentionality must be spontaneous in any of its functions, including sensibility.[3] If there is to be any determinate thing at all and, thus, if the

---

3 It is worth noting that intentionality, the definitive capacity of a mind to present things, is itself a thing (viz., a capacity). If, on the Humean-Kantian view of the world and its structure, intentionality must be active, it is constrained. This raises the question of how it can be so. The only answer available on the Humean-Kantian view, namely that the constraint comes from a mind, will not do, for the capacity of intentionality is necessary for there to be minds at all. Therefore, whatever constraint limits the capacity to being active is prior to minds. This is inconsistent with the Humean-Kantian view and corroborates my doubts about its coherence.

mind is to present one thing to the exclusion of all others, a mind must *do*, rather than just *be*. A mind must supply a condition that is then met by the world.

2.3 The Given

How intentionality can be is determined by the source of the constraints on things. The two views of the world, then, with their different accounts of the structure it contains, bring with them different accounts of intentionality. On the broadly Aristotelian view, intentionality is a capacity that is both active and passive; on the broadly Humean-Kantian view of the world, intentionality is only active. The given is an intentional state, to wit, the state of a mind in its primary engagement with the world, so the two views of the world allow different accounts of the given.

On the Aristotelian view of the world, because intentionality can be passive, an instance of the given can be an unstructured state of acquaintance. As such, it can be simple and unconditional, imposing no restriction on the world. (Note that the Aristotelian view can accommodate intentional states that are complex and conditional; however, the key point here is its compatibility with a given that is simple and unconditional.) On the Humean-Kantian view, however, because intentionality must be active, arising from a certain spontaneity, the given must be structured. Each instance of a mind in its primary engagement with the world must be complex, having some internal structure that imposes a condition that might (or might not) be met by the world.

3 The Given as Epistemically Idle

The two accounts of the given have significant epistemological consequences. Since sensory (i.e., perceptual) states, those intentional states of primary engagement with things in the nearby environment of a subject, have traditionally been the focus of interest in the given, I confine my attention to these. On the account of the given required by the Humean-Kantian view of the world, such sensory states cannot serve as one's epistemic basis for knowing the world. This conclusion is reached by employing a venerable style of argument purporting to show that the claim that the given is epistemically efficacious—that an instance of the given can provide some justification for taking the world to be a particular way—is a myth. This more general conclusion is not correct. However, the argument does show that any instance of the given structured as it must be on the Humean-

Kantian view is indeed epistemically idle, providing no justification for taking the world to be one way rather than another. In support of this, I present the argument and consider an instructive attempt, that of John McDowell, to found an epistemology on a given that is structured in this way.

If the primary state of engagement between a mind and the world is epistemically idle, one might well wonder with what sort of epistemology this account of the given leaves one. I maintain it leaves one with none at all: the spontaneity required by the given on the Humean-Kantian view, with the account of the source of the constraints in the world accompanying this view, undermines the very project of epistemology.

3.1 An Argument That an Epistemically Efficacious Given is a Myth

Concerns about the given as an epistemic foundation are long-standing, but have their contemporary origin in an exchange between two Logical Positivists, Moritz Schlick and Carl Hempel. Both accept that a judgment is an attitude towards a *proposition*, an entity that represents the world. Schlick maintains that one can compare propositions with *facts*, things in the world, and that the "*only ultimate reason*" (Schlick 1935: 70. Emphasis in original.) to accept a proposition as true is an experience of the fact(s) it represents. Thus, the basis of all one's judgments are those mental states that present things in the world. Hempel disagrees, holding that only propositions can epistemically support a proposition and, hence, a judgment. He holds this because he believes that any relation of epistemic support must be a logical one: one proposition supports another only if the former entails the latter given the rules of the representational system to which they belong.[4] Facts are not the right sort of thing to support propositions; they are not representational, nor even formal, and so cannot stand in logical relations. Moreover, Hempel presumes, one's experiences of facts, that is, things in the world, do not have the proper form to support propositions. This leads him to accept a version of coherentism.

The crux of these original concerns regarding the epistemic efficacy of the given are about *fit*, whether a primary state of engagement with the world fits with a relevant judgment in such a way that the former can indicate the appropriateness of the latter. It is taken for granted in discussions of the given that one's judgments have a *propositional* or *conceptual structure*. Thus, in taking the

---

4 Hempel 1934/5b: 94. See, as well, Schlick 1934, Hempel 1934/5a.

world (or some part thereof) to be as it is, one judges *that some thing is so-and-so*—e.g., that the door is open, that the moon is full, that the water is boiling—or that some thing satisfies the (general) concept such-and-such. If a judgment does have such a structure, than an instance of the given would fit with it in the requisite way only if that state indicates the relevant thing is, indeed, so-and-so (or satisfies such-and-such). If the given itself has propositional (or conceptual) structure, then it might seem unproblematic that such states support one's judgments about the world.

In fact, the predominant view in recent discussions of perception is that the given does have such structure. I return to this point below. For present purposes, it is more important to recognize that on the Humean-Kantian view of the world, with the account of intentionality it requires, the given *must* have propositional structure. It might seem, then, that on this view it is unproblematic to take the given as one's epistemic basis for knowing the world. This is, however, mistaken. Although, originally, concerns regarding the epistemic efficacy of the given turned on considerations of fit (between one's primary states of engagement with the world and one's judgments about it), further reflection led to more sophisticated criticism. This is captured in a dilemma, only half of which pertains to fit: if an instance of the given is not of the right structure and, hence, cannot fit with a relevant judgment in such a way as to indicate the appropriateness of the latter, then that state of primary engagement cannot be a suitable epistemic basis (of that judgment). On the other hand, if an instance of the given does have the appropriate structure, that is, it presents some thing as so-and-so, and so can indicate the appropriateness of the relevant judgment, then that state of primary engagement itself requires some epistemic support—to indicate that that thing is indeed so-and-so—and, therefore, cannot be one's ultimate justification for accepting that thing is so-and-so. Either way, states of the given cannot be a suitable epistemic foundation.[5]

3.2 One (Unsuccessful) Response: The Given is Efficacious if it has the Right Structure

The Myth of the Given is supposed to be revealed by the foregoing argument. To accept the Myth is to accept that it is merely mythical and, so, false that one's

---

[5] Variants of essentially this argument can be found in several influential discussions. Its most famous version can be espied in Sellars 1956. Others can be found in Rorty 1979; Davidson 1986; BonJour 2001: 23–24; Fumerton 2001: 13; Pryor 2014: 207.

primary states of engagement with the world are epistemically efficacious. Although I do not think the argument demonstrates this, I do take it to show that if the given has a certain structure, namely, one presenting that some thing is so-and-so, it is epistemically idle. It seems, however, that some fail to recognize the complexity and force of the argument, consequently holding that the given is epistemically efficacious *precisely because it has this structure*. A prominent example is John McDowell.

McDowell has devoted much effort to attacking the Myth of the Given. He believes that one's primary states of engagement with the world are indeed the bases of one's knowledge. However, this is not always appreciated for, according to McDowell, some misunderstand what these instances of the given are, in particular, how they arise and the structure they have. If one is confused about what the given is, it will seem that such states offer only "exculpations where we wanted justifications".[6] In other words, if one fails to recognize the provenance and structure of the given, one will regard such states as, at best, forcing one to take the world (or part thereof) to be a certain way without also providing some justification for judging that it is in fact that way.

In light of this understanding of the motivation for accepting the Myth of the Given, McDowell maintains the Myth can be avoided—and the epistemic efficacy of the given recognized—by articulating the correct account of one's states of primary engagement with the world. His objective, then, is to articulate an account on which an instance of the given is constrained by the world, and thereby apt to reveal how that part of the world is, where it is this constraint that is one's justification for judging the world to be as revealed. (It is clear that this is how the given must be if it is to be epistemically efficacious.) Yet McDowell's account is problematic for just the reason presented in the second horn of the dilemma against an epistemically efficacious given.

McDowell couches his discussion of the Myth of the Given in Sellarsian terms of the problematic interface between the *space of nature* and the *space of reasons*. The latter is all those contexts in which claims are susceptible to justification, capable of being shown to be appropriate in light of how things are. Within this space, one must employ concepts, the capacities one has to discriminate and thereby identify, recognize and sort things in the world. This is because in the space of a reasons, one must judge that some thing is so-and-so, a way it might not be, then seek or offer justification for that thing in fact being so-and-so. In the space of nature, there are no claims and, hence, no justifying anything; there just is whatever there is, doing whatever it does. This space seems to be that of the

---

6 McDowell introduces the Myth of the Given in these terms in Lecture I of McDowell 1994.

world per se. If the given is merely engagement with the space of nature, it is engagement with what is not susceptible to justification. Such engagement would not be the presentation of the world, or some part thereof, as being some particular way, otherwise this engagement would be susceptible to justification. If, however, the given does not present some thing as being so-and-so, then it cannot fit with any state from within the space of reasons, each of which does present something as being so-and-so, in such a way as to justify the latter. Any such instance of the given is, therefore, epistemically idle.

According to McDowell, then, conceptual capacities must be operative in one's states of primary engagement with the world per se, the space of nature. If they are, they provide the structure that enables each of these states to present some thing(s) as being so-and-so. Consequently, an instance of the given could fit a judgment within the space of reasons that some thing is so-and-so in a way that would justify this judgment. As he puts it:

> Conceptual capacities, whose interrelations belong in the *sui generis* logical space of reasons, can be operative not only in judgments—results of a subject's actively making up her mind about something—but already in the transactions in nature that are constituted by the world's impacts on the receptive capacities of a suitable subject; that is, one who possesses the relevant concepts. Impressions can *be* cases of its perceptually appearing—being apparent—to a subject that things are thus and so. (McDowell 1994: xx)

In sum, McDowell states: "Avoiding the Myth requires capacities that belong to reason to be operative in experiencing itself, not just in judgments in which we respond to experience."[7]

McDowell maintains, then, that if the given is to be epistemically efficacious it must have the right fit with one's judgments; in order to have this fit, one's conceptual capacities must be operative in one's primary states of engagement with the world. However, if each instance of the given has conceptual (or propositional) structure, so that it presents some thing as so-and-so, then this raises the question of whether what is presented by that state is in fact so-and-so. McDowell avoids one horn of the dilemma against the epistemic efficacy of the given, but only by embracing the other. Clearly, this is insufficient to establish that the given is epistemically efficacious.

---

[7] McDowell 2009: 258. McDowell's account of the given in this later paper is different in significant respects from the one propounded in McDowell 1994. However, it is still one on which the given is structured—hence, conditional—and so is impugned by my argument below, which applies to any such account.

If a mental state is structured, it has some complexity, some arrangement of parts. If that state is representational, purporting to present how something beyond itself is, it is apt only if its parts correspond in some way to those things it presents. The complexity of the state, then, captures some condition—one that must be met by the world if that state is to be a successful representation. In particular, then, if a state is structured in such a way that it presents some thing as so-and-so, that state might or might not be apt with respect to that thing. It is apt if what it presents is, in fact, so-and-so, inapt if this is not the case. The conditional nature of the (representational) state makes this question of aptness ineluctable.

If the given, one's state of primary engagement with the world is structured so as to present some thing as so-an-so and is, therefore, conditional, then one's very engagement with the world brings with it a question: whether what is presented as being so-and-so is indeed so-and so. If each instance of the given brings with it this question, there is no way of answering it. The given is supposed to provide one's primary, one's most basic and intimate engagement with the world. If this engagement itself is questionable, there are no more basic or intimate means of engaging with the world to resolve the question. One has no more direct and revealing way of getting at the world than what one has in the given. Hence, if an instance of the given is conditional, it itself cannot provide justification for taking the world to be one way rather than another and so is epistemically idle. This problem, which confronts any account of the given on which it has propositional or conceptual structure, seems insuperable. Reflection on the problem shows that not only is an instance of the given presenting that some thing is so-and-so epistemically idle, but an instance with any inherent structure is idle, as well. This is important below.

It is odd that McDowell thinks his account of the given is satisfactory, for he seems to be aware of the critical problem, at least in the offing. If the given employs concepts, presenting something as so-and-so, such a mental state would have representational content. Yet as McDowell acknowledges, "The very idea of representational content brings with it a notion of correctness and incorrectness: something with a certain content is correct, in the relevant sense, just in case things are as it represents them to be." (McDowell 1994: 162) A notion of correctness or incorrectness attached to the given is just the problem. Perhaps McDowell thinks he avoids this problem because he regards instances of the given as passive: "In fact it is precisely because experience is passive, a case of receptivity in operation, that the conception of experience I am recommending can satisfy the craving for a limit to freedom [i.e., a constraint on judgment provided by the world itself] that underlies the Myth of the Given." (McDowell 1994: 10)

McDowell seems to assume that the passivity of a state makes the question of aptness and, hence, of justification otiose. I belief it does, and this is crucial to my own account of the given. There are, however, different notions of passivity. There is the one introduced above, in terms of an utter lack of contribution. McDowell, though, construes passivity as a lack of conscious effort or deliberateness on the part of a subject. But one's mind can be active in the sense of making a significant contribution to a mental state even if there is no conscious effort or deliberateness required on the part of the subject to be in that state. On McDowell's account of the given, such states are not passive in the first sense, even if they are passive in the second. On his account, any instance of the given involves essentially the operation of one's conceptual capacities and, therefore, involves spontaneity; this spontaneity contributes a condition to any instance of the given. Indeed, it is the conditional nature of the given, resulting from this spontaneity, that renders them epistemically idle.

3.3 Another (Unsuccessful) Response: The Given is Efficacious Because it is the Given

In connection to this last point about passivity, one might hold that the second horn of the dilemma against the epistemic efficacy of the given, concerning its structure, is illusory, because instances of the given, as sensory states, simply are not the sort of mental state for which any question of justification can arise. Therefore, once an account of the given is provided on which these states fit appropriately with one's judgments, and so can support the latter, there is no further problem regarding the epistemic efficacy of the given. Such a view is suggested by James Pryor: "Yet, unlike beliefs, experiences aren't the sort of thing which *could be*, nor do they *need to be* justified. Sure, *beliefs about* what experiences you have may need to be justified. But *the experience themselves* do not."(Pryor 2014: 210. Emphasis in original.)

The view that the given itself needs no justification simply because it is the given is misguided. Whether one's states of primary engagement with the world themselves require justification depends on what these states are. To resolve this issue, then, one must have some account of what the given is. As I discuss below, if the given is an unstructured, passive state of acquaintance, such a state is not amenable to justification, for it either exists, and thereby relates a mind to something, or fails to exist. It cannot exist and yet fail to be apt, as any structured state that purports to represent can. However, if the given is structured and so conditional, it brings with it the question of aptness. If it is taken to justify some judgment, the issue of its own aptness and basis becomes pressing. Here, it is assumed that instances of the given have propositional (or conceptual) structure and fit straightforwardly with judgments so as to be capable of justifying them. But it is exactly the conditionality attendant upon such structure, I maintain, that makes instances of the given themselves require justification and renders them epistemically idle. To baldly insist, in the face of such argument, that such states do not need justification, are not even amenable to justification, will not do.

3.4 The End of Epistemology

On the Humean-Kantian view of the world and its structure, intentionality requires spontaneity. This spontaneity imparts a certain propositional (or conceptual) structure and, hence, conditionality to any instance of the given. Such an account of the given is embraced by some who defend the epistemic efficacy of one's primary states of engagement with the world. However, as I argue, the conditionality inherent to each of these states raises the question of whether that state aptly presents the world, rendering it itself epistemically idle. As a state of primary engagement with the world, there are no other means of revealing the world available to justify it. McDowell writes: "What we wanted was a reassurance that when we use our concepts in judgment, our freedom—our spontaneity in the exercise of our understanding—is constrained from outside thought, and constrained in a way that we can appeal to in displaying the judgments as justified."(McDowell 1994: 8) But such reassurance is precisely what is precluded by a structured, conditional given.

Traditionally, concerns about the epistemic efficacy of the given have been taken to support some sort of *coherentism* regarding justification, whereby a judgment or belief is justified to the extent that it coheres with other judgments (or beliefs). If, as I have argued, on the Humean-Kantian view of the world, any instance of the given is itself epistemically idle, then it seems clear that coherentism is the only account of justification compatible with such a view. I have not the space here to discuss coherentism in any great detail. I take it as obvious, though, that any coherentist view does not comport with an epistemology the objective of which is to illuminate one's knowledge of the world per se. All one's judgments (or beliefs) about the world might cohere and yet be incompatible with how the world in fact is. One might concede the point and simply forgo knowledge of the world per se, acknowledging that all that can be known about the world is how a mind constrains it to yield the experiences one has. This, one might assume, can be revealed by determining which of one's judgments cohere. Such a position stands to reason in light of the Humean-Kantian view of the world, for, after all, on this view, there is nothing determinate in and so nothing in particular to know about the world per se.

However, a project of this sort, one directed at determining which of one's judgments regarding a Humean-Kantian world cohere, does not seem to be genuinely epistemological. A genuinely epistemological project must be at least normative, prescribing how one ought to judge or acquire beliefs, if one is to have a correct view of the world (either the world per se or as experienced). If a project is (epistemically) normative, there must be some norm arising from its subject matter, lest there be no way to go wrong (or right) with respect to that subject matter. A norm is a constraint. If the world per se is structured, the things it comprises provide all the constraints needed for a properly epistemological project. If structure is imposed on the world, coherence with respect to one's mental acts and states is supposed to be the constraint (what coheres must be consistent, if nothing else). Yet on this view of the world, the only constraints it contains are those imposed on it by a mind. What judgments (or beliefs) cohere, then, is determined ultimately not by those judgments themselves, but by a mind. On this Humean-Kantian project, then, the requisite norm does not arise from the subject matter—one's judgments or beliefs per se – but from a different source – a mind. Since the source of the norm is removed from the subject matter, which the norm is supposed to constrain, that norm is hardly a proper constraint on that subject matter. Thus, this sort of project is in no straightforward way (epistemically) normative and, consequently, is not epistemological.

On the Humean-Kantian view of the world, not only is knowledge of the world per se forsaken, but the very possibility of epistemology, in any familiar form, seems to be, as well. The root of these epistemological problems is ontological, in the claim that constraints are not concomitant with existence, and so a mind is the ultimate source of the structure in the world. Therefore, if one is to do epistemology at all, one must eschew this view of the world.

4 The Given as Foundational

The Humean-Kantian view of the world requires spontaneity in intentionality and, hence, structure and conditionality in the given. This leads to some sort of coherentism that, on this view of the world, seems to thwart epistemology. If one is to avoid this outcome, one must adopt a broadly Aristotelian view of the world on which each thing is constrained in itself and the structure in the world is a corollary of the things that exist. This view is compatible with utter passivity in intentionality. The given, then, can be an unstructured, unconditional relational state of acquaintance. But, if it is, it is far from obvious how the given can be epistemically efficacious in light of the first horn of the dilemma above: if an instance of the given is not of the right structure – or structured at all – and, hence, cannot fit with a relevant judgment in such a way as to indicate the appropriateness of the latter, then that state of primary engagement cannot be a suitable epistemic basis (of that judgment, or any other).

Some who have taken the given to be epistemically efficacious, and foundational to all one's knowledge of the world, believe there is a way of avoiding this horn without succumbing to the second. Laurence BonJour, for example, holds that the given has structure, though it is not propositional (or conceptual); nevertheless, he maintains, this structure makes the given suitable to support one's judgments. However, reflection on my argument above against propositional structure in the given indicates that this sort of view, too, is problematic, and for essentially the same reason. Consequently, the given, if it is not to be epistemically idle, cannot be structured at all. If this is so, and these primary states of engagement with the world are indeed the basis of one's knowledge, the only way to avoid both horns of the dilemma against the epistemic efficacy of the given is to reject the orthodox account of what it is to make a judgment (at least with respect to primary cases).

4.1 Traditional Foundationalism

BonJour is an erstwhile coherentist, moved to the position by precisely the sort of dilemma against an epistemically efficacious given central to the present discussion.[8] Recognizing the futility of coherentism, though, BonJour became an "old-fashioned" foundationalist, accepting that some beliefs are justified immediately by one's states of primary engagement with the world (and that all justification for one's further beliefs can be traced to these foundational ones).[9] However, BonJour's version of foundationalism is unsuccessful. Despite his claim to the contrary, on his position, the given is epistemically idle. Seeing why this is so reveals that the given must be unstructured if it is to be epistemically efficacious.

BonJour maintains that each sensory experience, i.e., each instance of the given, includes constitutively a "built-in" awareness of itself. This feature makes

---

[8] See BonJour 1985, 1978.
[9] See BonJour 2001. For other contemporary foundationalist views, see Fumerton 2001 and Fales 1996. I have not the space here to discuss what I find problematic about these latter two views.

that state available to the subject when the state exists. Such states are, in Roderick Chisholm's term, one endorsed by BonJour, "self-presenting". These states of primary engagement with the world are supposed to be so rich in content that they are "nonpropositional and nonconceptual in character". (BonJour 2001: 29.) They are also supposed not to be themselves susceptible to justification; as sensory experiences, they are supposed to be one's originary, direct presentations of things in the world and, as such, not open to the question of being right or wrong. Such states justify beliefs about them, and the beliefs are foundational in that their justification comes from mental states, instances of the given, that are not themselves beliefs.

Even granting all this, one is far from a position on which one has justification for judging the mind-independent world to be as it is. One's foundational beliefs are about one's own mental states, those instances of the given taken to reveal the world. BonJour is aware of this significant limitation.[10] Setting it aside, there is a more pressing problem for the position. In light of the dilemma against the epistemic efficacy of the given, BonJour is concerned about the epistemic fit between one's states of primary engagement with the world and one's judgments. He presumes the orthodoxy that judgments (and the beliefs they yield) are propositional: one accepts (and then goes on to believe) that some thing is so-and-so. But, on his position, instances of the given do not have this structure; they are not propositional and so seem incapable of supporting the judgment that some thing is so-and-so. BonJour addresses this problem by maintaining that a propositional judgment, though structured differently, can nonetheless *describe* a nonpropositional state, which the given is supposed to be. Thus, a foundational judgment, which describes an instance of the given, can be supported by a direct awareness of that (self-presenting) latter state. The descriptive fit between the two, which can be more or less apt, is, BonJour maintains, sufficient for an epistemic relation between them.

In this way, BonJour addresses the first horn of the dilemma against the epistemic efficacy of the given. He does not even consider the second, because he takes for granted that instances of the given do not themselves need or even admit of justification. Yet this cannot be taken for granted. As argued above, any instance of the given that has propositional (or conceptual) structure is conditional and, as such, brings with it the question of whether the world meets that condition, whether the thing presented as so-and-so is in fact so-and-so. Such an instance of the given is in need of justification. Note, however, the crucial point

---

10 See, in particular, BonJour 2001: 34–37.

here can be generalized and so pertains not merely to propositional (or conceptual) structure. In general, if a mental state is structured—in any way—it has some complexity. If that state purports to present how something beyond itself is, it is apt only if its parts correspond in some way to those things it presents. The complexity of the state, then, captures some condition, one that must be met by the world if that state is to be an apt representation.

There has been much recent discussion about what exactly a state with nonconceptual (or nonpropositional) content is. Nevertheless, no one denies that such a state is representational; it is supposed to just represent differently than a proposition (pictorially, more vividly, in greater detail, etc.). If a nonpropositional (representational) state is structured, it is conditional—if it does not have truth conditions, then it has accuracy conditions or some such—and so can be apt or not depending on whether the world meets those conditions. Pictures can fail to be apt just as propositions can. But if the given, a state of primary engagement with the world, is conditional and, hence, of questionable aptness, there is no way of settling this question. Any such state, therefore, is epistemically idle and not a suitable epistemic basis. It makes no difference that the state is nonpropositional or nonconceptual, rather than propositional (or conceptual). The problem is that it is inherently conditional and it is so because it is structured.

4.2 The Given as Unstructured and the Orthodox Account of Judgment

If any structured state purporting to present the world is conditional and, hence, raises the question of whether the condition it captures is met, then if the given is to be epistemically efficacious – capable of supporting judgments without raising the question of its own aptness – it must be unstructured, unconditional. But if this is so, one is immediately confronted by the first horn, concerning fit, of the dilemma against an epistemically efficacious given.

Concern about the fit between one's states of primary engagement with the world and the judgments one makes in light of these is long-standing. It goes back at least to early modern empiricist views of sensations on which they are "raw feels" and supposed not to be representational at all. Davidson's famous critique of the epistemic efficacy of the given along these lines is that if a state of primary engagement with the world is unstructured and so significantly different in nature from a judgment, then the only interesting relation that the former can bear to the latter is causal.[11] One has a sensory experience, an instance of the given, then one judges that the world is a certain way. There is no justification here. The connection between the given and one's judgments might be explanatory, but it is not justificatory. If, as I have argued, an instance of the given must be unconditional and, thus, unstructured—but such a state is incapable of fitting epistemically with a judgment—then, insofar as one maintains that the given is indeed the basis of one's knowledge of the world, one must reconsider what a judgment is.

As observed in passing above, the orthodox account is one on which each judgment is an act of accepting that some thing is so-and-so (which then yields the persisting dispositional state of belief that that thing is so-and-so). If this is what a judgment is, then the problem with an unstructured, primary state of engagement with the world is obvious and insurmountable: such a state cannot present a thing taken in some way (as, for example, so-and-so), it can merely present a thing itself. Thus, the given does not present a thing in any specific way—so-and-so or otherwise—even when that thing is in fact so-and-so, and so cannot justify the specific judgment that that thing is so-and-so. If one judges that the desk is brown, the (brown) desk per se, or even its particular brownness, is unable to justify this judgment. Justification for accepting this would, it seems, have to come from a state presenting the desk as brown or its particular brownness as belonging to this desk. The specificity of the judgment is achieved through a certain complexity—a structure inherent to it—that demands a corresponding complexity (and structure) in an instance of the given, if the latter is to justify the former. An unstructured, unconditional relational state of acquaintance that merely presents a thing does not have the requisite complexity.

If, however, not all judgments are complex, if what one accepts in some judgments is not structured and, hence, conditional, then a judgment can indeed be supported by an instance of the given that is unstructured and unconditional.

4.3 A Reistic Account of Judgment

There is a heterodox view of judgment, the neglected account of Franz Brentano, on which judgments are not structured (and, hence, are unconditional).[12] On this account, in making a judgment, one accepts (or rejects) a thing—not that that

---

11 See Davidson 1986: 311.
12 See Brentano 1874, Book Two, Chapter VII. For an excellent overview of this account, see Brandl 2014.

thing is so-and-so, but simply *the thing itself*. Such a judgment is true or apt if what one accepts exists. I will not do much more here than introduce this sort of account, motivate it and show how it bears on the question of whether the given can be epistemically efficacious.

There has recently been some discussion and defense of non-propositional attitudes.[13] It is plausible to maintain that fear and desire, for example, are relations to non-representational things, rather than propositions. So one fears the dog (itself) and one desires the lovey (itself). But even among supporters of such attitudes, it has been assumed that judgment (and belief) is propositional. Given the predominance of the orthodox account, it certainly seems odd to hold that one can judge, in the relevant sense, the dog (itself), rather than, say, that the dog exists, or the lovey (itself), rather than, say, that the lovey is soft. Nevertheless, setting aside the oddness of unfamiliarity, such an account of judgment is not obviously untenable.

Indeed, if one assumes a broadly Aristotelian view of the world, on which all there is is intrinsically constrained things, among them minds, a Brentanian view of judgment seems to me quite plausible. This view of the world permits an account of the given on which it is an unstructured, unconditional relational state of acquaintance. Thus, one's primary encounters with the world are via states of engagement in which some thing simply impresses itself upon one's mind. To aptly take the world (at least part thereof) to be as it is, one needs only to accept that thing; one need not accept that it is any specific way. If the world is just an array of things, it is not implausible that in first engaging the world, as one begins to devise a view of how the world is, one begins with states *of this* and *of that*, rather than *that this is so-and-so* or *that that is such-and-such*. On this basis, one develops the conceptual capacities to make more sophisticated and specific judgments, to refine one's view of how the world is. Such specificity and any structure in one's intentional states it might require, with the attendant conditionality of structure, need not be present in one's primary encounters with the world (and, it seems, cannot be[14]). Nor, then, need specificity (or structure) be present in one's primary judgments about the world.

My goal in the present discussion is to articulate an account of the given on which it is epistemically efficacious, justifying judgments that are the basis of one's knowledge of the world. If the given is an unstructured, unconditional relational state of acquaintance with the things in the world, and at least some judgments are reistic, the acceptance of things, one has such an account. This

---

[13] See, for instance, Grzankowski 2016, Montague 2007.
[14] As I argue in Fiocco 2015.

account of the given is compatible with an Aristotelian view of the world and this account of judgment is plausible in light of the view. On this account of one's states of primary engagement with the world, they are indeed epistemically efficacious. An instance of the given itself has no structure and so imposes no condition, it simply relates one to a thing in the world. If the state exists, one is related to a thing; that very thing is constitutive of that very state. There is, therefore, no question of the aptness of the given. Consequently, such a state provides impeccable justification for one's judgment with respect to that existent thing, which is merely an acceptance of it. One could be in no better epistemic position vis-à-vis that thing. One then knows how the world is, at least in part: it includes that thing. On this primary knowledge of things, all one's other knowledge is founded.

Of course, much more needs to be said about the sort of heterodox account of judgment adopted here. It raises many questions – like how to understand the more specific (seemingly conditional) judgments about the world that one can surely make, and how these judgments are justified on the basis of one's foundational judgments of existing things – but such questions are beyond the scope of this discussion.

5 The Upshot

The world is experienced as structured. What the world per se is and, hence, how it comes to be structured determines how a mind must be – what it must do – to engage the world at all. If the things in the world are themselves unconstrained, unstructured, the structure experienced must be provided by a mind. The given, then, must involve spontaneity, an active contribution on part of a mind that yields constraints and with them structure. If each instance of the given must involve spontaneity and is, then, structured, each such state imposes a condition, a reflection of its inherent structure, that might not be met by the world. There is no way to ascertain whether this condition is met, for there is no more basic epistemic state that resolves the matter, nor any other means. Thus, each instance of the given is epistemically idle, providing no justification for taking the world to be one way or the other. If, however, the things in the world are constrained in themselves and so are the source of the structure one experiences, then the given need not involve spontaneity nor any structure. The primary engagement between a mind and the world can be utterly passive, unconditional. If the given can be a passive, unstructured, unconditional state that merely relates a mind to the world, such a state can be epistemically efficacious, providing some justification for taking the world to be a certain way. Indeed, if there is such a state, the world must be as presented.

If the world is itself unstructured, the given is epistemically idle; worse, there is no genuine epistemology (as I argue above). Therefore, the only tenable approach to epistemology requires a certain account of what a thing per se is and a corollary view of the world. This approach provides a foundationalist account of knowledge, one on which all one's knowledge is based on direct (i.e., passive, unconditional) acquaintance with the things in the world. Yet, to do this, the approach also requires a heterodox account of judgment, one that conforms with one's states of primary engagement with the world. Instances of the given acquaint one with things; one's primary judgments must, then, be of these things, simply accepting them. This account of the given indicates that the appropriate view of perception is naïve realism: it is the things in the world and not representations thereof that is fundamental to perception. Although there have been some fine contemporary discussions of naïve realism[15], proponents of this position have not recognized that the view must be accompanied by a non-propositional, reistic account of judgment. This is, I presume, because the complexity and force of the argument against the epistemic efficacy of the given has not been appreciated.

Others have defended naïve realism. The present discussion, however, is intended to corroborate the view from a novel and particularly secure position, one that begins with radical ontological considerations regarding what the world per se is and what things are. These considerations illuminate what a mind is and how to understand intentionality. As a result, they also cast light on some key issues related to naïve realism. It is often taken for granted that what it is for a state to be intentional is to be representational.[16] This is incorrect. An intentional state is a manifestation of the capacity of intentionality. Since intentionality can be utterly passive and, hence, purely relational, an instance of the given that simply acquaints one with a thing in the world is intentional without being representational. *Content* is a term of art, so one can say that such a state has content—it presents a thing in the world, and this is its content—or one can deny that it is has content, since it does not represent anything or have associated truth (or accuracy) conditions. The important thing to recognize is that a perceptual state

---

15 See, in particular, Brewer 2011, Travis 2004, Martin 2002.
16 See Crane 2009 for just one example of a philosopher who conflates being representational with being intentional.

of acquaintance is no less a state of engagement with the world, and so intentional, for not being representational. Some defend so-called reconciliatory views of perception, on which it is fundamentally both representational and relational.[17] The foregoing considerations show why such views are untenable. If a perceptual state—an instance of the given—is representational, in that it has associated truth (or accuracy) conditions, it is epistemically idle. If perception is supposed to reveal the world in an epistemically efficacious way, it is in no way representational.

In conclusion, it is worth noting that the sort of considerations here that lead to naïve realism, radically ontological ones concerning the world per se and the things it comprises, can be brought to bear on what many regard as the main problem with this view of perception, namely, providing a satisfactory account of illusion and hallucination. Cases of perceptual error, which certainly seem to include representations, lead many to maintain that perception must be representational, rather than relational, insofar as states of perceptual error are crucially similar to genuine perceptions. Of course, I, like any naïve realist, maintain that the former are significantly different, despite obvious phenomenological similarities, from the latter, and so am committed to some sort of disjunctivism. Here, I merely note that I argue for naïve realism on ontological and epistemological grounds that are far more basic than considerations of perceptual error (or the most intuitively satisfying way of individuating mental states). These most general grounds lead to the conclusion that perception is not representational. This motivates a position on which, if illusory and hallucinatory states must be representational, these are quite different from perceptual ones. Similarly, if the world just is an array of (natured) things, perceiving one of them, and thereby being acquainted with – directly related to – that thing, is clearly a different sort of state than, say, merely hallucinating such a thing when none is in fact there.[18]

References

BonJour, Laurence (2001): "Toward a Defense of Empirical Foundationalism". In: DePaul, Michael (Ed.): *Resurrecting Old-Fashioned Foundationalism*. Lanham, MD: Rowan & Littlefield, pp. 21–38.

---

17 See, for instance, Schellenberg 2014 and Logue 2014.
18 I would like to thank Giuliano Bacigalupo, Gordon Bearn, Sven Bernecker, Johannes Brandl, Matt Duncan, Guillaume Fréchette, Christopher Gauker, Christoph Limbeck-Lilienau, Howard Robinson, and Karl Schafer for helpful discussion pertaining to the contents of this paper.

BonJour, Laurence (1985): *The Structure of Justification*. Cambridge, MA: Harvard University Press.
BonJour, Laurence (1978): "Can Empirical Knowledge Have a Foundation?". In: *American Philosophical Quarterly* 15, pp. 1–13.
Brandl, Johannes (2014): "Brentano's Theory of Judgment". In: *The Stanford Encyclopedia of Philosophy* (Summer2014 Edition), Edward N. Zalta (ed.), URL = http://plato.stanford.edu/archives/sum2014/entries/brentano-judgment/, visited on 13 November 2017.
Brentano, Franz (1874): *Psychology from an Empirical Standpoint*, Rancurello, Antos C.; Terrell, Burnham; and McAlister, Linda L. (Trans.) London and New York: Routledge (1995).
Brewer, Bill (2011): *Perception and its Objects*. Oxford: Oxford University Press.
Crane, Tim (2009): "Is Perception a Propositional Attitude?". In: *Philosophical Quarterly* 59, pp. 452–469.
Davidson, Donald (1986): "A Coherence Theory of Truth and Knowledge". In: LePore, Ernest (Ed.): *Truth and Interpretation: Perspectives on the Philosophy of Donald Davidson*. Oxford: Blackwell, 307–319.
Fales, Evan (1996): *A Defense of the Given*. Lanham, MD: Rowman & Littlefield.
Fiocco, Marcello Oreste (2015): "Intentionality and Realism". In: *Acta Analytica* 30, pp. 219-237.
Fumerton, Richard (2001): "Classical Foundationalism". In: DePaul, Michael (Ed.): *Resurrecting Old-Fashioned Foundationalism*. Lanham, MD: Rowan & Littlefield, 3–20.
Grzankowski, Alex (2016): "Attitudes Towards Objects". In: *Noûs* 50, pp. 314–328.
Hempel, Carl (1934/5a): "On the Logical Positivists' Theory of Truth". In: *Analysis* 2, pp. 49–59.
Hempel, Carl (1934/5b): "Some Remarks on "Facts" and Propositions". In: *Analysis* 2, pp. 93–96.
Logue, Heather (2014): "Experiential Content and Naïve Realism". In: Brogaard, Berit (Ed.): *Does Perception Have Content?*. Oxford: Oxford University Press, pp. 220–241.
Martin, Michael (2002): "The Transparency of Experience". In: *Mind & Language* 17, pp. 376–425.
McDowell, John (2009): "Avoiding the Myth of the Given". In: *Having the World in View*, Cambridge, MA: Harvard University Press, pp. 256–272.
McDowell, John (1994): *Mind and World*, Cambridge, MA: Harvard University Press.
Montague, Michelle (2007): "Against Propositionalism". In: *Noûs* 41, pp. 503–518.
Pryor, James (2014): "There Is Immediate Justification". In: Steup, Mattias; Turri, John; and Sosa, Ernest (Eds.): *Contemporary Debates in Epistemology*, 2nd edition. Malden, MA: John Wiley & Sons, Inc., pp. 202–222.
Rorty, Richard (1979): *Philosophy and the Mirror of Nature*. Princeton: Princeton University Press.
Schellenberg, Susanna (2014): "The Relational and Representational Character of Perceptual Experience". In: Brogaard, Berit (Ed.): *Does Perception Have Content?*. Oxford: Oxford University Press, pp. 199–219.
Schlick, Moritz (1934/5): "Facts and Propositions". In: *Analysis* 2, pp. 65–70.
Schlick, Moritz (1934): "Über das Fundament der Erkenntnis". In: *Erkenntnis* 4. No.1, pp. 79–99.
Sellars, Wilfrid (1956): *Empiricism and the Philosophy of Mind*. Cambridge, MA: Harvard University Press.
Travis, Charles (2004): "The Silence of the Senses". In: *Mind* 113, pp. 57–94.

Guillaume Fréchette
Brentano on Perception and Illusion

Abstract: Brentano's philosophy of perception has often been understood as a special chapter of his theory of intentionality. If all and only mental phenomena are constitutively intentional, and if perceptual experience is mental by definition, then all perceptual experiences are intentional experiences. I refer to this conception as the "standard view" of Brentano's account of perception. Different options are available to support the standard view: a sense-data theory of perception; an adverbialist account; representationalism. I argue that none of them are real options for the standard view. I suggest that Brentano's conception of optical illusions introduces a presupposition that not only challenges the standard view – the distinction between the subjectively and objectively given – but that also makes his account more palatable for a naïve understanding of perception as openness to and awareness of the world.

Keywords: Brentano, perception, intentionality, illusion, sensation

1 The Standard View

Thanks to his account of mental acts, Brentano is usually acknowledged as the philosopher of intentionality. What characterizes mental acts is their intentionality, that is, their directedness towards an object.[1] Another important contribution of Brentano to contemporary philosophy lies in his conception of consciousness. In his view, mental acts are not only characterized by their intentionality with regard to their objects, but are also concomitantly self-directed.[2] This self-directedness is what makes them conscious.

Since intentionality and consciousness are two central marks of the mental, they also apply to perceptual acts as well. An act of sensory perception, insofar as it is mental, is intentional and conscious. It is worth noting, however, that while many readers of Brentano have acknowledged in recent years the intentionality mark for the mental, the consciousness mark is rarely challenged.[3] This perhaps explains in part why Brentano's account of perception has received so

---

1 Brentano (1874/1973: 68/124).
2 Ibid., 180/98.
3 See Textor (2017) on disputing the intentionality mark.

https://doi.org/10.1515/9783110657920-007

little attention in the secondary literature. If, following his view, perception has to be intentional *and* conscious, then it seems that the conditions for any mental state to be a perception are very strict, perhaps too strict: we may want to say that there is *always* an (intentional) object in every perceptual act, but we may want to dispute that every perceptual act is *therefore* also conscious. Or conversely, we may want to say that every perceptual act is *conscious*, but we may want to dispute that every perceptual act *therefore* has an (intentional) object.

Another possible explanation for the recent lack of interest in Brentano's philosophy of perception may be found in one common interpretation of his conception of intentionality, according to which the objects of intentional acts are immanent objects, that is objects that have "some kind of reality in the mind."[4] Following this interpretation, if intentionality is the mark of the mental, then perception is nothing but a special case of intentionality, understood as a relation between a mental act and an immanent object. In other words, following the common interpretation of Brentano's conception of intentionality, what one perceives is merely an intentional object, that is an object in the mind; it is not an ordinary spatiotemporal object. On this interpretation, it seems as if Brentano would defend a view of perception along the lines of the argument from illusion.[5]

2 Tenets of the Standard View

Let us summarize in a few general theses the gist of Brentano's conception of perception according to the standard interpretation.

T1: *Perception is a special case of intentionality*

T1 is simply a repetition of the common interpretation of Brentano's theory of intentionality, according to which intentionality is a relation to an immanent object. Since all mental phenomena are intentional in Brentano's view, and since perceptual experiences (hearing a sound, seeing a colour, etc.) are mental phenomena, it follows that all perceptual experiences are intentional.

---

[4] At least following one common reading of "intentional inexistence" propounded most notably by Chisholm (1967) and Smith (1994).
[5] Hume (1748) had a first version of the argument. See Smith (2002), and Crane and French (2016) for a reconstruction.

T2: *Perception is of something that truly exists*

T2 is a foundationalist thesis insofar as it restricts the use of "perception" to the perception of things that *truly* exist. If only mental phenomena *truly* exist (this thesis is expressed in the basic idea that physical phenomena exist only intentionally (or better: inexist) in the mind, while mental phenomena truly exist), and if perception (*Wahrnehmung*) is, by definition, perception of something that *truly* exists, then only *inner* perception (that is perception of mental phenomena) is perception in the relevant sense of the term.

T2 imposes obvious epistemological restrictions on the application of the term "perception": if there is a strong sense of perception in which what we perceive is what truly exists, then only inner perception is perception in the true sense.[6] Following the standard account, this thesis may explain Brentano's rejection of Berkeleyan idealism, Machian phenomenalism, and Lockean realism, since it acknowledges that there is a domain of what it innerly perceived, which is perceived *as it is*.

T3: *What we truly perceive is a mental-phenomenon-containing-something*

T3 addresses in part the issue that was left undetermined in T2, namely the actual contents of so-called sensory perception. Brentano comes to T3 from the following premises: (a) only mental phenomena truly exist (i.e. only mental phenomena are objects of *inner* perception); and (b) objects of mental phenomena are inexisting objects (colours, chairs, landscapes, etc. as "intentionally contained" in the mental phenomenon). Therefore, what we "truly" (or *innerly*) perceive is what one could call a mental-phenomenon-containing-something. The hyphens here are meant to stress, first, the fact that what is innerly or "truly" perceived is not simply the seeing, the hearing, etc., but the hearing as the hearing of some specific tone, the seeing as the seeing of a specific colour, etc.; and second, that sensory contents are perceived only to the extent that they are intentionally contained in a mental phenomenon, which is the actual object of perception. Sensory contents are only indirectly perceived, so to speak, that is, as part of a mental phenomenon.

---

6 Brentano (1874/1973: 119/70).

3 The Naïve Understanding of Perception

On the face of it, these three theses leave no room for anything but a restricted concept of perception, namely, that of inner perception. It is easy, on the basis of T1–T3, to understand why most readers of Brentano take him literally when he writes at numerous places that only inner perception is perception (*Wahrnehmung*) in the proper sense.[7] Characterizing inner perception as the only kind of perception (and characterizing outer perception as the mere reception of physical phenomena) seems to lead Brentano to reject the naïve understanding of perception (or perceptual experience) in terms of "openness to the world" (McDowell 1994: 112), according to which we are presented, in perceptual experiences, with ordinary mind-independent objects, and that in such experiences we are aware of such objects.[8] This would support an understanding of Brentano's position as defending the argument from illusion. Following the account at the basis of the three theses, it seems that no mind-independent objects are directly involved in perceptual acts. Moreover, T3 in particular makes it clear that Brentano would reject the transparency intuition that is often shared by philosophers who believe that our experience gives us features of mind-independent objects. In short, it seems that Brentano's account of perception, following the standard view, cannot account for the basic intuition that perception is *primarily* of something other than itself.

Is this a plausible reading? I doubt it. Taken literally, it would mean that what I truly perceive when I am seeing a barn is not the barn but the seeing. While this view may capture in some way the intuition that we are *aware* of something in perceptual experiences, it leaves out too much from our naïve understanding of perception in order to count as a plausible account of perception. After all, when I see the barn and when I see a church, there are some obvious differences in my perceptions. Cashing out these differences simply in terms of modulations in the seeing implausibly downplays the naïve intuition that these perceptions give me some information (erroneous or not) about the world, not merely indirectly as what is contained in a mental act, but perhaps even directly about the location and various features of certain objects. If Brentano does reject the positions of

---

7 Ibid. This was already the case with Husserl in the *Logical Investigations* (Husserl 1901/2001), who set the tone for the interpretation of Brentano in the phenomenological tradition, in Heidegger (1992[1925], 46) for instance, and later on in Føllesdal (1969: 680–81) and Jacquette (2006: 107) among others. See Hickerson (2007: 42ff.) for a discussion of the problems raised by this reading.
8 On awareness, see Crane and French (2016).

Berkeley, Locke, Mill, and Mach on perception, then he should have more to say about this naïve intuition than simply dismissing it. He ought to acknowledge some kind of perceptual process through which my sensory organs gather information (both correct and incorrect) about my environment. The existence of such process could hardly be denied if the hypothesis of an external world is to be justified at all.

Although T1–T3 plausibly explain the lack of interest in Brentano's account of perception, they are neither a plausible rendering of Brentano's view of perception, nor are they compatible with some important insights by Brentano on the nature of perception that are rarely discussed in the secondary literature. Although it is true that for Brentano, inner perception has a priority over outer perception in the order of investigation, this priority does not imply that there is no outer perception properly speaking, or that "perceiving your sensing" is the only case of perceiving. In the rest of this paper, I will argue that T1–T3 are meant to provide an account only of *inner* perception: that they are meant to provide instances of "good" perception, not paradigmatic cases.

4 Two Options for the Standard View

For a defender of the standard view, there are two main options in interpreting Brentano's theory of perception, both of which would account for the idea that truly perceiving the barn is actually perceiving the seeing (which contains, in some special way, the barn as its intentional object). The first option is a relational account, which can be spelled out in two different ways. (1) First, one could argue that we directly perceive mental images (or physical phenomena, in the Brentanian sense) which are dependent on the mind, and that these have the properties that perceptually appear to us. Such a view basically amounts to a sense-data theory. We have already seen that Brentano would not endorse such a view in the framework of phenomenalism.[9] The problem with such an account is that it introduces a veil of perception which makes our relation to the world highly problematic. Here again, it would make Brentano a defender of the argument from illusion, which does not fit with his critique of similar positions.

---

9 Of course, there is another option that is at least technically open: one could also accept the sense-data theory without accepting phenomenalism, as in causal theories of perception for instance (e.g., Price 1932). But such theories are usually designed as a justification of our belief in the external world. Brentano's account, however, both in the standard view and in the view argued for here, takes our belief in the external world to be primitive and unjustifiable.

(2) Second, one could also try to argue for the relational account in terms of some variety of representationalism or intentionalism, conceiving of perception as a special kind of relation between one's mind and the intentional object, mediated by the representational content. Crane (2009, 2009a, 2013) defends a similar view, though he maintains that his view is *not* relational as such: I can represent a golden mountain although there is no such thing; However, he seems neutral as to whether it actually fits with Brentano's. Following this view, in perception a given object seems to me in a particular way: the "seeming to me in a particular way" can be explained in different ways. It might be explained in terms of representational content alone; for example, I see the barn as an old and unoccupied brownish building in the middle of the field. It may also be cashed out, at least partly, in terms of the mode or attitude of a specific experience: seeing the barn is in this respect a different experience from merely imagining or remembering it. Independently of the question whether or not the mode or attitude plays a role in determining the phenomenal character of an experience, a representationalist account of Brentano's position should lead one to consider perception as (at least partly) determined by the representational content, that is, by the physical phenomenon. There might be an object which is represented – there might actually be such a barn in the field – but the experience represents a barn not in virtue of the existence of such a barn, but rather in virtue of being more or less accurate: for instance, an experience such as seeing the barn as floating above the field is likely to be less accurate than an experience such as seeing the barn as standing on the field.

Whether Brentano would agree that representations (or rather, presentations, *Vorstellungen*) represent in virtue of being more or less accurate can remain an open question for now, but if intentionalism is an option for the standard view, then it seems that only judgements of inner perception (of the form "A seeing exists," for instance), and not presentations per se, have correctness conditions and can be assessed for accuracy. Intentionalism therefore seems (at least on the face of it) not to be a real option for the standard view.

Even if we put this concern aside, it is also questionable whether Brentano would agree that representations represent in virtue of being the bearer of some semantic information, which is an essential component of a representationalist or intentionalist account. In the best case, intentionalism would fit only loosely with the standard view: Brentanian physical phenomena, in the standard view, are not really bearers of semantic information: they are not representational, and they are not, properly speaking, *about* the world in the sense that my seeing is about the "green as perceived." Certainly, Brentano sometimes calls them "signs of something real,"[10] in a way which evokes Helmholtz's theory of perception, but unlike Helmholtz he rejects the idea that these signs carry information about the actual localization of the external stimulus, information which according to Helmholtz is processed by unconscious inferences.[11] In short, Brentano's physical phenomena are signs of an outside reality, simply on the (highly probable) assumption of the existence of an external reality; however, if one sticks with the standard view, they do not seem as such assessable for accuracy, nor do they *represent* something else.

Finally, and most obviously, intentionalism cannot account for the non-distinction view between content and object which is presupposed by the standard view.[12] In the intentionalist account, intentional objects are *not* identical with the contents of mental acts, as presupposed by the standard view.

For these reasons, a relational (in this case representationalist) reading of Brentano's views on perception seems not to be very helpful for the standard view. Against such a reading, one can favour a non-relational reading of perception along the lines of adverbialism. According to this account, intentionality is quasi-relational, that is, the intentional content of one's mental act should be understood as a property of the perceptual experience itself rather than as some kind of object with a particular kind of existence. According to adverbialism, I do not see coloured objects, since colours are strictly phenomenal properties (and such a view fits well with Brentano's own view of colours). On this view, there is a common core between my seeing a yellow truck and my hallucinating a pink elephant, for in both cases phenomenal properties appear in the same way. The main problem with the application of this account to Brentano's views on perception is that while it fits well with his reism, in which *irrealia* are banned from the ontology (and therefore we present things in this or that way), it cannot account for the idea that what is presented are *intentional objects* (and not merely modes of presenting), and that these are in some relation with the outer world (not as representations, but as signs). If we consider Brentano's reism as his final word, not only in ontology, but in perception as well, then adverbialism may have some potential, but it entails the rejection of T3; adverbialism therefore seems not to be a real option for the standard view.

Thus, it seems that the only way to make sense of the standard reading of Brentano's view of perception is the relational account. It involves either ways

---

10 Brentano (1874/1973: 24/14).
11 See Brentano (1979: 69) for a critique of Helmholtz's position. More on this below.
12 I discuss the non-distinction view and propose an alternative based on Brentano's view in his lectures on descriptive psychology in Fréchette (2017).

however serious reconstruction under theoretical presuppositions that are not always plausible; this suggests that the alleged three tenets on perception (T1–T3) are perhaps giving a wrong picture of Brentano's actual views on perception.

5 The Background to Brentano's Views on Perception

To give a plausible reconstruction of Brentano's view, it might help to take a quick look at the background to his views on perception and his take on perceptual illusion. Let us start with the background. Johannes Müller (1837) thought that his law of specific nerve energies, according to which every sensory nerve reacts specifically and differently (as a light nerve, a sound nerve, a smell nerve, etc.) to a stimulation s, had the consequence that sensory perception is not perception of a quality of an external body, but of a quality of our nerves. This suggests that sensations cannot be seen as copies of external objects, but rather that they have a representational nature. This idea was also followed by Helmholtz, who argued that contents or sensations are rather *signs* that "completely depend on our organization" (Helmholtz 1878: 225f). Consequently, Helmholtz argued, perception should be seen as the result of this interpretation, this result being sometimes obtained through unconscious inferences.

Brentano accepted Müller's conclusion in his account of perception: it is not the quality of the external stimulation that determines sensation, but the specificity of the stimulated sensory organ. But does Brentano accept this simply on the basis of T2? In order to answer this question, it might be helpful to recall the views of Helmholtz and Hering, which both influenced Brentano to different extents. According to Helmholtz, Müller's law also confirms that there is a distinction between sensation and perception. Sensations are produced by the stimulation of the nerves and are fully specified, following Müller's law, by the specific characteristics or modalities of the sensory organs; nevertheless, we do interpret our sensations as giving us information about the position and form of objects in space (1867, 427). This interpretation is what Helmholtz calls "perception." Perceptions, and only perceptions, are mental acts: sensations merely provide the material upon which perception operates.

Hering, on the other hand, rejects the distinction between sensation and perception. For him, the spatiality of our sensations is not something superimposed by the "perceptions" of Helmholtz; rather, spatiality (or a sense for spatiality) is built into sensings themselves. Hence, sensations are not unorganized raw material, but sensing itself, as an activity, has access to spatiality as a primitive quality of what is given in sensations. Hering has no need for a further concept of perception as does Helmholtz, and can accommodate Müller's law by simply adding that objectual space, the space of objects, is something that we think on the basis of our experience and of our inferences. We *see* the trees in a row of trees as being bigger from a short distance, and getting smaller at a greater distance, but we *think* them as being of relatively equal heights. Characterizing this "thinking" as a perception, as does Helmholtz, suggests that in vision itself, for instance, purely hypothetical thought-like processes are involved (e.g., Helmholtz's unconscious inferences), a consequence rejected by Hering.

Where does Brentano stand? Like Hering, Brentano seems to draw the conclusion that Müller's law shows that a distinction between perception (of external objects) and sensation is superfluous. Sensations are specifically and spatially determined, and so is outer perception. According to him and similarly to Hering, I *see* the Müller–Lyer lines as being of equal lengths, but I think (or judge) them as being of unequal lengths. As far as outer perception is concerned, Brentano follows Hering's reading of Müller and rejects the distinction between perception and sensation. But in contrast to Hering, Brentano still wants to argue for perception as a mental process different from sensation (sensory stimulations). This view is expressed in T2, in which perception (i.e. *inner* perception) is only of something that truly exists. This explains the restriction made that the only veridical perception is inner perception (i.e. the perception of one's own mental acts).

In other words, Brentano wants to stress the two following points. First, perception in the strong sense of T2 is not to be confused with the reception of sensory stimulation which we experience as physical phenomena. Second, the distinction between perception and sensation does not take place at the level of sensory stimulation and its processing (as Helmholtz would have it). Rather, sensings themselves already provide information about quality and localization; this information is not processed in a further step, called "perception" by Helmholtz. Therefore, in order to avoid misunderstanding, the term "perception" should be reserved for "inner perception."

At bottom, this second point seems more terminological than philosophical. Brentano made this exact point in 1889:

> The term "perception" has degenerated in an almost similar way [to the term "pleasure"]. Only really appropriate in respect of knowledge, it came to be applied in the case of the so-called external perception – i.e. in cases of a belief, blind, and in its essential relations, erroneous – and consequently would require, in order to have scientific application as a

terminus technicus, an important reform of the usual terminology, one which would essentially narrow the range of the term (Brentano 1902: 83).[13]

What this terminological remark suggests is that "perception" as a technical term simply covers too much. While Brentano prefers the traditional, Cartesian use of "perception" to designate cases of self-evident knowledge, and only such cases (the German *Wahr-nehmung* suggests it more clearly than its French or English equivalents), he does not deny that we have some kind of access to the external world. He simply points out a terminological confusion arising from the use of a single term to designate two different processes. This point should not be taken as denying any kind of access to the external world. What I have called above "sensory perception," in the broader or naïve sense of openness to and/or awareness of the world is not challenged in any sense by this remark.

Taking the background of his views in consideration, we can summarize Brentano's views on perception with these three general ideas: (i) there is a general meaning of "perception" according to which it characterizes our openness and/or awareness of the world; (ii) inner perception is the only case of perception in which all cases of perception are cases of self-evident knowledge (and all these cases are exclusively cases of awareness); and (iii) outer perception is typically a case of perceptual experience in which physical things of the external world appear to us. All these cases are exclusively cases of openness. I will argue for the third idea in more detail in the next section.

6 Perception and Illusion

If we restrict the application of T2 to point (ii) mentioned above, it leaves open the possibility of accounting for perception in the naïve sense of openness and awareness of the world in Brentano's conception. One obvious way of doing so would be to look at his conception of the physiology of perception, which I have to leave here aside. Another way is to consider the explanation of the Müller–Lyer illusion that Brentano championed: on the face of it, his explanation follows the thesis defended by Helmholtz (1867: 566) of the perceptual overestimation of wide angles and the underestimation of narrow angles. But this similarity is only superficial. Helmholtz's model of explanation belongs basically to the category of physiological theories of illusions. Such models provide an explanation of the

---

[13] The English translation here (and in many other places) uses "impression" instead of "perception" as a translation of *Wahrnehmung*. I have corrected the translation here.

illusion on the basis of a disturbance in the information channels: it is merely the result of a physiological disturbance, which we describe as the overestimation of wide angles and the underestimation of narrow angles.[14]

While Helmholtz's model is based on the supposition of physiological disturbances, Brentano's model seems to be based on the supposition of an inappropriate application of the signalled information. Indeed, Brentano considers the Müller–Lyer illusion a case of "illusion of judgement" (*Urteilstäuschung*). In his view, this illusion of judgement is not to be confused with illusions "in which our phenomena do not correspond to the objectively given" (2009: 25). The broken stick illusion is such an illusion in the latter sense, and it is *not* an illusion of judgement, while the Müller–Lyer illusion is based on "a false evaluation of relations given phenomenally" (ibid.).[15] The optical paradox emerges because the judgement that the lines are unequal conflicts with the initial phenomenon in which the lines are of equal lengths.

It is quite remarkable here that both sorts of illusion presuppose a distinction between the objectively and the subjectively (or phenomenally) given. Müller–Lyer cases are such that the subjectively given actually matches the objectively given (two lines of equal lengths), but the paradox comes from the wrong judgemental evaluation of the subjectively given. In other words, the paradox comes from our *rejection* of ($a_{\text{subj. given}} = a_{\text{obj. given}}$), where a stands for the lines of equal lengths. Broken stick cases are such that the subjectively given simply does not match the objectively given; the paradox here comes from the *acceptance* of ($b_{\text{subj. given}} \neq b_{\text{obj. given}}$), where b stands for the unbroken stick. In the first case, the paradox arises only at the level of the judgement, while in the second case, it seems to come from a conflict which is intrinsic to the given itself.

---

14 On these theories, see Gregory (1970: 142), who labels them "physiological confusion theories."
15 In the phenomenology lectures of 1888/89, Brentano is a little more explicit on this distinction: "[Optical illusions] are of two sorts: (1) of the sort like when a stick in water appears broken, or an object appears misplaced in a mirror. Here, we have a real modification of the phenomenon; but this modification is caused by light waves which make their way to me in an unusual manner from the body from which they are sent and make me conclude to the existence of the object. [In this case], habitude leads me to deceptive hypotheses on its position and form. If I contented myself in designating the phenomenon as a different one, I would make no mistake. (2) The cases are different when I deceive myself about the subjective phenomenon itself; when it appears to me for example modified in a certain way, while the phenomenon is unmodified. [...] [This is the case with] the Zöllner figures. The appearance is so powerful that the modification of the phenomenon could barely be said to be more powerful. Even knowledge doesn't suspend the appearance." (Brentano, forthcoming).

It is also quite remarkable that Brentano here uses the expression "the given" (*das Gegebene*), which is quite unusual in his vocabulary. What he means by "objectively given" and "subjectively given" is sometimes also described in terms of objective and subjective sensations. In his phenomenology lectures from 1888/89, he lists under subjective sensations the presentations of fantasy, but also the sensory feelings, the muscular sensations, reflex sensations, sensations of darkness, after-images, simultaneous contrast, and concomitant sensations. These sensations have a common and complex cause: they are the result of the conjunction, according to his student Marty, between innate and acquired dispositions.[16] And most importantly, they are not caused by external stimulation. Only objective sensations are caused by external stimulation.

Given this distinction, the Müller–Lyer case would be a case in which (a) I have an objective sensation of the lines as of equal lengths; (b) the subjectively given is identical with the objectively given; (c) I incorrectly reject the identity in (b). The broken stick case would be a case where (a) I have an objective sensation of the stick as unbroken, which (b) is not identical with the subjective sensation of the stick as broken and (c) I correctly accept that (a) and (b) are not identical.

There are two obvious questions here. First, how do we know that objective sensations are always accurate (i.e. that the nerve signal which we experience as a physical phenomenon is produced by the appropriate external stimulation)? If objective sensations are always correct or appropriate signs of external reality, then we must admit that it is at least possible to directly perceive (in a relevant sense of "perception") external reality (ordinary mind-independent objects), otherwise the distinction between objective and subjective sensations would be purely arbitrary.

The second question is the following: is the distinction between objective and subjective sensation accessible in inner perception? If it is accessible, then I do have access in inner perception to the source of the stimulation. This would make T1, T2 and T3 false. T1 would be false because the external stimulation cannot be the target object of the intentional relation, and T2 and T3 would be false because if the distinction is accessible in inner perception, then inner perception would not be only perception of what truly exists (mental phenomena), and not only the perception of a mental phenomenon containing something (the physical phenomenon), but it would also give the correctness conditions of outer perception: an outer perception is correct when the external stimulation corresponds to the physical phenomenon, and it is incorrect when it does not correspond.

---

[16] See Marty (1889). Stumpf also uses the same distinction in his lectures on psychology (Stumpf 1886).

If the distinction is not accessible to inner perception, then T1, T2, and T3 would be quite implausible or in need of serious improvements. T1 would be implausible if the possibility of perceiving external stimulation is granted. T2 and T3 would not make much sense if one argues that there are correctness or accuracy conditions for outer perception which are not accessible to inner perception (correctness is, after all, something which one experiences in inner perception). If, in outer perception, we are able to discriminate between subjective and objective sensations, it would be implausible to hold that this ability to discriminate disappears in inner perception.

What Brentano's interpretation of the Müller–Lyer illusion suggests is that there are illusions, some of which (like the Müller–Lyer one) are illusions of judgement, but others emerge from a conflict between the subjectively and the objectively given. This distinction is incompatible with the central premise of the argument from illusion, which Robinson calls the phenomenal principle:

> Phenomenal principle: "If there sensibly appears to a subject to be something which possesses a particular sensible quality then there is something of which the subject is aware which does possess that sensible quality. (Robinson 1994: 32)

In order for him to agree with the principle, he would have to abandon the thesis that in perceiving the stick in the water, the unbroken stick is objectively given to me. If his take on perceptual illusions gives us an important insight on his conception of the nature of perception, then T1–T3 are simply not a correct rendering of this conception and should be given up.

7 The Alternative to the Standard View

I believe that the grain of truth in the standard view of Brentano's conception of perception consists in the two following claims:

(1) Understanding perceptual processes in the right way presupposes knowing what is the nature of perception. Hence, descriptive psychology is prior to genetic psychology in the order of investigation.

(2) In order to investigate the nature of perception, the best place to start is with inner perception, since all cases of inner perception are "good" cases: they show us things (i.e. mental phenomena) as they really are.

However, we have seen here that these claims must be supplemented in order to conform with what Brentano actually says on perception:

(3) Cases of inner perception should not be taken as paradigmatic cases of perception, as T2 suggests; they are simply instances of "good" cases.

(4) There might well be cases of outer perception which could be included under the "good" cases[17] – and there definitely need to be a few of them if the distinction between subjectively and objectively given is supposed to serve its purpose – but understanding cases of outer perception correctly is a far more complex task, since it requires an empirical investigation of their conditions of emergence.

(5) Perception in the naïve sense of awareness, that is, in the sense that it sometimes gives us perceptual awareness of ordinary mind-independent objects, is not challenged by Brentano's views. When I veridically see a blue patch, I have an objective sensation which is identical with the subjective sensation; when I see the broken stick in the water, I have an objective sensation of the unbroken stick. Having such a sensation presupposes, by definition, a regularity of the relation between the external object and the sign (the content of the objective sensation), which can be explained only if the possibility of having perceptual awareness of external objects is granted.

(6) Perception in the naïve sense of openness, that is, the idea that in perceptual experiences we are presented with ordinary mind-independent objects, is not challenged either. The most basic form of perception is presentation (*Vorstellung*), and its presenting mind-independent objects is granted on the same basis as perception in the sense of awareness (5).

If this alternative is correct, it seems that Brentano could agree with the intentionalist tenet that representations (or rather presentations, *Vorstellungen* in his terminology) present or represent at least partly in virtue of being more or less accurate. Such an interpretation, even if it means abandoning the standard view, would be welcome at least for a proper understanding of the motivations and details of Brentano's descriptive psychology, of his realist ontology of his middle

---

17 Nothing rules out that outer perception could be of something as it truly is: but if there are such cases, then these will not be cases of evident knowledge.

period, of his conception of time perception, and of his conception of mental dispositions.[18]

References

Brentano, Franz (1874/1973): *Psychologie vom empirischen Standpunkt.* Leipzig: Hirzel. English trans., *Psychology from an Empirical Standpoint.* London, Routledge.
Brentano, Franz (1902): *The Origin of the Knowledge of Right and Wrong.* Westminster: Constable.
Brentano, Franz (1979): *Untersuchungen zur Sinnespsychologie.* Hamburg: Meiner.
Brentano, Franz (forthcoming): *Phänomenologie und Psychognosie: Vorlesungen 1888/89 und 1890/91.* Dordrecht: Springer.
Chisholm, Roderick (1967): "Intentionality". In: Edwards, Paul (Ed.): *Encyclopaedia of Philosophy.* London: MacMillan.
Crane, Tim (2009): "Intentionalism". In: *Oxford Handbook to the Philosophy of Mind* (ed. A. Beckermann and B. McLaughlin), Oxford: Oxford University Press, pp. 474–493.
Crane, Tim (2009a): "Is Perception a Propositional Attitude?". In: *The Philosophical Quarterly* 59, pp. 452–469.
Crane, Tim (2013): *The Objects of Thought.* Oxford: Oxford University Press.
Crane, T. and French, C. (2016): "The Problem of Perception". In *The Stanford Encyclopedia of Philosophy,* https://plato.stanford.edu/entries/perception-problem (consulted on March 15, 2018).
Føllesdal, Dagfinn (1969): "Husserl's Notion of Noema". In: *Journal of Philosophy* 66, pp. 680–687.
Fréchette, Guillaume (2017): "Brentano on Content and Object". In: *IfCoLog: Journal of Logics and their Applications,* 4, no. 11, pp. 3609–3628.
Gregory, Richard (1970): *The Intelligent Eye.* London: Weidenfeld and Nicolson.
Heidegger, Martin (1992[1925]): *History of the Concept of Time. Prolegomena.* Bloomington: Indiana University Press.
Helmholtz, Hermann (1867): *Handbuch der physiologischen Optik.* Leipzig: Leopold Voss.
Helmholtz, Hermann (1878): "Die Thatsachen in der Wahrnehmung". In H. Helmholtz, *Vorträge und Reden,* vol. 2, Braunschweig: Vieweg, pp. 217–271.

---

18 This is an expanded and reworked version of a paper presented first in Kirchberg, then in Munich and Guarapuava in 2017. I thank the Kirchberg audience for its input, especially those who took part in the workshop on Brentano and the Myth of the Given: Marcello Fiocco, Uriah Kriegel, Michelle Montague, and Hamid Taieb for stimulating interactions on the first version, Johannes Brandl for the discussions in Kirchberg and Munich, and Mark Textor for his input in Munich. Thanks also to Evandro Brito, Ernesto Giusti, André Leclerc, Mario Gonzáles Porta, Gleisson Schmidt, Jean Siqueira, Wojciech Starzyński, and the other participants at Universidade Estadual do Centro-Oeste do Paraná (Guarapuava) for stimulating discussions during the Brentano conference there. This paper was written as part of the research project "Brentano's Descriptive Psychology" funded by the Austrian Science Fund (FWF, P-27215).

Hickerson, Ryan (2007): *The History of Intentionality: Theories of Consciousness from Brentano to Husserl*. London: Continuum.
Hume, David (1748): *Philosophical Essays Concerning Human Understanding*. London: Millar.
Husserl, Edmund (2001): *Logical Investigations*. Vol. 1, London: Routledge.
Husserl, Edmund (2001a): *Logical Investigations*. Vol. 2, London: Routledge.
Husserl, Edmund (1901): *Logische Untersuchungen. Band I*, Halle: Max Niemeyer.
Husserl, Edmund (1901): *Logische Untersuchungen. Band II, zweiter Teil*, Halle: Max Niemeyer.
Jacquette, Dale (2006): "Brentano's Concept of Intentionality". In: *The Cambridge Companion to Brentano* (ed. D. Jacquette), Cambridge: Cambridge University Press, pp. 98–130.
Marty, Anton (1889): "Genetische Psychologie". Unpublished lecture notes, Husserl Archives, Leuven (Q 10).
McDowell, John (1994): *Mind and World*. Cambridge, MA: Harvard University Press.
Müller, Johannes (1837): *Handbuch der Physiologie des Menschen*. Vol. 2, Koblenz: Hölscher.
Price, Henry Habberley (1932): *Perception*. London: Methuen.
Robinson, Howard (1994): *Perception*. New York: Routledge.
Smith, David (2002): *The Problem of Perception*. Cambridge, Harvard University Press.
Smith, Barry (1994): *Austrian Philosophy. The Legacy of Franz Brentano*. Chicago: Open Court.
Stumpf, Carl (1886): "Vorlesungen über Psychologie". Unpublished lecture notes, Husserl Archives, Leuven (Q 11).
Textor, Mark (2017): *Brentano's Mind*. Oxford: Oxford University Press.

Sofia Miguens
The Problem with J. Searle's Idea That 'all Seeing is Seeing-as' (or What Wittgenstein *did not* Mean With the Duck-Rabbit)

Abstract: In *Seeing Things As They Are – A Theory of Perception* (Searle 2015) John Searle claims that all seeing is seeing-as. The thesis in fact encapsulates his intentionalism about perceptual experience. In what follows I suggest that Searle's intentionalism embodies what Wittgenstein thought should not be said about seeing-as (Wittgenstein 2009). Based on recent interpretations of Wittgenstein on seeing-as (Schulte 2016, Baz 2016, Travis 2016). I try to spell out the nature and the implications of the head-on clash between Searle's and Wittgenstein's positions regarding seeing-as. I finish by discussing whether an alternative to intentionalism as a view of perception does indeed emerge from Wittgenstein's remarks on seeing-as.[1]

Keywords: Searle, Wittgenstein, seeing-as, silence of the senses, undeterminateness

1 All Seeing is Seeing-as

In Chapter 2 of his 2015 book *Seeing Things as They Are,* entitled 'The intentionality of perceptual experiences', John Searle very briefly brings in Wittgenstein's use of the duck-rabbit in paragraph 118 of the *Investigations* (Searle 2015: 74). What is remarkable about the duck-rabbit, he says, is that without any phenomenon of illusion, hallucination or delusion occurring you can have different experiences, produced by exactly the same stimulus: you see the duck-rabbit as a

---

[1] This article was motivated by some of the approaches to Wittgenstein on Seeing-as gathered in the 2016 volume *Wollheim, Wittgenstein and Pictorial Representation – Seeing-as and seeing-in* edited by Gary Kemp & Gabriele Mras. My basic intention was to use them against John Searle's claim that all seeing is seeing-as. I thank Gabriele Mras for the opportunity to participate in the Conference on John Searle's 2015 book, as well as on the 2013 conference *Wittgenstein and Wollheim: Seeing-as and Seeing-in* (both in Vienna at the WU). A further motivation for the article was the absence of the discussion of seeing-as from a debate in the philosophy of perception I have been working on, the debate between Charles Travis and John McDowell on perception and representation.

https://doi.org/10.1515/9783110657920-008

duck, and then you see the duck-rabbit as a rabbit. Searle goes on to say that because of the *intentionality* of visual experience, all seeing is seeing-as, as is the case with the duck-rabbit. And he goes on: "All visual intentionality is a matter of presentations, presentations are a subspecies of representation, and representation is always under some aspect or other." (Searle 2015: 75) The crucial claim that 'All seeing is seeing-as' in the 2015 book on perception thus translates the fact that for Searle all perception is representational, which he then takes to mean that all perception is of something under an aspect.

When Searle claims that 'all seeing is seeing-as' he obviously means to include ordinary visual experiences, not just seeing the duck-rabbit as a duck and then as a rabbit, or seeing a similarity between two faces (PI 2009: 113),[2] or seeing a triangle as a triangular hole, or as a solid, or as standing on its base, or as hanging from its apex, or as an arrow or a pointer, or as pointing downwards or upwards (PI 2009: 162). These are (some of) Wittgenstein's examples in Part II of the *Investigations* (now *Philosophy of Psychology – a Fragment*). If all seeing is seeing-as as Searle claims, then ordinary visual experiences such as my seeing you now, or my looking out of the window in Kirchberg and seeing a cow or a tree, or a duck or a rabbit, or a building, are also cases of seeing-as. This is a position about perception in general. This is part of what I will be taking issue with.

2 Two Things to Notice About Wittgenstein's Remarks

Searle is not alone in identifying Wittgensteinian seeing-as with the idea that all perceptions are under an aspect. To give just one example, Stephen Mulhall, in *On Being in the World – Wittgenstein and Heidegger on Seeing Aspects*, defends the idea that *continuous aspect perception* characterizes our normal perceptual relation to the world, i.e. our perception in general.

Yet two things are to be noticed about Wittgenstein's own remarks on seeing-as when we look close: first, that ordinary visual experiences do not seem to be what he has in mind and then that he does not intend to be putting forward a position about perception in general. Both come off clearly in recent interpretations of Wittgenstein on seeing-as (Schulte 2016, Baz 2016, Travis 2016).

---

[2] All references to the *Philosophical Investigations* are references to the Hacker-Schulte 2009 edition.

As for not having ordinary visual experiences in mind, Wittgenstein puts it quite directly: it makes little sense at the sight of a knife and fork to say 'Now I see this as a knife and fork':

> It would have made as little sense for me to say "Now I see it as ...." as to say at the sight of a knife and fork "Now I see this as a knife and fork". This utterance would not be understood. Any more than "Now it is a fork for me" or "It can be a fork too" (Wittgenstein 2009: 122)

This is precisely to be contrasted with the case of the duck-rabbit; there it is indeed the case that I, as it were, exclaim to myself "Now I see it as a rabbit" (or "Now I see it as a duck!"). As Joachim Schulte stresses, in *Seeing aspects and telling stories about it*, if seeing x as y is replaced with seeing x as x, then to say I see x as x makes no sense (Schulte 2016: 39). You can try it, facing an ordinary duck, i.e. a real life duck: say to yourself – "now I see it as a duck!" Or find a rabbit, look at it and say to yourself: "now I see it as a rabbit!" There is some sense of comedy to it. Of course if ordinary perception is not even Wittgenstein's focus in his approach to seeing-as we may doubt that ordinary perception will be directly illuminated by the remarks on seeing-as.

Anyway Searle could not have missed that Wittgenstein himself observes that it makes little sense, at the sight of a knife and fork, to say 'Now I see this as a knife and fork'. But then how can he, with such good conscience, say that all seeing is seeing-as? Does he really mean to say that seeing a knife and fork is seeing them as a knife and fork?

To understand Searle's good conscience we have to understand his position about perception in general. Unlike Wittgenstein he does have one. Let me call it intentionalism since the key to it is what Searle calls intentionality.

Searle's global position on perception is not new; his 2015 views are a corrected extension of his views on intentionality and consciousness put forward before, namely in Chapter 2 of his 1983 book *Intentionality*. For Searle intentionality is the feature of the mind by which the mind is directed at objects and states of affairs in the world (or is *about*, or *of*, them). It is also 'a biological phenomenon' occurring inside an organism, common to humans and other animals. In contrast with e.g. Husserlian Phenomenology, causality is involved in Searle's story about intentionality. The most basic forms of intentionality are biologically primitive forms of conscious perception such as hunger or thirst, or emotions such as anger, lust and fear. Intentional states such as beliefs are derived forms of intentionality. Regardless of this difference, all intentional states are caused by the brain and realized in the brain and they have, according to Searle, directions of fit (mind-world, or world-mind), and so they are satisfied, or not satisfied.

The idea of conditions of satisfaction is key to understand Searlean intentionality in general. Still, he carefully distinguishes perceptual experiences from beliefs. Beliefs are the most philosophically interesting of intentional states, he thinks (Searle 2015: 34), because they have entire propositions as contents. Yet "Unlike *[what is the case with]* our beliefs and statements, we do not say that our visual experiences are true or false" (Searle 2015: 57). Even if beliefs are philosophically interesting because they have entire propositions as contents and so can be said to be true or false, Searle is careful to point out that beliefs are not attitudes towards a proposition. In fact, the most essential thing when we are thinking about intentionality according to Searle is that we should distinguish between *content* and *object*. Beliefs (well, most beliefs[3]) are not about propositions: propositions are the contents of beliefs, or a way to speak of content of beliefs, not their objects. And the same content-object distinction applies to perceptual experience: if I see a computer in front of me the content of my perceptual experience is *that there is a computer* in front of me, whereas the object is the computer itself. One never just sees an object, Searle says (Searle 2015: 110). This allows him to say that the content may be exactly the same in this case, as in any case of visual perception, and in a corresponding hallucination – the content will be be same, but not the object. The Bad Argument, which is the main target of Searle's 2015 book, is precisely the systematic confusion of content and object when thinking about perception: it amounts to mistaking the content of a perceptual experience for its object. Mistaking the content of a perceptual experience for its object is a *faux pas* common to many people, from sense data theorists to disjunctivists, according to Searle. But no, says Searle, you don't experience perceptual contents, you *have* them.

When it comes to the *specific* intentionality of perceptual experiences in contrast to beliefs, another idea is crucial for Searle. Perceptual experiences have a different phenomenology from that of beliefs: they have phenomenal properties; they are not just representations but also presentations. For Searle intentionality is not mysterious and does not have to be reduced to anything else. Yet things are not that simple with the phenomenology. He speaks of visual phenomenology as extending from the top of my forehead down to my chin. He says it is an 'area': I don't have visual consciousness behind my head or under my feet (Searle 2015: Introduction), he claims, but I still have it in front of my head even with my eyes closed. This area is what he calls *subjective visual field*. As Charles Travis put it in

---

[3] This is Searle's own example: "If I believe Bernouilli's principle is boring, than I do have an attitude towards a proposition – namely the proposition that states Bernouilli's principle – I think it is boring." (Searle 2015: 39).

"Eyes Wide Shut" (Travis 2015), his review of Searle's 2015 book, for Searle visual experience is a subjective experience that takes place inside the head; the question is what inside the head means. According to Searle, if I open my eyes the *subjective visual field* fills up, since I become visually aware of the *objective visual field*. This he identifies with objects and states of affairs around me. He insists much on this difference between subjective visual field in your head and objective visual field outside your head: the 2015 view of perception proceeds by telling us how subjective and objective visual fields relate. And the key idea for this relating is that all seeing is intentional:

> The fact that the processes in the subjective visual field, the experiences, have intentionality has two important consequences (...) : all seeing is *seeing as* and all seeing is *seeing that*. (Searle 2015: 110)

It is because all perceptual experiences are intentional that all seeing is (or rather becomes, for Searle) seeing-that. And then Searle identifies seeing-that and seeing-as, i.e. he takes seeing-as to simply mean the same as seeing-that. What is happening here? One thing that is happening according to Travis is that Searle is being deaf to the difference between what is meant by 'seeing' and what is meant by 'seeing-that':

> Unfortunately, Searle neglects a (...) distinction: that between what 'see' speaks of in, e.g., 'see the *Wildschwein* digging up the garden', and what it speaks of in 'see *that* the *Wildschwein* is digging up the garden'. One can watch a *Wildschwein* digging. One cannot watch *that* a *Wildschwein* is digging. *That* it is digging, as opposed to its digging, neither goes on for a long time nor is very brief. Though it may be digging next to the roses, such is not where *that* it is digging is. Nor is any other spot. (Travis 2015: par. 12)

We speak of seeing, or watching, a *Wildschwein* when we are, say, facing it, here and now. It is a different thing though when it comes to speaking of 'seeing that a *Wildschwein* is digging'. There is no duration or location of such (in Searle's term) content. Content is not a *Wildschwein*. It is not (it cannot be) in front of me, or behind a tree. Travis goes on: "*That* it is digging, unlike its digging, does not form images on retinas, is not seen, does not *look* any particular way." (Travis 2015: par.12)

Travis point is then that only by neglecting a distinction present in our practice of speaking of seeing –the distinction between seeing (a pig, or a tree) and seeing that a pig is digging or that a tree is a cedar–, can Searle make it that *that the pig is digging* looks like a possible object of sight. But this, he argues, cancels Searle's own good point that a content *cannot* be an object of sight, a point Travis fully agrees with.

3 Wittgenstein's Seeing-as: *Erfahrung* and Shareability

Back to Wittgenstein and to evidence of the fact that, in contrast with Searle, it is not perception in general, or ordinary perception, that he is interested in. For Wittgenstein when an aspects dawns, e.g. when I see the ambiguous figure, the duck-rabbit, as a duck, or when I see a similarity between two faces, or when I see the triangle as pointing upwards, this is quite an unusual case. It is an experience, an *Erfahrung* or *Erlebniss*, in a very specific sense, as Joachim Schulz stresses (Schulte 2016: 42), reflecting, as a translator, on the fact that English has only one word here, the word *experience*. The dawning of an aspect is not something we are continuously undergoing as we perceive things around us; it is rather fleeting, lasting only as one is occupied with the object in a special way. It is, in Gary Kemp and Gabriele Mras' terms, a *transitory event* rather than an *enduring state* (Kemp & Mras 2016: xiv. Also Baz 2016). It is such sudden change of aspect that the indicator of time expresses linguistically, when we say "*Now I see a duck!*"/ "*Now I see a rabbit!*" Yet in readings of seeing-as such as Searle's (or Mulhall's), i.e. readings according to which any perceptual experience is an experience of seeing (or hearing)-as, perceiving anything (e.g. a color, or a shape) is perceiving an aspect. But just think of seeing a figure painted in Yves Klein blue: it is there, in front of you, you see its colour. It is not the case that this suddenly dawns on you, as a fleeting *Erfahrung* or *Erlebnis*, lasting only as your are occupied with the object in a special way. You see a figure painted in Yves Klein blue. It is not a transitory event.

Also, if we consider Wittgenstein's examples, is there even anything like a unified phenomenon of seeing-as? The duck-rabbit, the triangle seen as pointing upwards, the resemblance between two faces, the Necker cube, the white cross on black background / black cross on white background– are they in all respects similar? Joachim Schulte doubts that they are (Schulte 2016: 43), as does Charles Travis (Travis 2016: 15), as does Avner Baz (Baz 2016: 56). The duck-rabbit is different from the case of seeing a similarity between two faces in that in the second case there is no shifting back and forth. Also not in every case is there a determinate aspect competing, as there is in the case of the duck-rabbit – there is no such thing in the case of seeing the similarity between two faces, or the triangle pointing up, or hanging from above. Granted, thinking about seeing-as, Wittgenstein was interested in what we might call a kind of conceiving which is extremely close to perceiving which may at a certain point in time not be shared by two people who look at the very same picture, say. I may be seeing the duck-rabbit as a rabbit, or the two faces as similar, or the triangle as pointing upwards whereas you are not. Yet you are looking at the very same pictures and do not see them as similiar. Yet does that make seeing-as an unified phenomenon? Not *per se*. And especially is this – the fact that we are looking at the same picture and I might be seeing it as x and you not – the sort of thing that should lead us to think that a subjective experience of seeing is taking place inside one's head? For one, I can certainly call your attention to it – I can say "Look! Can you not see the similarity between the faces?" or "Can you not see this triangle as pointing upwards?" That this is possible is in fact the reason why people such as Richard Wollheim were interested in recruiting the phenomenon of seeing-as for dealing with aesthetic matters. It is an important phenomenon for the way we experience paintings, or experience art in general (in fact for Wollheim, the dawning of Wittgensteinian aspects is revelatory of a feature of human perception). Anyway, the seeing-as may not be shared just now (i do not see the similarity between the two faces) yet it is shareable. But if it is shareable then it is not inside my head (certainly not in the same sense that my brain is inside my head since I definitely cannot share my brain with you).

By now we have some traits of Wittgensteinian seeing-as. What Wittgenstein is interested in his remarks on seeing-as is not ordinary experience, but rather something more specific: an *Erfahrung*, a transitory event. His examples of seeing-as are disparate; they may not point at a unified phenomenon. Yet they do point at something which is sharable. If it is sharable then it cannot be inside our head. In these circumstances Wittgensteinian seeing-as does not even seem to be something from which to generalize to a view of perception; it is a phenomenon both more specific and less central in ordinary perception that the people who claim that 'All perception is perception under an aspect' need it to be.

4 Does an Alternative to Searle's Intentionalism Arise From Here?

Things are very different with Searle: he simply recruits seeing-as as a side illustration of his views on intentionality. What he is really interested in is ordinary perception, perception in general. The fact is, Searle does have a general position about perception – what about Wittgenstein? Does he have one? We must be very careful here – Wittgenstein is certainly not involved in current discussions in philosophy of perception.[4] But Searle is, or is in a way.[5] What I suggest can be done, then, is isolate basic claims by Searle in order to get what Wittgenstein might not want to say about perception. So: Searle claims that all seeing is seeing-as and that perceptual experience takes place inside our heads. It is cautious enough to say that Wittgenstein did not want to say that all seeing is seeing-as or that perceptual experience takes place inside our heads. What Wittgenstein's remarks on seeing-as may do then is open a path to think of perception very different from Searle's. But then, what next, once we are persuaded that not all seeing is seeing-as? I already put forward the beginning of a suggestion from Charles Travis; I also want to look at a suggestion from Avner Baz. These are two ideas that might do work in thinking about perception once we put aside Searle's claim that all seeing if seeing-as.

Travis thinks Searle's view according to which all seeing is seeing-that works only by being voluntarily oblivious to a genuine difference between senses of seeing, seeing and seeing that. He claims that Searle has not shown that all seeing is seeing-as (or seeing-that); what he is doing is simply equivocating with 'seeing'. It is only by neglecting the different senses of 'see' that *that the flower has five petals* (what Searle calls content) may ever be taken to be a possible object of sight. But then this cancels Searle's own good point that a content cannot be an object of sight. Travis' general attack on Searle thus has the following shape: if Searle is not himself a sense-datum theorist (remember that his whole book on perception is aimed against the Bad Mistake of mistaking content for object, and sense datum theorists are supposed to have been guilty of it...), then he is separated from being a sense-datum theorist by a *very* thin line. Also, according to Travis, Searlean 'intentionality' gets Searle conditions of satisfaction for free: because perception is intentional it is representational and thus has conditions of satisfaction. For Travis, though, a positive account is needed of how something truth-evaluable gets into the picture when there is perceiving, lest one is conflating a sentence such as "This (tree) is a cedar" with visually perceiving what is there before me. Travis' claim is that an environment is needed for there to be accuracy conditions; this will do away with the idea that perceptual experi-

---

4 Ch. Travis claims (Travis 2016: 32) that whereas if it would be anachronistic to see Wittgenstein as a disjunctivist, he is certainly opening space for the position– the very position Searle finds 'beyond the pale' in his 2015 book on perception.
5 One may of course complain that he misreads what goes on around him in the philosophical discussions on perception (for instance under the name of disjunctivism).

encings themselves have anything like accuracy conditions, conditions of satisfaction. For Travis only judgments have accuracy conditions. What experiencing does is (just) to bring our surroundings into view. In a image Travis himself has used, our senses are like a CCTV; they register. They do not take it *that the flower has five petals* or *that a robber has just entered the room*, or *that the sun has set*. They are simply registering. This is the idea of silence of the senses. Thinking that the senses are silent, like Travis does, is the beginning of an alternative path to the idea that all seeing is seeing-as. It emphasizes the non-determinateness of what one is presented with; determinateness (e.g. *that the flower has five petals* or *that a robber has just entered the room*, or *that the sun has set)* comes only with our judging-that. Conditions of satisfaction are in the picture here, not with experiencing *per se*.

Another idea besides Travis' silence of the senses which might do work if we stop thinking of Searle's 'All seeing is seeing-as' as uncontroversial is something I want to call *undeterminateness* of perception. Notice that it is part and parcel of Searle's view that perceptual experience of reality presents it as determinate (Searle 2015: 69). He does not recoil from saying that 'as Leibniz told us, reality itself is determinate' (he seems to forget Leibniz' very self-conscious appeal to God's eyeview in saying this). Avner Baz thinks that in his remarks on seeing-as Wittgenstein is trying to bring forth the fact that precisely this is not so, that reality in itself is not determinate, in a sense to be explained. He thinks that in this Wittgenstein's view of perception converges with Merleau-Ponty's (Baz 2016).

For Baz, like for Wollheim, the dawning of Wittgensteinian aspects is indeed revelatory of a feature of human perception. But the feature revealed is not that all seeing is seeing-as, in particular if that is read as saying that all seeing is conceptual. According to Baz this would be an overintelectualization of the phenomenon Wittgenstein is interested in. It is true that Wollheim himself went as far as saying (at some point, in his first book, although he then retracted the view) that for any perceived object x whenever I perceive x there is always some concept f such that I perceive x as f (Baz 2016: 57). This amounts to assuming that what can be seen-as is something that can be judged or known to be that way. Baz completely disagrees with this, as well as with the idea that Wittgensteinian seeing-as amounts to that. Let us think of Wittgenstein's examples again: which concept is being applied when the similarity between two faces strikes me? Under what concept am I perceiving the duck-rabbit before I see it as duck, and then as a rabbit? (what are concepts, anyway?)

What the dawning of Wittgensteinian aspects reveals according to Baz is not that for any perceived object x whenever I perceive x there is always some concept f such that I perceive x as f. It is something else. What the dawning of Wittgensteinian aspects reveals is the power to perceive unity and sense anew. This for Baz was something Kant was interested in in his approach to beauty in the *Critique of Judgement*,[6] and something Merleau-Ponty is after in the *Phenomenology of Perception*.

> It is one thing to see something as x and quite another thing to conceive of it as x, or to judge it to be x. And seeing something as x – I mean, the perceptual phenomenon that Wittgenstein investigates under that title – cannot be continuous. The dawning of a Wittgensteinian aspect, especially when it happens in the natural course of everyday experience, is the momentary emergence, more or less willed or invited, of relative determinacy – a particular way of momentarily taking hold of what encounters us in our experience (…) Wittgenstein's investigation of aspect perception, far from showing, or trying to show, that everything we see is under some particular concept, as Wollheim proposes, rather suggests that the more or less indeterminate unity of the perceived world is neither brought about nor secured by the application of concepts. (Baz 2016: 72)

What, according to Baz, both Kant and Merleau-Ponty and Wittgenstein are after then, are occasions when a pre-conceptual and pre-objective level of human experience gets revealed and *we stop doing as if there was one thing which is the one and one only way thinks look in a particular perceptual experience and see it anew* (imagine that we look at layout of this very same conference room, with all of us here now, and see it as an installation in an art gallery). That there is such possibility is what I am calling undeterminateness, after Baz. According to Baz, who is following Kant and Merleau-Ponty here, such underdeterminateness is characteristic of perceptual experience: pointing out the phenomenological–grammatical nature of Wittgenstein's remarks on seeing-as Baz observes that this might be something that cannot be captured in a Wittgensteinian *grammatical, and thus linguistic,* investigation.

5 Conclusion

In this article I approached John Searle's recent book on perception (Searle 2015) from a Wittgensteinian viewpoint. In his book Searle claims that because all mental phenomena are intentional, visual experiences are intentional, and thus all seeing is seeing-as. I argued that such an idea does not stand. It is simply not the

---

[6] Which counters the idea, based mostly in an interpretation of the first Critique, that Kant is a representationalist regarding perception. See Miguens 2017 and 2019.

case that all seeing is seeing-as. On the one hand some seeing might be simple seeing what is there before your eyes, on the other there are reasons not to conflate the very specific phenomenon of seeing-as as Wittgenstein characterizes it with Searlean seeing-that. This is one thing Wittgenstein's remarks remind us of. Searle's intentionalism, which rests on an unargued identification of seeing with seeing-as, and of seeing-as with seeing-that, turns out to embody precisely what Wittgenstein thought should not be said about seeing-as. Wittgenstein's remarks on seeing-as show us that, in contrast with what Searle thinks, seeing-as is not a characteristic of perception in general, or ordinary perception, but a particular phenomenon. Wittgensteinian seeing-as is a matter of dawning of aspects, which is a fleeting experience (*Erfahrung* or *Erlebnis*). In other words, seeing-as as the dawning of aspects is not something we are continuously undergoing as we perceive things around us. It is not characteristic of just any perceptual experience. In fact Wittgenstein's examples of seeing-as are not even anything like a unified phenomenon. The duck-rabbit, the triangle seen as pointing upwards, the resemblance between two faces, the Necker cube, the white cross on black background / black cross on white background are not similar in all respects. Still, there is one common characteristic to all of them: although the seeing-as they involve may be not shared just now (e.g. I do not see the similarity between the two faces that you see) it is shareable. But then if such seeing-as is shareable it is not inside my head. A close look at Wittgenstein's remarks on seeing-as thus leads to a head-on clash with Searle's main tenets.

From this it does not follow, though, that a clear alternative to intentionalism as a view of perception emerges from Wittgenstein's remarks on seeing-as *per se*. More work needs to be done, since Wittgensteinian points about seeing-as are mostly negative. What can be done, if we accept the Wittgensteinian points about seeing-as, is to search for alternatives to intentionalism which might accomodate them. At the end of the article I identify two ideas that might be instrumental to start devising such alternatives to Searlean intentionalism: Travis' idea of the silence of the senses and Baz' idea of undeterminateness. Interestingly, they lead in quite different directions in the philosophy of perception. In Travis' case we are led to to a disjunctivist opposition to representationalism (and disjuntivism, for at least some of its proponents, comes along with naïve realism). In the case of Baz we are led to Merleau-Ponty's view of '*le sensible*'[7], allowing for meaningfulness in perception itself. It is particularly interesting that in spite of their as it were initial agreement (both believe that it is not the case that all seeing is seeing-

---

7 This is Merleau-Ponty's term for the world.

as) the implications of Travis' and Baz' ideas of silence of the sense and undeterminateness cannot easily be brought together. This might show the limits of a Wittgensteinian, i.e. grammatical, and thus language-bound, investigation, when it comes to perception. But that would be the topic for another article.

References

Baz, Avner (2016): "Aspects of perception". In: Gary Kemp and Gabriele Mras (Eds.): *Wittgenstein, Wollheim and Pictorial Representation: seeing-as and seeing-in*, London: Routledge, pp. 49–76.

Benoist, Jocelyn, (2006): "Voir comme quoi? II, xi". In: S. Laugier & Ch. Chauviré (Eds.): Lire les Recherches Philosophiques, Paris: Vrin, pp. 237–253.

Miguens, Sofia (2017): "Apperception or environment – J. McDowell and Ch.Travis on the nature of perceptual judgement" (Apercepción o ambiente. J.McDowell y Ch. Travis sobre la naturaleza del juicio perceptivo"). In: *ConTextos Kantianos – an international journal of philosophy* 6, Diciembre 2017, pp. 79–92

Miguens, Sofia (2019): "Is seeing judging? Radical contextualism and the problem of perception". In: David Zapero and Eduardo Marchesan (Eds.): *Objectivity, Truth and Context*. London: Routledge, pp. 124–158.

Mras, Gabriele and Kemp, Gary (2016): "Introduction". In: Gary Kemp and Gabriele Mras (Eds.): *Wittgenstein, Wollheim and Pictorial Representation: Seeing-as and Seeing-in*. London: Routledge, pp. xiii–xv.

Mulhall, Stephen (1990): *On Being in the World – Wittgenstein and Heidegger on Seeing Aspects*. London: Routledge.

Schulte, J. (2016): "Seeing aspects and telling stories about it". In: Gary Kemp and Gabriele Mras (Eds.): *Wittgenstein, Wollheim and Pictorial Representation: Seeing-as and Seeing-in*. London: Routledge, pp. 37–48.

Searle, John, (2015) *Seeing Things as They Are: A Theory of Perception*. Oxford: OUP.

Searle, John (1983): *Intentionality*. Cambridge: Cambridge University Press.

Travis, Charles (2015): "Eyes Wide Shut", Review of John Searle Seeing Things as They Are: A Theory of Perception, *Notre Dame Philosophical Reviews* (http://ndpr.nd.edu/news/59294-seeing-things-as-they-are-a-theory-of-perception/)

Travis, Charles (2016): "The room in a view". In: Gary Kemp and Gabriele Mras (Eds.), *Wittgenstein, Wollheim and Pictorial Representation: Seeing-as and Seeing-in*. London: Routledge, pp.3–33

Wittgenstein, Ludwig (2009): *Philosophische Untersuchungen/Philosophical Investigations*. Revised 4th edition by P.M.S. Hacker and Joachim Schulte, Oxford: Wiley-Balckwell.

3 **Perception, Cognition and Images**

Uriah Kriegel
The Perception/Cognition Divide: One More Time, With Feeling

Abstract: Traditional accounts of the perception/cognition divide tend to draw it in terms of subpersonal psychological processes, processes into which the subject has no first-person insight. Whatever betides such accounts, there seems to *also* be some first-personally accessible difference between perception and thought. At least in normal circumstances, naïve subjects can typically tell apart their perceptual states from their cognitive or intellectual ones. What are such subjects picking up on when they do so? This paper is an inconclusive search for an answer. At its end, I conclude, without joy, that we may have to simply accept the perception/cognition distinction as a primitive and inexplicable bright line within the sphere of conscious phenomena.

Keywords: Perception, cognition, attitudinal properties, phenomenology

1 Introduction: The Perception/Cognition Divide from the First-Person Perspective

Suppose you are in a conscious mental state that represents a brown dog, and an omniscient authority assures you that your mental state is either a *perceptual experience* of a brown dog or an *occurrent thought* about a brown dog – it is not a memory of a brown dog, not an imagination of a brown dog, not a fear of a brown dog, and so on. Then the authority asks you whether, in your opinion, your mental state is in fact a perceptual experience or a thought.

There are two assumptions about this scenario that I would like to make from the outset. The first is that you should be able to answer the authority's question fairly effortlessly and immediately, with a considerable degree of reliability. Perhaps you will not be infallible in answering such questions, and perhaps a sufficiently inventive evil demon or scientist could put you in sufficiently atypical circumstances that you would get it wrong often. But in typical circumstances, it seems most of us will, most of the time, be right about whether our brown-dog-representing state is a perceptual experience or a thought.

The second assumption I want to make is that you can answer the authority's question without access to any third-person evidence. For present purposes, this includes four types of evidence: verbal report, nonverbal behavior, third-party testimony, and brain scans. Typically, when asked whether *someone else* is perceiving a brown dog or thinking about a brown dog, you need access to at least one of these four types of information to take any informed view; but when asked whether *your own* mental state is a perceptual experience or a thought, you can have justified belief on the matter even in the absence of evidence from any of these four groups.

I do not think these two assumptions are beyond reasonable doubt, and will in fact take a more critical approach to them in the final section of this paper. But the two assumptions are on their faces rather plausible. And if we accept them both, we face the following question: What feature(s) of your mental state do you pick up on when you answer the authority's question? If we can answer such questions relatively effortlessly and reliably, despite having no *third-person* evidence of relevance, it would seem that we must have *first-person* insight into the perceptual or cognitive character of our conscious states. But what is the exact content of this first-person insight?

In the 1970s and 80s, philosophers of mind developed a number of sophisticated accounts of the perception/cognition divide. However, these accounts tended to draw the distinction in terms of subpersonal or architectural features of mental states and processes, ones into which naïve subjects do not seem to have any first-person insight. Consider the Fodorian notion that perceptual processes are 'modular' whereas cognitive ones are 'central.' Fodor (1983) adduced a number of features distinguishing the former from the latter, notably domain-specificity and informational encapsulation. However, these do not seem to be features into which we have first-person insight (nor did Fodor intend them to be such). Domain-specificity is a matter of responsiveness to a limited range of inputs, hence a matter of the origin of the processes producing the relevant mental states; informational encapsulation is a matter of susceptibility to cognitive penetration, that is, to influence from certain top-down processes. Clearly, an ordinary subject may have no pertinent information about the processes in which her current mental representation of a brown dog originated, or the processes to which it is susceptible, and yet have the kind of first-person insight into certain features of her current mental state that makes it possible for her to reliably tell whether that state is perceptual or cognitive.

In what follows, I will call such features *first-personally manifest* features. The question I want to raise, then, is this: What are the first-personally manifest features that distinguish perceptual experiences and occurrent thoughts? The architectural and subpersonal approaches from a generation ago may not answer this question (or if they do, we would still need to get clear on what the answer *is*). What might?

2 The Perception/Cognition Divide and Intentional Character

One straightforward approach to our problem might be: perceptual experiences have one kind of phenomenal character, thoughts have another, and this is what a naïve subject picks up on when forming a justified belief on the matter. Ultimately, this answer may well be right. But absent further elaboration, all it says is this: perception has a perceptual phenomenal character, cognition has a cognitive phenomenal character. This does not yet illuminate the nature of the perceptual/cognitive divide.

Indeed, this helps us see our problem from another angle. In the 70s and 80s, the debate on the perception/cognition divide was conducted against the background of a widespread assumption that while perceptual experiences have phenomenal character, thoughts are non-phenomenal states. Since those days, many philosophers have come to countenance a proprietary kind of cognitive phenomenology, that is, a sui generis phenomenal character proper to thought (see, e.g., Siewert 1998, Pitt 2004). But once we recognize cognitive phenomenology alongside perceptual phenomenology, we incur the theoretical debt of accounting for the phenomenal *difference* between the two. So, even if the features our subject picks up on, when classifying her occurrent mental representations as perceptual or cognitive, are certain phenomenal properties, there is still a legitimate kind of curiosity we might have about the *nature* of these phenomenal properties – and of the difference between them. Suppose all and only perceptual experiences instantiate phenomenal property P, while all and only occurrent thoughts instantiate phenomenal property T. It is natural to want to know *what P and T are*. On the assumption that phenomenology is by its nature first-personally manifest, providing an account of the difference between P and T – between perceptual and cognitive phenomenology – is also answering the question of what is the first-personally manifest difference between perception and thought.

It is also possible, of course, to *deny* the existence of any proprietary cognitive phenomenology. If one does, one instantly acquires a straightforward answer to our question: perceptual experiences have phenomenal character, thoughts do not – that is the first-personally manifest difference between them. I will be assuming here, however, that thoughts do have a phenomenal character proper to them. I concede that it is only against the background of this assumption that our question becomes pressing.

Now, at one level, I think the phenomenal feature that distinguishes a perceptual experience of a brown dog from a thought about a brown dog is pretty straightforward. The problem is that the most natural ways of capturing this feature are metaphorical. We say, for example, that in perceptual experience objects are *directly* present to us, whereas in thought they are not. But what does 'directly' exactly *mean*? Husserl puts it nicely when he says that while perceptual experiences present their objects *in the flesh* ('*in persona*,' he writes), thoughts do not. But that is just a compelling metaphor. Our question is how to get underneath such suggestive expressions and provide a substantive, informative account of the first-personally manifest difference between perception and thought.

There are many 'leads' one might consider. One might, for example, be visited by a hunch that perception is crucially 'perspectival' whereas thought is 'objective'; or one might feel that the key difference is that perception is in some sense passive whereas thought is active ('receptivity' vs. 'spontaneity'); or one might be impressed by the fact that perception seems to be phenomenally rich whereas thought is phenomenally sparse at best. I cannot hope to follow up here on *all* the possible leads of relevance. To restrict the group of options to be considered in a principled way, I will focus on features of perceptual experiences and occurrent thoughts that pertain to their *intentional character*. By this I mean both (i) these states' intentional *content* and (ii) the kinds of *attitude* they take toward these contents. (There are different views on the relationship between content and attitude. One model treats contents and attitudes as distinct features that combine together to form intentional characters; another model takes the basic intentional structure to be that of taking-attitude-A-toward-content-C and treats content and attitude as theoretical abstractions of some sort. Although I lean toward the second understanding, I will take no official stand on this question here. What matters to me is that not only content but also attitude be examined when we consider the intentional profile of mental states.)

The restriction to intentional character is not *too* restrictive. Many philosophers today are impressed by the idea of the 'transparency of experience' (Harman 1990). As is well known, though, some very different claims have been associated with this label. Most strongly, some hold that when we first-personally attend to our own conscious states, we are only aware of the external objects and/or properties these states are intentionally directed at. More weakly, some hold that what is first-personally manifest when we attend to our conscious states are properties of these states themselves, but only properties of the form having-such-and-such-intentional-content. More permissively yet, someone might hold that among the first-personally manifest properties of conscious states are not only content properties but also attitudinal properties. Indeed, this view is *so* permissive that many might consider it not to qualify as a transparency view at all.

Thus in considering both content and attitude views we are imposing a relatively permissive restriction on the space of possible approaches.

It is possible, of course, that although perceptual experiences and occurrent thoughts are different in a first-personally manifest way, they are so in virtue of features that are neither content features nor attitudinal features. This possibility will not be ruled out by anything I will say hereafter – that is the cost of our restriction.

In what follows, I will devote more attention to attitudinal approaches to the first-personally manifest divide between perception and cognition, because elsewhere (Kriegel forthcoming) I argue in some detail against content approaches. Nonetheless, I start, in §3, with a summary of my case against content approaches. In §4, I introduce and motivate the attitudinal approach. In §§5–6, I consider two specific attitudinal accounts, arguing against each. In §7, I consider our options given the failure of both the content and attitudinal approaches examined here; I conclude, without joy, that we may be forced to adopt a primitivist position according to which there is simply two distinct first-personally manifest features, a sui generis phenomenology of perceptuality and a sui generis phenomenology of cognitivity, such that perceptual experiences exhibit the former whereas conscious thoughts exhibit the latter.

Before starting, three clarificatory comments are in order. First, I will use the expressions 'cognition' and 'thought' interchangeably, and have in mind such phenomena as thinking to oneself that the weather is nice, considering the likelihood that Spain will win the next world cup, and realizing that the deadline for submitting a grant proposal is only ten days away. There is a use of the term 'cognition' that makes it considerably wider, covering also phenomena of mental imagery, episodic memory, and any other stimulus-independent mental phenomenon (see Phillips 2019). Indeed, there is a use of 'cognitive' where it means essentially the same as 'mental' (see under: 'cognitive science'). I will not be using the term 'cognitive' in these more extended senses. For that would effectively turn the question before us into the more general one of what distinguishes perceptual from non-perceptual mental phenomena. But *that* question is really an amalgam of a number of separate questions: (a) what distinguishes perception from imagination?; (b) what distinguishes perception from episodic memory?; (c) what distinguishes perception from thought?; and so on. I think the right approach here is to take up each of these more focused questions in its own turn and give it the time of day. Running them together risks papering over important distinctions and producing a more confused picture of the main bright lines within the overall field of mental phenomena.

Secondly, it is important in some contexts to distinguish between three very different kinds of thought reports. The locution 'thinking *that*' tends to figure in reports of mental states that take a stand on the truth of that-which-is-thought-about, such as judging that p and believing that p. In contrast, the locution 'thinking *of*' tends to figure in reports of mental states that do *not* take a stand on the question of truth, such as entertaining p and contemplating p. Entertaining or contemplating p does not constitutively involve taking p to be true, but judging or believing that p does. There is also a locution that tends to be neutral on the matter, namely, 'thinking *about*.' In any case, in what follows I will restrict myself to the think-that and think-about locutions, and have in mind only the committal, belief-like states, not the neutral, entertaining-like states. The reason for this is that I take perception to be likewise committal regarding the reality of its objects – more on this in §4. Therefore, it is for the contrast between perception and *committal* thought that the question of distinguishing the two presents itself most urgently.

Third comment: the discussion to follow ignores entirely the phenomena of *unconscious* perception and thought. I will not consider such phenomena as blindsight or even subliminal perception, nor tacit or dispositional belief. The reason for this is that I do not expect there to be any *first-personally manifest* difference between such mental states. For these, the sub-personal and architectural approaches from the 80s will do just fine. The residual problem I have identified at the opening does not arise for them. So although I will for the sake of brevity speak of perception and thought, I really just mean conscious perceptual experience and conscious occurrent thought ('cognitive experience'). (Note: for the sake of flow I use 'perception' to cover veridical, illusory, and hallucinatory perceptual experiences alike; that is, I bracket the fact that the term is, in its most central usage, a success term.)

3 The Content Strategy

There is a natural temptation to distinguish perception and thought in terms of what they represent. In particular, we might think, perception characteristically represents *low-level* properties, such as color and shape, whereas thought typically represents *high-level* properties, such as being a dog and being Parisian. More generally, the idea is to start by dividing represented entities into *sensibles* and *intelligibles*, then explain the difference between perception and thought in terms of representing the former versus representing the latter.

The main problem here is that while there may be restrictions on what perception can represent, there appear to be no restrictions on what thought can represent. In particular, it is unclear why, whatever the property one's perception represents, one could not simply think about the-property-one's-perception-represents, if only under that description. In that scenario, there might be a difference in the *description used to pick out* this property, but there will be no difference in the property being picked out.

Note that it is beside the point that there is still a difference here insofar as certain things perception cannot represent whereas thought can represent anything representable. For that only helps us to distinguish the faculties of thought and perception, but does not help us distinguish two token mental states, one perceptual and one cognitive, which both represent F. Yet a normal subject in normal conditions can tell whether her mental state is a perceptual experience of red or a thought about red.

The reasoning so far suggests that the content strategy would do well to draw the perception/cognition distinction not in terms of what properties are being represented, but in terms of something like the *modes of presentation* used to represent those properties. Of course, it would be uninformative to simply state that perception employs a perceptual mode of presentation whereas thought employs a cognitive mode of presentation. It would likewise be of limited help to say that perception employs an in-the-flesh mode of presentation whereas thought does not. What we want is to capture the psychological reality underlying that metaphor. It is more informative to unpack mode of presentation either in terms of abstract entities in Frege's 'third realm' or in terms of functional role. But both of these do not seem like first-personally manifest features. Certainly abstract objects cannot be *introspected*, since introspection directs itself at one's *current* stream of consciousness, not at a realm of timeless beings. And arguably, functional role cannot be introspected either, since functional role is a *dispositional* property, whereas introspective awareness presents only categorical properties. (Compare: you cannot see the vase's fragility, even if in some sense you can see *that* the vase is fragile. Likewise, I would argue, you cannot introspect your experience's disposition to elicit such-and-such behaviors and inferences, even if you can introspect *that* your experience has such a disposition.)

It is hard to see, then, how to produce an informative-yet-adequate characterization of the alleged difference between the modes of presentation employed by perception and by thought. Might one suggest that perception employs *perspectival* modes of presentation, whereas thought employs non-perspectival ones? This is problematic without further explanation of what makes a mode perspectival. If we understand it, as is common, in terms of *indexical representation*, then the resulting account would be extensionally inadequate: many thoughts have indexical content as well. In addition, it is unclear that indexicality and perspectivality characterize *all* perception. For example, an olfactory experience of the odor of freshly ground coffee (without a clear sense of where the odor is coming from, say) is certainly perceptual, but in what sense is it perspectival? We are still left with the question of what distinguishes that experience from a conscious occurrent thought about the odor of freshly ground coffee.

It might be suggested that the key difference between perceptual and cognitive content is more structural: thought employs *conceptual* modes of presentation, perception *nonconceptual* ones. The notion that perception has *nonconceptual* content whereas thought has *conceptual* content is a recurring theme in contemporary philosophy of mind (e.g., Dretske 1995). There are several different ways this notion can play out (Heck 2000), but the main one is probably this: a perceptual experience of a brown dog is a representational state we can be in even when we do not possess the concepts BROWN and DOG, whereas an occurrent thought about a brown dog is a representational state that we cannot be in unless we possess BROWN and DOG.

An immediate concern is that the suggestion offers only a *negative* characterization of perceptual experience: it is a certain kind of lack, or absence, that makes a mental state perceptual. This seems at best incomplete, as there also seems to be something positive *present* in perceptual experience – all those vividly present colors and sounds we experience! Arguably, it is precisely this 'something positive' that a naïve subject picks up on when classifying her conscious state as perceptual. One could of course use the label 'nonconceptual' for something positive, but one would also have to make sure that that positive feature is first-personally manifest. Stalnaker (1998), for instance, understands nonconceptual content in terms of functions from worlds to extensions; but surely we cannot *introspect* such functions, so it is unclear in what sense they might be first-personally manifest.

In fact, it is questionable in general that the conceptual/nonconceptual distinction is first-personally manifest. On many accounts, it is ultimately a difference in *functional role*: a conceptual representation of a hexagon implicates certain capacities, such as to recognize and reidentify hexagons across time, as well as trigger certain inferences that nonconceptual representations of hexagons do not. But to repeat, functional role, as a dispositional property, is not an introspectible feature.

The biggest problem with the account under consideration, however, is that the nonconceptual character of our perceptual experiences appears to be a merely contingent and accidental feature of theirs. Imagine a supersentient creature – call it Lynceus – who possesses a concept for every shade of red and every polygon. Lynceus can discriminate red_{273} from red_{274}, recognize a red_{273} sample a year after seeing it, and draw appropriate inferences about objects' color properties. Imagine now that Lynceus is presented with a red_{273} megagon (in good lighting conditions etc.). It would be strange to say that Lynceus cannot perceptually experience the red_{273} megagon, but can only *think* about it, on the grounds that his perceptual acuity and processing power is so much better than ours. Perceptual acuity helps us see more, not less! But if Lynceus possesses the concepts for the properties he perceives, then it is not *in the nature* of perception to outstrip the perceiving subject's conceptual capacities. Crucially, there is no reason to expect that someone like Lynceus be unable to distinguish his perceptual experiences of red_{273} megagons from his thoughts thereabout. So he must pick up on some first-personally manifest difference between them that has nothing to do with whether concepts are used to pick out the properties of being red_{273} and being a megagon. Upshot: it is a merely contingent fact about *us* that we fail to possess concepts for many features we can perceive, a fact that tells us nothing about the nature of perception as such.

For the same reason, it is implausible to draw the perception/cognition distinction directly in terms of what often *motivates* the conceptual/nonconceptual approach, namely, the notion that perceptual experience is informationally rich whereas thought is informationally sparse. It is true that a typical perceptual experience of a yellow cornfield contains much detail that goes beyond yellowness and corniness, whereas a thought to the effect that the cornfield is yellow, or that there is a yellow cornfield about, does not. But again, this seems merely contingent: a Laplacean demon may have extremely detailed thoughts, while a perceptual experience of a yellow Ganzfeld boasts a rather sparse content – yet there is obviously something different, manifest to the first-person perspective, between such states and their perceptual and cognitive counterparts. In addition, a richness difference would be a difference in degree, not a difference in kind; whereas the experiential difference between thought and perception seems to be rather a difference in kind. Perception does not seem to be cut of the same cloth as thought but just have much more of that cloth, so to speak. This calls for some *categorical* distinction between the two.

There are other possible content approaches to the perception/cognition divide. As noted, I provide a more indulging discussion of the approach in Kriegel Ms. Here I will rest content with what I have said so far against the content approach, moving now to consider the attitudinal approach.

4 The Attitudinal Strategy: Background

If the contents of perception and thought could be shown to always allow a perfect match, then the first-personally manifest difference between perceptual experience and thought would be proven not to be a content difference. But it would still not follow that it is not an intentional or representational difference. For it might be a difference at the level of *attitude*. So-called impure intentionalists (Chalmers 2004, Crane 2009) have held that some phenomenal features of conscious states pertain to attitude. Since phenomenal features are paradigmatically first-personally manifest, this has the potential to yield a satisfactory approach to our problem.

Obviously, construals of attitude in terms of functional role will raise the aforementioned problems concerning introspectibility. And such construals have certainly been prominent in philosophy of mind. When we construe the difference between belief that *p* and desire that *p* in terms of whether *p* is in the 'belief box' or the 'desire box,' the background picture is the kind of boxes-and-arrows psychology that characterizes mental phenomena in terms of their functional role within the overall economy of mental life.

But functional role is not the only way to construe attitudes. Thus, it is sometimes said that whereas belief that *p* represents *p as obtaining*, desire that *p* represents *p* rather *as good*, in some suitably generic sense of 'good.' Thus, Dennis Stampe writes:

> [W]hile the belief and the desire that *p* have the same propositional content and represent the same state of affairs, there is a difference in the *way* it is represented in the two states of mind. In belief it is represented *as obtaining*, whereas in desire, it is represented as a state of affairs *the obtaining of which would be good*. This *modal* difference explains why a desire that *p* is a reason to make it true that *p*, while the belief that *p* is not. (Stampe 1987: 355; see also Tenenbaum 2009: 96)

Note that this way of describing attitudinal facts casts them as clearly *representational facts*: they are facts about belief's and desire's distinctive manners of representing their content. To be sure, the content of the belief that the weather will be nice in April is simply <the weather will be nice in April>, not <the state of affairs of the weather being nice in April obtains>. But this is precisely why the information about the state of affairs' obtaining is encoded into the very attitude of believing, not the belief's content. We may put this by saying that the belief *represents-as-obtaining* the content <the weather will be nice in April>. In the expression 'represents-as-obtaining,' the 'as obtaining' denotes a modification of the representation relation; it does not qualify that which is being represented.

The desire that the weather will be nice in April, meanwhile, *represents-as-good* the same content. Representing-as-obtaining and representing-as-good are the distinctive attitudinal characters of belief and desire, on this approach, and they are *representational* facts about belief and desire – though not facts about the representational *contents* of belief and desire.

This way of thinking of 'attitudinal character' may open the door to an attitudinal account of the first-personally manifest difference between perceptual experiences and occurrent thoughts: given a perception and a thought that represent the same state of affairs (e.g., a rectangle's being red), the task is to identify the right P and T, such that the perception represent-as-P the rectangle's being red whereas the thought represents-as-T the rectangle's being red.

One general objection to this approach is that the nature of properties of the form representing-as-F is unclear. However, while this is a legitimate complaint, I will set it aside here and argue that there are more specific problems with concrete attitudinal accounts of the perception/cognition divide.

We have already mentioned in passing that the attitudinal character of belief is probably that of representing-as-obtaining. Plausibly, belief that *p* shares its attitudinal character with such mental states as judging that *p* and thinking that *p*. For all of these, it is natural to assign representing-as-obtaining as attitudinal character.[1] If we could identify a *different* attitudinal character associated with perceptual experience, this would give us an initial account of the first-personally manifest perception/cognition divide.

One suggestion might be that perceiving a red rectangle is a matter of representing-as-*existent*, or representing-as-*real*, the red rectangle. Perhaps this would be claimed to explain, for example, the phenomenal contrast between perceptual experience of a red rectangle and (sensory) imagination of a qualitatively indistinguishable rectangle: while the former represents-as-*real* the rectangle, the latter represents-as-*unreal* the rectangle (Kriegel 2015a). If this is right, then the cognition/perception divide is to be drawn in terms of representing-as-obtaining vs. representing-as-real/existent.

---

[1] I think we can say this with confidence without a full account of the exact relationship between beliefs, judgments, and thoughts(-that). Some hold that beliefs are never conscious, and thoughts are their conscious counterparts. Others hold that beliefs are dispositional states and thoughts are occurrent manifestations of them. Both these models, and others, suggest that if belief that the triangle is red represents-as-obtaining the triangle's being red, then thinking that the rectangle is red does so as well. There is an additional question of what *distinguishes* these mental states, but let us set it aside here; the answer may not have to do with attitudinal character.

But this account of the perceptual attitude is doubly problematic. While representing-as-existent is suitable for perception *of concrete particulars*, but arguably, there is also such a thing as perception *of states of affairs*. Looking in the relevant direction, you see not only the rectangle but also its redness, indeed you see the redness as being *the rectangle's* redness. Presumably, perception of states of affairs would involve representing-as-obtaining rather than representing-as-existent, insofar as the mode of being of states of affairs is that of obtaining rather than existing. To that extent, the proposed suggestion could only work against the background of the assumption that states of affairs cannot be perceived. But this is an odd commitment to take on board from the outset. (Note well: if we think that the difference in mode of being between concrete particulars and states of affairs is terminological and insubstantive, then the proposed account would itself become insubstantive, since what it proposes is distinguishing thought and perception in terms of representing-as-obtaining vs. representing-as-existent.)

The general point is: for at least some thought about a's being F (e.g., some rectangle's being red), there is a corresponding perceptual experience of a's being F. In that scenario, the two mental states represent the very same entity, indeed both represent-*as-obtaining* that entity; yet there is intuitively a stark difference between seeing and thinking of some rectangle's being red, one that should be introspectively manifest to any subject capable of having either state.

5 Spatiotemporal Attitudinal Characters

A mental state's attitudinal character goes with a specific kind of correctness conditions. If p obtains but is bad, for example, then it is correct to represent-as-obtaining p but not to represent-as-good p, hence to believe but not to desire that p. If instead p is good but fails to obtain, then it is correct to desire but not to believe that p. This creates an interesting problem for ascribing to perceptual experiences the attitudinal character of representing-as-obtaining. Imagine you are hallucinating a rectangle, and hallucinate its being red. Imagine further, however, that, as it happens, there really is an intrinsically indistinguishable red rectangle, but on Mars rather than in front of you; or perhaps there really was such a rectangle exactly where you hallucinate it to be, but a year ago rather than now. Intuitively, your perceptual experience is *incorrect*. That is, its correctness conditions are not met. But if the experience's attitudinal character were that of representing-as-obtaining, then given that the Martian rectangle *exists*, and the state of affairs of its being red obtains (as does, at least by eternalist lights, the yesteryear state of affairs of the rectangle's being red), the experience would be correct. Thus the proposed account returns the wrong result that your hallucination is correct. This is what we might call *thought-experimental disconfirmation* of the account.

This problem may inspire the following suggestion: the difference between a perceptual experience of and a thought about some rectangle's being red is that the perceptual experience represents-as-obtaining-*here-and-now* the rectangle's being red, whereas the thought represents-as-obtaining-*simpliciter* the rectangle's being red. Here the distinction is between two ways of representing-as-obtaining a state of affairs: an unrestrictive way characteristic of thought, and a spatiotemporally restrictive way we find in perception. We might say that perception exhibits an *egocentric* form of representing-as-obtaining, whereas thought exhibits an *allocentric* form of representing-as-obtaining.

The advantage of this account is that it neutralizes the Martian and yesteryear red rectangles, and allows the perception of states of affairs. Having a perceptual experience as of a rectangle's being red is incorrect, on the account, if no rectangle is red *here and now*. If a rectangle is red on Mars, but not here, then the experience's correctness conditions are not met; if a rectangle *was* red here, but a year ago rather than now, then again they are not met. Meanwhile, representing-as-obtaining-here-and-now is a kind of representing-as-obtaining, so can target states of affairs unproblematically.

For this account to enjoy any plausibility, however, it is important *not* to understand 'represents-as-obtaining-here-and-now' as denoting a species, or determinate, and 'represents-as-obtaining-*simpliciter*' as denoting the corresponding genus or determinable. For perception is not a species or determinate of thought. Accordingly, we should interpret the expression 'represents-as-obtaining-*simpliciter*' rather as meaning something like 'represents-as-obtaining-*somewhere-and-somewhen*'; and consider that both representing-as-obtaining-here-and-now and representing-as-obtaining-somewhere-and-somewhen are species of representing-as-obtaining. So understood, perception and thought can be seen to employ *incompatible* attitudinal characters – an egocentric one and an allocentric one.

To increase the account's plausibility, we might also consider weakening its characterization of the attitudinal character distinctive of perception as follows: instead of claiming that it is the character of representing-as-obtaining-here-and-now, one would put forward the disjunctive thesis that it is either representing-as-*obtaining*-here-and-now or representing-as-*existing*-here-and-now. The point of this is to allow perceptual experiences not only of states of affairs but also of individual objects. (Obviously, if we have positive reasons to think that perception of individual objects is impossible, at least outside the context of their being constituents of states of affairs, then this move is unnecessary.)

Even with these provisos in place, however, the 'here-and-now' account faces a number of difficulties. Note, to start, that the account does nothing to rule out the possibility of *thoughts* about the here and now. Fortunately: we can clearly *think* that there is a brown dog *here and now*. It is just that the here-and-now information conveyed by such a thought must be conveyed as part of its *content*. That is, while the perception of a rectangle's being red represents-as-obtaining-here-and-now the state of affairs of the rectangle's being red, the thought that the rectangle is red here and now represents-as-obtaining-*simpliciter* the (different) state of affairs of the rectangle's being red here and now. The first problem with the account under consideration is that it is far from clear that the difference between *content-based* here-and-now information and *attitudinally encoded* here-and-now information is first-personally manifest. Introspection alone does not seem to reveal whether a mental state represents x as F or represents-as-F x.

Another problem with the account under consideration is that it seems to get the extension wrong in certain cases. Someone may sit in a sports bar in Tokyo and watch a live broadcast of a basketball game taking place in Chicago. It is natural to say that this person is *seeing the game* – even though the game is not 'here' relative to this Tokyo-bound individual. Likewise, a person who looks at Mars through a telescope is naturally described as *seeing Mars*. But Mars is not here, unless we are so generous about what counts as here that we risk eroding the very distinction between 'here' and 'somewhere.'

These considerations raise a deeper problem for the here-and-now account: the account owes us some elucidation of what 'here' and 'now' actually *mean*, and while it is natural to elucidate 'now' as meaning something like 'simultaneous with the perceptual experience,' it is less clear what 'here' means. We can say that it means 'compresent with the experience,' or 'collocated with the experience,' but this is a vague and relative notion. We can imagine a superman with 'bionic vision' who, sitting among us, can see specific pebbles on the moon. What would count as 'here' for him would presumably be very different from what would count as 'here' for us. And this raises the specter of an even more extraordinary superwoman, one who can see to the end of the cosmos. Although the cosmos has been expanding very rapidly during the upward fifteen billion years since the Big Bang, the distances involved are still small potatoes for this superwoman. Such is the extraordinary strength of her vision, that only in another five billion years she would start losing the ability to see certain faraway objects!

(Note: it is of no consequence to this reasoning if this superwoman is nomologically impossible – so long as she is metaphysically possible.) It seems that even for our superwoman there is a difference between *thinking about* a specific grain of dust on Jupiter and *seeing* that grain of dust. And yet there is no part of the cosmos that is so far away from her that it could no longer be said to be 'here' relative to her – since all parts of the cosmos are *visible* (as well as audible etc.) to her.

In response, it might be suggested that we simply drop the 'here' part of the account, adopting the view that perception's distinctive attitudinal character is simply that of representing-as-now. Given an understanding of 'now' in terms of simultaneity, this would amount to the following view: a perceptual experience represents-as-obtaining-simultaneously-with-its-own-occurrence the relevant state of affairs. Observe that this makes perceptual experience (but not thought) *token-reflexive*: each token perceptual experience figures in its own correctness conditions. However, the token-reflexivity here is due to perception's attitude rather than content (compare Kriegel 2015b), and is a temporal rather than causal kind of token-reflexivity (contrast Searle 1983 Ch.2).

Unfortunately, there are many problems with this account. First, it brings back to life the problem of the Martian rectangle's being red, which obtains now but fails to render your hallucinations of a rectangle's being red correct or appropriate.

Secondly, there may be temporal analogs of the spatial problems generated by live broadcast and telescopic perception. A person may miss a concert due to a traffic jam, but be fortunate enough to still hear the concert, thanks to a recording played on the radio the next day. Another person, watching the sunset over the Mediterranean, sees the sun where and how it was almost eight minutes earlier (given that the sun lies almost eight light minutes away from Earth).

Most importantly, perhaps, the difference between representing-as-obtaining-now and representing-as-obtaining-*simpliciter* just does not seem like the right difference for capturing the distinctively 'in the flesh' character of perception. All those vivid colors and sounds directly present to the perceiving mind, but not to the thinking intellect, do not seem to have much to do with the simultaneity between perceptual experience and its objects. (I am using 'object' here widely, to cover any type of entity that may be targeted by a mental state, not only concrete particulars.)

A final objection, which applies to both the hic-et-nunc account and the nunc-only account, has to do with so-called veridical hallucinations. Suppose that, under the influence of effective hallucinogens, you have a visual experience as of a butterfly fluttering exactly one meter straight ahead; and that while you are having this hallucination, a butterfly just like the one you are hallucinating enters the room and starts fluttering just where, and how, your hallucinated butterfly 'does' (Searle 1983 Ch.2). This seems like an incorrect visual experience. However, both the hic-et-nunc and nunc-only accounts return the result that the experience is a correct one. For the experience represents-as-obtaining(-here-and)-now the state of affairs of such-and-such a butterfly fluttering so-and-thus, and indeed such-and-such a butterfly is fluttering so-and-thus here and now.

6 Causal Attitudinal Character

On the face of it, the problem with the real butterfly before you is that it is in no way responsible for the experience you are having. For a perceptual experience to be correct, this suggests, it must be *caused by* the perceived object. Accordingly, we might opt for an account of perception that focuses not on a here-and-now condition on perceived objects, but on a *causal responsibility* condition – still understood as a condition imposed by the attitude, not content (see Recanati 2007 Ch.17). On this view, while the thought that the rectangle is red represents-as-obtaining the rectangle's being red, the corresponding perception represents-as-obtaining-and-causing-that-very-perception the rectangle's being red. On the plausible assumption that a state of affairs cannot cause something without obtaining, we might just say: the perception represents-as-causing-that-very-perception. Again we have a token-reflexive picture of perception (but not thought) here, and again this token-reflexivity is attitudinally grounded. It is just that here the token-reflexivity is causal rather than (spatio)temporal.

This causal-attitudinal account has several advantages. First, the notion of causality invoked here is easier to pin down than the notion of compresence or collocation suggested by 'here.'[2] Secondly, the causal account captures the pretheoretically appealing idea that perception is stimulus-dependent in a way thought is not (Beck 2018, Phillips forthcoming), but instead of involving the *actual* stimulus-dependence of perceptual states – something which is presumably not *introspectively* manifest – it adduces an attitudinally imposed stimulus-dependence condition on perceptual objects. Thirdly, and most importantly, the

---

[2] There are of course rather involved philosophical debates on the deep nature of causality (see under: counterfactual dependence, production, manipulation). But those will presumably be more or less extensionally equivalent. So the notion of causality invoked here can be neutral between them.

causal account handles elegantly the cases of telescopic and live-broadcast perceptions (as well as the recording and sunset cases): in all these cases, although the perceived object is not in any useful sense here (or now), it is still causally responsible for the occurrence of the perceptual experience. For example, Mars is *causally responsible* for our stargazer's experience as she looks through the telescope; the basketball game in Chicago causes the broadcast, which in turn causes the Tokyo barfly's experience as she watches TV (and causation is transitive).

Of all the accounts we have considered in this paper, this one appears to me the most defensible. Nonetheless, there are three considerations that make me suspect it is ultimately unsatisfactory as well.

Perhaps the most important is the following. We have noted that a difference in temporal token-reflexivity between perception and thought does not seem to be the right difference to capture the special presence to the perceiving mind of colors, sounds, motion, and so on. But it is unclear in what way *causal* token-reflexivity fares any better here. To see the point, consider that thoughts too can represent their objects as causing them, they just have to do so via their content rather than attitude. It is perfectly possible to think *that* the rectangle is red *and* its being red causes one's thought to that effect. Obviously, however, such content-based causal token-reflexivity does *not* make the thought-about red rectangle present to one 'in the flesh.' So it must be part of the story that there is something special about imposing a causal token-reflexivity requirement *through the attitude* that makes the red rectangle 'present' in the relevant way. It is hard to see why this should be so.

In addition, some work would need to be done to show that the difference between attitude-based and content-based causal token-reflexivity is really first-personally manifest.

Finally, I think the causal token-reflexivity account is on reflection ill motivated. The account is motivated chiefly by the case of veridical hallucinations. Something is *wrong* with these, clearly, but the diagnosis of what is wrong is up for debate. The account under consideration offers us a way to capture theoretically what is wrong with them, by casting them as representationally defective. When the token-reflexivity is built into the content, as in Searle 1983, the relevant experiences turn out to be *non*-veridical; when it is built into the attitude, as in Recanati 2007, they turn out to be incorrect (or inappropriate). But on both accounts, they turn out to be 'representationally defective.' However, an alternative diagnosis would cast them rather as *epistemically* defective. To see why, compare the case of so-called veridical hallucination with the following doxastic case. Suppose a person believes that there is a God, not on the basis of any evidence however, but on the basis of her emotional needs, or because she was brainwashed as a child. And suppose further that, as it happens, there really is a God. This person's belief lacks some of the epistemic qualities highlighted by reliabilists (e.g., it is not *sensitive*: the person's having the belief does not counterfactually depend on the belief's truth). More fundamentally, God's existence is causally unrelated to the person's *having* the belief in God. Nonetheless, intuitively the belief is still true, and therefore correct/appropriate. To cast the belief as incorrect and perhaps false is to mistake the belief's *intentional* character with its *epistemic* character. It should be possible to reach true beliefs by sheer luck! By the same token, I suggest, it should be possible to luck into correct perceptual experiences. And this is just what happens with veridical hallucinations: they are hallucinations because, despite representing the world the way it really is, they are not linked to the world in a way that would bestow on them the relevant positive epistemic property; but they are veridical nonetheless, precisely because they present the world as being a certain way, and the world really is that way. To cast veridical hallucinations as incorrect is thus to confuse their intentional and epistemic profiles.

If the epistemic diagnosis of what is wrong with so-called veridical hallucinations is more accurate than the representational diagnosis, then the causal token-reflexivity account of the intentional character of perceptual experience is unmotivated. As we have seen, it is also far from clear that the account really delivers a first-personally manifest difference between perception and thought, let alone the kind of difference suited for capturing the distinctive 'in the flesh' character of perception.

With this I close my discussion of attitudinal approaches to the (first-personally manifest) perception/cognition divide. As with the content approaches, I do not pretend to have considered all possible options. For example, I have not considered the notion that perception represents-as-*appearing*-to-obtain whereas thought represents-as-*really*-obtaining (was this Aristotle's view?). I have not considered it essentially because here too the difference does not seem to me to be the right kind to capture the distinctive in-the-flesh character of perception. But the view, as others too, surely deserves treatment in a fully comprehensive examination of possible attitudinal theories of the perception/cognition divide. Still, it is significant that, having considered several prominent or natural content-based and attitudinal approaches, we have found all of them wanting.

7 Conclusion: What Next?

If none of the aforementioned accounts of the first-personally manifest difference between perception and thought is satisfactory, what are our options?

One option is to look for a *non-intentional* difference. We have considered only accounts adverting to intentional character, understood as including both content and attitude. But this leaves open the possibility of an account that adverts neither to content nor to attitude. Perceptual and cognitive states have many other properties, after all. The old idea that perception is experienced as passive or 'receptive' whereas thought is experienced as active or 'spontaneous' may be one example. That particular idea is problematic, as the tendency of thoughts to involve a feeling of agency or authorship may not be a universal characteristic – think of cases where a thought 'pops up' in your mind unbidden ('I haven't paid yet the phone bill!'). But some other altogether non-intentional characteristic(s) may prove essential to perception or thought.

Recall, however, that our concern here is with finding a *first-personally manifest* difference between perception and thought. So what we would need to find are first-personally manifest properties of perception and thought that go beyond its content properties and attitudinal properties. As noted in §2, however, this may run afoul of an extremely modest version of transparency, one which allows not only content but also attitudinal intentional properties to be manifest to introspection. Thus an immediate challenge to the non-intentionalist strategy is to show that perceptual experiences and thoughts *have* altogether non-intentional properties that are first-personally manifest.

A related option is to retain an intentionalist approach to thought but adopt naïve realism about perceptual experience. In this approach, the difference between perceptual experience and thought is that perceptual experience is constitutively related to the perceived object, so that the perceived object is in fact a constituent of the perceptual experience, whereas none of this is true of thought. This thought seems particularly well suited to capturing the distinctive in-the-flesh character of perceptual experience.

The obvious problem for this approach is that envatted brains with mental lives phenomenally indistinguishable from ours will perforce experience the exact same in-the-flesh-ness, despite lacking any kind of constitutive connection to external objects being perceived. What this brings out is that we need to distinguish the *experience* of in-the-flesh encounter with an object, which is a first-personally manifest feature of perceptual states, from *actual* encounter with an object, which goes beyond what is manifest to the subject's first-person perspective. What the naïve realist has to show is that she is well positioned to capture not only actual encounter but also the experience of encounter; for it is only the latter that seems relevant to drawing the first-personally manifest perception/cognition divide.

A third option we have is to *deny the datum*. In a particularly radical form, this would be to deny that there is a substantive distinction between perception and cognition. In a milder form, it might be granted that there is such a distinction, but denied that it has a first-personally manifest dimension. If no account of the first-personally manifest difference between perception and thought seems to work, this may rationalize revisiting the starting assumption that there *is* such a difference. Perhaps *only* the third-person subpersonal difference in underlying functional architecture is psychologically real.

The immediate challenge for this approach is to explain, or explain away, the fact (as I claim it is) that naïve subjects with no insight into the functional architecture underlying their mental life can still – reliably, effortlessly, immediately, and confidently – determine whether certain of their mental states are perceptual or intellectual.

A fourth option is to go *primitivist* about the first-personally manifest difference between perception and thought. Here the idea is to accept, however reluctantly, that we cannot give an informative account of the perception/cognition divide as it appears to the first-person perspective. Some mental states exhibit a phenomenology of perceptuality, some exhibit a phenomenology of cognitivity, each of us is first-personally acquainted with the difference between the two, and that is all there is to it – there is no way to 'get underneath' the difference between perceptuality and cognitivity and anchor it in more fundamental or more specific features of conscious experiences. This sort of no-theory theory is unsatisfactory in an obvious way, as it leaves us with no deeper (personal-level) understanding of a basic bright line in our mental life. Nonetheless we may have to learn to live with this sorry predicament. The pill may be made less bitter if the primitivism at the level of the first-personally manifest is married with a substantive subpersonal story about the mechanisms underlying the instantiation of these sui generis features of perceptuality and cognitivity.

A final option, of course, is that there is some content or attitudinal difference between perception and thought, subtler than any considered here, that does anchor the first-personally manifest difference between the two. We just have to employ greater invention to identify it than I have managed here. For my part, I am rooting for this 'hidden factor' option – while preparing myself for life as a primitivist.[3]

References

Beck, Jacob (2018): 'Marking the Perception-Cognition Boundary: The Criterion of Stimulus-Dependence.' In: *Australasian Journal of Philosophy*, 96, pp. 319–334.

Chalmers, David J. (2004): 'The Representational Character of Experience'. In: Brian Leiter (Ed.): *The Future of Philosophy*. Oxford and New York: Oxford University Press.

Crane, Tim (2009): 'Intentionalism'. In: Ansgar Beckermann and Brian McLaughlin (Eds.): *Oxford Handbook of Philosophy of Mind*. Oxford: Oxford University Press

Dretske, Fred I. (1995): *Naturalizing the Mind*. Cambridge MA: MIT Press.

Fodor, Jerry A. (1983): *The Modularity of Mind*. Cambridge, MA: MIT Press.

Harman, Gilbert (1990): 'The Intrinsic Quality of Experience'. In: *Philosophical Perspectives* 4, pp. 31–52.

Heck, Richard G. (2000):'Nonconceptual Content and the Space of Reasons'. In: *Philosophical Review* 109, pp. 483–523.

Kriegel, Uriah (2015a): 'Perception and Imagination: A Sartrean Account'. In: Sofia Miguens, Gerhard Preyer, and Clara Bravo Morando (Eds.): *Prereflective Consciousness: Sartre and Contemporary Philosophy of Mind*. London: Routledge.

Kriegel, Uriah (2015b): 'Experiencing the Present'. In: *Analysis* 75, pp. 407–413.

Kriegel, Uriah (Forthcoming): 'Phenomenal Intentionality and the Perception/Cognition Divide'. In: Arthur Sullivan (Ed.): *Sensations, Thoughts, and Language: Essays in Honor of Brian Loar*. London and New York: Routledge

Phillips, Ben (2019): 'The Shifting Border Between Perception and Cognition'. In: *Noûs* 53(2), pp. 316–346.

Pitt, David (2004): 'The phenomenology of cognition; Or What is it like to think that P?' In: *Philosophy and Phenomenological Research* 69, pp. 1–36.

Recanati, François (2007): *Perspectival Thought*. Oxford and New York: Oxford University Press.

Siewert, Charles (1998): *The Significance of Consciousness*. Princeton: Princeton University Press.

---

3 This work was supported by the French National Research Agency's grant ANR-17-EURE-0017, as well as by grant 675415 of the European Union's Horizon 2020 Research and Innovation program. For comments on a previous draft, I am grateful to Géraldine Carranante, Ben Phillips, and Enrico Terrone. I have also benefited from presenting the paper at Columbia University, the University of Luxembourg, the University of Milan, and conferences on phenomenal intentionality (Paris, March 2017), perceptual awareness (Paris, July 2017), and perception and observation (Kirchberg, Austria, August 2017); I am grateful to the audiences there, in particular Davide Bordini, Géraldine Carranante, Marian David, Arnaud Dewalque, Anna Giustina, Gabriel Greenberg, Martin Lin, Tricia Magalotti, Olivier Massin, John Morrison, Takuya Niikawa, Elisa Paganini, Jesse Prinz, Susanna Schellenberg, Enrico Terrone, Alfredo Tomasetta, and Nick Young.

Stalnaker, Robert (1998): 'What Might Nonconceptual Content Be?' In: *Philosophical Issues 9*, pp. 339–352.
Stampe, D. (1987): 'The Authority of Desire'. In: *Philosophical Review* 96, pp. 335–381.
Tenenbaum, S. (2009): 'Knowing the Good and Knowing What One is Doing.' *Canadian Journal of Philosophy* 39 (supplement), pp. 91–117.

Pierre Jacob
Why Verbal Understanding is Unlikely to be an Extended Form of Perception

Abstract: Millikan's teleosemantic approach constitutes a powerful framework for what evolutionary biologists call an "ultimate" (as opposed to a "proximate") explanation of the continued reproduction and proliferation of intentional conventional linguistic signs. It thereby aims at explaining the stability of human verbal ostensive communication. This evolutionary approach needs to be complemented by particular proximate psychological mechanisms. Millikan rejects the kind of mentalistic psychological mechanisms posited by the Gricean tradition in pragmatics, according to which the task of the hearer is to recognize the speaker's intentions. Instead Millikan has persistently argued that verbal understanding is an extended form of perception. My paper is a critical assessment of Millikan's thesis that verbal understanding of a speaker's utterance enables the hearer to perceive whatever the speaker's utterance is about. I argue that Millikan's thesis rests on two fundamental assumptions. First, Millikan's notion of extended perception of the world is itself an extension of her semiotic approach according to which the process of ordinary perception (in humans and non-human animals) involves the translation of what she calls locally recurrent natural signs. Secondly, Millikan argues that only humans have the further capacity for flexible extended perception of what she calls detached signs, as opposed to attached signs or location-reflexive signs.

Keywords: Attached (vs. detached) sign, direct (vs. derived) proper function, natural sign, intentional representation, extended perception, translation, flexible perception

In this paper, I want to probe Millikan's provocative thesis that human verbal understanding is just direct perception of the world being spoken of by the speaker. As she puts it repeatedly, "during normal conversation, it is not language that is most directly perceived by the hearer, but rather the world that is perceived through language" (Millikan 2012) or else "understanding language is simply another form of sensory perception of the world" (Millikan 2004).[1] Of

---
1 "During *Normal* conversation, it is not language that is most directly perceived by the hearer but rather the world that is most directly perceived through language. Distal states of affairs are

course, not all human speech acts are *descriptive* or have a mind-to-world direction of fit. If a speaker utters a *prescriptive* request for action with a world-to-mind direction of fit, then the hearer's task is to form a desire or an intention to perform an action, not a perceptual task. Millikan's perception thesis narrowly construed should be restricted to a hearer's verbal understanding of descriptive utterances. In what follows, I will only consider a recipient's response to a speaker's testimony at the expense of a speaker's request.

Millikan's thesis directly challenges three *mentalistic* tenets of the approach to human ostensive communicative actions inspired by the Gricean pragmatic tradition:[2]

(1) A hearer's first task is to recognize the speaker's *communicative* intention, namely her higher-order intention that he recognizes her lower-order informative intention that she wants him (she intends to cause him) to acquire a new belief.[3]

(2) Secondly, the hearer's contribution to the success of the speaker's act involves two separable psychological steps (or processes): *understanding* and *acceptance*. The hearer understands the speaker's utterance if (and only if) he fulfills the speaker's communicative intention and thereby recognizes her informative intention. To accept the speaker's testimony is to further fulfill the speaker's informative intention, which the hearer will do only if he takes the speaker to be sufficiently trustworthy or competent on the topic at hand. Thus, the hearer's understanding of the speaker's testimony is *not* a sufficient condition for his acceptance, i.e. for his endorsement of the new belief that the speaker wishes him to accept.[4]

(3) Thirdly, the interests of the speaker and the hearer of a speaker's testimony overlap to a large extent, but they are *not* strictly identical. Furthermore, they clearly face different options. While the speaker faces the basic choice between speaking *truthfully* or not, the hearer faces the basic choice between *trusting* the speaker or not (cf. Sperber 2001). The speaker, whose main goal is to cause the hearer to accept a new belief, will be generally better off if her hearer trusts her rather than not, whether she is truthful or not. But the hearer, whose goal is

---

perceived through speech sounds just as they may be perceived, for example, through the medium of structured light during normal vision." (Millikan 2005: 207).
2 In the following, I spell out the mentalistic assumptions characteristic of the Gricean tradition in the terminology of Sperber and Wilson's (1986) relevance-based framework. For Grice's own views, see Grice (1957, 1969, 1989).
3 For purposes of clarification, I refer to the speaker as 'she' and the hearer as 'he'.
4 This second ingredient of what I broadly call the Gricean tradition in pragmatics is spelled out in greater detail in Sperber et al. (2010).

to receive truthful information from the speaker, will be generally better off if the speaker is truthful rather than not, whether he is trustful or not.

I accept the mentalistic framework inspired by the Gricean pragmatic tradition and I wish to examine Millikan's challenge.

In the language of evolutionary biologists and philosophers of biology,[5] Millikan's thesis that verbal understanding of a speaker's testimony consists in the hearer's perception of what the speaker's testimony is about can be construed as a purported *proximal* psychological mechanism, whereby human recipients contribute to the success of human verbal communicative actions. Millikan's proposal is that a speaker's communicative action is successful if and only if the hearer can *perceive* the state of affairs the speaker is talking about. This purported proximal mechanism is meant to supplement Millikan's teleosemantic approach to the continued proliferation of conventional linguistic signs, which in turn can be construed as a potential *ultimate* explanation of human verbal communication. In my opinion, Millikan's teleosemantic account of the re-production of conventional linguistic signs is one of the outstanding landmarks of naturalistic philosophy of mind and language of our time. It purports to answer such questions as: Why do humans engage in verbal communication at all? What are the biological and/or the cultural functions of human verbal communication? What selectional advantages does the capacity to perform verbal communicative actions confer to human agents and recipients?

This paper is comprised of four main sections followed by a short concluding section. In the first section, I briefly sketch Millikan's insightful teleosemantic account of the continued proliferation of human conventional linguistic signs, which in turn stands as the background to her thesis that verbal understanding is an extended perception of the world. As I explain in the second section, much of Millikan's argument for the view that verbal understanding is an extended form of perception involves three crucial assumptions, the first of which is that both ordinary perception and verbal communication rest on processes of *translation*. Her second assumption is that the relation of being a *natural sign* of something is *transitive*. Her third heterodox assumption is that, not just intentional signs but natural signs as well, may have *constituent structure*. In the third and penultimate section, I examine her responses to an obvious pair of objections to her thesis that verbal understanding is an extended form of perception. Finally, in the fourth main section, I examine a pair of arguments used by Millikan to undermine the mentalistic picture of verbal understanding inherited from the Gricean tradition.

---

[5] Cf. Scott-Philipps et al. (2011).

1

Millikan's teleosemantic account rests on her adoption of a cooperative sender-receiver framework, according to which a sign can be an *intentional representation R* only if it is a *relatum* in a three-place relation involving two cooperative mechanisms, one of which (the *sender* mechanism) produces R, and the other of which (the *receiver* mechanism) consumes R.[6] The producer and the consumer mechanisms are further taken to have co-evolved so that the *Normal* conditions for the performance of the *proper* function of one are also parts of the *Normal* conditions for the performance of the *proper* function of the other.[7] On this approach, an intentional representation R has a *derived* function, i.e. derivative from the respective proper functions of the sender (or producer) and the receiver (or consumer). In short, the derived function of an *inner* (*mental*) intentional representation is to achieve the *coordination* between the producer and the consumer mechanisms when they are located *within* the brain of a *single* organism. The derived function of a *linguistic* (*conventional*) intentional representation is to achieve the *coordination* between the producer and the consumer mechanisms when they are located in the brains of *distinct* organisms (Millikan 1984; 2004). Although the derived function of an intentional representation (whether mental or conventional) is to achieve the coordination between the producer and the consumer mechanisms, Millikan takes the content of an intentional representation to reflect primarily the needs of the consumer at the expense of the capacities of the producer.[8]

Arguably there are two relevant differences between the proliferation of inner (mental or non-conventional) representations and the proliferation of linguistic (conventional or non-mental) representations, the first of which is perhaps underestimated by Millikan. First, only speakers and hearers (i.e. distinct individuals with distinct brains) face the choice between being respectively truthful or not and trustful or not. A producer mechanism does not face the choice between deceiving or not the consumer mechanism if and when the two mechanisms belong to a single brain. Nor does the consumer mechanism face the choice between trusting or not the producer mechanism when both mechanisms belong to a single brain.

---

6 As I will explain soon, unlike an intentional representation, a natural sign is not a *relatum* of a three-place relation.
7 On Millikan's (1984) etiological approach, the proper function of a mechanism is one of its selected effects.
8 Cf. Neander (1995; 2017), Pietroski (1992), Jacob (1997) for critical discussions.

Secondly, Millikan has offered a powerful two-tiered naturalistic account of *conventional patterns*, which of course does not apply to the reproduction of inner mental representations. A pattern is conventional if it is the output of a continued process of reproduction (or replication). What makes it conventional (and to a large extent arbitrary) is that the reproduction is "owing to precedent determined by historical accident, rather than owing to properties that make them more intrinsically serviceable than other forms would have been" (Millikan 2005: 188).

Given this framework, conventional linguistic forms turn out to be tools or *memes* in Dawkins's (1976) sense: they have been selected and have accordingly been reproduced because they serve *coordinating* functions between a sender (the speaker) and a receiver (the addressee), whose interests overlap.[9] But like any other tool, in addition to the *direct memetic* (or 'stabilizing') proper function of its *type*, which explains the continued reproduction of its tokens, a particular *token* of some public language form may also have a *derived* function or purpose, i.e. derived from the purpose (or intention) of the speaker who produced it at a particular place and time. The direct or memetic purpose and the speaker's derived purpose may or not coincide (cf. Millikan 1984, 2004, 2005 and Jacob, 2016 for further discussion).

2

Millikan's thesis that understanding another's testimony is an extended perception of the world is itself an extension of her *semiotic* approach to the ordinary perception of what she calls *locally recurrent natural signs* (Millikan 2004). Unlike an inner or a conventional representation, a natural sign lacks a *function*. It carries information about what it is reliably correlated with within a highly restricted (i.e. *local*) spatial and temporal *domain*. For example, in one geographical area, tracks made by quail are locally recurrent natural signs of quail. But in a neighboring spatial area, visually indistinguishable tracks made by pheasants are locally recurrent natural signs of pheasants, not of quail (Millikan 2004: 32). Locally recurrent natural signs also carry information over limited *temporal* domains. For example, the position of the needle of a gas gauge in a particular car is a locally recurrent natural sign of the amount of gas in the same car "from the time it is initially installed until the time it first breaks down" (Millikan 2004: 51).

---

9 As I noticed earlier, overlapping interests are not identical interests.

Ordinary visual perception is the process of interpreting locally recurrent natural signs by *tracking* their informational source through a semiotic cascade generated by the *transitivity* of the relation of being a locally recurrent natural sign of a state of affairs over a restricted spatial and temporal domain. For example, retinal patterns on a human (or non-human) eye can be locally recurrent natural signs of distinctive shapes, colors and textures at a location, which in turn are locally recurrent natural signs of earlier fresh goose droppings at this location, which in turn are locally recurrent natural signs of geese flying over this location at the time of the droppings, which in turn are locally recurrent natural signs of upcoming Winter into this location (Millikan 2004: 54–55). As Millikan (2004: 55) puts it, in virtue of its transitivity, the natural sign relation can be "interpreted at any level of embedding or at more than one level of embedding."

On Millikan's teleosemantic account of the proliferation of conventional linguistic signs, the task of the hearer of a verbal communicative act is parallel to a perceptual task to the following extent: the hearer must *track* the correct memetic family (lineage or type) to which a particular conventional sign (e.g. 'clear' or 'the dog') belongs. Thus, both ordinary perception and verbal understanding turn out to be processes of *translation* (*not inference*). While the former is guided by the capacity to track the spatial and temporal domain over which a natural sign can be deemed to be locally recurrent, the latter is guided by the capacity to track the spatial and temporal domain of the memetic family or type of conventional signs to which a particular token belongs.

Arguably Millikan's assumption that perception is a process of *translation* sheds light on her puzzling statement that "the perceptual and cognitive systems of every animal are deeply dependent on the local information found both in the environment and within the organism itself. Without information there could not be any intentional signs or intentional information" (Millikan 2004: 32). This is puzzling in light of Millikan's repeated rejection of informational teleosemantics on the grounds that it could not be the etiological function of an intentional representation to carry information (cf. Millikan 1989a; 2004; 2013). What she has in mind is not that it is the function of an intentional representation to carry information, but instead that it is the task of perception (and cognition) to build intentional representations by means of translating natural signs.

Clearly, whether translation counts as an inferential process or not, the idea of translation paradigmatically applies to the interpretive process whereby a structured sequence of *conventional* signs uttered by a speaker for the purpose of expressing her thought is being mapped onto another structured sequence of conventional signs. The types of conventional signs used by the speaker belong to one natural language. The complex meaning of the sequence of conventional signs uttered by the speaker depends on the meanings of its constituents and the syntactic rules of combination. The speaker uses the complex compositional meaning of the sequence of conventional signs from her language to express the propositional content of her thought. The translation process maps the sequence of conventional signs used by the speaker onto a sequence of distinct conventional signs whose types belong to a different natural language. The mapping is expected to preserve enough of the complex meaning of the sequence of conventional signs used by the speaker so that the translation can count as an alternative expression of the propositional content of the speaker's thought. Upon understanding the complex meaning of the translation of the speaker's initial utterance, the hearer is likely to entertain a thought that appropriately resembles the speaker's own thought.

Millikan construes Normal verbal communication between a sender and a receiver as a two-step translation process involving one and the same structured sequence of conventional signs produced by the speaker. First, the speaker translates her belief into a sentential conventional sign, which is uttered by the speaker. Secondly, the hearer (who speaks the same language as the speaker) translates the content of the speaker's utterance of conventional signs into his own new belief. By proposing to assimilate perceptual processes to processes of translation, Millikan means to reject an *inferential* model of perception, whereby she seems to assimilate inferential processes and processes of deliberate reasoning from explicitly entertained premises to conclusions via explicitly known rules of inference. As Millikan (2017: 186) puts it, "reading a sign does not require understanding why it corresponds to its signified but only how it corresponds."

In other words, when Millikan (2017: 185–186) rejects the inferential approach to visual perception, what she really objects to is the claim that successful visual perception requires the ability to understand and reason explicitly about the causal mechanisms of visual processing: the light being reflected by a distal stimulus hits the retina where it is converted into electrical impulses. Visual information is carried from the retina through the optic nerve to various dedicated areas of the visual cortex, where it is ultimately transformed into a unified visual percept. Thus, it looks as if Millikan takes this perceptual process to be a process of translation, not inference, because she assimilates inference to conscious reasoning (or even theorizing) from explicit premises to explicit conclusion via explicitly known rules of inference. In a sense, Millikan's skeptical attitude with respect to the role of inferential (or computational) processes in perceptual psychology goes hand in hand with her skeptical attitude with respect to the role assigned to mindreading (i.e. the attribution of mental states) in verbal understanding by the neo-Gricean tradition.

Millikan takes perceptual processes to be translation processes unfolding within a single brain and mapping locally recurrent natural signs onto inner mental representations of what the signs are signs of. Not only does the transitivity of the relation of being a natural sign of something makes natural signs interpretable at any level of embedding, but locally recurrent natural signs also have an unexpected feature that Millikan takes to support her thesis that perceptual processes are translation processes. While natural signs (unlike conventional signs) have no function, like conventional linguistic signs, they have *constituent structure*: they exhibit significant variables (or determinables). For example, if tracks in the mud are locally recurrent natural signs, then not only will they be locally recurrent natural signs of e.g. pheasants (not quail), at a determinate location and a determinate time, but the size of the tracks will further be a natural sign of the size of the pheasants that caused them and the distance between the tracks will also be a natural sign of how fast the pheasants were moving (Millikan, 2004: 47–48). Mapping chains of locally recurrent natural signs onto a perceptual representation of some distal state of affairs may involve filling in a determinate value for the significant variables or determinables that are parts of the constituent structure of the natural signs. By stressing the constituent structure of natural signs, Millikan intends to close much of the gap between natural signs and intentional representations and to hereby pave the way for her semiotic thesis that both perception and verbal understanding are processes of translation.

On Millikan's approach, an organism's sensory (e.g. visual) mechanisms could not efficiently translate deeply embedded natural signs into ordinary perceptual intentional representations of distal states of affairs unless the organism were able to reliably *track* the spatial and temporal domains over which the relevant natural signs are indeed locally recurrent natural signs of what they are signs of. What makes tracking these spatial and temporal domains reliable in turn is the invariance of the physical, chemical and neurophysiological laws governing the sensory mechanisms of animals (including humans) endowed with visual perceptual capacities on the surface of the Earth. Light is reflected by the surface of objects onto the retina of the perceiver's eye where the energy of photons is converted into electrical impulses, which are carried to the visual cortex via the optic nerve and so on. Thus, the capacity to reliably track the spatial and temporal domains of natural signs relevant for ordinary perception is likely to be built in the brains of humans and non-human animals by biological evolution by natural selection.

Tracking the memetic family of types of linguistic signs, however, is an entirely different matter. Humans at the surface of the Earth speak different languages comprised of different memetic families of conventional signs that are not natural signs. According to Millikan, linguistic signs have proliferated via processes of *conventional* re-production. Thus, the reliability of the human capacity to track the memetic family of types of conventional signs cannot be taken to reflect the invariance of deep physical, chemical and neurophysiological laws. What Chomsky (2000) calls "universal grammar" may have been built into the brains of humans by evolution by natural selection, but what Millikan calls the ability to track the memetic families of types of conventional signs used by different human groups in different geographical areas cannot be built into the brains of humans as a result of evolution by natural selection. For example, tacit knowledge of universal grammar by itself cannot provide children with the knowledge that what is called "dog" in one language community is called "chien" in the next.

3

On the face of it, Millikan's thesis that verbal understanding is a form of perception faces an obvious pair of objections. There is a major difference between the content of a visual representation of some fact or actual state of affairs and the verbal understanding of the content of another's testimony describing the very same state of affairs. At an appropriate distance and in good lighting conditions, one could not see a cup resting on a table without also seeing its shape, size, color, texture, orientation and spatial location with respect to the table, to any other object resting on the table, and especially to oneself. Moreover, the spatial relation of a perceived object to the self is likely to change over time as one moves with respect to the object and it must be updated especially if one uses the visual information for acting on a seen object. However, if an addressee located in the next room understands the content of the speaker's utterance of the sentence "There is a cup on the table," he may endorse the belief that there is a cup on some salient table without having any definite expectation about the shape, size, color, texture, orientation and spatial location of the cup with respect to the table or anything else, and especially himself. Nor does the addressee need update his understanding of what the speaker said about there being a cup in the next room as he moves around inside his own room.

Furthermore, unlike the content of an individual's perceptual experience, the content of an agent's testimony is not restricted to objects, events and properties with which the hearer stands in a direct causal relation. It is precisely a distinctive purpose of human testimony that it enables a hearer to learn about things that are *not* directly observable by him because either he is not at the right place at the right time or else he simply could not perceive them at all. For example, numerals can, but numbers cannot, be perceived at all. A speaker's testimony can be about e.g. abstract numbers or theoretical entities posited by scientific theories. Numbers are not observable at all. Theoretical entities posited by scientific theories (e.g. quarks) can only be indirectly tested through long chains of reasoning and complex measuring instruments, neither of which might be accessible to the hearer. The point here is that some topics that are not open to an individual's perceptual experience can be conveyed by a speaker's verbal testimony for the benefit of a recipient.

One interesting way Millikan proposes to bridge the gap between perception and verbal understanding is by arguing that humans have a distinctive capacity for flexibly *perceiving* things and events *without* encoding their direct spatial and temporal relations to the self, i.e. to the spatial and temporal location of the perceiver's own body. Millikan (2017) deals with this putatively distinctive human capacity for flexible extended perception in terms of what she insightfully calls "detached signs," as opposed to "attached signs" or "location-reflexive" signs. Ordinary perception (available to both humans and non-human animals) involves the translation of "location-reflexive" (or attached) natural signs into intentional representations, where the attached or location-reflexive signs carry information about the spatial and temporal relation between what they are signs of and the perceiver's own spatial and temporal context. For example, when the surface of an object reflects light onto an animal's retina, the retinal image is a location-reflexive or attached sign: it carries information about the relation between the spatial and temporal location of the reflecting surface and the spatial and temporal location of the perceiver's own body. This is why an inner perceptual representation that is mapped by translation from a chain of attached (or location-reflexive) signs can be a representation of an *affordance*, i.e. why it can guide the perceiver's *action*.

By contrast, on Millikan's (2017) account, flexible perception by verbal understanding is typically translation of *detached* signs, where a detached natural sign does *not* carry information about the relation between the spatial and temporal location of the things or event that the sign is about and the spatial and temporal location of the hearer's own body. Millikan (2004, 2017) further argues that there are cases of typically human flexible perception other than verbal understanding, whereby humans can perceive events by translating detached signs that fail to carry information about the relation between the spatial and temporal location of the signed events and the spatial and temporal location of the perceiver's own body.

For example, humans can visually derive information from the image of an object that is reflected by a mirror. Light reflected from the mirror to the perceiver's eye directly carries information about the relation between the spatial location of the mirror and that of the perceiver's body. But it carries only *indirect* information about the relation between the spatial location of the reflected object and that of the perceiver's body. Nonetheless a human agent can learn to use information derived from an image of herself reflected by a mirror for the purpose of combing her hair or shaving (Millikan 2004: 122). A human driver can also learn to use information derived from an image of a blue car that was initially seen through the rear-view mirror of her car to re-identify the blue car that just passed her own car on the left and is now moving in front of her own car (Millikan 2004: 132). Similarly, humans can visually extract from a photograph the mental representation that there once existed sometime and somewhere or other e.g. an apple looking so and so, while the relation between the spatial and temporal location of the apple and the spatial and temporal location of the perceiver's body is not encoded at all by the photograph.[10] Humans can also see events depicted on a television screen: the relation between the spatial and temporal location of the depicted events and that of the perceiver's body is not encoded either by the pictures on television. In a nutshell, images reflected by a mirror, photographs and pictures on television are what Millikan (2017) calls *detached* natural signs, not attached (or location-reflexive) natural signs.

Millikan takes it that ordinary perception, which is based on the capacity to track the relevant domains of *attached* signs, is shared by human and non-human animals. However, Millikan (2004: 122–124) strongly suggests that unlike ordinary perception, flexible extended perception is like verbal understanding in being uniquely human: both extended perception and verbal understanding rest not only on "a marvellous flexibility in accommodating new semantic functions, but also [on] the capacity mentally to represent… information that does not include the relations to you of the things the information is about." Millikan (2004: 122–124) further assumes that flexible perception, including verbal understanding, is no more a mentalistic task than ordinary perception is. In other word, the hearer of another's testimony must be able in *all* cases to track the relevant appropriate memetic family of the type of conventional linguistic signs used by the speaker *without* representing any of her psychological states.

---

10 Arguably, non-human animals can discriminate pictures of living entities from pictures of non-living entities, but Millikan would likely argue that this is part of ordinary non-flexible perception.

The challenges for this assumption seem, however, quite overwhelming. For example, Millikan claims that there are many ways to flexibly recognize rain, all of which are perceptual. There is a way that rain feels on one's skin and a way it looks when one sees it fall out the window. There are distinct ways it sounds when falling either on the rooftop or on the ground. There is still another way it sounds when falling on English speakers: 'It's raining!' But this last statement cannot be strictly true for this English sentence could clearly be used by an English speaker who is talking about a raining event somewhere in the universe where no English speaker is present. Similarly, it is quite unclear how a hearer could understand what a speaker means by her utterance of the definite description 'the dog' or some universally quantified sentence e.g. 'Everybody is asleep' or the possessive 'John's book' without representing the speaker's beliefs and intentions. Only if the speaker's recipient is part of a narrow circle of well-known relatives (e.g. one's spouse and/or children) could the contextual common ground for such utterances be taken for granted by the speaker without requiring the hearer to represent the speaker's beliefs and intentions. However, human verbal communication is not so restricted to a narrow circle of in-group members. A speaker's use of these linguistic forms (possessives, definite descriptions or universally quantified expressions) is not restricted to a narrow circle of in-group recipients. When a speaker uses such expressions, her recipients may be foreigners and members of cultural communities far different from hers. It is likely that in many cases, a recipient could only make sense of the speaker's utterance involving such expressions if he was able to retrieve the speaker's communicative intention. Thus, Millikan's picture of verbal understanding seems to rest on a *parochial* view of human verbal communication, where common grounds between a speaker and a recipient can be taken for granted.

4

I now turn to two separate arguments used by Millikan to undermine the neo-Gricean mentalistic picture of human verbal communication, the first of which rests on what it takes to achieve a task of flexible extended perception. Her second argument rests on findings from the experimental psychological (especially developmental) investigation of false-belief understanding.

Millikan's first argument rests on a questionable analogy between ordinary and flexible extended perception. One stage of a rabbit's ordinary visual perception of a fox involves the processing of retinal images of the fox, which are natural signs of the fox. Seeing the fox, however, does not require the rabbit to form intentional representations *of* her retinal images. Millikan makes a somewhat similar claim about flexible extended perception. For example, she claims that the successful use of binoculars or televisions and the extraction of abstract information from photographs do not require a flexible perceiver to "understand the innards" of binoculars, televisions or cameras. She concludes that a hearer need not either represent the speaker's beliefs and intentions in order to perceive what the speaker's testimony is about.

There is arguably a stronger and a weaker version of Millikan's premise that successful flexible extended perception does not require any understanding of the relevant visual tools. On the stronger reading, Millikan denies that an individual must have scientific knowledge of the natural laws underlying its construction for successfully enrolling a visual tool in a task of flexible extended perception. On the weaker reading, she denies that an individual could successfully enroll a visual tool (such as binoculars) *without* making *any* assumption or other about them.

While I agree with Millikan's rejection of the stronger claim, I don't think that she can easily reject the weaker claim. A human perceiver could hardly calibrate the bilateral acuity of her binoculars, switch her television on or extract relevant abstract information from a photograph without making some assumptions or other about the function of binoculars, televisions and cameras. For example, a human perceiver could not switch a TV on unless he or she assumed that it is an electrical appliance. He or she could not calibrate the acuity of binoculars unless he or she assumed that it is an optical device whose function is to enhance the visual perception of objects at a distance. Nor could he or she extract from a photograph the information that there once existed sometime and somewhere or other an apple looking so and so unless he or she knew something about how a camera can be used to take a picture of an apple. Arguably, what the weaker claim highlights is that flexible extended perception rests on human cultural learning, which in turn rests on human mindreading capacities, in accordance with the neo-Gricean mentalistic picture of human verbal communication. If so, then acceptance of the weaker claim about flexible extended perception would seem to vindicate, not to undermine, the neo-Gricean picture.

Finally, I turn to Millikan's repeated thesis that experimental developmental evidence shows that young children reach proficiency in tasks of verbal communication much before they are able to read others' minds, which she also takes to undermine the neo-Gricean assumptions. As she nicely puts it, "the infants learn what kitties look like in various postures, what they feel like, the sounds they make and what they sound like through language. There seems no reason why this last would require that the infants employ a theory of mind or concepts of mental states." As Millikan recognizes, human adults and older children have the reflective resources needed to represent a speaker's mental states. However, if infants don't need to represent a speaker's beliefs and intentions, then neither does an adult hearer in a normal conversation. Only if the normal flow of verbal communicative information breaks down and the meaning of the speaker's utterance is puzzling for one reason or another must an adult hearer reflect upon the speaker's beliefs and intentions.

Millikan's two-pronged strategy against the neo-Gricean picture rests on two intimately related assumptions about mindreading (or theory of mind), the first of which is that the experimental developmental investigation of false-belief understanding has established that young children still lack a theory of mind (or the ability to read others' minds) when they are already proficient in tasks of verbal communication. Her second related assumption is that for human adults, mindreading is a demanding (or effortful) cognitive task, which requires reflective thinking.

Taking Millikan's second assumption first, it may seem as if what makes her diagnosis that mindreading, unlike perception (including extended flexible perception), is effortful for human adults is that mindreading has a *metarepresentational* architecture. However, the fact that the best scientific (or proto-scientific) characterization of some cognitive capacity has a complex structure does not entail that the use of this cognitive capacity is effortful. For example, the best current scientific characterization of human vision is complex. But this does not entail that visual processing is effortful for humans.

In fact, some empirical evidence suggests that human adults perform tasks of mindreading, if not automatically, at least spontaneously. For example, in the context of a psychophysical study, Kovács (2010) and colleagues found evidence that adults automatically compute the content of a protagonist's false expectation about the presence of a ball behind an occluder on a computer screen, even if the protagonist is a blue smurf and his expectation is irrelevant to their psychophysical task, which is to press a button as fast as possible if they detect the ball behind the occluder. In a (2010) study on Level 1 visual perspective-taking in adults, Samson and colleagues also found that participants automatically compute the number of dots that an avatar can see on the walls of a room, as shown by the fact that they were slower to respond and made more mistakes about the number of dots that *they themselves* could see, if the number of dots that they could see was different from, rather than equal to, the number of dots that the avatar could see.

I finally turn to Millikan's appeal to the developmental investigation of false-belief understanding in human childhood. Millikan appeals to evidence based on explicit change-of-location false-belief tasks, in which participants who know the location of a mistaken agent's toy are asked to predict where the mistaken agent will look for her toy. This evidence shows that most 3-year-olds fail and incorrectly point to the toy's actual location. Not until they are 4,5 years of age do most children pass these tests (cf. Wimmer and Perner 1983; Baron Cohen et al. 1985; Wellman et al. 2001). However, much recent evidence based on implicit change-of-location false-belief tasks, in which participants are not asked any question, also shows that preverbal infants expect an agent to act in accordance with the content of her (true or false) belief (Onishi and Baillargeon 2005; Baillargeon et al. 2010). The puzzle is: how to reconcile these discrepant findings?

So far as I am aware, everything Millikan has written on this topic suggests that she accepts the assumption that only success on explicit false-belief tasks can demonstrate false-belief understanding. I think, however, that this assumption is demonstrably false. If only success on explicit false-belief tasks could demonstrate false-belief understanding, then conversely false-belief understanding should be sufficient for success on explicit false-belief tasks. But this is clearly not true: a monolingual adult Russian speaker might fail to answer the canonical English sentence "Where will Sally look for her toy?" and still be fully able to ascribe false beliefs to others.

Suppose on the contrary that we take the findings based on implicit false-belief tests at face value as showing that preverbal infants can represent the contents of others' false beliefs. The question then is: why do most 3-year-olds find explicit false-belief tasks so challenging? Here is one possible pragmatic answer. In order to correctly *predict* where a mistaken agent will look for her toy, it is sufficient to know where she last placed it. In typical explicit false-belief tasks, however, participants are provided by the experimenter with much information about the relocation of the toy and its actual location, which is strictly irrelevant to the prediction task. Preschoolers should simply ignore this irrelevant information and focus on the only relevant information, namely where the mistaken agent last placed her toy. But they are likely to find it difficult to ignore irrelevant information provided by an adult that looks like a benevolent and competent speaker. Thus, one possible way preschoolers might make this irrelevant information relevant is if they turn the experimenter's *prediction* question "Where *will* Sally look for her toy?" into the *normative* question "Where *should* Sally look for her toy?" If they do, then the correct answer to this normative question is the toy's actual location, which is exactly where most preschoolers point in answer to the experimenter's question. If this explanation of the findings based on explicit false-belief tasks is on the right track, then preschoolers' failure in these tasks is consistent with preschoolers' (and also infants') ability to ascribe false belief to others.

5

As I have argued in the first section of this paper, Millikan's major teleosemantic contribution has been to open an entirely novel approach to the continued reproduction of intentional conventional public-language signs. This contribution is best construed as a potential *ultimate* explanation of human ostensive verbal communication, i.e. as an answer to the question "Why do humans engage in ostensive verbal communicative actions?" Millikan's teleosemantic approach to the proliferation of intentional conventional public-language signs must be supplemented by some *proximate* psychological mechanism. Millikan proposes that the basic proximate psychological mechanism whereby a human recipient understands and accepts an agent's verbal testimony is *perception*.

As I have argued in the second section of this paper, Millikan makes three fundamental assumptions about ordinary perception. She assumes that ordinary perception is a process of translation mapping natural signs onto intentional representations. She further assumes that the relation of being a natural sign is transitive. Finally, she assumes that natural signs, just like intentional representations, also have constituent structure. In a nutshell, Millikan's semiotic approach to perception paves the way for her thesis that verbal understanding is an extended form of perception.

As I have explained in the third section of the paper, in response to obvious objections to her thesis that verbal understanding is ordinary perception, Millikan argues that humans have a distinctive capacity for flexible extended perception that enables them to flexibly perceive things and events (e.g. on a television screen) without encoding their direct spatial and temporal relations to the self, i.e. to the spatial and temporal location of the perceiver's own body. In particular, Millikan claims that successful flexible extended perception through visual tools (e.g. binoculars) does not require the flexible perceiver to have any understanding of the relevant visual tools. By parity of reasoning, she further claims that the success of verbal understanding does not either require a recipient to recognize a speaker's informative intention, let alone to fulfill it.

Finally, Millikan has repeatedly argued against the mentalistic Gricean approach to human verbal understanding that the developmental evidence about false-belief understanding shows that human children can reach proficiency in tasks of verbal communication much before they are able to read others' minds. In the fourth section of the paper, I have distinguished between a stronger and a weaker reading of her claim that successful flexible extended perception through visual tools (e.g. binoculars) does not require the flexible perceiver to have any understanding of the relevant visual tools. I have argued that she cannot easily reject the weaker version of the claim that successful flexible perception requires some assumptions about the function of visual tools. I have also taken issue with Millikan's interpretation of the developmental evidence about false-belief understanding and I have argued that the failure of preschoolers on explicit false-belief tasks is compatible with their mentalistic capacity to attribute false beliefs to others. My overall conclusion is that verbal understanding of a speaker's testimony is unlikely to be an extended form of perception of what the speaker is talking about.[11]

References

Baillargeon, Renée, Scott, R. M., & He, Z. (2010): "False-belief understanding in infants." In: *Trends in Cognitive Sciences*, 14, pp. 110–118.
Baron-Cohen, S., Leslie, A., & Frith, U. (1985): "Does the autistic child have a 'theory of mind?'" In: *Cognition*, 21 (37), p. 46.
Chomsky, Noam (2000): *New Horizons in the Study of Language and Mind*. Cambridge: Cambridge University Press.
Dawkins, Richard (1976): *The Selfish Gene*. Oxford: Oxford University Press.
Grice, H.Paul (1957): "Meaning". In: *Philosophical Review*, 66, pp. 377–388.
Grice, H.Paul (1969): "Utterer's meaning and intentions". In: *The Philosophical Review*, 78(2), pp. 147–177.
Grice, H.Paul (1989): *Studies in the Way of Words*. Cambridge, MA: Harvard University Press.
Jacob, Pierre (1997): *What Minds Can Do*. Cambridge: Cambridge University Press.
Jacob, Pierre (2016): "Millikan's teleosemantics and communicative agency". In: Metzinger, T. & Windt, J.M. (Eds.): *Open Mind, Philosophy and the Mind Sciences in the 21st Century*. Cambridge, MA: MIT Press, pp. 767–788.
Kovács, Ágnes, Téglás, E., and Endress, A. (2010): "The social sense: Susceptibility to others' beliefs in human infants and adults". In: *Science*, 330, pp. 1830–1834.

---

[11] I am grateful to Christoph Limbeck-Lilienau for inviting me to the 40th International Wittgenstein Symposium "The Philosophy of Perception and Observation" as well as for his comments on a draft of this paper, and to members of the audience for their questions and comments. I acknowledge support from the European Research Council (ERC) under the European Union Seventh Programme (FP/2007-2013)/ERC Grant 609819.

Millikan, Ruth G. (1984): *Language, Thought and Other Biological Categories*. Cambridge, MMA: MIT Press.
Millikan, Ruth G. (1989a): "Biosemantics". In: *The Journal of Philosophy*, 86, pp. 281–197.
Millikan, Ruth G. (1989b): "In defense of proper functions". In: *Philosophy of Science*, 56, 2, pp. 288–302.
Millikan, Ruth G. (1990): "Seismograph reading for 'Explaining Behavior.'" In. *Philosophy and Phenomenological Research*, 50 (4), pp. 807–812.
Millikan, Ruth G. (1995) : "Pushmi-Pullyu Representations". In: *Philosophical Perspectives*, 9, pp. 185–200.
Millikan, Ruth G. (1998): "Conventions made simple". in: *The Journal of Philosophy*, 95(4), pp. 161–180.
Millikan, Ruth G. (2000): *On Clear and Confused Ideas*. Cambridge: Cambridge University Press.
Millikan, Ruth G. (2004): *Varieties of Meaning*. Cambridge, MA: MIT Press.
Millikan, Ruth G. (2005): *Language: A Biological Model*. Oxford: Oxford University Press.
Millikan, Ruth G. (2010): "Learning language". https://production.wordpress.uconn.edu/philosophy/wp-content/uploads/sites/365/2014/02/Spracherwerb-Learning-Language.pdf
Millikan, Ruth G. (2013): "Reply to Neander". In: Ryder, D., Kingsbury, J. & Williford, K. (Eds.): *Millikan and her Critics*. Oxford: Blackwell.
Millikan, Ruth G. (2017): *Beyond Concepts, Unicepts, Language, and Natural Information*. Oxford: Oxford University Press.
Neander, Karen (1995): "Misrepresenting and Malfunctioning". In: *Philosophical Studies*, 79, pp. 109–141.
Neander, Karen (2017): *A Mark of the Mental, in Defense of Informational Semantics*. Cambridge, MA: MIT Press.
Onishi, Kristine, Baillargeon, Renée (2005): "Do 15-Month-Old Infants Understand False Beliefs? " In: *Science* 308 (5719), pp. 255–258.
Pietroski, Paul (1992): "Intentionality and Teleological Error". In: *Pacific Philosophical Quarterly*, 73(3), pp. 267–282.
Samson, D., Apperly, I., Braithwaite, J. J., Andrews, B. J. and Bodley Scott, S. E. (2010) : "Seeing it their way: Evidence for rapid and involuntary computation of what other people see". In: *Journal of Experimental Psychology: Human Perception and Performance*, 36(5), pp. 1255–1266.
Scott-Philipps, Tom C., Dickins, T.E., & West, S.A. (2011): "Evolutionary theory and the ultimate-proximate distinction in the human behavioral sciences". In: *Perspectives on Psychological Science*, 6(1),pp. 38–47.
Sperber, Dan (2001): "An evolutionary perspective on testimony and argumentation". In: *Philosophical Topics*, 29, pp. 401–413.
Sperber, Dan, & Wilson, Deirdre (1986): *Relevance, Communication and Cognition*. Cambridge, MA: Harvard University Press.
Sperber, Dan, Clément, F., Heintz, C., Mascaro, O., Mercier, H., Origgi, G., and Wilson, D. (2010): "Epistemic Vigilance". In: *Mind and Language*, 25(4), pp. 359–393.
Wellman, Henry M., Cross, D., & Watson, J. (2001): "Meta-analysis of theory of mind development: the truth about false belief". In: *Child Development*, 72, pp. 655–684.
Wimmer, Heinz, & Perner, Josef (1983): "Beliefs about beliefs: representation and constraining function of wrong beliefs in young children's understanding of deception". In: *Cognition*, 13 (1), pp. 103–128.

Mark Eli Kalderon
Sound and Image

Abstract: We hear sounds, and their sources, and their audible qualities. Sounds and their sources are essentially dynamic entities, not wholly present at any given moment, but unfolding through their temporal interval. Sounds and their sources, essentially dynamic entities, are the bearers or *susbtrata* of audible qualities. Audible qualities are qualities essentially sustained by activity. The only bearers of audible qualities present in auditory experience are essentially dynamic entities. Bodies are not, in this sense, essentially dynamic entities and so are not present in our auditory experience. Though absent in auditory experience, we may, nonetheless, attend to bodies in audition, when an audible sound-generating event in which they participate presents a dynamic aural image of them.

Keywords: Audition, sound, source of sound, audible qualities, body

Suppose that the bearers of audible qualities, such as pitch and timbre, are essentially dynamic entities such as events or processes, not wholly present at any moment, but unfolding through time. If we suppose further that only audible qualities and their bearers are present in auditory experience then a puzzle arises. For we seem to be able to attend to bodies in audition. We can listen to an animal's approach, say. But bodies are not essentially dynamic entities, nor do they inhere in such. But only audible qualities and their bearers are present in auditory experience. Which means that bodies, being neither, are absent. But if bodies are absent in auditory experience how may we attend to them in audition?

I believe that this puzzle may be resolved without rejecting the central claim upon which it rests, that the bearers of audible qualities are essentially dynamic entities. In the first part of this talk, I try to motivate that claim. I do so both directly and indirectly by criticizing an alternative. I end with a speculative resolution of our puzzle.

What are the bearers of audible qualities? What are the kinds of things in which such qualities inhere? I claim that the bearers of audible qualities are essentially dynamic entities such as events, as opposed to bodies. If the bearers of audible qualities are essentially dynamic entities, then audible qualities are qualities essentially sustained by activity.

Consider the following analogy: Colors are spatially extended, at least in the sense of being instanced only by spatially extended things. We can imagine smaller and smaller things being colored, but we cannot conceive of a thing without extension exhibiting color. Audible qualities are temporally extended, at least in the sense of being instanced only by temporally extended things. We can imagine hearing briefer and briefer occurrences of pitch, but we cannot conceive of a thing without duration exhibiting pitch. The temporal dimension of the bearers of audible qualities is not exhausted by their having a beginning and end, sounds have a distinctive way of being in time. Like events, at least as the three-dimensionalist conceives of them, sounds unfold in time. Unlike states that are wholly present whenever they obtain, sounds are not wholly present at every moment of their sounding. They are spread over the interval of time through which they unfold.

We hear sounds, and their sources, but we also hear their audible qualities. Audible qualities, such as pitch, are not essentially dynamic entities unfolding through time. Rather, their mode of being is more akin to the mode of being of states. Nevertheless, sounds and their sources, conceived as essentially dynamic entities, not wholly present at any moment, but unfolding through time, are bearers of audible qualities. That the bearer of an audible quality is an essentially dynamic entity is manifest in the conditions under which that quality may be instantiated. There is no instantaneous pitch since there is nothing instantaneous to instantiate it. For pitch to exist, it must persist over time. And that is because audible qualities are qualities essentially sustained by activity. The audible qualities of a sound will vary and extinguish as the sound's activity varies and extinguishes. Sounds without audible qualities would be inaudible, but audible qualities without sound would simply not be (or at least, those audible qualities that modify sounds, as opposed to other audible *substrata*, such as sources). Audible qualities, while not essentially dynamic entities, are qualities that audible activity gives rise to. They are qualities of audible events or processes or phases of these.

Kulvicki (2008) has argued that the bearers of audible qualities are not events but bodies. Like Aristotle, *De anima* 2 11 422b31–32, he accepts that an audible quality has a bearer. Being quality instances, they must inhere in something upon which they existentially and ontologically depend. However, unlike Aristotle, he denies that sound is the bearer of audible qualities. Audible qualities inhere in bodies but these bodies are not themselves sounds. Rather, they are ordinary material substances. Instead, sounds are the audible qualities that inhere in these bodies and are manifest in their audible activity. Thus, like Pasnau (1999) and Leddington (2014), Kulvicki endorses a broadly Lockean metaphysics that identifies sounds with audible qualities. However, it is not the Lockean metaphysics of sound that is our present focus, but whether bodies are bearers of audible qualities.

Bodies have resonant modes determined by their material structure. Because of their resonant modes, bodies are disposed to vibrate at certain natural frequencies when "thwacked". According to Kulvicki, the sound a body has, an audible quality of it, is the stable disposition to vibrate when thwacked. Just as the energy of the illuminant reveals the colors of things to sight, the energy of thwacking reveals the sounds of things to hearing. And just as bodies retain their colors even when unilluminated, bodies retain their sound even when unthwacked. The stable disposition to vibrate when thwacked is a sound that a body has. Not every sound that a thing makes is a sound that a thing has. Stereo speakers when thwacked produce a dull thud, but when played they can make a wide variety of sounds.

Why think that sounds are qualities of material bodies that are associated with their natural frequencies? Kulvicki provides an argument from perceptual constancy that, while not conclusive, is meant to speak strongly in favor of his view. Kulvicki draws our attention to an interesting feature of speech perception, our ability to recognize voices. A speaker's voice will vary in pitch, timbre, and so on, as they speak. And yet despite these variable auditory appearances, we seem to be presented with a constant voice in our experience of their speech. This is due, in part, to the resonant modes of the special parts of the speaker involved in speech production, such as their vocal cords and nasal cavities. And this is just the kind of auditory constancy one would expect if the sounds that we hear were stable dispositions of objects to vibrate when thwacked.

We have our voices. At least as we ordinarily speak. But do we have them, as well, in Kulvicki's extraordinary sense? Or are they sounds that we make but do not have? The sound of a stereo speaker playing is a sound that it makes but does not have. I suspect that a person's voice is more like the sound of a stereo speaker playing than the sound that it makes when thwacked. Through a series of unfortunate events, I have first hand experience of what I sound like when thwacked. I can attest it sounds nothing like my voice. Like a stereo speaker, I produce a dull thud when thwacked. When playing, a stereo speaker produces the sounds that it makes but does not have by an internal activity driving the vibration of special parts of it. When speaking, I produce the sounds that I do by an internal activity driving the vibration of special parts of myself. Are these not sounds that I make but do not have? If the sound of my voice is something that I make but do not have, then its being the constant element in an auditory experience provides no reason for thinking that sounds are stable dispositions to vibrate when thwacked since these are sounds that bodies were meant to have rather than make.

Kulvicki is right to emphasize that auditory experience can disclose the stable dispositions of bodies to vibrate at their natural frequencies and so auditorily manifest, albeit partially and imperfectly, material properties of those bodies. But in hearing that, is what we hear a sound or its source? Suppose that we hear sounds and their sources. And suppose that the sources that we hear are sound-generating events. A body's participation, if not the body itself, is part of the audible structure of that event. And those aspects of the body relevant to its participation in the event are reflected, partially and imperfectly, in its audible structure. Stable dispositions of bodies to vibrate at their natural frequencies given their resonant modes as determined by their material structure are aspects of bodies relevant to their participation in audible activities, such as being thwacked. When Dr Johnson, outside of the church in Harwich, kicked the stone, his boot rebounding despite its mighty force, the stone was well and truly thwacked. Doubtless, it could be heard as well as felt. And Dr Johnston could hear, as well as feel, that it was a stone, and not a log, that he was kicking. He could hear his boot kicking a stone as opposed to a log because of their distinctive timbre. Their different resonant modes are relevant to their participation in audible activities such as being kicked. Kulvicki is right to emphasize that auditory experience can disclose the stable dispositions of bodies to vibrate at their natural frequencies and so auditorily manifest, albeit partially and imperfectly, material properties of these bodies. But he was wrong to suggest that this requires bodies to be the bearers of audible qualities.

We hear sounds and their sources. These are essentially dynamic entities, not wholly present at any given moment, but unfolding through time, or so I claim. Sounds and their sources have audible qualities, qualities essentially sustained by activity. Are sounds and their sources, as well as their audible qualities, really all that we can hear?

According to Broad (1952: 4), we ordinarily speak of hearing bodies. So when Big Ben strikes the time, and is in earshot, we may say that we can hear Big Ben. However, Broad concedes little in acknowledging this point of usage since he also observes that it takes but a little pressure to convince "the plainest of plain men" that "hearing Big Ben" is shorthand for hearing the striking of Big Ben. If we accept Broad's suggestion, then we only hear Big Ben insofar as it is a participant in a sound-generating event or process. And when we do, what we strictly speaking hear is Big Ben's striking and not Big Ben, that is, not the body, but an event the body participates in. We hear not the body in a condition of activity, but the activity of the body.

Allow me to engage in speculation about a hypothetical sense in which we may be said to hear bodies consistent with the principle, if true, that audition only presents bearers of audible qualities with the distinctive temporal mode of being of events or processes.

Both sounds and the sources that we hear are like events in that they are not wholly present at every moment of their occurrence. Perhaps this is a general feature of the bearers of audible qualities present in audition. Perhaps for a bearer of an audible quality to be present in auditory experience it must have a particular temporal mode of being, it must unfold through time. This would preclude, by their very nature, entities such as bodies from being present in auditory experience. First, by hypothesis, bodies lack the requisite temporal mode of being of bearers of audible qualities. And second, bodies do not inhere in essentially dynamic entities the way that audible qualities do. But if what is present in auditory experience is either essentially dynamic or an audible quality that the essentially dynamic *substratum* gives rise to, then bodies are not present in auditory experience. Earlier we noted Broad's helpful suggestion that perhaps "hearing Big Ben" is elliptical for hearing Big Ben's striking.

As plausible as this may be, a worry may still persist. One of the uses to which audition may be put is to track a body's progress through the natural environment. We can listen to an animal's approach, say. And it might be thought that we are attending to the animal in audition in listening to them. Moreover, it might seem insufficient for the body to be attended to that an event in which that body participates is present in auditory experience. Not every part of a visible body is seen, so why assume that every participant of an audible event is heard? How can we listen out for bodies even though they are precluded from being present in auditory experience?

Bodies may not be present in auditory experience, but perhaps they figure in auditory experience in another way, if not as the intentional object of experience, then something very much like it. Bodies are, on the speculative hypothesis that we are entertaining, not present in auditory experience. Thus bodies are absent in auditory experience. And yet we can attend to bodies in audition. How could this be?

Aristotle uses this kind of puzzle or aporia about presence in absence to argue for, as we might put it, the intentional character of memory (*De memoria et reminiscentia* 450a25–451a1, for discussion see Sorabji 2004). The Peripatetic response to the puzzle is to straightforwardly accept the claim of absence and reinterpret what purported to be a presentation instead as a kind of re-presentation. When one remembers Corsicus in his absence one contemplates a *phantasma* caused by a previous perception of Corsicus and one conceives of the *phantasma* as a likeness and reminder of Corsicus as he was perceived. How might the Peripatetic response, so abstractly described, be applied to the perceptual case of attending to bodies in audition?

Perhaps what is present in auditory experience may constitute a natural image of what is absent. That is, perhaps we can understand hearing the body's sound-generating activity as providing the listener with a dynamic aural image of the body otherwise absent in audition. It is an image, indeed, as I have suggested, a natural image, like a fossil or a footprint. But unlike paradigmatic images it is not a visual image but an aural image. And while visual images are static, aural images, if such there be, would be dynamic as befitting their aural character. Hearing Big Ben's striking, while not the presentation of Big Ben in auditory experience, would nevertheless provide the listener with a dynamic aural image of Big Ben. We do not so much as hear Big Ben in a condition of activity as we hear Big Ben in its audible activity. In order for this to be so, the auditory presentation of a sound-generating event must involve at least the partial disclosure of the event's participants. Audition partially discloses an event's participant by presenting it's participation in the audible event. It is the body's participation in the event, and not the body per se, that is part of the event's audible structure. The disclosure of such audible structure is partial. Only those aspects of the body that are manifest in its participation in the audible event are disclosed, and perhaps only some of those. Furthermore, there is no guarantee that if a perceiver hears an event, they hear each of its participants, if any. But that is consistent with audition, in certain circumstances of perception, partially disclosing at least some of the participants in the unfolding audible event. It is only if we can hear Big Ben's participation in its striking that we can use that hearing to attend to Big Ben. It is only if we can hear Big Ben's participation, can that hearing provide us with a dynamic aural image of Big Ben and its activities that we exploit in attending to Big Ben in audition.

References

Broad, C.D. (1952): "Some elementary reflections on sense-perception". In: *Philosophy*, 27 (100). Reprinted in Broad 1965.
Broad, C.D. (1965): "Some elementary reflections on sense-perception". In: Swartz, Robert J. (Ed.): *Perceiving, Sensing, and Knowing*, Anchor Books, Garden City, NY: Doubleday & Company, Inc., pp. 29–48
Kulvicki, John (2008): "The nature of noise". In: *Philosophers' Imprint*, 8 (11), pp. 1–16.
Leddington, Jason (2014): "What we hear". In: Richard Brown (Ed.): *Consciousness Inside and Out: Phenomenology, Neuroscience, and the Nature of Experience*, volume 6 of *Studies in*

Brain and Mind, chapter 21, Dordrecht Heidelberg New York London: Springer, pp. 321–334.
Pasnau, Robert (1999): "What is sound?" In: *Philosophical Quarterly*, 50 (196), pp. 309–324.
Sorabji, Richard (2004): *Aristotle on Memory*. Bristol: Classical Press, second edition.

4 The Cognitive Penetrability of Perception

Berit "Brit" Brogaard
Bias-Driven Attention, Cognitive Penetration and Epistemic Downgrading

Abstract: It has been argued that dogmatism, the view that experience alone can justify belief, has no way of explaining why experiences that are epistemically downgraded by irrational thinking should not play the same justificatory role as experiences that haven't suffered this fate. In this paper I argue that a recent, initially promising response to this challenge has limited applicability, as it cannot accommodate the experiences that are epistemically downgraded by bias-driven attention. I then argue that dogmatism can be salvaged by denying that genuine high-level properties are presented in experience.

Keywords: Attention hijacking, cognitive penetration, epistemic downgrade, evidence insensitivity, implicit bias, phenomenal conservatism, phenomenal dogmatism, presentational phenomenology, selection effects

1 Introduction

The question of whether cognitively penetrated sensory experience is epistemically downgraded has been under fierce scrutiny in recent years (Steup 2004: 415–416; 2013, section 6; Goldman 2008: 72–3; 2009: 330; Markie 2005: 356–7, 2013; Lyons 2011: 299–300; Siegel 2012, 2017; McGrath 2013; Tucker 2014).[1] Susanna Siegel (2017) provides a book-length defense of the view that it is. On her view, an experience may be epistemically downgraded when its content has been shaped by doxastic and affective states that lack justification.[2] When this is the case, the justification (if any) that it might otherwise have provided for a perceptual belief is degraded to a point that falls below a sensible threshold for justification.[3] Here is one of Siegel's core cases. Jill believes that Jack is angry at her for

---

[1] Tucker (2014) argues convincingly that all epistemic theories are potential targets of the cognitive penetration objection.
[2] For discussion of the cognitive penetrability of experience, see e.g. Lyons 2011, Macpherson 2012, Siegel 2012, 2015, Tucker 2014, Brogaard & Chomanski 2015, Firestone & Scholl 2016, Brogaard & Gatzia 2017.
[3] This is a key assumption in Siegel's (2017) argument for the view that experience itself is assessable for rationality. It is uncontroversial that experience plays an epistemic role. However,

no good reason. The next time Jill sees Jack, Jill's irrational belief cognitively penetrates her visual processing of Jack's face, and this leads her to perceive him as angry. In cases like this where an experience is significantly altered by wishful thinking, irrational belief or irrational affect, the experience is said to be 'hijacked'.

The possibility of hijacked experiences presents a prima facie problem for phenomenal dogmatism (also referred to as 'phenomenal conservatism' and 'dogmatism'). Phenomenal dogmatism is the view that experiences can confer immediate prima facie justification on perceptual belief. The core case cited above presents a prima facie objection to dogmatism insofar as the view would seem to imply that Jill's initially unjustified belief can become justified by an experience that is hijacked by that very belief.

Elijah Chudnoff (in press) argues in response to Siegel that not all forms of phenomenal dogmatism are subject to this worry. On Chudnoff's view, only experiences with what he calls 'presentational phenomenology' can serve as immediate justifiers of perceptual belief (Chudnoff 2012, 2013, 2014, 2018; Chudnoff & Chomanski 2018). An experience has presentational phenomenology just when its phenomenology makes it seem to the perceiver that she is directly aware of a truth-maker for the content of the experience.[4] On this view, experience serves as an immediate justifier of perceptual belief as a result of intrinsic properties of its phenomenology. Let's call this view 'intrinsic phenomenal dogmatism', and let's refer to Chudnoff's particular version of this position as 'presentational dogmatism'.

According to Chudnoff (in press), there are two ways in which Jill's experience may be hijacked. Jill's unjustified belief may cause Jill to experience Jack as

---

the latter view does not imply that experience itself is assessable for rationality. In fact, dogmatists tend to take experience to be unjustified (or a-rational or epistemically basic). This is what enables it to serve as a foundation for immediately justified perceptual belief. If experience can be downgraded to a point where it can no longer serve as a justifier of belief, as suggested by Siegel, then experience itself appears to be in need of epistemic justification in order for it to immediately justify belief.

4 For this notion of presentational phenomenology, see also Yablo (1993: 64), Chalmers (2002: 150) and Chalmers (2006: 65). Only (Chalmers 2006) uses the term 'presentational phenomenology'. On Chalmers' view, '*presentational phenomenology* of perceptual experience [is] the way that it seems to directly and immediately present certain objects and properties in the world' (2006: 65). In his (2002) Chalmers speaks of a perceptually imagined situation *verifying* [i.e., making it true] that pigs fly. This mental event is differentiated from one where one is supposing that pigs fly or entertaining the proposition that pigs fly. Also addressing perceptual imagination, Steve Yablo notes that 'to imagine that there is a tiger behind the curtain, for instance, I imagine a tiger, and I imagine it as behind the curtain' (1993: 64).

angry, even though she does not experience him as having facial features indicative of anger (e.g., a frowning mouth). This is what he calls the 'just high' case. Alternatively, Jill's unjustified belief may cause her to experience Jack as having facial features indicative of anger *and* as being angry. This is the 'high + low' case (Fig. 1).

Fig. 1: Just High, High + Low Cases - In the 'just high' case only the high-level property processed by the visual system is modified by Jill's prior belief. In the high+low' case, the high-level property and the low-level properties signaling an angry face are modified. From Chudnoff (In Press).

Chudnoff then argues that the 'just high' case is unproblematic because Jill's experience does not have the right kind of phenomenology to serve as an immediate justifier for her belief that Jack is angry. This is because without the low-level facial features indicating anger, Jill's experience of Jack does not have presentational phenomenology. Since presentational dogmatism requires that experiences have presentational phenomenology in order for them to serve as immediate justifiers of belief, presentational dogmatism correctly implies that Jill's belief is not immediately justified.

The 'high + low' case does not present a problem for phenomenal dogmatism either, Chudnoff argues. Presentational phenomenology is an essential property of experience. So, presentational dogmatism implies that there cannot be any case of epistemic downgrading. Epistemic downgrading would require that experience can be more or less of a justifier of perceptual belief depending on intrinsic properties of its phenomenology. But given presentational dogmatism, this is not an option. Experiences can differ in what Jack Lyon's calls 'epistemic potency' (Lyons 2016). They can be very bright, not too bright, fleeting, long lasting, etc. An experience that is not very epistemically potent with respect to a particular property, however, will simply fail to justify a belief that this property is instantiated rather than justify the belief to a certain degree. For example, if the experience washes out the colors but not the shapes of the objects in a scene, then the experience may be able to confer justification on shape beliefs but not on color beliefs. But this is not epistemic downgrading. Since epistemic downgrading cannot happen, an experience either confers justification on a belief, or it doesn't. In the 'high + low' case Jill has an epistemically potent experience that represents facial features indicating anger as well as the high-level property of being angry. So, she is prima facie justified in believing that Jack is angry in virtue of having that experience.

Let it be granted for now that this reply succeeds in solving the problem raised by Siegel's (2017) core cases. Here I want to argue that there are other cases of hijacked experiences that at first glance raise problems for phenomenal dogmatism yet turn out to be unresponsive to the kinds of considerations Chudnoff (in press) appeals to in his refutation of the alleged challenge of epistemic downgrading. I will then discuss some options available to the phenomenal dogmatist for dealing with the new challenges. Ultimately, I will conclude that the new challenges do not ultimately threaten phenomenal dogmatism because they appeal to beliefs that are not candidates to be immediately justified by experience. In the last section I argue that the core cases Siegel (2017) discusses fail to challenge dogmatism for the same reason that other cases of hijacked experience fail to do so, and that this is so, even if we share the intuition that the envisaged beliefs in her core cases are *not* prima facie justified.

2 Attentional Modulation and Implicit Biases

Sensory experience can be hijacked in others ways than by direct cognitive penetration (Siegel 2013; Wu 2017). Wayne Wu (2017) argues that attention itself can be cognitively penetrated by irrational thought processes. The type of attention that Wu has in mind is endogenous (top-down) attention. Because endogenous, or goal-driven, attention is oriented by the task to be solved by the perceiver, Wu argues, the focus of endogenous attention is manipulated by the perceiver's interests, goals and desires. There is thus an important sense in which attention can be seen as being cognitively penetrated by the perceiver's attitudes. The perceiver's attitudes could be irrational, however. In that case, biased attention can modify how sensory stimuli are processed downstream. This type of cognitive penetration of sensory processing differs from traditional forms by being a type of *indirect* influence. Yet it seems just as problematic as direct hijacking.

Wu's conception of top-down attention is in line with traditional thinking. In traditional theoretical work on attention, endogenous attention is contrasted with exogenous, or stimulus-driven, attention, which is typically described as operating independently of the perceiver's desires, intentions and goals (for a review see Corbetta & Shulmann 2002). The latter type of attention is sometimes said to proceed 'bottom-up', so as to accentuate its dissociation from top-down, or goal-driven, attention.

Exogenous attention, however, is unlikely to operate entirely independently of the perceiver's interests (Corbetta & Shulman 2002). External stimuli will summon attention only if they are important to the subject. What is important to the subject can be heavily influenced by the perceiver's implicit biases, wishful thinking or irrational affective states.

Here is one way that this can happen. The thalamus in the subcortical layers of the brain functions as a gate that controls the quantity and quality of the information that enters into the visual cortex and other sensory areas (Kentridge & Brogaard 2017; Watzl 2017). The gating mechanism in the thalamus receives input directly from higher cortical areas. If, for instance, you are thinking about what to make for dinner while driving, then the visual cortex may not generate a *conscious* experience on the basis of visual information about the road because the gating mechanism in the thalamus withholds information that is necessary for the generation of visual consciousness.[5]

In light of these considerations, consider now the following case. Your implicit bias about black people's math abilities influences the attentional gating mechanism in the thalamus in such a way that you do not hear any of the correct answers made by the black students in your algebra class. You only hear correct answers made by white students. Based on your experience, you form the belief that only the white students in your class know the answers to your math questions.

The thought that our implicit racial biases can indirectly contribute to, or even bring about, the epistemic justification of our prejudices makes us feel uneasy (Siegel 2013, 2017; Tucker 2014). In some respects, such cases appear more atrocious than those in which more innocent yet tenacious beliefs, emotions or desires contribute to the perceptual justification of belief. However, intrinsic phenomenal dogmatism appears to have the consequence that many of our prejudices are indeed justified. Consider again presentational dogmatism. Your bias-driven experience represents the white students in your class as providing the correct answers to your questions. You are completely unaware of the black students having answered any of your questions correctly. So, on the face of it, your

---

[5] The main reason that lack of attention may block the generation of conscious experience is that brightness processing requires a certain amount of attentional input via the gating mechanism in the thalamus (Kentridge & Brogaard, 2017).

bias-driven experience makes it seem to you that you are aware of a truth-maker for the content *only the white students know the answers to my questions*. It would seem to follow that your bias-driven experience confers immediate prima facie justification on your belief that only the white students know the answers. In the absence of a defeater, your belief is ultima facie justified. It looks like something has gone awry. At least, my own inclination is to say that the belief that only the white students know the answers does not merit any epistemic justification—not even prima facie justification.

Other versions of intrinsic phenomenal dogmatism do not seem to fare any better. In the past I have defended the view that *phenomenal* (as opposed to *epistemic*) seemings can provide immediate prima facie justification for perceptual belief (Brogaard 2013; Brogaard 2018b, c; Brogaard 2019, In Press). Phenomenal and epistemic seemings can be contrasted as follows (cf. Chisholm 1957; Jackson 1977):

Phenomenal Seemings
A seeming S is phenomenal just in case S is evidence *in*sensitive.

Epistemic Seemings
A seeming S is epistemic just in case S is evidence sensitive.

To a first approximation, a seeming is evidence insensitive just in case, if the perceiver were to acquire information suggesting that the seeming is inaccurate, the seeming would persist. Conversely, a seeming fails to be evidence insensitive just in case, if the perceiver were to acquire information suggesting that the seeming is inaccurate, the seeming would cease to persist. Consider the Müller-Lyer Illusion (**Fig. 2**). In the illusion, the two line segments visually appear as if they have different lengths. After measuring them, we might discover that they have the same length. However, even when we know that the line segments have the same length, the line segments in the initial image on the left continue to visually appear as if they have different lengths. So, the visual appearance the line segments in the initial image have different lengths is evidence insensitive. By the tentative definition of 'phenomenal seeming' provided above, the seeming that the line segments in the initial image have different lengths is thus phenomenal as opposed to epistemic.

Fig. 2: The Müller-Lyer Illusion. Even when you learn that the line segments on the left have the same length, they continue to appear as if they have different lengths. So, the visual seemig is evidence insensitive.

Epistemic seemings are belief-like but they do not typically have the same high credence as belief. Here is an example of an epistemic seeming. I hear on the radio that Hurricane Maria may make landfall in Miami. As a result, it comes to seem to me that I ought to evacuate. Later that day the radio station informs me that the hurricane took a different course and will not make landfall in South Florida after all. At this point, it no longer seems to me that I ought to evacuate. So, my seeming fails to be evidence insensitive and hence is epistemic.

Evidence insensitivity is not usually understood as an intrinsic feature of the phenomenology of experience or seemings (Brogaard 2013a, 2018a). However, it might be conceived of in this way (cf. Brogaard 2018b; Brogaard & Gatzia 2018). Here is one way to articulate the notion of evidence insensitivity, when understood as intrinsic to phenomenology:

Phenomenal Evidence Insensitivity
A seeming S that p is evidence insensitive just in case, if the perceiver were to gain awareness of evidence suggesting that p is false, S would persist in virtue of its intrinsic properties.

A view that requires experiences to be phenomenally evidence insensitive in order for them to confer immediate prima facie justification on perceptual belief is a kind of intrinsic phenomenal dogmatism. Accordingly, it encounters the same problems as other versions of this view. In the implicit bias case, as it has been detailed, your bias-driven seeming that only white students answered your math questions correctly is phenomenally evidence insensitive. So, on the face of it, the seeming provides immediate prima facie justification for your belief that only white students know the answers to your math questions. This result, however, seems misguided.

3 Phenomenal Dogmatism and Inferential Justification

How can the phenomenal dogmatist respond to this worry? One option is to deny that the phenomenon of hijacking can occur. Whether or not it can only be determined empirically and the empirical evidence indicates that many alleged cases of hijacking are not as they appear (see e.g., Firestone & Scholl 2016). However, it may turn out not to matter to epistemology whether hijacking is actual or merely possible. It is plausible to think that epistemic hijacking is at least psychologically possible. If phenomenal dogmatism is a necessary theory about perceptual justification of human belief, and there are psychologically possible instances in which the theory yields the wrong predictions, then the view is false. So, denying the possibility of hijacked experience may well be futile.

It may be argued, of course, that in order for epistemic hijacking to present a threat to phenomenal dogmatism, this phenomenon must actually occur. The threat to dogmatism then is a conditional one: if epistemic hijacking does indeed occur, then phenomenal dogmatism is false. Since it is still an open empirical possibility that hijacking phenomena occur, the phenomenal dogmatist should still take an interest in addressing the challenge that hijacking presents (Siegel 2013; Siegel 2017).

One way for the phenomenal dogmatist to address this challenge is to put further constraints on the class of experiences that can provide immediate prima facie justification for perceptual belief. The phenomenal dogmatist may argue on philosophical grounds that prejudices are not the kinds of psychological state that can alter the epistemic role of experience. So, if prejudices contribute to the content of an experience by modulating sensory processing, then that experience cannot confer immediate justification upon belief.

Cases of prejudice-driven experience, however, are not the only test cases that the dogmatist ought to worry about. Suppose that prior to viewing **Figure 3**, you have a hypothesis to the effect that only the white geometrical figures in **Figure 3** are square. Suppose further that this hypothesis affects sensory processing in such a way that a non-square shape is attributed to the black square. As a result, your experience confers immediate justification on your hypothesis in virtue of having been shaped by that very hypothesis. In this case, your experience is not problematic because it is driven by implicit bias or prejudice in the standard sense but because it is rooted in a kind of confirmation bias.

Fig. 3: Black and white squares. In our thought experiment, your hypothesis that only the white figures are square drives the information processing of the squares. As a result, what you experience when looking at Figure 3 confirms your hypothesis.

A third way for the dogmatist to address these challenges is to argue that experiences that have their justificatory status as a result of irrational processes cannot serve as immediate justifiers of perceptual belief (Brogaard 2013a, 2018a, 2018b). For example, we might characterize seemings that are evidence insensitive and can serve as immediate justifiers in virtue of being the result of rational or a-rational processes as follows:

> *Rational Evidence Insensitivity*
> A seeming S that p is evidence insensitive just in case, if the perceiver were to gain awareness of evidence suggesting that p is false, S would persist as a result of internal rational or a-rational processes.

It may be thought that the processes that go into generating common optical illusions are irrational and that the proposed modification therefore rules out that optical illusions can provide immediate prima facie justification for perceptual belief. However, upon further scrutiny, this is not so. Consider again the Müller-Lyer Illusion in **Figure 2**. One explanation of the illusion is that it is the result of intra-perceptual principles that determine depth perception (Pylyshyn 1999; Howe & Purves 2005). These intra-perceptual principles estimate that the upper line segment is located further away from us than the lower, as illustrated in **Figure 4**. The reason that the intra-perceptual principles misfire in the Müller-Lyer Illusion is that the line segments must have the same length two-dimensionally in order for the upper line segment to be perceived as being located behind the lower segment in a three-dimensional sketch.

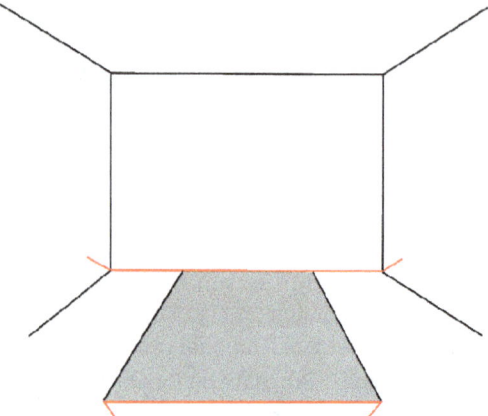

Fig. 4: The Müller-Lyer Illusion. Illustration of how the arrow "head" and the arrow "tail" generate the appearance of the upper line segment in the Müller-Lyer Illusion being further away from us than the lower line segment.

Since the intra-perceptual principles inherent to the visual system are neither rational nor irrational, the Rational Evidence Insensitivity constraint is indeed satisfied in the Müller-Lyer Illusion.

This alternative formulation of phenomenal dogmatism involves taking the experiences that can serve as immediate justifiers to be constrained by their etiology or causal history. The etiology of experience is not an intrinsic feature of its phenomenology. So, since intrinsic phenomenal dogmatism requires that experiences that serve as immediate justifiers do so *solely* in virtue of their intrinsic phenomenal properties, this way of handling the problem cases requires denying *intrinsic* phenomenal dogmatism.

The intrinsic phenomenal dogmatist need not throw in the towel yet, however. The argument in the previous section rests on the assumption that sensory experience can have quantificational content (e.g., 'all', 'only the', 'there are 48', etc) that can confer immediate justification upon a belief with the same quantificational content. But the phenomenal dogmatist need not commit to this claim. In fact, there are good reasons to think that at least some quantificational contents are not the sorts of contents that can be contents of experience. To see why, consider the speckled hen problem (Chisholm 1942; Tucker 2010). The speckled hen problem is sometimes alleged to pose a problem for phenomenal dogmatism. Matthew McGrath outlines the problem the speckled hen case supposedly presents as follows:

> When you look at the hen with exactly 48 clearly visible speckles, you aren't justified in believing it has 48 speckles, at least without counting. Nor do you seem to have prima facie justification that is somehow defeated. But each speckle is clearly visible and it might seem therefore that your experience represents the hen as 48-speckled. If this is right, we have a counterexample to [phenomenal dogmatism] (Mc Grath 2016: 5).

Arguably, we cannot acquire justification for the belief that the speckled hen has exactly 48 specks by simply glancing at it. If, however, the experience represents the hen as having 48 specks, then the phenomenal dogmatist seems to be committed to the claim that a quick glance at the hen can give us justification for our belief that the hen has 48 specks.

One way for the phenomenal dogmatist to respond to this problem is to deny that the speckled-hen experience represents the hen as 48-speckled. The experience may turn out to represent each of the 48 specks, but this does not entail that the property of being 48-speckled is a constituent of the content of the experience. Where 'X' is a plural variable ranging over pluralities and 'S' refers to the perceiver, we can articulate the difference between the two types of content that the speckled-hen experience might be thought to have as follows:

> *Wide-Scope*: There are 48 specks (X) such that S has an experience as of the hen instantiating *them* (X).

> *Narrow-Scope*: S has an experience as of there being 48 specks (X) such that the hen instantiates *them* (X).

The phenomenal dogmatist can argue that the speckled-hen experience has the content specified by the wide-scope claim, that is, the experience represents the hen as having a plurality of specks rather than a precise number of specks. Because the experience does not represent exactly 48 specks but merely a plurality of specks, the experience is accurate. This is as it should be.

If the experience has the content specified by the wide-scope claim, then the speckled-hen case is not a problem for the phenomenal dogmatist. This is because an experience with this content does not provide immediate justification for the perceptual belief that the hen has 48 specks. The experience can provide justification for this belief only together with a justified belief to the effect that the totality of specks adds up to 48.

An analogous response can ward off the problem presented by confirmation bias-driven experience. The problem was this. If the visual cortex only correctly processes shape information for the white squares, it may seem that we come to have an experience with the (false) quantificational content *Only the white geometrical figures are squares*. The dogmatist, however, need not accept this claim.

As in the speckled-hen case, she can draw a distinction between the following two experiential contents ('X' and 'Y' are plural variables ranging over pluralities, the predicates 'white-geometrical figures', 'squares' and 'white' are distributive plural predicates):

> *Wide-Scope*: There are some Xs such that white-geometrical-figures(X), and for all Ys, if white-geometrical-figure(Y), then Y = X, and **S** has an experience with the content: square(X).

> *Narrow-Scope*: S has an experience with the content there are some Xs such that white-geometrical-figures(X), and for all Ys, if white-geometrical-figure(Y), then Y = X, and square(X).

The dogmatist can say that the content of the biased experience of the geometrical figures is best articulated by the wide-scope claim. This sort of solution preserves the intuition that maximality can be presented in perceptual experience without committing us to quantifiers being presented in experience. The maximality presented in experience is the maximality of items visually processed. So, the experience is accurate. Elsewhere I have argued that experiences that are accurate can fail to be successful (Brogaard 2018a). This can happen when the experience fails to make the subject directly aware of the object represented by the experience. This is not the sort of case we are encountering here, however. In this case, the lack of success consists in the experience's epistemic shortcomings. Because the experience has the content specified by the wide-scope claim, it does not provide immediate justification for the perceptual belief that only the white geometrical figures are square but only for the weaker claim that a plurality of white geometrical figures in **Figure 3** are white. In order for the perceptual belief that all the white geometrical figures are square to be justified, the perceiver would need to possess the additional information that she has given sufficient attention to all the geometrical figures.

A similar point applies to the case of racial bias. In this case, when a black student provides a correct answer to a question, the gating mechanism in the thalamus filters out the information, so it fails to be processed. Here too the dogmatist can say that the content of the experience is best specified by the wide-scope claim ('X' and 'Y' are plural variables ranging over pluralities, the predicates 'students who answered correctly', 'white' and 'correct' are distributive plural predicates:

> *Wide-Scope*: There are some Xs such that students-who-answered-correctly(X), and for all Ys if students-who-answered-correctly(Y), then Y = X, and S has an experience with the content white(X).

Narrow-Scope: S has an experience with the content there are some Xs such that students-who-answered-correctly(X), and for all Ys if students-who-answered-correctly(Y), then Y = X, and white(X).

A perceptual experience with the content specified by the wide-scope claim does not confer immediate justification on the belief that only the white students correctly answered the questions but only on the weaker claim that a plurality of white students answered the questions correctly. The experience can confer justification on the belief that all the students who answered the questions correctly are white only together with a justified belief to the effect that you paid equal attention to what the black and the white students had to say.

This takes us back to the case of Jack and Jill. We can resolve this problem as follows. Jill's experience of Jack does not present Jack as being angry, we might say. It presents Jack as instantiating a certain holistic facial expression—call it an 'anger gestalt property' (Brogaard 2013; Brogaard 2017). Many distinct configurations of anger-indicating low-level (e.g facial) features can be a cause of an anger gestalt being presented in experience. But anger gestalts can come to be presented in experience *only* in the presence of a number of other conditions, for instance a particular visual system, visual detection of the low-level features and innate or perceptually learned capacities to recognize certain facial expressions holistically, and so on (Brogaard 2017). Putting up an angry face is the anger gestalt property most relevant to the case at hand. But it is not the only example of an anger gestalt property. Other examples—at different levels of generality—are: looking angry, shouting angrily, scowling at someone, shaking one's fist, smashing plates, slamming the door, punching the wall, interrupting with a cutting remark, giving someone the stink eye.

Jill's experience of Jack instantiating an anger gestalt property does not confer immediate justification on her false belief that Jack *is* angry. It provides justification for the belief that Jack instantiates an anger gestalt property (e.g., putting up an angry face).

Given innate or learned information about which gestalt properties (e.g., putting on an angry face) typically correlate with anger, the experience as of John putting up an angry face may also confer justification on the belief that Jack *is* angry. But the belief that John *is* angry is not *immediately* justified. Its justification relies on acquired background information about the correlations between configurations of low-level properties and anger. Suppose Jill's twin sister Joy has a poorly developed theory of mind. Blessed with knowledge of her own condition, Joy attends theory of mind classes. The instructor is highly reliable. However, in a lesson that covers material about the facial expressions that typically correlate with disgust, the teacher accidentally presents a slide with a person putting up an angry face. As a result, Joy comes to believe that anger gestalt property, which others normally take to correlate with anger, correlates with disgust. Like Jill, Joy unjustifiably believes that Jack is angry at her. When she later encounters him, her unjustified belief modifies her low-level feature processing. Accordingly, she comes to have an illusory experience of Jack exhibiting facial features that most others would perceive as an angry face. Indeed, the particular anger gestalt property is presented in Jill's experience (even though she would not report on her experience using the word 'angry'). Yet owing to the teacher's one-time mistake, Jill takes this particular anger gestalt property to be indicative of disgust. Accordingly, she comes to believe that Jack is not angry at her but is disgusted by her. Joy's experience together with her background belief about the correlation between the particular anger gestalt property presented in her experience and disgust confer mediate justification on her belief that Jack is disgusted by her.

An opponent of phenomenal dogmatism may raise the following objection to my reply to the Jill and Jack case.[6] Suppose the following exchange ensues between Jill and her friend Jasmine after they have both seen Jack:

Jill: I think Jack looks angry.
Jasmine: Are you kidding? He doesn't look angry at all.
Jill: Yes, he does.
Jasmine: No. None of the others I talked to thinks that he looks angry. In fact, his face is perfectly neutral.

Jasmine has no beliefs about Jack's mindset prior to seeing him. So, it is natural for her to counter Jill's belief that Jack looks angry. Jack apparently only looks angry to Jill, not to Jasmine or anyone else. So, it seems that Jill's initially unjustified belief that Jack *is* angry is a significant contributor to the justification of her belief that he *looks* angry. Because Jill's experience that John looks angry confers *mediate* justification on her belief that Jack is angry, her initially unjustified belief ends up being a major contributor to its own justification. So, phenomenal dogmatism still faces a circularity objection.

My reply to the envisaged objection turns on the distinction between looking angry to the perceiver and looking angry to an unbiased observer in normal viewing conditions. Jack doesn't look angry to an unbiased observer in normal viewing conditions (e.g., Jasmine). He looks angry to Jill. So, Jill's experience represents Jack as looking angry to her. It should be fairly uncontroversial that Jill's experience of Jack looking angry can provide justification for her belief that Jack

---

[6] Thanks to Jake Beck and Mike Martin for raising this objection.

looks angry to her. Of course, Jasmine's remarks give Jill a reason to doubt that Jack *is* angry. So, she is not ultima facie justified in believing that Jack *is* angry.

The phenomenal dogmatist who pushes this line of argument can make a partial concession to those who appeal to wishful thinking and irrational belief and desire in support of the conclusion that experience does not provide immediate prima facie justification for beliefs about genuine high-level properties (e.g., *being angry*). Experiences can represent gestalt properties (e.g., an angry face, a smiley face or a frowning face) but it cannot represent genuinely high-level properties (e.g., being angry). Experiences that represent gestalt properties can confer immediate prima facie justification upon belief about configurations of low-level properties (e.g., facial expressions). However, they can provide justification for beliefs about genuine high-level properties only together with justified beliefs about typical correlations between the low-level configurations and genuine high-level properties.

4 Concluding Remarks: The A-Rationality of Experience

What I have called 'intrinsic phenomenal dogmatism' takes experience to confer prima facie immediate justification upon belief in virtue of intrinsic properties of the experience's phenomenology. Cases in which the experiential content is modified via cognitive penetration or bias-driven attention present a prima facie problem for this view. For example, if you are biased against black people, you may fail to experience any of the black people in your class as having correctly answered your questions. This may lead you to believe that only the white people in your class have provided correct answers. If intrinsic phenomenal dogmatism has this implication, then the view is fundamentally flawed.

In this paper I have argued that phenomenal dogmatism can ward off this objection by denying that genuinely high-level properties (including quantificational properties) are presented in experience. If only gestalt properties (i.e., appearance properties caused by configurations of low-level properties) are presented in experience, then intrinsic phenomenal dogmatism does not have this implication. If you experience a plurality of white students in your class provide correct answers to your questions but you completely fail to pay attention to any of the answers provided by black students, your experience can confer immediate justification on the belief that a plurality of white students in your class have correctly answered your questions. But you do not have immediate justification for the belief that *only the* white students in your class have answered your questions correctly. Your experience can provide justification for this belief only if you justifiably believe that you have paid equal attention to (and given equal credit to) what the white and the black students had to say. You may believe that you have done so, but this belief is in all likelihood not justified.

The view presented here has the implication that experiences hijacked by implicit biases can nonetheless still confer immediate justification on perceptual belief. If hijacking could result in epistemic downgrade, experience itself would be in need of justification in order for it to play the desired epistemic role. A hijacked experience would thus fail to be properly basic because hijacking causes epistemic downgrade. On the view presented here, experience is not itself in need of justification and can thus be taken as properly basic in a foundationalist theory of justification.[7]

References

Brogaard, Berit (2013a): "Phenomenal Seemings and Sensible Dogmatism". In: Tucker, Chris (Ed.): *Seemings and Justification: New Essays on Dogmatism and Phenomenal Conservatism*. Oxford: Oxford University Press, pp. 270–289.

Brogaard, Berit (2013b): "Do we Perceive Natural Kind Properties?". In: *Philosophical Studies* 162, Issue 1, pp. 35–42.

Brogaard, Berit (2018a): *Seeing & Saying*, New York: Oxford University Press.

Brogaard, Berit (2018b): "Phenomenal Dogmatism, Seeming Evidentialism and Inferential Justification". In: McCain, Kevin (Ed.): *Believing in Accordance with the Evidence: New Essays on Evidentialism*, Synthese Library Book Series, pp. 53–70.

Brogaard, Berit (2018c): "In Defense of Hearing Meanings". In: *Synthese* 195 (7), pp. 2967–2983.

Brogaard, Berit (In Press): "Seeing and Hearing Meanings. A Non-Inferential Approach to Utterance Comprehension". In: Chan, Timothy / Nes, Anders (Eds.): *Inference and Consciousness*, Routledge.

Brogaard, Berit / Chomanski, Bartek (2015): "Cognitive Penetrability and High-Level Properties in Perception: Unrelated Phenomena?". In: *Pacific Philosophical Quarterly* 96, pp. 469–486.

Brogaard, Berit / Gatzia, Dimitria (2017): "Is Color Experience Cognitively Penetrable?". In: *Topics in Cognitive Science* 9, pp. 193–214.

---

[7] For helpful comments on a previous version of this paper, I am grateful to Tim Bayne, Jake Beck, Ned Block, Christoph Limbeck-Lilienau, Jack Lyons, Fiona Macpherson, Mike Martin, Michelle Montague, Anders Nes, Pär Sundström, Charles Travis, Sebastian Watzl and audiences in Kirchberg, Oslo, and Miami.

Brogaard, Berit / Gatzia, Dimitria (2018): "The Real Epistemic Significance of Perceptual Learning". In: *Inquiry* 61:5–6, pp. 543–558.
Chalmers, David John (2002): "Does Conceivability Entail Possibility?". In Szabó Gendler, Tamar / Hawthorne, John (Eds.): *Conceivability and Possibility*, New York: Oxford University Press, pp. 145–200.
Chalmers, David John (2006): "Perception and the Fall from Eden,". In Szabó Gendler, Tamar / Hawthorne, John (Eds.), *Perceptual Experience*. Oxford: Clarendon Press, pp. 49–125.
Chisholm, Roderick Milton (1942): "Discussions: The Problem of the Speckled Hen". In: *Mind* LI, pp. 368–373.
Chisholm, Roderick Milton (1957): *Perceiving: A Philosophical Study*. Ithaca: Cornell University Press.
Chudnoff, Elijah (2012): "Presentational Phenomenology". In Miguens, Sofia / Preyer, Gerhard (Eds.): *Consciousness and Subjectivity*. Frankfurt: Ontos Verlag, pp. 51–72.
Chudnoff, Elijah (2013): *Intuition*. Oxford: Oxford University Press.
Chudnoff, Elijah (2014): "Review of Tucker (Eds.) Seemings and Justification". In: *Notre Dame Philosophical Reviews*.
Chudnoff, Elijah (2018): "Epistemic Elitism and Other Minds". In: *Philosophy and Phenomenological Research* 96 (2), pp. 276–298.
Chudnoff, Elijah (In Press): "Experience and Epistemic Structure: Can Cognitive Penetration Result in Epistemic Downgrade?" In: T. Chan and A. Nes (Eds.): *Inference and Consciousness*.
Chudnoff, Elijah & Chomanski, Bartek (2018): "How Perception Generates, Preserves, and Mediates Justification". In: *Inquiry* 61 (5–6), pp. 559–568.
Corbetta Maurizio & Shulman Gordon L. (2002): "Control of Goal-Directed and Stimulus-Driven Attention in the Brain". In: *Nat Rev Neurosci.* 3 (3), pp. 201–15.
Firestone, Chaz & Scholl, Brian J. (2016): "Cognition Does Not Affect perception: Evaluating the Evidence for 'Top-Down' Effects". In: *Behavioral and Brain Sciences* 39, pp. 1–72.
Goldman, Alvin (2008): "Immediate Justification and Process Reliabilism". In: Smith, Q. (ed.). *Epistemology: New Essays*. Oxford: Oxford University Press, pp. 63–82.
Goldman, Alvin (2009): "Internalism, Externalism, and the Architecture of Justification". In: *Journal of Philosophy* 106, pp. 309–38.
Howe Catherine Q. & Purves Dale (2005): "The Müller-Lyer Illusion Explained by the Statistics of Image-Source Relationships". In: *PNAS* 102(4), pp. 1234–1239.
Jackson, Frank (1977): *Perception: A Representative Theory*. Cambridge: Cambridge University Press.
Kentridge, Bob & Brogaard, Berit (2017): "The Functional Roles of Attention". In Nanay, Bence (Ed): *Current Controversies in Philosophy of Perception*. New York: Routledge, pp. 139–147.
Lyons, Jack (2011): "Circularity, Reliability and the Cognitive Penetrability of Perception". In: *Philosophical Issues* 21, pp. 289–311.
Lyons, Jack (2016): "Inferentialism and Cognitive Penetration of Perception". In: *Episteme* 13 (1), pp. 1–28.
Macpherson, Fiona (2012): "Cognitive Penetration of Colour Experience: Rethinking the Issue in Light of an Indirect Mechanism". In: *Philosophy and Phenomenological Research* 84(1), pp. 24–62.
Markie, Peter (2005): "The Mystery of Perceptual Justification". In: *Philosophical Studies* 126, pp. 347–73.

Markie, Peter (2013): "Searching for True Dogmatism". In: Tucker, Chris (Ed.): *Seemings and Justification: New Essays on Dogmatism and Phenomenal Conservatism*. Oxford: Oxford University Press, pp. 248–269.
McGrath, Matthew (2013): "Phenomenal Conservatism and Cognitive Penetration: the 'Bad Basis' Counterexamples". In: C. Tucker (Ed.): *Seemings and Justification: New Essays on Dogmatism and Phenomenal Conservatism*. Oxford: Oxford University Press, pp. 225–247.
McGrath, Matthew (2016): "Looks and Perceptual Justification". In: *Philosophy and Phenomenological Research*, First published online: 1 April 2016. DOI: 10.1111/phpr.12289.
Pylyshyn, Zenon Walter (1999): "Is Vision Continuous with Cognition? The Case for Cognitive Impenetrability of Visual Perception" In: *Behavioral and Brain Sciences*, 22, pp. 341–423.
Siegel, Susanna (2012): "Cognitive Penetrability and Perceptual Justification" In: *Noûs* 46(2), pp. 201–222.
Siegel, Susanna (2013): "Can Selection Effects on Experience Influence Its Rational Role?" In: Szabó Gendler, Tamar and Hawthorne, John (Eds.): *Oxford Studies in Epistemology* 4. Oxford: Oxford University Press, pp. 240–270.
Siegel, Susanna (2015): "Epistemic Evaluability and Perceptual Farce". In: J. Zeimbekis & A. Raftopoulos (Eds): *The Cognitive Penetrability of Perception: New Philosophical Perspectives*. Oxford: Oxford University Press, pp. 405–424.
Siegel, Susanna (2017): *The Rationality of Perception*. New York: Oxford University Press.
Silins, Nicholas (2016): "Cognitive Penetration and the Epistemology of Perception". In: *Philosophy Compass* 11, 1, pp. 24–42.
Steup, Matthias (2004): "Internalist Reliabilism". In: *Philosophical Issues* 14, pp. 403–425.
Steup, Matthias (2013): "Does Phenomenal Conservatism Solve Internalism's Dilemma?" In: Tucker, Chris (Ed.): *Seemings and Justification: New Essays on Dogmatism and Phenomenal Conservatism*. Oxford University Press, pp. 135–153.
Tucker, Chris (2010): "Why Open-Minded People Should Endorse Dogmatism". In: *Philosophical Perspectives* 24, 1, pp. 529–545.
Tucker, Chris (2014): "If Dogmatists Have a Problem with Cognitive Penetration, You Do Too". In: *Dialectica* 68 (1), pp. 35–62.
Watzl, Sebastian (2017): *Structuring Mind: The Nature of Attention and How it Shapes Consciousness*. Oxford: Oxford University Press.
Wu, Wayne (2017): "Shaking Up the Mind's Ground Floor: The Cognitive Penetration of Visual Attention". In: *Journal of Philosophy* 114 (1), pp. 5–32.
Yablo, Sthephen (1993): "Is Conceivability a Guide to Possibility?" In: *Philosophy and Phenomenological Research* 53, pp. 1–42.

Athanassios Raftopoulos
Pre-Cueing, Early Vision, and Cognitive Penetrability

Abstract: I have argued that early vision is cognitively impenetrable because its processes do not operate over cognitive contents. Recently it has been argued that pre-cueing guided by cognitively driven attention affects early vision rendering it cognitively penetrated. Since the signatures of these effects are found in early vision, early vision is directly affected by cognition since its processes use cognitive information. Here, I defend the cognitive impenetrability. First, I define early vision and cognitive penetrability. I argue that a set of perceptual processes is cognitively penetrated only if cognition undermines the epistemic role of these processes in grounding empirical beliefs. Second, I discuss the problems cognitive penetrability causes for the epistemic role of perception and relate them to the impact of cognitive penetrability on the sensitivity of perception to the data. Third, I examine the epistemic role of early vision and argue that the cognitive effects underpinning pre-cueing do not undermine this role and, thus, do not render early vision cognitively penetrable. In addition, they do not entail that early vision uses cognitive information; they are indirect effects similar to the shifts of overt or covert attention.

Keywords: Pre-cueing, early vision, cognitive Penetration, epistemic role of perception, sensitivity to the data

1 Introduction

In previous work (Raftopoulos 2009, 2015), I argued that a stage of visual processing, early vision, is not directly affected by cognition since its processes do not draw on cognition as an informational resource, which is at the core of the claim that perception is cognitively penetrated (CP). Early vision is cognitively impenetrable (CI).

It has been argued by philosophers (Cecchi 2014; Ogilivie and Carruthers 2015), and cognitive scientists (Goldstone et al. 2015; Lupyan 2015; Vetter and Newen 2014) that various pre-cueing attentional effects directly modulate early visual processing, in that the signatures of these effects are found in early vision and since these effects involve cognition, early vision is CP.

I defend the CI of early vision, in three steps. First, I define the main terms used in this paper, that is, early vision, and CP. In relation to CP, I argue that whether a set of perceptual processes is CP hinges on whether there are cognitive effects that undermine the epistemic role of these processes in grounding empirical beliefs. In the second section, I elaborate on the problems the CP of perception causes for the epistemic role of perception in grounding perceptual beliefs. Note that the epistemic role of perception is not threatened only by the cognitive effects that are cases of CP. It is also threatened by all sorts of cognitive effects on perception. (This thesis presupposes that not all cognitive effects on perception are cases of CP, but since this is the view endorsed in the vast majority of the discussions I will take it for granted.) I will concentrate on the way CP affects the epistemic role of perception. In the third section, I examine the epistemic role of early vision and argue that the cognitive effects that act through pre-cueing do not undermine this role and, thus, do not render early vision CP. Furthermore pre-cueing does not affect early vision directly. Thus, even if one does not endorse the epistemic criterion of CP and thinks that there should be direct cognitive effects on perceptual processes for CP to occur, pre-cueing does not entail that early vision is CP. The discussion suggests that the epistemic criterion for CP and the definition of CP according to which CP occurs when cognition directly affects perceptual processing are inextricably linked.

2 Defining the Key Terms

2.1 Early Vision

Early vision includes a feed forward sweep in which signals are transmitted bottom-up. In visual areas (from LGN to IT) the feed forward sweep lasts for about 100ms. It also includes a stage at which lateral and recurrent processes that are restricted within the visual areas and do not involve signals from cognitive centers occur. Recurrent processing in early visual areas starts at about 80–100 ms and culminates at about 120–150 ms. Lamme (2003) calls it local recurrent processing. The unconscious feed forward sweep extracts high-level information that could lead to categorization, and results in some initial feature detection. Local recurrent processing produces further binding and segregation. Many studies show that there are early feedback loops from LGN or V1 to MT/V5 and then back to V1, where the recurrent signals engage the neurons of V1 to perform different tasks than those performed when V1 received feedforward signals from the LGN (Drewes et al. 2016; Heinen et al. 2005).

In Raftopoulos (2009), I argued that early vision processing is not affected directly by cognitively driven attention although attention may affect pre-early vision and post-early vision stages of visual perception. This entails that signal transmission during early vision is not affected by top-down signals produced in cognitive areas and is restricted within the visual areas of the brain. Thus, the processes of early vision do not use cognitive information as an information resource and this makes early vision CI.

The processes of early vision retrieve from the environment the information that will eventually allow perception to perceive a visual scene with as much accuracy as possible. To do so, early vision gradually constructs representations of increasing complexity (from variations in light intensities it extracts edges, from edges blobs, from blobs it extracts two-dimensional surfaces, and from these it infers the 21/2 sketch). The representations formed in early vision comprise information about spatio-temporal and surface properties, the shape of the object as viewed by the perceiver, color, texture, orientation, motion, and affordances of objects, in addition to the representations of objects as bounded, solid entities that persist in space and time.

2.2 Cognitive penetrability

The term CP is intended to cover the cognitive influences on perception such that the contents of cognitive states affect the contents of perceptual states through the causal interaction of the cognitive and perceptual states that carry these contents. It is unanimously agreed upon in the relevant literature (the reasons for this are beyond the scope of this paper) that this interaction, in order to signify CP, must be purely mental and should not involve any eye or bodily movements.

For Siegel (2011: 5–6; 2013; 2017: 4), CP is a term covering all cases of influences on the contents of experience by prior mental states, including cognitive and emotive states, which causally affect the content of perception. CP occurs when cognitive effects influence how things look, or, more generally, when the cognitive effects affect not the selection of the input but perceptual processing itself.

According to Siegel (2011, 2017), selection effects where attention selects the input are not cases of CP. I think that Siegel is wrong to exclude attention as a potential source of CP but I do not discuss this problem here. I simply assume that when cognitively driven attention directly modulates perceptual processing, this process is CP.

Siegel's view that CP occurs when cognitive states affect perceptual processing itself if conjoined with the thesis that when they do so the affected perceptual processes operate upon cognitive information, accords with one of Pylyshyn's (1999) themes on CP. This is the thesis that cognition affects perception if cognition causally influences perception directly, that is, if the perceptual processes operate upon the information contained in the affecting cognitive states establishing a semantic coherence between cognitive and perceptual contents.

To understand better what is at stake with CP, one should go back in time. Hanson (1958), Kuhn (1962), Churchland (1988) and others interpreted findings in psychology and neuropsychology as showing that cognitive states involving propositional/conceptual contents affect perception. This was used as a springboard to mount an attack on the received view in the philosophy of science that there is a theory neutral observational basis on which a rational choice for empirical adequacy between competing theories could be made. If perception is CP, perception becomes theory laden (perception is theory laden if perceptual processing is affected by some background theory) and the choice between two alternative and mutually exclusive theories cannot be based on empirical testing. Since the two theories belong to different comprehensive conceptual frameworks the observations being interpretations made under the influence of the two alternative frameworks differ across them. It follows that there is not a common empirical basis on which to base the choice between the two competing theories.

Sellars (1956) sought to undermine one of the tenets of classical empiricism, to wit, the view that one could introspect perception independently of concepts and get to the world, which, thus, is revealed in its own guise without any conceptual influences. This 'given' can be used as a neutral basis on which to determine the adequacy of perceptual beliefs. Since the CP of perception undercuts the possibility of such a given, the justificatory role of perception is undermined.

The thread connecting these views is that perception cannot play the epistemological role assigned to it by empiricism because it does not provide a neutral ground on which to decide which of our cognitive schemes is true or false; to the extent that perception is CP, perception's role in grounding perceptual beliefs is undermined. CP affects the epistemic role of perception because it lessens the sensitivity of perception to the data, or because it introduces some sort of irrationality in perceptual processing.

CP, therefore, was thought to undermine the epistemic role of perception, that is, to undermine the extent to which experience could justify some belief. It follows that a cognitive influence on perception is a case of CP if it undermines the epistemic role of perception. Not all cases of CP undermine the epistemic role of perception, however, and some may even benefit it. One should extend, thus, the definition of CP so that any and only cognitive influences that affect the epistemic role of perception should be deemed as cases of CP independent of whether they diminish or enhance this role.

Following this, Raftopoulos (2009, 2014) and Stokes (2015) argue that CP should be understood in terms of its consequences. Consequentialism captures what is important in all discussions of CP, namely, the consequences of CP for the epistemic role of perception, theory-ladenness of perception, rationality in science, etc. An adequate account of CP should describe a class of phenomena that has implications for the rationality of science, the epistemic role of perception, etc.

This sets the following condition for CP:

Epistemic Criterion for CP: If perception (or a stage of it) is cognitively influenced in a way that renders it unfit to play the role of a neutral epistemological basis, by vitiating its justificatory role in grounding perceptual beliefs, perception (or a stage of it) is CP. If perception (or a stage of it) is cognitively influenced in a way that does not affect its epistemic role in justifying perceptual beliefs, it is CI.

The epistemic criterion for CP entails that to determine whether a perceptual stage is CP one should examine whether there are cognitive or emotive influences on this stage that affect its epistemic role in grounding perceptual beliefs. For the purposes of this paper, I will run this definition in parallel with the more standard definition that we discussed before, namely that a cognitive effect on perception is a case of CP if it affects perceptual processing directly in the sense specified above. In this paper, I will not address in depth the problem of the relations between the two definitions, although the discussion suggests that the two definitions are inextricably linked.

3 The Impact of CP on the Epistemic Role of Perception

It is intuitive to think that perceptual experience provides defeasible evidence, or warrant, or rational support, or grounds, for endorsing beliefs. It does so directly without any intermediate mental states just because it is perceptual experience. Perceiving p provides prima facie justification, i.e., rational support, for the proposition p. There are many views concerning the way perception justifies perceptual beliefs, which are roughly divided into two main categories; those that fall within internalism and those that fall within externalism.

According to internalism, the justification of perceptual beliefs by perception is independent of truth-related factors. Externalists reject this thesis. The two camps differ on the way they interpret and account for the problems that CP engenders for the epistemic role of perception. Within internalism, the most classical view of perceptual justification is called perceptual or phenomenal conservatism or dogmatism (Huemer 2007; McGrath 2013; Tucker 2014), which holds that if it perceptually seems to S that p, then, thereby, S has *prima facie* perceptual justification for the proposition p. Having an experience with content p suffices to give S immediate (meaning that S does not have to believe anything else) *prima facie* justification for p.

The problem that the CP of perception poses for the epistemic role of perception is that it threatens the role of perception in justifying perceptual beliefs. If prior beliefs affect perceptual processing, this arguably affects the justificatory role of perception. It is intuitive to argue that if the belief that X is F causally affects perceptual processing of a visual scene in which an X is present and as a result a viewer has an experience with content "X is F" on which the viewer subsequently bases the belief that X is F, one has a right to suspect that the role of the prior belief in affecting the content of perception undermines the rational support for the perceptually based belief; the belief is epistemically compromised.

Siegel (2013: 702–703) calls the phenomenon of CP leading to epistemically compromised beliefs, the *downgrade principle*. The experience E that results from, among other factors, the causal influence of a prior belief and owing to this casual influence has its justificatory role diminished, is epistemically downgraded. According to Siegel (2013: 707), when the CP of an experience downgrades the experience by diminishing its justificatory role, this happens because the experience is formed through an irrational process; it is the irrational etiology of the experience that epistemically downgrades it (Siegel 2013: 699–700). The experiences that are generated through an irrational process, i.e., those that are causally affected by prior mental states in a way that diminishes their justificatory role, generate ill-formed beliefs on account of their etiology.

It is contestable that there are discursive inferences either in early or late vision (Hatfield 2009; Raftopoulos 2011). This undermines the argument that some perceptual processes could be deemed with less rationality on account of their structural affinities to less rational discursive inferences. For the rest of this paper, I assume that only taking into consideration externalistic notions, such as the sensitivity of perception to the data, could one hope to achieve an adequate account of the role of CP in downgrading perception. Externalists hold that to understand the epistemic role of perception, one need invoke truth-related factors, such as the sensitivity of perception to the environmental data and the extent to which perception faithfully reflects the environment.

CP may be epistemically damaging because it creates insensitivity to the distal stimulus, and it may be epistemically beneficial if it increases this sensitivity. Wishful seeing, for example, leads through perception to unjustified beliefs because a viewer's beliefs influence her perception to such an extent that she may see that X is F independent of whether this is true or not. CP downgrades perception because it makes a viewer's beliefs insufficiently dependent on her environment and bases them more on her prior mental state; this may make the viewer, simply put, see things that are not there.

4 The Epistemic Role of Early Vision, Pre-cueing, and CP

The epistemic criterion for CP entails that to determine whether a perceptual stage is CP one should examine whether there are cognitive influences that affect its epistemic role. To do that, one should delineate first the epistemic role of the perceptual stage. The epistemic role of perception in grounding perceptual beliefs centers on, but is not exhausted in, the percept because it is the percept that ultimately grounds the perceptual belief whose content matches the content of the percept. The percept that O is F is formed in late vision because it presupposes that the object and the features in a visual scene have been identified and this takes place in late vision. It follows that the onus of perceptual justification is on late vision. The details of the processes by which late vision forms the percept have been discussed elsewhere (Raftopoulos 2011). For the purposes of my arguments here suffices it to say that the epistemic role of late vision is affected by cognitive influences and, thus, late vision is CP.

The epistemic role of early vision is determined by the fact that early vision retrieves from the visual scene information that is fed to late vision and is used for the construction of the percept. The iconic information delivered by early vision (the proximal image or stimulus) provides the support basis on which the various hypotheses concerning the identity of objects in the visual scene are formed and tested in late vision. Thus, the role of early vision is to retrieve from the environment the information that will be used by late vision. Early vision delivers a structural description of the visual scene that contains information about the 3D shape as viewed from the perceiver, spatio-temporal and surface properties, color, texture, orientation, motion, and affordances of objects, in addition to the representations of objects as bounded, solid entities that persist in space and time.

I have argued (Raftopoulos 2009, 2015) that early vision is CI because it is not directly affected by cognition since the processes of early vision do not operate over the contents of any cognitive states. My arguments were based on empirical evidence showing that object/feature based attention and cognitively driven or endogenous spatial attention are delayed and affect the visual areas of the brain (from V1 to IT) after 150–170 ms poststimulus, which means that their effects are felt in the visual areas of the brain after the time frame of early vision.

Recently, some philosophers and cognitive scientists argued against the view that early vision is CI on the grounds of empirical evidence suggesting that cognitively driven object/feature-based and spatial attention modulate perceptual processing during early vision. Many studies show that when subjects are instructed to attend to a certain location or attend for a certain object/feature to appear, the neuronal assemblies in the visual brain whose receptive fields are withing the attended location, or the neuronal assemblies that encode the feature indicated by these instructions receive a boost in their activation as a result of these instructions before the appearance of the stimulus. This means that cognitive effects affect perceptual processing from its inception, and, hence, they affect early vision rendering it CP.

Cognitive effects are involved in this process because the instructions determine attentional commands (wait for a red latter A to appear, or attend to the upper left part of the screen) to be carried out and these commands require that the subject understand them. When subjects are instructed that a red object will appear on a screen, they use their cognitive resources to understand the instruction and activate their knowledge concerning the color red by activating the neuronal assemblies in the cognitive centers of the brain that store this knowledge. The activation is spread top-down and increases the baseline activation of the neuronal assemblies in the visual areas of the brain that encode the color red. Such instructions function as cues directing attention and, since they are given before stimulus presentation, the experimental setting is called pre-cueing. Pre-cueing can occur by cues presented on a screen without any accompanied verbal instructions, such as the arrow 'up'. These cues generate attentional commands because the subject understands them and the ensuing attentional effects are cognitively driven.

The problem is to decide whether pre-cueing effects entail that early vision is CP. To do so, one should examine them and determine whether they satisfy the epistemic criterion for CP, that is, whether pre-cueing effects influence the epistemic role of early vision. Since this epistemic role consists in retrieving visual information from the environment, the epistemic role of early vision would be affected if pre-cueing could influence the processes of information retrieval during early vision, because, then, it would affect the sensitivity of early vision to the environmental data.

There is also a related problem that pre-cueing creates for the thesis that early vision is CI. Pre-cueing effects are found early in perceptual processing in ERP components, which seems to entail that the processes of early vision operate over cognitive information. This is a problem because the standard definitions of CP hinge on whether some perceptual process operates over cognitive information; should such evidence be found, this would entail that early vision is CP.

4.1 Pre-Cueing and Early Vision

The cognitive effects on early vision that I discuss are the cases of pre-cueing effectuated by covert shifts of attention. I do not discuss the indirect cognitive effects consisting in shifts of cognitively driven overt attention because these effects are realized through eye- or body-movements introducing an external factor in the causal chain by which cognition affects perception and the existence of an external factor is almost unanimously thought not to entail CP. Whenever viewers are instructed to attend to a certain location or a certain feature or object to appear, or when they implicitly or explicitly expect some object or feature to appear on a certain location or they expect a specific object or feature to appear on the screen, attention affects perception by modulating the internal on-goings biasing the baseline activation of the neurons that encode the expected stimulus or location. By being internal and not external, this sort of attentional effects is a viable candidate as a cause of CP of early vision.

Studies of the effects of spatial cues before stimulus presentation show early modulation of perceptual processing (Carrasco 2011; Reynolds and Chelazzi 2004). Attending to a location may enhance the base-line activation of the neuronal assemblies tuned to the attended location in specialized extrastriate areas V2, V3, V3a, V4, and in parietal regions (Heeger and Ress 2004; Hopfinger et al. 2004; Kastner and Ungerleider 2000) and in striate cortex V1 (Kastner et al. 1999) by an average of 30–40%, although the increase is more pronounced in V4 and less evident if V1 (Kastner et al. 1999; Ling et al. 2009). Following target onset, spatial attention increased the amplitude of early visual responses to cued targets at about 100 ms after target onset (Wyart et al et al. 2012).

This phenomenon refers to the enhancement of the baseline activity of neurons at all levels in the visual cortex that are tuned to a location that is cued and thus this location is attended before the onset of any stimuli. It is called *attentional modulation of spontaneous activity*. The spontaneous firing rates of these neurons are increased when attention is shifted toward the location of an upcoming stimulus before its presentation.

This cueing reflects the effects of the neural processes that occur in response to cues to orient attention to a location before the stimulus appears. Spatial attention enhances the sensitivity of the neurons tuned to the attended spatial location by improving the signal-to-noise ratio of the neurons tuned to the attended location over the neurons with receptive fields outside the attended location that contribute only noise. Spatial pre-cueing operates by boosting the gain of the neuronal responses, that is, it increases by a multiplicative factor the overall neuronal response of all the relevant neurons, and, thus, increases the response of all feature detectors independent of which features are the targets and the nontargets (Ling et al. 2009). This effect does not determine what is perceived in that location because by enhancing the responses of all neurons tuned to the attended location independent of the neurons' preferred stimuli keeps the differential responses of the neurons' unaltered and thus does not affect what is perceived. "The increase in baseline activity might be due, for example, to an activation of large populations of neurons containing the attended spatial location within their receptive fields and responding relatively nonspecifically to the various features of the expected stimuli" (Kastner et al. 1999: 758).

What is perceived depends on the relative activity of appropriate assemblies of neurons that selectively code the features of the stimulus compared to the activity of assemblies that do not code the features of the stimulus and contribute noise. Since the percept depends on the differential response of these assemblies, the effects of spatial attention by not evoking differential responses leaves the percept unchanged. Spatial attention makes detection of the objects/features in the scene easier but does not determine the percept.

Evidence (Carrasco, 2011; Kok et al. 2014; Liu et al. 2007) suggests that through pre-cueing of features (a particular color or a particular grating) feature-based attention modulates prestimulus activity in the visual cortex. In fMRI experiments designed to examine the effects of feature attention to color and motion on the visual, frontal, and parietal areas, a cue appeared 1 s before the stimulus. The activity within the color sensitive visual areas and the motor sensitive visual areas was increased by attention to color and motion, respectively. This resulted in the relevant visual areas that encode color showing enhanced activation as early as 80 ms after stimulus presentation.

The effects of feature-based attention in feature pre-cueing may act either as a preparatory activity to enhance stimulus-evoked potentials and, thus, the sensitivity to the cued feature, within feature sensitive areas, or they may act to modulate stimulus-locked transients suppressing neural noise; feature-based precueing operates by both boosting the and sharpening the tining of the neuronal response. In either case, they make the detection of the target easier, less expensive, and faster. Thus, the preparatory activity that occurs through pre-cues that rely on feature/object based attention increases the baseline firing rate of the neurons preferring the cued stimulus. These effects are widespread from V1, V2 to upper levels of perceptual processing.

Research (Itti & Koch 2001; Montemayor and Haladjian 2015: 41–42; Raftopoulos 2009: chapter Two) suggests that visual objects are individuated by the early visual stage irrespective of whether they are targets or non-targets, which means that early vision retrieves the required information and individuates all objects in a visual scene, despite the modulation of the prestimulus activity due to object/feature-based pre-cueing. Further research suggests that there is rich information from a visual scene stored in early visual circuits independent of storage limitations of visual working memory and outside of the focus of attention; non-cued or suppressed items are perceived and processed despite the fact that they are not attended to. In addition, it is very likely that subjects have phenomenal awareness of some of these items (Block 2014; Bronfman et al. 2014; Frassle et al. 2014; Vandenbroucke 2014). Therefore, despite feature- or object-based pre-cueing, both non-cued and cued items are all perceptually represented in early vision.

Both effects of pre-cueing reflect a change in background neural activity. They are called anticipatory effects established prior to viewing the stimulus. In this sense, they do not modulate processing during stimulus viewing but they bias the process before it starts; they do not affect perceptual processing on-line. There are various interpretations of the effects of pre-cueing on the neural activity in the occipital areas of the brain. They may act so as to increase the base line firing rates of the neurons that encode the pre-cued stimuli; these are cases of gain modulation (Kastner et al. 1998). Alternatively, they may act so as to suppress noisy neural activity rather than to increase the activity of the neurons that encode the information contained in the pre-cueing signal (Hegde & Kersten 2010). It may also be that a variety of mechanisms are available and which one is chosen depends on the task at hand, which means that attention can flexibly solicit different ways to modulate the activity of neurons (Gilbert & Li 2013). The net result is the same: anticipatory activity sharpens and optimises the response properties of the affected neurons according to anticipated stimulus independent of whether a stimulus is expected as more likely to appear, or attended to as more relevant to the viewer's purposes. As such, anticipatory effects do not emerge as part of perceptual competition and in this sense they are not intrinsic to perceptual processing, which is otherwise unaffected by top-down effects. During the feedforward processing and local recurrent processing there are no top-down cognitive effects due to pre-cueing; the perceptual processes are data-driven.

What pre-cueing does is to set up the values of some parameters of the transformation rules in FFS processing. When they set the parameters of the transformation rules, the pre-cueing effects highlight some information, by enhancing the activation of the neurons that encode this information, but they do not create the proximal image or stimulus. In the case of object/feature pre-cueing, although anticipatory effects enhance the activity of the neurons responding preferentially to the pre-cued object or feature increasing the likelihood that they will be selected eventually for further processing, early vision still retrieves in parallel information concerning all the objects and features present in the visual scene so that these objects be individuated independently of whether they are targets or non-targets. What they essentially do is to modulate early perceptual filters; in this sense, they act "as a 'filter' that 'selects' the information for downstream processing, which may itself be impervious to cognitive influence" (Firestone and Scholl 2016: 23–24). These parameters can be construed as the attentional parameters that weight the effect of sensory signals postulated in computational models of perceptual attention. Pre-cueing may increase the value of some parameter and decrease that of another and this results in some input being given priority in terms of subsequent processing but this does not mean that early vision does not retrieve all information in the visual scene. Pre-cueing effects do not select which information is retrieved from the visual scene once the visual scene has been determined; all information from the visual scene is retrieved in parallel in early vision.

When attention is used on-line, that is, during visual processing, cognitively-driven selective attentional control selects for further processing a specific feature or object in a visual scene by increasing the firing rates of neurons that have a stimulus-evoked response to a particular stimulus; in this case, top-down signals modulate perceptual processing during stimulus viewing. In pre-cueing, processing during stimulus viewing in early vision relies solely on bottom-up processing or top-down and lateral processing restricted within visual areas. This is different from the role of attentional control during visual processing that involves a top-down attentional control of the perceptual input.

If pre-cueing does not affect the information retrieved from the visual scene, cognition does not affect the selection of the 'evidence' or the information against which hypotheses concerning object identity will be tested in late vision. It follows that pre-cueing and the various cognitive effects underlying it do not affect the epistemic role of early vision; pre-cueing does not entail the CP of perception.

There is an additional question that needs to be answered. CP goes hand in hand with the thesis that cognition directly affects early vision in the sense that the processes of early vision use cognitive contents as an informational resource. The question, thus, is the following. Do pre-cueing effects suggest that cognition affects directly early vision?

In view of the fact that the electrophysiological signatures of pre-cueing effects are found within the time frame of early vision, one must examine these electrophysiological signatures. O'Shea et al. (2004), for example, found early latencies for target/distractor discrimination tasks, as in their study the discrimination by FEF neurons was effective after 100–120 ms after stimulus onset. O'Shea et al. (2004: 1063) note that the early latencies discrepancy may be explained by the fact that the repetition of the same target/distractor combination likely resulted in feature priming across the 10 blocks of 80 trials in their experiment and such priming has been shown to produce earlier target discrimination peaks in monkey FEF. This priming leads to expectations about the upcoming stimulus and is, thus, a sort of feature priming. One first response, thus, may be that in some experimental settings, the early latencies due to pre-cueing reflect some sort of priming effects. Priming effects belong to the category of perceptual learning that does not, being data- rather than cognitive-driven, signify cognitive influences on perception.

Another response could be that they are carry-over effects of the initial enhanced activation of the relevant feature sensitive areas owing to pre-cueing, that is, of the anticipatory effect of pre-cueing. This means that the fact that they are found during early vision processing does not entail that the processes of early vision operate over cognitive contents. Even though pre-cueing effects set the attentional parameters that we discussed in the previous paragraphs and these parameters in turn affect perceptual processing, the pre-cueing effects act so as to set some initial values but they do not alter the equations that govern the state transformation in which the processing consists. It follows that pre-cueing does not affect the processes of early vision themselves, and, thus, does not affect early vision directly.

This conclusion is reinforced by a recent study examining the effects of TMS on FEF in relation to precueing (Taylor and Nobre 2007), who applied TMS to the right FEF during the spatial cueing period of a covert attentional task. They found that inducing activity in the right FEF with TMS during the cueing period of a rule-guided covert endogenous attentional orienting task modulated ERPs recorded over visual cortex, which suggests that the TMS applied to FEF altered functional processes related to perception and attention in the visual cortex. FEF TMS had a causal impact on visual activity measured with ERPs. The earliest effect of TMS was a sustained negative deflection during the interval between the cue and the visual stimulus. This negativity remained until 200 ms after stimulus onset. The data were normalized to a pre-TMS baseline period to emphasize ERP shifts occurring after warning cue onset but before visual stimulus presentation. The normalization shows that this negativity remained present in the ERP until 200 ms after stimulus presentation, which means that this negativity can be interpreted as an effect on visual processing at the time of the attentional modulation of the ERP. Thus, the enhancement of the neural activity does not simply reflect the increase in baseline activity but also reflects the attentional modulation of the visually evoked activity. This is important because it speaks against attempts to deflate the role of attention by arguing that attention merely determines the where and what viewers focus their attention on but otherwise leaves perceptual processing unaffected; attention is merely a selection effect (Firestone & Scholl 2016; Siegel 2011, 2013; Pylyshyn 1999). Note that the attentional enhancement of the baseline activity and the attentional modulation of visually evoked activity are not tightly coupled suggesting that they might derive from different but overlapping populations of neurons (Kastner et al. 1999: 758).

In view of the fact that the spatial attention modulation of the occipital visual areas is delayed in time and occurs after 170 ms post stimulus, one would expect that TMS applied to FEF would affect the neuronal activity in early visual areas with a similar time delay, if TMS effects on FEF affected online visual processing by controlling top-down attention. Indeed, when Taylor and Nobre (2007) isolated the stimulus-evoked activity by using the peristimulus period as the baseline, ERPs differed significantly as a function of FEF TMS starting at 200 ms.

This study shows that TMS on FEF is affecting ongoing visual cortical activity prior to visual stimulation, and it is not just affecting the visual cortex's generation of an ERP. These results mean that

(a) FEF TMS affects neuronal activity in the posterior visual areas prior to the presentation of the stimulus, in accordance with the view that FEF activity causally affects the visual activity in posterior visual areas when spatial attention is being allocated. Note, that the fact that the enhancement of FEF activity after the spatial cue but before stimulus presentation does not increase after stimulus presentation (unlike in areas V2, V4 and IT), that is, the fact that no additional activity is evoked in FEF by the onset of visually stimuli (Kastner et al. 1999), possibly means that FEF activity is related more to the attentional demands and operations of the task rather than to perceptual processing.

(b) TMS on FEF continues to affect the visual cortical activity generated by the visual stimulus for about 200 ms after stimulus presentation, which refutes the view that visual stimulation causes the immediate cessation of the cortical processes that were started by TMS; the pre-stimulus stimulation of FEF keeps playing a role in the control of top-down spatial attention even after stimulus onset;

(c) the effects on visually evoked activity of the FEF controlled top-down attention are felt on the posterior visual areas at about 200 ms after stimulus onset, which means that their latencies fall within late vision but outside early vision. This last result is very important because it shows that the cognitive states that drive cognitively-driven attention do not affect early vision but only late vision.

A third possible response is that the attentional parameters in perceptual computations exemplify a way of how cognitive contents can be accessed and operated over without their role in the computation being appropriately inference-like, that is, without there being a logical, semantic, relation between the cognitive contents that issue the attentional commands that set the values of the attentional parameters and the contents of the relevant perceptual states. This is important because one of the reasons adduced to support the view that early vision is CI is that CP requires that the cognitive and the perceptual contents stand in a semantic, quasi-logical relation of the sort found in discursive inferences. Even though a computational transition might itself be deemed an inference, or inference-like, not all elements of the computation, the attentional parameters, for example, need be quasi-semantic. The attentional weights that are computationally relevant affect computations in a way that does not presuppose that the cognitive contents that set them stand in the appropriate semantic relation required by CP.

5 Conclusion

I have argued that pre-cueing does not diminish the sensitivity of early vision to the distal data since all data in the visual scene are retrieved and form the proximal image. Pre-cueing does not affect the information that early vision retrieves from a visual scene and is subsequently used in late vision to establish object identity; the information retrieved from the visual scene reflects only the environment and the perceptual makeup of the viewer. The epistemic role of early vision is not affected by the cognitive effects due to pre-cuing and, thus, early vision is not the source of the epistemic downgrade of perception owing to CP. When such an etiology emerges, it is due exclusively to the CP of late vision and the way late vision functions. In addition, pre-cueing does not affect the ongoing perceptual processes and, thus, does not entail that early vision uses cognitive information; it does not affect early vision directly

References

Block, N. (2014): "Rich conscious perception outside focal attention". In: *Trends in Cognitive Science, 18.* No.9, pp. 445–447.
Bronfman, Z Z., Brezis, N., Jacobson, H., & Usher, M. (2014): "We see more that we can report: 'cost free' color phenomenality outside focal attention". In: *Psychological Science,* 25. No. 7, pp. 1394–1403.
Carrasco, M. (2011): "Visual attention: the past 25 years". In: *Vision Research,* 51, pp. 1484–1525.
Cecchi, A. (2014): "Cognitive penetration, perceptual learning, and neural plasticity". In: *Dialectica,* 68. No.1, pp. 63–95.
Chelazzi, L., Miller, E., Duncan, J., Desimone, R. (1993): "A neural basis for visual search in inferior temporal cortex". In: *Nature,* 363. No, 3, pp. 45–347.
Churchland, P. M. (1988): "Perceptual plasticity and theoretical neutrality: a reply to Jerry Fodor". In: *Philosophy of Science,* 55, pp. 167–187.
Drewes, J., Goren, G., Zhu, W., & Elder, J/H. (2016): "Recurrent processing in the formation of percept shapes". In: *The Journal of Neuroscience,* 36. No.1, pp. 185–192.
Firestone, C., & Scholl, B. (2016): "Seeing and thinking: foundational issues and empirical horizons". In: *Behavioral and Brain Sciences, Behavioral and Brain Sciences,* DOI: http://dx.doi.org/10.1017/S0140525X15000965.
Frassle, S., Sommer, J., Jansen, A., Naber, M., & Einhauser, W. (2014): "Binocular rivalry: frontal activity relates to introspection and action but no to perception". In: *The Journal of Neuroscience,* 34. No. 1, pp. 1738–1747.
Gilbert, C. D., and Li, W. (2013): "Top-down influences on visual processing". In: Nature *Reviews Neuroscience* 14. No. 5, pp. 350–363.
Goldstone, R. L., de Leeuw, J. R., & Landy, D. H. (2015). "Fitting perception in and to cognition". In: *Cognition,* 135, pp. 24–29.
Hanson, N. R. (1958): *Patterns of Discovery.* Cambridge: Cambridge University Press.
Hatfield, G. (2009): *Perception and Cognition: Essays in the Philosophy of Psychology.* Oxford: Clarendon Press.
Hegde, J., & Kersten, D. (2010): "A link between visual disambiguation and visual memory". In: *The Journal of Neuroscience,* 30. No. 45, pp. 15124–15133.
Heeger, D. J., and Ress, D. (2004): "Neuronal correlates of visual attention and perception". In: Gazzaniga, M. S. (Ed.): *The Cognitive Neurosciences* (third edition). Cambridge, MA: The MIT Press, pp. 339–350.

Heinen, K., Jolij, J., & Lamme, V.A. (2005): "Figure-ground segregation requires two distinct periods of activity in V1: a transcranial magnetic study". In: *Neuroreport*, 16. No. 13, pp. 1483–1487.
Hopfinger, J. B., Luck, S. J., & Hillyard, S. A. (2004): "Selective attention". In: Gazzaniga, M. S. (Ed.): *The Cognitive Neurosciences* (third edition). Cambridge, MA: The MIT Pres], pp. 561–574.
Huemer, M. (2007): "Compassionate phenomenal conservatism". In: *Philosophy and Phenomenological Research*, 74, pp. 30–55.
Itti, L., & Koch, C., (2001): "Computational modelling of visual attention". In: *Nature Reviews Neuroscience*, 2, pp. 194–204.
Kastner, S., and Ungerleider, L. G. (2000): "Mechanisms of visual attention in the human cortex". In: *Annual Review of Neuroscience*, 23, pp. 315–341.
Kastner, S., Pinsk, M. A., De Weerd, P., Desimone, R., & Ungerleider, L. (1999): "Increased activity in human visual cortex during directed attention in the absence of visual stimulation". In: *Neuron*, 22, pp. 751–761.
Kok, P., Failing, M., & de Lange, F. (2014): "Prior expectations evoke stimulus templates in the primary visual cortex". In: *Journal of Cognitive Neuroscience*, 26, pp. 1546–1554.
Kuhn, T. S. (1962): *The Structure of Scientific Revolutions*. Chicago: Chicago University Press.
Lamme, V. A. F. (2003): "Why visual attention and awareness are different". In: *Trends in Cognitive Sciences*, 7. No. 1, pp. 12–18.
Ling, S., Liu, T., & Carrasco, M. (2009): "How spatial and feature-based attention affect the gain and tunning of population responses". In: *Vision Research*, 49, pp. 1194–1204.
Liu, T., Stevens, S. T., & Carrasco, M. (2007): "Comparing the time course and efficacy of spatial and feature-based attention". In: *Vision Research*, 47, pp. 108–113.
Lupyan, G. (2015): "Object knowledge changes visual appearance: semantic effects on color afterimages". in: *Acta Psychologica*, 161, pp. 117–130.
McGrath, M. (2013): "Phenomenal conservatism and cognitive penetration". In: Tucker, C. (Ed.): *Seemings and Justification*. Oxford: Oxford University Press, pp. 225–247.
Montemayor, C., & Haladjian, H. (2015): *Consciousness, Attention, and Conscious Attention*. Cambridge, MA: The MIT Press.
Ogilivie, R., & Carruthers, P. (2015): "Opening up vision: the case against encapsulation". In: *Review of Philosophy and Psychology*, DOI: 10.1007/s13164-015-0294.
O'Shea, J., Muggleton, N.G., Cowey, A., & Walsh, V. (2004): "Timing of target discrimination in human front eye fields". In: *Journal of Cognitive Neuroscience*, 16. No. 6, pp. 1060–1067.
Pylyshyn, Z. (1999): "Is vision continuous with cognition?" In: *Behavioral and Brain Sciences*, 22, pp. 341–365.
Raftopoulos, A. (2009): *Cognition and perception: How do psychology and neural science inform philosophy?* Cambridge, MA: MIT Press.
Raftopoulos, A. (2011): "Late vision: its processes and epistemic status". In: *Front Psychol*. 2 (382). Published online 2011 November 30: doi: 10.3389/fpsyg.2011.00382.
Raftopoulos, A. (2014): "The cognitive impenetrability of the content of early vision is a necessary and sufficient condition for purely nonconceptual content". In: *Philosophical Psychology*, 27. Vol. 5, pp. 601–620.
Raftopoulos, A. (2015): "The cognitive impenetrability of perception and theory-ladenness". In: *Journal of General Philosophy of Science*. 46. No. 1, pp. 87–103
Reynolds, J.H. & Chelazzi, L. (2004): "Attentional modulation of visual processing". In: *Annual Review of Neuroscience*, 27, pp. 611–647.

Roelfsema, P. R., Lamme, V. A. F., & Spekreijse, H. (1998): "Object-based attention in the primary visual cortex of the macaque monkey". In: *Nature,* 395, pp. 376–381.

Sellars, W. (1956): "Empiricism and the philosophy of mind". In: H. Feigl, H., and M. Scrive, M (Eds.): *Minnesota Studies in The Philosophy of Science, Vol. I.* Minneapolis, MN: University of Minnesota Press, pp. 253–329.

Siegel, S. (2011): "Cognitive penetrability and perceptual justification". In: *Nous,* 46, pp. 201–222.

Siegel, S. (2013) "The Epistemic Impact of the Etiology of Experience". In: *Philosophical Studies,* 162 (3), pp. 697–722.

Siegel, S (2017): "How is wishful seeing like wishful thinking?". In: *Philosophy and Phenomenological Research,* 9 (2), pp. 408–435.

Stokes, D. (2015): "Towards a consequentialist understanding of cognitive penetration". In: Zeimbekis, J. & Raftopoulos, A. (Eds.): *Cognitive Penetrability of Perception: New Philosophical Perspectives.* Oxford; Oxford University Press, pp. 75–100

Taylor, P. C. J., & Nobre, A. (2007): "FEF TMS affects visual cortical activity". In: *Cerebral Cortex,* 17, pp. 391–399.

Tucker, C. (2014): "If dogmatists have a problem with cognitive penetration, you do too". In: *Dialectica,* 68. No. 1, pp. 35–62.

Vandenbroucke, A. R. F., Fahrenfort, J. J., Sligte, I. G., & Lamme, V. A. F. (2014): "Seeing without knowing: neural signatures of perceptual inference in the absence of report". In: *Journal of Cognitive Neuroscience,* 26. No. 5, pp. 955–969.

Vetter, P., & Newen, A. (2014): "Varieties of cognitive penetration in visual perception". In: *Consciousness and Cognition,* 27, pp. 62–75.

Wyart, V., Dehaene, S., & Tallon-Baudry, C. (2012): "Early dissociation between neural signatures of endogenous spatial attention and perceptual awareness during visual masking". In: *Frontiers in human neuroscience,* 10, https://doi.org/10.3389/fnhum.2012.00016.

Ophelia Deroy
Predictions do not Entail Cognitive Penetration: "Racial" Biases in Predictive Models of Perception

Abstract: According to predictive accounts of the mind, our brains do not simply process information upstream- but constantly predict the upcoming signals, to only process the difference between these predictions and the incoming information. But does the role of these top-down processes mean that all perception is influenced by cognition? Or does it rather suggest that the distinction between cognition and perception collapses, as every level of processing now integrates predictions?
While the later suggestion is embraced by most interpreters of, and contributors to, predictive accounts, I argue that cognition, or thought, remains distinctive by being the only level that is not predicted by a level above. Using this definition and the example of the «race-lightness» effect, I show that the problem of cognitive influence of perception can be reframed in a graded manner, and make us ask how much perception can be affected by a change in these higher level cognitive predictions.[1]

Keywords: Predictive accounts, cognitive penetration, perceptual bias, racial bias, metacognition, cognition

1 Introduction

Racial perceptual biases are, rightly so, among the most discussed in the literature. Not only do they confirm that our perception of the world is not always ac-

---

[1] Versions of the present paper were presented at the 40th International Wittgenstein Symposium in Kirchberg, the PLM conference in Bochum, the ECAP in Munich, and at departmental seminars in Salzburg and Magdeburg. Thanks to the organisers and audience of these events, for their very insightful and helpful comments. Particular thanks to Christopher Gauker, Sascha Fink, Christoph Limbeck-Lilienau, Albert Newen and Jesse Prinz for comments. I also thanks Merle Fairhurst and Eoin Travers for their indispensable contribution to the empirical and theoretical arguments exposed in this paper. The ideas reflected here do not engage them, but would not have emerged without our collaboration.

https://doi.org/10.1515/9783110657920-014

curate, but their inaccuracy comes with worrying ethical consequences. This concern starts with the suggestion that racial categories – whose use and even mention are highly questionable – have a pervasive influence on our mental lives, including the most basic perceptual processes. Among the most concerning biases to be documented in perception is the tendency to categorise an ambiguous object as a gun when it is carried by a black man, and as a mere phone or tool when carried by a white man (Correll et al. 2002; Payne 2006; see also Ofan et al. 2011 for a priming study). Another, no less sadly significant bias, is the 'cross-race' recognition deficit (Levin 2000; Hugenberg et al. 2007). This well-documented effect shows that individuals tend to perceive members of another ethnic group as more similar to one another than members of their own – a bias which has also impact on re-identification of criminals in court cases (Sporer, 2001).

However important to the ethicists, these biases are not the ones that attract most attention from philosophers of perception. One bias, documented by Levin & Banaji in 2006, has been the object almost of a monopolistic interest from experts in perception: This so-called 'race-lightness' bias shows that the perceived lightness of skin is influenced by the morphology of the face it belongs to, depending on whether it corresponds to a typically African or a typically European morphology. Though human faces present a high degree of distinction, there is evidence that their morphological and skin tone differences correlate between humans (Jablonski & Chaplin 2000, Stepanova & Strube 2012) making it likely, that this correlation is learned by human perceivers. The authors' hypothesis was to test whether this prior knowledge about the reflectance of faces also affects their perceived lightness.

In the most telling of their experiment, participants were asked to adjust the luminance of a test face to match the luminance of a target face. The target face could present either a typically African or typically European morphology, and vary in luminance (five values). The response face was also either of the same morphology or a different one, to counter-balance the design. What the results show then is that faces with the same objective luminance were not perceived as equally light or dark depending on the facial features of the target: Faces with typically African morphology were consistently matched to a darker shade than faces with typically European morphology, though their mean objective luminance was similar.

In another experiment, participants were presented with the same face, accompanied either by the label 'Black' or 'White', and similar biases were observed: Here, both luminance and morphology being equal, a face was perceived as darker when labeled as 'Black' rather than 'White'.

The reason why this bias is so important is that, by contrast with the gun/tool bias, it does not correspond to a difficult situation of perception. The stimuli are presented without time constraints, and the response is also possibly slow. By contrast with the cross-race recognition deficit, it is clearly about perception, and not memory. More crucially, this bias is also a good case of non-motivated perception. Research has indeed shown that the responses in the gun / tool task were largely driven by fear responses (Azevedo et al. 2017). Last but not least, the bias here affects a continuous variable (the judgement of brightness) and can itself be manipulated parametrically (by manipulating the morphological features through morphing).

The philosophical challenge arises then from this perceptual manifestation, as mentioned by Firestone and Scholl (2016): "it is, to our knowledge, the only purported top-down effect on perception that readers can experience for themselves simply by looking at the stimuli." While most experiments on top-down influences show effects on reports or judgements, which remain problematic, this effect shows a clear influence on perceptual experience (see Deroy 2013 for discussion). The influence of thought, or its conceptual constituents, on perceptual experience is at the core of what philosophers have in mind when discussing cognitive penetration of perception (e.g., MacPherson 2012, Siegel 2012, Newen & Vetter 2017) though it is certainly not the only version of cognitive penetration that is discussed (e.g., Pylyshyn 1999, Raftopoulos 2001, Zeimbekis & Raftopoulos 2015 for discussion).

What's more, because the effect is not timed, nor dependent on a special attentional scanning of the scene, attentional explanations are more easily ruled out. However, in this paper, I want to show that interpreting the 'race-lightness' effect as a case of cognitive penetration is problematic. What's more, framing this as a case of cognitive penetration is not helpful. I want to suggest that this case raises a different problem.

2 Three Issues with the Cognitive Penetration Interpretation of the Bias

2.1 What is the Source of Influence?

Cognitive penetration accounts need to provide a plausible candidate for the source of the cognitive influence. However, it is really unclear what that can be in the case of the race-lightness effect.

The strength of the perceptual effect studied by Levin & Banaji (2006) does not seem to correlate with explicit racist or essentialist attitudes: The effect is seen in individuals who don't endorse the idea that there is more to ethnic categories than surface differences, and may object to the concept of race. Can we identify other explicit beliefs that would generally explain, through a cognitive influence, the observed tendency to perceive faces with African facial features as darker than faces with European facial features? The challenge here is that the belief, if it is to be responsible for the effect, must account for the graded character of the effect, as well as its probabilistic nature. It must also remain within the reasonable grounds that no one denies the existence of African people with comparatively light skin colour, and Europeans with comparatively dark skin colour. Supposing that anyone really believes that "All Africans have darker skin colour than Europeans", taking the universal quantifier strictly, attributes to them an ungrounded belief.

Take then the following candidate: People may believe that "Africans have darker skin-complexion than Europeans ". We know from previous research that people hold this type of generic beliefs, even though they do not believe that there cannot be exceptions. If this is the case, this may explain a generic bias, but not explain the fine-grained character of the darkness enhancement as a function of how marked the morphological traits are, either toward a typical African or typical European face. A better candidate here would be to suppose that perceivers hold the belief that "the more pronounced the African facial features, the darker the skin; the more pronounced the European features, the lighter the skin." Though this belief might do better in terms of relating to the effect, it is less plausible than the generic belief mentioned above: This idea of a positive correlation between the markedness of certain facial features, and the skin colour, does not seem to correspond to what people actually believe.

The difficulty, not to say the failure, of identifying a good explicit cognitive candidate pushes one toward other, implicit, candidates. Empirical evidence in the domain of other racial biases points at the role of implicit and associative biases (e.g., as measure by the Implicit Association tests, or IAT, Greenwald et al. 2015 for recent review). Whether implicit bias points toward a single cognitive entity and whether they should be considered as conceptual associations, rather than affective responses, remains debated (e.g. Holyrod & Sweetman 2016). This point leads to a second challenge.

2.2 Is the Influence Genuinely Cognitive?

Besides the problematic role of implicit associations, the literature on biases also points at the role of intermediate levels of categorization, which are pretty different from what we mean by the contents of thoughts (Deroy 2019). Those categories are inherently probabilistic, continuously and quickly updated through exposure, and not consciously accessible (Rigoli et al. 2017, for review).

Several people (including myself, see Deroy 2013) have highlighted the fact that not all top-down influences should count as cognitive in some of the discussed cases of 'cognitive penetration'. Of course, this recommendation is only to be taken seriously if there is a good account of the non-cognitive candidates. As it happens in the race-lightness bias, there is.

2.3 Is this Top-down at all?

An independent challenge, however, has arisen in the case of the race-lightness bias: Do we need to resort to top-down explanations at all? In a recent study, Firestone and Scholl (2014) used blurred faces instead of clear ones. Blurry African faces are still perceived as comparatively darker than blurry European faces by 70% participants, and this despite the reported absence of awareness of racial differences between the two types of faces. In this case, it seems that the distribution of darker and lighter pixels in the blurred versions of the faces drives the effect, turning the bias actually into a reflection of a true difference between the stimuli. As the authors conclude, if differences in the stimuli are sufficient to explain the effect, there is no need to appeal to top-down influences, cognitive or not. The results of this study have been challenged, and discussed, but this is actually beside the point. First, from the evidence provided by the authors, one can exclude that there is a conscious recognition of the differences between the two types of faces, but not that there is a non-conscious one, triggering eventually a high-level conceptual association, or racial categories which exert an influence on the perception of skin lightness. The results are still compatible then with a top-down influence whose source remains unconscious. There is a second issue, this time independent of some alternative explanation of the effects. For even if one grants the conclusion that differences in the distribution of luminance in the blurred stimuli drive the difference in perception, this conclusion does not necessarily generalise to non-blurred cases. In other words, if one does not have sufficient information to categorise or recognize African faces as African, and European faces as European, when the stimuli are blurred, this information becomes available when the faces are not blurred. Then, it is perfectly possible that the low-level differences do not play much role in the non-blurred case tested by Levin & Banaji (2006), and that top-down influences from the categories or concepts triggered by the stimuli do drive the effect. The role of bottom-up differences with blurred faces, when ethnic categorisation is not available, does not preclude that, when ethnic categorisation is possible, with non-blurry faces, there is no role for top-down influences. Indeed, it is even possible to consider that the two explanations are then still valid: The effect in the non-blurry case could be due to a combination of both sensory differences and top-down influences.

2.4 Intermediate Summary

The race-lightness is a robust example of perceptual bias, where differences in the final percept seem to be driven by prior expectations, rather than by differences in the world. Though the effect is most interpreted as an instance of cognitive penetration, this interpretation, however, is problematic in at least three aspects:

First, it is unclear which cognitive state can be cited as a good candidate for the cognitive influence;

second, it is not fully justified why cognitive candidates should be privileged over other top-down non-cognitive influences;

finally, it is not even fully established that top-down influences are at all needed as an explanation.

Each of these problems points at different weaknesses of the account. Some, it could be argued, are conditioned on some empirical evidence still missing, that could eventually be provided by cognitive neuroscience studies. Others, however, seem to be more fundamentally problematic, such as to establish whether unconscious non-cognitive candidates operate or not. There is, undoubtedly, no way to predict what future experimental designs will be able to do, but the primary issue for 'strict' cognitive penetration accounts is that they face a competitive explanation, which can overcome all these difficulties.

3 Predictive Accounts, and the End of the "Cognition Influences Perception" Debate?

3.1 Why Predictive Accounts Count as Best Available Explanation for a Bias Like Race-Lightness

Predictive coding accounts, which are being defended by researchers like Friston[2], in the neurosciences, and Clark, Hohwy, Lupyan in philosophy, provide a way to accommodate all the previous evidence and lack of determinate answer regarding the cause of the race-lightness bias. Perceptual processing is redefined in such accounts as a combination of top-down and bottom-up factors, and includes several layers of top-down influences, ranging from the high-level cognitive influences, with explicit beliefs and propositional attitudes supported by language at the top, to low level, usually precise predictions at the bottom. At each level, predictions are matched to the incoming sensory signal, with only the error (the mismatch between predictions and input) being transferred to the higher level. This model is supposed to explain both the stability of perception and its flexibility in front of new evidence.

In the case of the race-lightness bias, predictive accounts can accommodate both some differences in the stimuli and multiple sources of top-down influences, now redefined as predictions. The higher-level predictions, being the most abstract and general, cascade down to more and more specific predictions about basic sensory features, such as, eventually, brightness processing.

This interpretation overcomes the dilemmas in which the cognitive penetration interpretation was drowning. It raises, however, one problem – at least for philosophers: It seems to dissolve all problems of thought influencing perception, leaving us to understand only how different levels of predictions and error signals explain the perceived bias. More importantly, predictive accounts are usually considered as initiating 'a collapse of perception and cognition' (Lupyan 2015). This diagnosis is echoed by philosophers, such as Andy Clark when he states that predictive coding "makes the lines between perception and cognition fuzzy... In place of any real distinction between perception and belief we now get variable differences in the mixture of top-down and bottom-up influence..." (Clark 2016) and by neuroscientists supporting predictive accounts, such as Karl Friston and Chris Frith, who admit that "within this framework, there is no qual-

---

[2] See Friston (2009), (2010) Clark (2013) and Hohwy (2014) for overviews.

itative distinction between perception and belief, since both involve making inferences about the state of the world on the basis of evidence" (Frith & Friston 2013).

This diagnosis, I want to argue, is mistaken: The cognition/perception divide persists in predictive coding accounts, and therefore, the question of whether thought influences perception still makes sense for a proponent of those accounts.

3.2 The Cognition/Perception Divide in Predictive Accounts

I do not want to deny that predictive coding accounts raise a challenge for the dominant (or once dominant) model of how perception works. Contrary to the dominant model, predictive accounts stress that, right from the earliest level of processing, what is processed is not the whole incoming sensory information, but the mismatch between a prediction coming from a higher level in the hierarchy, and the incoming sensory signal. Still, besides this significant redefinition, every level, in this respect, receives some signal from the level below: The first level receives input from sensory epithelia, and sends the mismatch between the prediction and this signal to the second level; the third level receives then the signal that results from the difference between the second level prediction and the signal it received from the first, and so on and so forth, until the result of the mismatch between prediction and incoming signal from the previous level reaches the last level. In this hierarchy, however, not all levels, however, receive predictions from the level above. Each level receives predictions which integrate the information from the level above, but the upper one. By necessity, predictions must start somewhere, and this upper level of the hierarchy is then the one which predicts but is not predicted by anything else. What I suggest is to call this "thought."

Importantly, the almost trivial observation that the upper level is not predicted by anything else means that, instead of challenging the cognition/perception distinction, predictive coding accounts provide a substantial characterisation of thought. Thought is the process that contributes to predicting other things, but is not itself predicted by anything else.

Obviously, thought gets updated by the flow of error signals coming from the immediately inferior level, which we can generally equate to the perception of objects and scenes. Depending on what one believes perception to be (i.e., akin to or different from beliefs) then the characterisation of the level below thought might change, but this point is orthogonal to our current question. We can expect then that, exposing people to a large number of faces where morphology is not correlated with skin luminance, or where it presents an inverse relation to the present one (i.e., African faces appearing with lighter facial luminance, and European faces with darker facial luminance) will slowly correct the predictions. It is still not obvious how to measure how this change will impact thought. To do so, we have to move to a positive, rather than negative characterisation of thought in predictive coding accounts.

However, by saying that the upper level, i.e., thought, is not predicted by anything else, we are not obliged to say that thought can only be updated by the levels below, for instance by sensory perception. Predictive accounts do not entail this kind of perceptual empiricism. There are at least two other ways in which thought can be updated, that are consistent with this hierarchical model and the 'upper' status of thought: First, thought can be updated by itself – reflectively, so to speak. Second, thought can be updated by other thought contents, linguistically communicated by others. The first possible kind of updating would correspond quite well to what is currently being studied as 'metacognition', or thinking about thinking (e.g. Shea 2018; Deroy et al. 2016, Proust 2013). It is debatable whether metacognition exhausts the kind of self-reflective updating that one can perform on his or her own thought ; it is also debatable whether the working of metacognition rests on predicting thoughts (in which case it should perhaps be called the real 'upper' level) or simply, as more often put, in monitoring thoughts. The question can be left for later. For the immediate purpose, I want to focus on the second kind of updating, which comes from linguistic communication. By contrast with perceptual evidence, which should lead to a slow updating of the predictions, linguistic statements can change one's thought through single exposure (though quantifying this is a delicate matter). The prediction about racial biases now becomes more substantial: If higher-level cognition is involved in predictions, which cascade down to influence lower-level brightness processing, then by initiating a change at this level, by providing the perceiver with a linguistic testimony and/or a set of new instructions, the change should have repercussions all the way down, and change the effect. Because of the stability of lower-level predictions, and because of persisting differences in the initial stimuli, one would also expect a reduction, rather than a disappearance of the bias. This is indeed what is observed with participants who are told about their biases. Travers et al. (2017) ran a variant of the race-lightness effect, inspired by Levin & Banaji (2006), with 90 participants. The first 70 trials confirmed the existence of a robust bias, where morphology would influence the perceived luminance of faces. After those first trials, however, participants were divided in three groups: The first group was informed that they were relying on morphology in their judgements, and advised to do better in the next trials; the second group was informed that they were relying on racial stereotypes in their judgements, and also advised to do better in the next trials. The third group of participants acted as a control, and were just asked to take a rest and to try and do better in the next trials. The results show that the first two groups, whose thoughts and goals had been reset by instructions, showed a significant reduction of the perceptual bias in the next set of trials. Importantly, the time-course of the responses suggest that the reduction of the bias is not due to an inhibition of responses, but to a genuine lowering of the weight given to morphology. In other words, the experiment successfully demonstrates that a change in one's thoughts (or higher-order level cognition) triggers a change in the race-lightness effect, in a way which is congruent with the predictive coding accounts and the idea of a possible, yet indirect influence of thought on perception.

4 Conclusions

I have here argued for two things. First, perceptual biases, instead of fuelling debates about the direct influence of thought on perceptual experience and processing, should be interpreted in a more distributed way, as revealing a partial (not total) influence, of thought on perceptual processing and experience. In other words, the question we should be asking is not "Does thought (or higher-level cognition) influence perceptual experience and processing?" but "How much does thought influence perceptual experience and processing, if it does at all?"

Second, this question suggests that we should be testing the difference that thought can make to perception, rather than focusing only on trying to attribute effects to possible cognitive causes - in a way that might be subject to an over-attribution bias. The right question to ask, in this respect, is not just "How much does *thought* influence perceptual experience and processing?" but "How much will a *difference in thought* change perceptual experience and processing, other things being equal?". Here, I believe we start to have good evidence, in the case of the race-lightness effect, that a change at the higher level of cognition can trigger a moderate change in perception. This reconciles the role of both bottom-up factors, and top-down ones, and only sees the cognitive part of the perceptual bias as one of the many top-down influences which explain its occurrence.

Although I have framed the argument around one specific bias (the 'race lightness bias') it should be valid for others. The argument also rests on predictive accounts but is possibly detached from some of their assumptions (such as the fact that all types of processing in the brain are predictive and Bayesian)[3]. Though I am positively convinced that the predictive models are robust and enable us to approach the mind/brain better than other models, the arguments involved here do not require a specific form of realism or exclusivity toward such models. What matters still is to show that, when working within such models, we are not asked to give up the distinction between perception and cognition, but asked to re-consider new hypotheses and ways to approach it.

References

Azevedo, R.T, Garfinkel, S.N, Critchley, H.D, & Tsakiris M. (2017): "Cardiac afferent activity modulates the expression of racial stereotypes". In: *Nature Communications*, 8, pp. 138–154

Clark, A. (2013): "Whatever next? Predictive brains, situated agents, and the future of cognitive science". In: *Behavioral and Brain Sciences*, 36(03), pp. 181–204.

Clark, A. (2016): *Surfing uncertainty*. Oxford: Oxford University Press.

Correll, J., Park, B., Judd, C. M., & Wittenbrink, B. (2002): "The police officer's dilemma: Using ethnicity to disambiguate potentially threatening individuals". In: *Journal of personality and social psychology*, 83(6), pp. 1314–1329.

Deroy, O. (2013): "Object-sensitivity versus cognitive penetrability of perception". In: *Philosophical Studies*, 162, pp. 87–107.

Deroy, O. (2019): "Categorising without concepts". In: *Review of Philosophy and Psychology*, pp. 1–14.

Deroy, O., Spence, C., & Noppeney, U. (2016): "Metacognition in multisensory perception". In: *Trends in Cognitive Sciences*, 20(10), pp. 736–747.

Firestone, C. & Scholl, B. J. (2014): "Can you experience 'top-down' effects on perception? The case of race categories and perceived lightness". In: *Psychonomic Bulletin and Review*, 22, pp. 694–700.

Firestone, C. & Scholl, B. J. (2016): "Cognition does not affect perception: Evaluating the evidence for 'top-down' effects". In: *Behavioral and Brain Sciences*, 39, pp. 1–77.

Friston, K. (2009): "The free-energy principle: a rough guide to the brain?". In: *Trends in cognitive sciences*, 13(7), 293–301.

Friston, K. J. (2010): "The free-energy principle: a unified brain theory?" In: *Nature Reviews Neuroscience*, 11(2), pp. 127–138.

Frith, C. D., & Friston, K. J. (2013): "False perceptions and false beliefs: Understanding schizophrenia". in: *Neurosciences and the Human Person: New Perspectives on Human Activities*, 121, pp. 1–15.

---

[3] See also Orlandi (2015) for an in-depth discussion of this issue. Though she reaches a more radical conclusion than the present one, she also argues that vision does not need to count as cognitive in any sense in predictive or Bayesian models.

Greenwald, A.G., Banaji, M.R, Nosek, B.A (2015): "Statistically small effects of the Implicit Association Test can have societally large effects". In: *Journal of Personality and Social Psychology*, 108, pp. 553–561.
Holroyd, J., & Sweetman, J. (2016): "The heterogeneity of implicit bias". In: Michael Brownstein & Jennifer Saul (Eds.): *Implicit Bias and Philosophy*. Oxford: Oxford University Press
Hohwy, J. (2014): *The predictive mind*. Oxford: Oxford University Press.
Hugenberg, K., Miller, J., & Claypool, H. M. (2007): "Categorization and individuation in the cross-race recognition deficit: Toward a solution to an insidious problem". In: *Journal of Experimental Social Psychology*, 43(2), pp. 334–340.
Jablonski, N. G., & Chaplin, G. (2000): "The evolution of human skin coloration. In: *Journal of human evolution*, 39(1), pp. 57–106.
Levin, D. T., Banaji, M. R. (2006). Distortions in the perceived lightness of faces: The role of race categories". In: *Journal of Experimental Psychology: General*, 135, pp. 501–512.
Levin, D. T. (2000): "Race as a visual feature: using visual search and perceptual discrimination tasks to understand face categories and the cross-race recognition deficit". In: *Journal of Experimental Psychology: General*, 129(4), pp. 559–574.
Lupyan, G. (2015): "Cognitive penetrability of perception in the age of prediction: Predictive systems are penetrable systems". In: *Review of Philosophy and Psychology*, 6, pp. 547–569.
Macpherson, F. (2012): "Cognitive penetration of colour experience: Rethinking the issue in light of an indirect mechanism". In: *Philosophy and Phenomenological Research*, 84(1), pp. 24–62.
Newen, A., & Vetter, P. (2017): "Why cognitive penetration of our perceptual experience is still the most plausible account". In: *Consciousness and Cognition*, 47, pp. 26–37.
Ofan, R.H., Rubin, N., & Amodio, D. M (2011): "Seeing race: N170 responses to race and their relation to automatic racial attitudes and controlled processing". In: *Journal of Cognitive Neuroscience*, 23, pp. 3153–3161.
Orlandi, N. (2015): *The innocent eye: Why vision is not a cognitive process*. Oxford: Oxford University Press.
Payne, B. K. (2006): "Weapon bias split-second decisions and unintended stereotyping". In: *Current Directions in Psychological Science*, 15, pp. 287–291.
Pylyshyn, Z. (1999): "Is vision continuous with cognition? The case for cognitive impenetrability of visual perception". In: *The Behavioral and Brain Sciences*, 22(3), pp. 341–365; Discussion pp. 366–423.
Proust, J. (2013): *The philosophy of metacognition: Mental agency and self-awareness*. Oxford: Oxford University Press. Oxford.
Raftopoulus, A. (2001): "Is perception informationally encapsulated?: The issue of the theory-ladenness of perception". In: *Cognitive Sciences*, 25(3), pp. 423–451.
Rigoli, F., Pezzulo, G., Dolan, R., Friston, K. (2017): "A goal-directed bayesian framework for categorization". In: *Frontiers in Psychology*, 8, p. 408.
Shea, N. (2018): "Metacognition and abstract concepts". In: *Philosophical Transactions of the Royal Society B: Biological Sciences*, 373(1752), pp. 2017–2133.
Siegel, S. (2012): "Cognitive penetrability and perceptual justification". In: *Noûs*, 46(2), pp. 201–222.
Sporer, S. L. (2001): "The cross-race effect: Beyond recognition of faces in the laboratory". In: *Psychology, Public Policy, and Law*, 7, pp. 170–200.

Stepanova, E. V., & Strube, M. J. (2012): "The role of skin color and facial physiognomy in racial categorization: Moderation by implicit racial attitudes". In: *Journal of Experimental Social Psychology*, 48(4), pp. 867–878.

Travers, E., Fairhurst, M. & Deroy, O. (2017): "Racial biases in social perception: Fast, unconscious, but still surmountable". psyarxiv.com/je7j4. [on-line]

Zeimbekis, J., & Raftopoulos, A. (Eds.) (2015): *The cognitive penetrability of perception: New philosophical perspectives*. Oxford: Oxford University Press.

5 Epistemology of Perception

Charles Travis
Boundless

Abstract: How can perceptual experience reveal the truth to us? How can it bear for us on what (or how) to think? Consider a way for something to relate to something such that, depending on how A is, for A so to relate to B may be, eo ipso, for B to be true. There is such a relation, for example, between the thought that Sid drinks and Pia writes and the thought that Pia writes. Here the way that first item must be is specifiable. The way it is: being true. The relation is thus truth-transmitting. In such a relation B, a potential truth, must be something conceptually structured. Now an idea: So, too, A; there are such relations only between conceptually structured things. An idea with some currency. On it, the conceptual is, so to speak, unbounded. In Wittgenstein's mocking words, "one cannot step outside it, one must always turn back again. There is no outside, outside there is no air to breathe" (Investigations §103). But this idea misconceives radically the business of representing-as, and it is disastrous. For, first, it erases the conceptual altogether. Second, it encourages a sort of desperate reverse-psychologism, with which empirical psychological theses masquerade as conceptual necessities. So the conceptual is bounded. Some relations are, not truth-transmitting, but truth yielding. All this the present brief.

Keywords: Truth, conceptual, perception, perceptual experience, reverse psychologism

> You cannot escape it. You must always turn back. There is no outside; outside there is no air to breathe. (Wittgenstein, 1953: §103)

Frege once wrote,

> One justifies a judgement either by tracing it back to already recognised truths, or without making use of other judgements. Only the first case, that of consequence, is the concern of logic. (n.d.: 190 (*Kernsatz* 13))

This essay's concern is with that second case. Perception, one would have thought, would provide a fertile field for justification of this second sort, a prime instance where such is to be found. For perception's main work, one would have thought, is to reveal (or confirm) to the perceiver how things are; notably (but not only) what is so. And thereby to inform the perceiver on what to do; on how to treat things (to reach his goals). (Of course, it may also entertain, or inspire (e.g., fear or awe).) But there has seemed to some to be a problem as to how such ever could be done, more specifically, how what one *perceived* (saw, heard, etc.) could ever be proof (thus proof for him) that such-and-such was so. This essay aims to explain why there is no such problem; also to begin to enquire why there might seem to be. In the course of this it will also identify a form of reverse psychologism into which a philosopher may fall, as at least one notable philosopher has; a form in which empirical hypotheses (if they are anything) may be mistaken for conceptual discoveries.

The main target here, regrettably, is John McDowell, who, anyway once, called the idea that

> there are relations of ultimate grounding that reach outside the conceptual realm altogether" a 'myth' (1994: 25), holding that "reality is not located outside a boundary that encloses the conceptual"; endorsing "an image ... in which the conceptual is unbounded; there is nothing outside it. (McDowell 1994: 44)

Such is the picture which I have appropriated Wittgenstein's words above to fit. The sort of view one is driven to by some (merely) apparent problem. Even our best prove not immune to some such picture. I do not think I can really say what the picture is with such a grip. At any rate, I cannot feel its *Drang*. This is, admittedly, a handicap. At least, though, the impression that there is some such problem—something which requires the conceptual to be unbounded in McDowell's sense—can be dissolved. Here I will rely heavily on Frege.

1 Prologue

Perception may gain us awareness that such-and-such is so (or true). Perceptual awareness may be awareness of what is proof of such; recognisably so to one suitably *au fait* with things. Or so we hope. The pig before us is, so *may* be for us, proof that there is a pig before us: that (palpable) presence leaves nothing for it but for that conclusion to hold true. Perception (we hope) may engender awareness *that* such-and-such. What one sees, one might have hoped, *may*, in a favourable case, be *proof* (for him) that things are thus and so. For, one *hopes*, objects of perception—collidables (Sid, that lamppost he barely missed), happenings (a sparrow falling), what thus occurs (its graceful fall) must be such that truth may depend on how they are; which must then bear, often enough recognisably, on what is so.

Suppose that A might be, or have been, such that for A to be as it thus was would be, *eo ipso*, for B to be true, and such that awareness of A's so being need not be *eo ipso* awareness that it so relates to B. Call the way A would thus stand towards B truth-relevant. For example, a way A might be (or have been) is shaped as it is (or would have been); B might then be the thought that A is spherical. If A relates truth-relevantly to B, and A *is* such that for it to be as it is is *eo ipso* for B to be true, let us say that A *yields* the truth of B. Two remarks. First, suppose that in addition, conversely, if B is true, then, A is such as to yield B's truth. Then the truth of B might reasonably be said to *turn on* how A is. A strong form of truth-relevance. Second, it is assumed here that B is eligible for truth (or falsehood). So it, anyway, represents things as a certain way: makes truth turn in a certain way on how things are; has the generality of a thought. It is *not* assumed (though it may turn out to be so) that A must also be eligible for being true (or false).

The point is not just to stipulate. Truth-relevance in present sense is meant to capture—in part only—that notion of *rational* relation on which there *is* proof only where rational relations hold between the proof and the proven. What still needs to be added for A to relate rationally to B, are two clauses. First, that and how A is truth relevant to B must be recognisable. Second, given this, A might sometimes be recognisably such as for B, *eo ipso*, to be true. Given all this, A's being as it was might sometimes (depending on *how* A was) be proof for someone that B is true: it might be recognisable that, given how A was, there was nothing for it but for B to be true; that no possibility of otherwise remained. Such just *is* proof. *Caveat*: we must not assume that having proof is *eo ipso* having *a* proof; nor that for one to have proof there must of necessity be *a* proof which is the one he thus has.

In a truth-relevant relation, the B-term is, *ipso facto* a truth-bearer—a thought. In one sort of rational relation, so, too, the A-term. Proof *here* would be recognisably truth-preserving. But does this exhaust the domain of truth-relevance?

Suppose that the A-term were a certain pig, now before Pia's eyes, rooting in her bed of crocuses and daffodils. Might it (or not) be that that pig's being as it then was, *eo ipso*, for there to be a pig among the crocuses? And might such not be made recognisable to Pia by looking, in the awareness she thus gained of the pig's being up to what it then was? This last question has proven not merely rhetorical. John McDowell, for example, once wrote,

> We cannot really understand the relations in virtue of which a judgement is warranted except as relations within the space of concepts: relations such as implication or probabilification, which hold between potential exercises of conceptual capacities.
> (McDowell 1994: 7)

Some might see this as a paradox, others as a result. Such, in one form, is the issue of this essay.

Consider Sid's left shoe (a candidate for an object of visual or olfactory, awareness). The shoe, as McDowell admits, is not *conceptually* structured, that is, a structuring of ways for things to be. Seen, it (or its untied state) might be proof that it is untied. Or so one might have thought. But neither it nor the way it is (its untied state) is, by McDowell's standard, eligible to be a term in a rational relation, the sort of relation which might constitute a proof. So what one *sees* when he looks cannot be proof that Sid's shoe is untied. Not that McDowell denies that seeing Sid's untied shoe may yield awareness that his shoe is untied. But the proof McDowell sees here lies in further elements in perception which McDowell feels the need to *posit*: not objects of perceptual awareness; things other than the untied shoe itself.

If the conceptual is unbounded, then proof consists, from the start and throughout, of conceptually structured proper parts; of things truth-evaluable, since, by his lights, it is only what one can, with right, so commit to which can bear on truth. But the point of perception is to *gain* us awareness which was not previously in our grasp, to *extend* awareness in a way other than that in which it is extended by deriving things from what we were aware of already. So these initial elements in the sort of proof McDowell envisions must be something we *come* to have available to include in proof only via, and thanks to our seeing, hearing, etc., what we do. Whence, then, these elements? And, more central to this essay, whence their credentials?

McDowell suggests a stratagem for addressing these issues. For a *res cogitans* (such as us), he holds, there is no such thing as visual awareness of Sid's left shoe which is not already accompanied by conceptual (sc. representational) content. In any instance of seeing the shoe, the shoe is presented to us as being such-and-such. Premises are thus made available from which to construct proof. What follows will argue that such a plan is unfit for purpose. In synopsis, such may serve as premises in a proof only if their truth may be taken as given. But what reason could there be to hold them true? If McDowell is right as to what a rational relation must be, I will argue, perception could provide none, and there could *be* none. If so, we must rid ourselves of McDowell's idea of an unbounded conceptual, correlatively of the idea that truth-preserving relations (or their probabilistic kin) exhaust the category *rational relation*. Such is first on the agenda here. To show how the trick is turned I turn now to Frege.

2 The Dawn of Truth

If its name may be our guide, the conceptual is made up of ways of conceiving things, of ranging what there may be to range under given generalities. It is something which belongs to thought, as opposed to history, that which provides things to think about. Thought and history meet in representing something as being something, for short representing-as. Such is one use of the English verb 'represent' (assuming there is just one such verb). One use among many. That man at the door may represent the Acme brush concern. That bar on the chart may represent the average income of an Icelander. Those circles under Sid's eyes may represent (the effects of) a hard night on the town. Suppose, now, that Pia says that Sid had a hard night on the town. She represents him as having so done. With this something entirely new comes on the scene. If Sid did not so cavort, then those circles under his eyes do not represent his having done. Something else is responsible. For all that he did not cavort, by contrast, Pia still did so represent him. The possibility thus arises of her having done so falsely. With which the further possibility arises of representing either truly or falsely. The new item on the scene now is thus the business of being true (*Wahrsein*).

Representing-as relates two terms. There is, so to speak, on its left hand, something to represent as being thus and so—as it may be, Sid (for one thing). On its right hand is something to represent such a left-hand term as being; a way for something to be which there might still be for something to be even if there were not just the same things (notably just the represented thing) so to be or not. With which, that right-hand term puts generality in play (in this representing-as) where the left-hand term does not. Having had a hard night on the town is a way for someone to be. There would still be that way *for* someone to be if the items which might be that way or not were not just the items there are (if, for example, Sid had never been born, if a new person had been), and if they were not just as they are. (Sid did not have a hard night on the town. But he might have. Or, if he did, he *might* have gone for the pale ale rather than the lager, or for the table to the right of the bar rather than that one to the left.) So in being the way for someone to be that it is, a right hand item must determine (so far as it is determined) just when, were things different, they would be such as to be a case of being it (just when it is a hard night on the town which would have been had). Whereas all a left-hand item need contribute to any particular project of representing *it* as being some way or other is just to be as it is, however that is.

The two parties in a representing-as—the represented (as being something or other), and the representer—are thus the two parties in that exclusively two-party enterprise, the pure business of being true (or false). Party of the first part (here the right-hand term) is here called on to make truth turn in a particular way on party of the second part—in the general case, on how things are; to fix how it matters to truth, in this particular case of representing, just how things are—and to do so such as to exclude any substantive role for third-parties. The role of the second part is simply being as it is—thereby being such as to make for truth or falsehood (of the representation thus in question).

We thus see how it is intrinsic to those *Umstände* of *Begriffsschrift* (see below section 5) to have generality, and thus *not* to be historical items (particular occurrences). The circumstance of Sid having been knighted, as we are to speak of such things for Frege's purpose, is what, for all of there being such a thing as that, might obtain or not. It is thus obliged, in being the circumstance that it is, to determine when it would have occurred, when not. We may speak of the historical circumstance of Sid having been knighted—when, if ever, he is knighted. Such a circumstance is something which transpired. It is datable, locatable. To be it is to be precisely *that* episode. Something may well be required of an episode for being *identical with* this one. But it is not for the episode itself to determine when such would be so. It is rather for that way for an episode to be, being identical with *that* one. (Just as Sid does not determine what it would be to be identical with Sid: the generality of this way for things to be is fixed by such things as what it would be to be (a given) person.)

3 Whole Thoughts First

Frege wrote,

> A thought always contains something which reaches over and beyond the particular case, by which it presents this to consciousness as falling under some given generality. (n.d.: 189 (*Kernsatz* 4))

He also wrote (more than once), "Without meaning to give a definition, I call a thought something by which truth can come into question at all." (1918: 60)

So a thought comes onto the scene exactly with truth, thus exactly with representing-as. One might usefully think of a thought as *the* representing of such-and-such as being thus-and-so. It engages in representing-as, not as a thinker does, but in that different aspect in which, in effect, it isolates, identifies, a particular way for one so to engage. *For present purpose, the thing to focus on is that distinction between the general and the particular*: that which has, and that which lacks, that generality which we have already encountered in the notion of representing-as.

a. *A* thought (*ein Gedanke*) is, at any rate, a countable, in McDowell's own term, a 'thinkable', something in particular which might be thought truly or falsely. It is means for articulating (in part) some corresponding mass. A prominent sort of such mass would be someone's (or some group's) thought (about such-and-such, or as to how things are). So, though a thought's proper bailiwick is logic (the pure business of being true), it also has some sort of presence in the psychological. With Frege holding the psychological and the logical apart, one question to ask here is what the relation might be between such a mass and the thoughts in terms of which it might articulate.

b. A thought is, by design, the prime locus of truth outright. 'Outright' is to contrast here with being true *of* such-and-such. If someone has been represented as indolent, or insouciant, or impecunious, there is as yet no saying whether such was representing truly, or rather falsely. For that we need a further bit of information: of *whom* such was said. For there to be truth outright is for there to be no such further question. It matters whether it was Sid, or rather Pia, who was represented as indolent. But where there is a way it takes a whole thought to represent things as being—say, such that Sid is indolent, or such that flies fly—it is otiose (or worse) to ask just *what* object (or item) was represented as being this way. There are not two thoughts—two questions of truth—each of which represents something as this way, but nonetheless different thoughts on grounds of a different something in each case. Which means this: if we think of a thought as a particular case of representing-as, each thought is identified as the thought it is *entirely* by the right-hand term in that enterprise. What the whole thought represents as *its* way to represent something as being (*vide* above examples) is always the same thing. That thing has had many names, e.g., sometimes 'Wirklichkeit'. I will simply call it 'things©', that 'c' for 'catholic' (small 'c').

c. A thought is *just* that by which truth can come into question at all. So two thoughts can differ only by features which change how the world must be to be as represented. Three corollaries matter most here. First, a thought is 'invisible'. It has no environmental profile: no visible features, no spatial or temporal ones (no location), and so on. As Frege points out, you can watch the sun rising, but you cannot 'watch that the sun is rising', or even catch a glimpse of this. There is no way *that the sun is rising* looks. A point of *grammar*. Second, relatedly, it has no indexical or demonstrative elements. (Imagistically, no pointing without fingers (and without location).) Third, it has no psychological profile. It is impersonal. It is not identified by some psychological condition one would have to be in to be thinking it (as nor by given words which would express it).

d. The *whole* thought comes first, both ontologically and logically. But a thought admits of decomposing, of being carved up into elements (constituents).

It can be structured. On one notion of a structure, one's attention in doing so is on the right side of representing-as. The thought poses a question of truth, makes truth turn in a particular way on how things are. To structure it is to articulate what is thus done into partial doings of it. To speak roughly, if the thought makes truth turn on whether Sid is indolent, one may find in it a part which makes truth turn in part on how Sid is; another part which makes truth turn, in part, on who is indolent. All these partial doings are in that same business of being true as the whole thought itself. Each, in its own way, engages partially in representing-as. If generality of the here-relevant sort is a feature of the right side of representing-as, such generality is distributed through all such parts. There is that range of cases which would be ones of Sid being some way or other, that range which would be ones of someone or other being indolent.

Now two points about ontological priority. The first is that the sort of partial doing which a thought-element might achieve is something which cannot be done on its own, but only in the context of the whole thought. There is no such thing as making truth turn on how Sid is, *Punkt* (and then skiving off to go sailing). For a thought-element to make truth turn on how Sid is is for it to relate in a particular way to the whole in which it is a part. The second point is that, as Frege insists, there is no reason to expect that there will be just one way of decomposing a thought. As a rule, at least, we ought to expect many. All that is needed is that the joint doing of the subtasks on a decomposition should be, *eo ipso*, the doing of the whole (that thought's task). So thoughts are not built up of building blocks. Accordingly, they are not structured in the same sense that a sentence of a language is—built up from the vocabulary of the language by its syntax. Perhaps language is compositional. But thought is not. (Signs here of how unlike language thought is.)

e. When we decompose a thought (in our present sense of 'decompose'), our concern is focussed on the right side of representing-as. What we find there, to begin with, is a way for things© to be. But to decompose a thought (to repeat) is to decompose what it does into partial doings of this. The thought makes truth turn in some given way on how things are; a part on a decomposition makes truth turn on this in part in that way. The right-hand item supplies the details. The thought is that Sid is indolent; a part makes truth turn in part on who is indolent. A part makes truth turn on how Sid is. The distinction between particularity (the historical) and generality (constancies around which the historical might vary) is not one between different sorts of right-side items (elements in a decomposition). These *all* have generality of the relevant sort. It is rather a distinction between the two sides of the representing-as relation.

The key point about a generality—that is, a way for things to be—is that there might still be that generality were things not just as they are. It is thus incumbent on that generality, in being the one it is, to fix *when* such might be so. Which is, *eo ipso*, a way for truth to turn (at least in part) on how things are. Trivially, things being as they are (or things©) would not be what it is were things not just as they are. So there is no call for it (absurdly) to fix *when* it would be so. It is not part of this bargain that things being as they are is something there may be cases of; no need to look to it to see when there would be such. Here, then, is something innocent of generality. And it is on just this that truth outright always turns; just this, then, that any whole thought—e.g., the thought that Sid got Benno's goat—represents as some way or other (a way for things© to be, not for *a* thing to be). To play its role in the business of being true all things© needs to do is simply to *be*, as it is (there is no other way); and, in so doing, to meet, or fail to meet, whatever demand the thought in question places on truth.

Such is the paradigm for a distinction between the particular (historical) and the general (ways, in thought, to let things vary). Consider, though, the thought that Sid ate the last *macaron*. Such is a way for things to be outright. So, like the thought that butter melts, it makes truth turn on how things© are. But, in another sort of decomposition, we can decompose the representing being done here in presenting it as representing something to be so of *Sid*, namely, that he ate the last one. Such *might* count as a way of being more specific as to on what, in this case, truth turns. What of Sid, then? Does *he* fall on the *particular* side of the general-particular distinction we are now drawing? The first thing to note here is this: we have already identified that on which the truth of the thought turns; and we have already seen that this—things©, or how things© are—belongs to the particular, is innocent of generality. We cannot change that on which truth turns by presenting it in some new way. So for the thought to turn on how Sid is must remain for it to turn on history, on that particular case, things being as they are. Things might have been other than they are while we still had Sid to kick around. Which shows that there is such a thing as (something) being (identical with) that very object, Sid. Here we have a definite generality, one involving the notion of identity. And this generality has, or can have, a role to play on the right side of the representing-as relation, in imposing the demand thus made for truth on things© being as they are. But it is the concept, *for an object to be Sid*, and not Sid the man, which does the work there. An object may be Sid. But no object can Sid. there is no such thing as 'Sidding'. *Sid* does not determine when there would be a case of something being him, though a concept of being him certainly does. Sid is, in the relevant sense, particular.

So far, the general-particular distinction we are limning distinguishes the left side from the right side of representing-as. *So far* it will do to suppose that what this distinction distinguishes are two different sorts of items—ones such as things©, or Sid, which simply lack generality full stop, and ones like being (that very one) Sid, or being an aromatic hydrocarbon, to which it is intrinsic to have a proprietary generality. But perhaps the wanted distinction here is actually functional, rather than categorical. What really matters, that is, is that the left side of representing-as—whatever gets cast in this role—contributes nothing to the generality of the representing-as thus done—that is, to determining when things would, or might, count as thus represented.

To see this, let us suppose, *pace* Frege, that one could represent a generality as being some way for it to be. For example, here is a thought: being a smoker is a way for a thing to be which there would not have been had tobacco not evolved. Suppose, for sake of argument, that in this thought *being a smoker* really does play the role of an object: it saturates the unsaturated, a way for a way for a thing to be to be, to form the unsaturated thought, something true or false outright. The generality of this thought would then be, as it were, the vector sum of two other generalities: being a way for a thing to be which depends on tobacco for its existence (I rephrase slightly here); and being that way for a thing to be *for one to be a smoker*. The first is instanced by, for example, that way for a thing to be *being subject to tobacco tax*. The second is instanced, of course, only by that way for a thing to be, being a smoker. Whereas being a smoker is instanced by, say, Benno, Beryl and Boris (the last of a dying breed). But *that* generality plays no role in the generality of the thought itself.

f. If the origin of truth is representing-as, what is the origin of generality? Things©, or the way things© are, is a sort of mass out of which to carve countables, particular specifiable ways things are. It is precisely in such carving that generality arises. *One* way for things to be is: such that Sid just got Benno's goat. Such is a start at articulation. And then there is the remainder; all the rest. What might that be? (How else might things© be?) So far anything at all so long as what is left intact is: things being such that Sid just got Benno's goat. It has not yet been said, for example, what Benno ate for breakfast. There are so many possibilities just here. And so on. Thus the generality of a way for things to be, and its absence in that mass from which we start. There is a parallel point about articulating someone's thought (still a mass term here, without plural) into *thoughts*. To this we will return in due course.

Remark: Wherever there is representing-as, there is a left-side term, and a right-side term, which may stand, or fail to stand, in a certain relation to each other. The right-side term determines how the left-side term was represented as being (where the representing itself is a case of representing truly or falsely, represented to be). The left-side term may then be, or not be, as thus represented. The right side of representing-as is always a way for something to be (an n-tuple of things, or just thing©). It presents something as falling under some given generality. Its identity consists in this generality. An object of perception, say, Sid's left shoe, lies without the bounds of the conceptual. It presents nothing as falling under a generality. It does not generalise at all over particular cases. But it lies within the bounds of truth (or falsity) yielding. For it to be as it is *is*, *eo ipso*, for indefinitely many thoughts to be true, and for indefinitely many to be false. Being as it is is a case of, instances, something being as indefinitely many thoughts represent it. For *it* to be those ways is for *those* thoughts to be true. *Mutatis mutandis* for being false. Instancing itself relates what lies beyond the conceptual to what lies within it: on the one hand, Sid's left shoe, as it is to be found; on the other a way for a shoe to be, e.g., untied: what does not generalise over cases, and what does. It is the fundamental such relation. The truth-yielding is thus not exhausted by the truth-preserving. Nor is truth-yielding confined to the conceptual. There is not *that* bar to what one sees being *proof* that things are thus and so.

4 Two Forms of Awareness

Perception is *of* our shared environment; in the visual case, of a scene in view, and (some of) its denizens: happenings, events and their protagonists, objects and the condition (*Zustand*) they are in. It is a form of awareness, afforded us, no doubt, largely thanks to the workings of various neural structures, but, where these are successful, enjoyed of what is (relevantly) before the eyes; and of this being visually as it is. Perceptual awareness differs from awareness-that, or related forms of thought, both in its objects and in its role.

Its objects belong to the environment. They are what can be seen, or heard, or smelt or touched. They are distinguished by their grammar. One sees a school of fish. One sees them swimming in the shallows near the river's mouth. One sees how they undulate, suddenly change directions. One sees their undulations. One hears the tintinnabulations welling from the bells. The objects of perception are thus historical; particular episodes of bell-clanking, or piscine swimming; particular fish at it again. One does not see *that* the fish are swimming, or at least such is not an object of *perception*. The word 'see' does indeed occur with 'that'. But then it has a sense akin to, or perhaps the same, as 'recognise' or 'realise'; a feat of thought, not of the eyes. One may see that the flower has five petals. One may do so by looking; by gaining something to recognise as a case of a flower having five petals. The eyes may give one something to recognise. But the recognition, that the flower has five petals, an exercise of a capacity to tell such things, is not done with the eyes. What one sees is how things are to be thought of.

That its objects are environmental means, for one thing, that perception is perfectly extensional. If you see Sid, and Sid is the one whose left foot you tripped over making your way out of *La Grenouille au Grenier* last night, then you see the one whose left foot, etc.. To do the one is *eo ipso* to do the other. If you witness *la Belle Hélène* at her toilette, and if this is the event that set sail a thousand ships, then you thereby witness the event that set said a thousand ships, whether you know it or not. The words, 'You don't know what you're looking at', said by the Pimpernel of the rock in his palm, make good literal sense. The thought that the diamond of the Queen is in the Pimpernel's palm is another matter.

As to its role, perception is a form of *informative* awareness. It *gains* for us authority as to how things are; puts us in a position to judge, in a best case, one in which we *ought* to know (whether there is a *Wildschwein* among the roses). What one gains hearing a familiar grunt from the garden, or of seeing the lay of the land where the ball lies, or that bulge around the breast pocket of that rather beefy specimen leaning nonchalantly on the wall may be proof that there is a *Wildschwein* among the roses, while the ball lies on a slope and that beefy specimen you face is carrying.

Along both these dimensions perceptual awareness contrasts with awareness-that. We need not now re-rehearse the difference in their objects. Nor is awareness-that a form of *informative* awareness (though one may be informed in being told that such-and-such: authority may be transmitted in the telling). Awareness-that is a product of informative awareness, a form of registration. It relates to perceptual awareness something as follows: awareness enjoyed in perception, awareness of the form that perceptual awareness is, works as a rule to modify the way a perceiver thinks of things, inclusive the way he takes things to be—his thought about the world, or the environment, 'thought' here a mass, not a count, term. A that-clause, or what it speaks of—a thought (count term), to put things one way—offers a particular form in which to articulate such a mass. Such articulation (partial as it may inevitably be) may serve various purposes. Notable among others: it may permit, or enhance, sensitivity to law-like features in things being as they are; a sensitivity which may be quite useful, often indispensable, in appreciating what the thing to do might be.

For the perceiver, then, aiming as we all inevitably do to guide his pursuit of goals, his execution of plans, in the light of what he sees, hears, etc., a capacity so to articulate his thought, and, *inter alia*, the objects of his perceptual awareness, is no doubt useful, desirable, even essential for thinkers of the sort we are.

What are the terms of such capacity? Its fruits are, by hypothesis, awareness-*that*; what it operates on are, for example, the objects of perceptual awareness. It is the sort of capacity exercised, for example, in recognising by that distinctive sound, or by looking (at sight), *that* there is a *Wildschwein* in the roses, or a shoulder holster beneath the blazer. What it is exercised on is thus the historical, *particular* events or cases of an object in its present condition; on things, such as objects of perceptual awareness, which are innocent of generality. Its fruits are precisely *not* so innocent. It is intrinsic to a 'that'-clause to speak, *inter alia*, perhaps, of a way for things to be. It is thus a capacity to recognise instancing by the way things are (something *not* conceptualised) of various ways *for* something to be (and to be represented as being).

5 A Rationale

Grammar tells us that objects of perceptual awareness are innocent of conceptual, or representational, content, even if not *entirely* unequivocally. Why should there be this to be told? In synopsis: to have conceptual/representational content is *eo ipso* to have generality: to be one under which for things to fall, or to represent something as so falling (or to be proper part of either, generality not to be found in the environment.)

Illusions of such may arise. In *Begriffsschrift* (1879: 3–4) Frege suggests a syntax for the content of a thought which cancels engagement in representing-as. The thought that Archimedes fell at Syracuse, he suggests, can be transformed into the thought *of* Archimedes falling at Syracuse. Frege labels what such mentions an *Umstand*, or circumstance. To revert to representing-as, predicate of the *Umstand* something such as *obtains*, or *is a fact*. Such adds nothing to the content, but simply puts it back in the business of being true. The *Umstand* is thus a way for things© to be, presented in a different light. So it is, or has, a generality under which for things to fall.

Were one there, he might have seen Archimedes falling at Syracuse. Here that (apparently) same phrase mentions an object of perception. Why does this not show that an object of perceptual awareness can have content? Because to mention a Fregean *Umstand* and then this last observable is to mention two different things. This last is an historical, datable, occurrence. It takes place, has a duration. Whereas a Fregean *Umstand* is what is liable to occur or not. *It* is just the same thing in either case. Which shows up in grammar, e.g., in this: where Archimedes' falling might be watched, there is also Archimedes' fall (parallel to that sparrow's fall into the soup); whereas for there to be such a thing as the *Umstand* of Archimedes falling there need be no such fall to watch. There is, e.g., such a thing as Sid swilling chardonnay, however unlikely this is to happen.

An *Umstand* is what might obtain or not. So for it to be the *Umstand* it is is for there to be answers to questions when it would be *that* which obtained on an occasion (or history being what it is), and whether such-and-such was its obtaining. When would what happened at Syracuse be a *fall*? When would something have happened at Syracuse. Such must follow from the *Umstand* being the one it is. Which is precisely not so of that historical event, in fact one of Archimedes falling. For the event to be *that* is for it to instance a certain generality. Whether it does so depends on what would count as so doing. But the *event* does not decide such questions. Archimedes' fall does not decide what it would be for something to be a fall. It is simply what there is so to count or not.

Generality is not visible (nor tangible, nor etc.). One sees this in what I will call *freedom of thought*. Start from a (further unspecified) way for an object to be, to be φ. Now consider a particular case—say, Sid being *just* as, doing just what, he now is. Let it be given that *this* is a case of an item being φ. Now take another case—say, Sid being as he *now* (later) is, or Pia being as she now is, or Sid as he soon will be. Is either of these a case of something being φ? Study Sid now as closely as you like. The answer is not to be found in his being as he is. For there are both generalities Sid now falls under which he still will fall under later, and/or which Pia now does, and generalities he now falls under of which such is not so. For any pair of particular cases there are ways of generalising which capture both, and ways of generalising which capture one but not the other. To say this is already to say that Sid's being as he now is cannot answer the question posed. Two cases of some given generality, or being some way there is to be, are thereby the same in some given respect; that is, on some given understanding of *same*. The understanding on which they must be the same to be two cases is not to be found in *them*, but rather in the generality they both instance—in how such things are to be thought of. *Such* one does not learn from the cases themselves. Thus that a generality, a way for things to be, is invisible. Thus, then, that objects of perceptual awareness cannot have generality, so nor conceptual structure. A simple point which has proven difficult to swallow. Thus that it is always in the cards for someone to see Sid sipping chardonnay, to be aware of that event, while missing entirely the fact *that* Sid is sipping chardonnay. The bounds of the conceptual always leave room for that sort of slip between cup and lip.

6 Boundlessness

The above sets out, first of all, a view of the relation of the things we think (or might) to the things we think this of; so, in particular, a view of the relation of the things we think to the things we see, or hear, or, more generally, the objects of the senses. It is a view drawn in large part from Frege. It is time now for a contrasting view. This view fits the slogan, 'The conceptual (the realm of generality) is unbounded', in a sense of 'unbounded' to be made out. Its most cogent exponent, it seems to me, is John McDowell. Two theses form the core of this view— the second, however, taking sometimes a benign, sometimes an aggressive, form.

The first thesis lies on the logical, as opposed to the psychological, side of Frege's distinction. It is about what truth-relevance might be. What might *recognisably* obtain remains to be discussed. It might be put thus:

1. Only what is conceptually structured can be a term in a rational relation.

Here is one clear statement of the view by McDowell:

> [W]e cannot really understand the relations in virtue of which a judgement is warranted except as relations within the space of concepts: relations such as implication or probabilification, which hold between potential exercises of conceptual capacities. (McDowell 1994: 7)

A rational relation, as explained above, is, first, a truth-relevant one which, second, sometimes holds recognisably between what stand in it to each other. It is thus one by which the first item of such a pair *may* sometimes be proof of the second.

The first thesis now tells us this: that the whole domain of rational relations, understood as above, contains nothing but relations between conceptually-structured items. Truth-*preservation* is, of course, a relation between conceptually structured, or at least structurable, items; items which bring things under generalities. Inference is thus, by this, a source of knowledge. And, in present parlance, any rational relation relates its first side to something which is conceptually structured; that is, to what might be true or false (or so or not). The first thesis tells us that justification never issues from anything other than relations between conceptually structured things; not ever simply from relations between objects of perception and things one might think (so). Just this is disputed here.

The benign form of the second thesis can be put thus:

2. An object of perception cannot bear rationally for the perceiver unless the perceiver's rational capacities are drawn on in his so relating to it.

As McDowell explains,

> What my condition disallows is the idea that something, for instance a piece of meat, can impinge on a subject's rationality without conceptual capacities, capacities that belong to reason, being drawn on in the subject's being thus related to it." (McDowell 2008: 259)

No one should doubt a thesis so benign. What one may doubt is McDowell's conception of what impingement on rationality would come to (thus of what rationality is). Many can, and often do, recognise a face, or a chilidog, or pit or Porsche, at/by sight. Such are the feats perception enables. So far, our achievements, and how we reach them, might be emulated by a trained dog, or by a smart phone app. We are sensitive to certain highly abstract visual features; in principle so might the app be. (Blue light for the porcine, red light for the rest.) As *res cogitans*, though, we can do something else for which the smart phone or dog is not yet enabled. The thing is, we all know that to look *just* like Sid, or a chilidog, or a Porsche, *need* not be to be him/one. Sid-clones, fake chilidogs, etc., are at least in the conceptual cards. Circumstances *might* prove, or turn, inhospitable to such means of recognising such things. What we then have, which the app does not, is a capacity to recognise when, how and why, what we in fact rely on would prove inhospitable, and to recognise effective replacements for it (or their impossibility) when such occurs. *Such* is rationality. Such capacities apply even when there is, in fact, no reason not to rely on those means of recognition incorporated in the app. When there *is* such reason, their application is evident. It is fair to say (or not here in dispute) that were these capacities not in play, poised to spring when called for, perception could not place us to *judge* that such-and-such is so, where to judge is to *commit* to something, to exercise authority as to what is so in the way a *res cogitans* does (or can). On this understanding, the benign version of McDowell's thesis is fine. But it gives no reason to posit conceptual content in seeing (hearing, etc.) things as such.

McDowell and I share a Cartesian conception of a *res cogitans*, the distinguishing mark of which is an unbounded capacity for critical examination of whatever it does, or thinks. But we differ in our elaborations of it. McDowell inserts an ingredient with sources in Davidson and Sellars: rational relations only relate the conceptually structured. So, consequently enough, experience, for such a being, must come already conceptually structured. As sketched above, a genuine capacity for critical self-examination renders such an ingredient otiose.

The benign thus disposed of, I turn to the aggressive.
A perceptual experience has both an object and a conceptual content.
Here is McDowell:

> The thinkable contents that are ultimate in the order of justification are contents of experiences. (Mc Dowell 1994: 29)

> [T]hinkables are not objects of sensory awareness...[which] does not exclude thinkables as contents of sensory awareness. (McDowell 2018: 35)

Here is a thesis about *how* rationality is in play in making its objects bear rationally for us on what to think. When, say, one sees Sid on the porch, chilidog in hand, what one sees is presented to the viewer as being given ways there is for such an object to be: the conceptual content of the experience. And it is thanks to this that the viewer may sometimes, through perception, gain awareness *that* what is before his eyes is thus and so (perhaps the first-cited ways, perhaps others).

If the first thesis were true this aggressive thesis would seem mandatory. Perception would have to provide, or bring with it, material to stand in rational relations on which the perceiver might operate, or at least to whose holding he might be sensitive. Such material would have to be conceptual, content for a thought, or for what might be true or false, so that, standing in those relations, it might then *justify* the perceiver (in his awareness of it) in judging that things in his surroundings were thus and so. All this would have to be for perception to yield awareness-that, *if* the conceptual were unbounded in McDowell's sense. For if it were, Frege's second case of justification (*Kernsatz* 13) would not exist. Only a judgement, or its content, could justify a judgement.

But the first thesis is false. This we have already seen. There is a relation which holds between the left side and the right in representing-as just where that left side is as that right side represents it. Were there no such relation, there would be no such thing as representing-as, nor, hence, as truth. So no such thing as a concept. This relation holds or not as objectively as truth is objective. And there is no reason why its holding should not sometimes be recognisable; detected by our app above when the app is doing what it is meant to; nor it be detectable by us when the app ceases so to function (when and how the environment proves inhospitable). Thesis 1 is thus flatly wrong. Representing-as (at least truly or falsely) is essentially of something distinct from it, which is as it is independent of how it is thought about. Without instancing, there would be no such thing as this; no such thing as a second party in that two-party enterprise, truth.

7 Futility

McDowell's proposal for making experience bear on what to think factors in two. One part is the idea that perception (or experience generally) has a suitable representational content, as set out above. The other part is that this content would, or might, actually justify judgements, confer on the subject awareness-that. This essay focusses on this second part, bracketing *pro tem* the first. But there are good reasons for thinking that that first part also could not be right. Their core is this: representing-as, where not simply the holding of an attitude, must be recognisable as the representing that it is; thus means for achieving this, which, then, are *correctly* taken (understood) as so representing. This, of course, remains to be argued; as does the idea that it is just such representing-as which McDowell's proposal requires. Space prohibits arguing this here (though my 2014 presents the core of a case). To begin on this second topic, then, let us note two requirements on the content McDowell posits if it is to do the required work. We may then pose three questions.

The first requirement is that the relevant conceptual content of an experience of perceiving must belong to the informative awareness which perceiving thus provides (us). It must arrive with the relevant perceiving. No doubt any experience is viewable as rife with content. Its enjoyer may think, and feel, all sorts of things with regard to what he is experiencing—say, loathing at the sight of Benno beneath the Jacaranda, or resentment as one watches him eat the last *courato*, or reveries of Benno stepping in front of a bus. But the content McDowell posits is meant to *enable* something which, formerly, was not within reach, *new* awareness as to how things are. So it cannot be the content of the viewer's thoughts or attitudes. Not ones he comes to in or by the experience. These, so far as rational, are what is to be explained. Nor ones he had already. The question is what perception *adds*.

Second, the relevant content must be something accessible to the perceiver in and by his having the relevant experience. For its role is to be reason for him, justification he has, for judging one thing or another. The objects of someone's perceptual awareness, e.g., the pig, it rooting in the tulip bed, its rooting, are not conceptually structured. But in experiencing them—in witnessing the mastication—these things must be presented *to him* as falling under one or another generality. Presented to *him*, and *presented* to him, not just thought by him; so that *they*, and not just (impossibly for McDowell) that masticating pig, or its masticating, itself, can become for him reason for judging what he does, *inter alia*, what he can *take* for reasons, recognise as ones he has, what justifies such judgement.

(Further, the occurrence of such representing must in fact *be* reason to think such-and-such (about the scene in view).)

Our three questions are now the following:
1. What is the source of this representing—of this content's presence?
2. What are the credentials of this source (and what would they need to be)?
3. (If the conceptual is unbounded), how could there *be* such credentials to be had?

As to the first, for a start, the relevant conceptual content could not lie in the object of perception itself—e.g., in Sid's left shoe, or the sight of him about to trip. For objects of perception are *not* conceptually structured. Sid's left shoe does not decompose into, *inter alia*, a proper part which decides what would count as a case of something. The shoe does not present anything as falling under a generality. At one time Wittgenstein seems to have thought otherwise (*vide* 1922: 2.18) And at one time McDowell seems to have endorsed him in this (*vide* 1994: 27). Neither, though, remained with the idea for long. Nor, equally, could the perceiver himself be the source of that content (or its relevant occurrence). For the content here is meant to be something which arrived with the relevant instance of perceiving, not something present all along.

So the source of the content, the responsible here, must be thought of as what is proprietary to the perceiver in some sense; some capacity of mind. Perhaps something like an *Einbildundskraft* (to speculate). But a capacity conceived as identified by how it enables what it does, on the model of a 'visual system', which, in its own species specific way enables its possessor to enjoy awareness of his surroundings. A capacity identified merely by what it was a capacity to do would, thus far, leave us without an explanation of what was here to be explained.

With which our second question. The point here is: the content of perceiving, to perform its appointed role, would need to carry the right force. Not, e.g., one borne by dadaist poetry, or a move in a game of 'What-if?', or CCTV art, in which the artist doctors tapes to make wry comments on society, 'the system', and all that. Not that of mere *plaisanteries*, or the force of '*zum Spass*'. Of course, if Sid suddenly launches into *plaisanteries,* this may mean that he has something to hide. And if some para-visual system larded visual experiences with flashes of dadaist poetry, this might mean something too. Factive meaning. But the justification for what is judged that the content of experience was to provide lies in its content. *That* a stout live animate collidable stands before us is meant to be at least evidence for their being a pig before us. For this the content of experience must come with the force of commitment; of underwriting taking what is thus represented as the way things are.

It is just here that questions may arise as to the credentials of the content's author. One might well suppose that representing-to-be, and thus representing-as *überhaupt*, was reserved for persons, or anyway for thinkers such as us, *res cogitans*. The origin of the representing/content here in question is to be, as per question 1, some sort of enabling device, so to speak a para-perceptual system, what does *work* something as (to speculate) an *Einbildungskraft* is billed as doing. The question is how such an enabling mechanism *could* have the right credentials for the here-needed underwriting. Not just that it is not the sort of thing to take a suave or supercilious tone, or to be arch. Here what is distinctive about a *res cogitans* (McDowell's rational agent) comes back to haunt. The underwriting we want from assertive force is the sort which could only be given by a being, or entity, which could stand back from what it was doing (say, telling pigs by those distinctive porcine features), recognise when this was jumping to conclusions, and thereby desist from so jumping; a being, or entity, which would rely on its ability to tell pigs by sight near enough only where this was to be relied on. For an enabler to be eligible to pretend to such authority, it would need to be sensitive to things to which we, by hypothesis, could not (without some conceptually structured items or other as cognitive prosthetic): to such things as to when the way a shoe visibly was was a case of something being untied. For if *we* could be so sensitive, the *content* of perceiving which McDowell posits would be otiose.

The main point here, though, is not that there could never be a non-personal device with a *res cogitans'* capacity to judge. On *this* we can remain agnostic. It rather turns on McDowell's conception of what a *res cogitans* could not do—what *we* could not do. On his view, a visual experience of a pig before us which was not in part constituted by conceptual content would leave us unable to recognise, to become aware *that* there was a pig before us. He has a very good reason for insisting on this, if it is true. The reason is that there *are* no rational (in present terms, no truth-relevant) relations between what is not conceptually structured and what is. Such is supposed to be what requires *our* perceptual experiences of pigs to have both an object—pigs, not themselves conceptually structured—and a content, in effect, a 'presenting-as'. The rub here is that if *we* are so handicapped, then so is whatever it is which ensures that *our* perceptual experiences of pigs do have content. This rests on a logical, and not a psychological, point. There simply *is* nothing for us to be sensitive to here other than the obtaining of relations between conceptually structured items. There *are* no other relations to whose obtaining anything might be sensitive. The device which was meant to enable us is no better off than we are. At this point, visions of world-bearing turtles swim before the mind.

Which brings us to our third question. How could *anything* have the right credentials for giving the wanted assurances as to which ways things visibly are? The answer: nothing could. To have the right credentials would be to be suitably sensitive to the holding of relations between what was not conceptually structured—a scene, say, before our eyes—and what was. But, on McDowell's story, there are no such relations to be sensitive *to*.

If the conceptual were unbounded, if there were no truth-relevant relations between what lay without it and what lay within, one could not so much as seriously *pretend* to authority as to what ways things are—as to where there are cases of what. There would be nothing to be authoritative about. Which is only to recall a truism lying at the foundations of the phenomenon of being true itself: representing-as (or what has truth-evaluable content) is *essentially* of something distinct from the representing, and of what is as it is independent of its so being.

8 Reverse Psychologism

It remains to identify a more radical way in which McDowell, and perhaps some of the above, has the phenomena at issue the wrong way around. I will dub this error *reverse psychologism*. Psychologism assigns empirical psychology the task of discovering the nature of the logical. Insofar as a capacity is species specific, one may look to facts about the species to identify that capacity's scope and workings. Where the species is human one may assign human psychology this task. Insofar as a capacity is not species specific, such an approach is inappropriate. For Frege, logic, part of the most general form of the business of being true, is not species-specific, hence not the business of psychology. Reverse psychologism moves in the opposite direction. It occurs where a philosopher, impressed by some very general, presumably non-species-specific features of the shape of the conceptual, presents as consequences of these what would be, if anything, empirical hypotheses (unrecognised as such because the real shape of the conceptual is not yet sufficiently in view).

To see the reverse psychologism in McDowell, one needs to attend to the relation between mass and count as it plays out in experience and its deliverances. Restricting ourselves to mass terms we may say: Experience, anyway perception, modifies one's view, *inter alia*, awareness, of how things are: how he takes things to be, what he is aware of as to how things are. Such masses are articulable into countables. The thought is one such countable, designed to serve logic's ends. We rational (discursive) beings enjoy capacities for such (*inter alia* auto) articulation. We may say (some of) what we think, articulated into discrete bits. Identifying such bits to relate to, we may ascribe to others, *inter alia*, discrete bits of taking-to-be-so; where applicable, discrete bits of such successes as awareness-that.

Perception, experience more generally, surely modifies such masses. There is Pia haggard and drawn. Taking in what one thus sees, he may become aware of her suffering from stress. There is how one took things© to be before seeing her; there is the way one takes them to be now. Similarly for observing the state of the fruit bowl, or of the lecture hall, increasingly a void at lecture time. Such transformations from then to now are the sort of thing which, in first instance, perception may effect.

Such masses as how Sid took and now takes things to be are, of course, articulable into countables, notably thoughts (*Gedanken*). For McDowell, some particular articulation or other is part of an experience of seeing how things are itself. For him some such articulation is a *sine qua non* for effecting articulable modification in the resultant mass. Seeing the lecture hall may place one to judge knowledgeably that attendance is declining. Seeing the red meat on the white rug may place one to judge that there is meat on the rug. But only, on McDowell's story, if what one sees is already presented to him as, say, a half-empty hall, or meat on the rug (or perhaps something more abstract). At best, though, such are empirical hypotheses. *That* such-and-such is *one* form in which to register what perception informs one of; one form among, perhaps, others. Plumping for that form, assigning it the importance McDowell does, is for a philosopher, in his capacity as such, to avoid (as McDowell surely would if he saw this as what he was doing).

One good reason for a philosopher to avoid such theses emerges when we look at the other end of the process: the resultant mass, how the thinker comes to take things to be. On what does correct articulation thus turn? Suppose it is Sid at the lectern whose take on things (*Auffassung*) is to be articulated. First question: what is there into which *for* it to be articulated? Well, into relations to one or another thing there is to be held true (or so). Observation: it is not *Sid* who determines what such things there are. One does not answer this question by examining that particular mass, how *Sid* takes things to be. But now, what determines which of those items Sid in fact thinks? Is there some articulation of the relevant mass which can claim objective priority as *the* way Sid himself articulates the mass? Is there something it would be for there to be *a* way which is the way he does so? *At best* this would be an empirical hypothesis; for various reasons, I suggest, hardly a promising one. To see which is to see McDowell again as treading where no philosopher ought to.

References

Frege, Gottlob (1983): *Nachgelassene Schriften* (2nd edition), H. Hermes, F. Kambartel, F. Kaulbach, eds., Hamburg: Felix Meiner, 1983.
Frege, Gottlob, n.d.: "17 Kernsätze zur Logik". In: Frege 1983, pp. 189–190.
Frege, Gottlob (1879): *Begriffsschrift: Eine der arithmetischen nachgebildete Formelsprache des reinen Denkens*, Halle: Louis Nebert, 1879.
Frege, Gottlob (1918): "Der Gedanke: Eine Logische Untersuchung". In: *Beiträge zur Philosophie des deutschen Idealismus*, V. 1, n. 2, pp. 58–77.
McDowell, John (1994): *Mind and World* (2nd edition), Cambridge MA: Harvard University Press.
McDowell, John (2008): "Responses". In: McDowell, John: *Experience, Norm, and Nature*, J. Lindgaard, ed., Oxford: Basil Blackwell, pp. 200–267.
McDowell, John (2018): "Travis on Frege, Kant and The Given: Comments on 'Unlocking the Outer World'". In: *In the Light of Experience – Essays on Reasons and Perception*, J. Gersel, R. Jensen, M. S. Thaning, S. Overgaard, eds., Oxford: Oxford University Press, pp. 23–35.
Travis, Charles (2014): "The Preserve of Thinkers". In: *Does Perception Have Content?*, Berit Brogaard, ed., Oxford: Oxford University Press, pp. 138–179.
Wittgenstein, Ludwig (1922): *Tractatus Logico-Philosophicus*, London: Routledge & Kegan Paul.
Wittgenstein, Ludwig (1953): *Philosophical Investigations*, Oxford: Basil Blackwell.

Johannes Roessler
The Manifest and the Philosophical Image of Perceptual Knowledge

Abstract: Explanations of knowledge of mind-independent objects in terms of perception can be used to validate or vindicate claims to knowledge: they provide us with reasons for thinking that we know what objects are like. In this paper I contrast two ways to think about this 'vindicatory role' of perception. The majority view in epistemology is that it must be understood by reference to the way perception explains and warrants beliefs. I argue that this is not how perception figures in our ordinary explanatory and dialectical practice. As ordinarily conceived, perception's role in vindicating a claim to knowledge that p turns on our ability to perceive that p. I suggest that this analysis enables us to adjudicate some entrenched disagreements over the sense, if any, in which perceptual knowledge is 'based on' sensory experience. I conclude with a suggestion about how to understand the conflict between the perspective of the commonsense psychology of perceptual knowledge and the perspective of the traditional philosophical project of explaining 'perceptual warrant'.

Keywords: Epistemic perception, perceptual experience, reason-seeking questions, attention, perceptual recognition, epistemology.

We can distinguish two ways in which perception bears on our justification for claims about mind-independent objects around us. First, it is a familiar observation that the question 'How do you know that p?' can be used as a challenge (a 'pointed question', in Austin's phrase). Used in this way, the question serves to probe the addressee's entitlement to a claim to knowledge that p, often in response to her asserting or telling someone that p. In effect, the question asks for a reason to think that you do know that p. And it seems possible to meet that request — to vindicate your claim to knowledge — by relating your knowledge that p to your current or past perception. Call this the 'vindicatory role' of perception. Second, we might ask about your justification or warrant for believing that p. 'Why do you believe that p?' is often used to press that question. And here too it is natural to think that a good answer can make reference, in various ways, to your current or past perception. Call this the 'warranting role' of perception.

My question in what follows is how the two sorts of justificatory role of perception are related to each other. The majority view in recent epistemology has been that 'perceptual warrant' comes first in the order of explanation. An account of *how you know* that the tile before you is blue (when you know this by sight), on this view, must put centre stage the explanation of your belief that the tile is blue. If your seeing what you see explains your knowledge this can only mean that it causes and warrants your belief, and that, in the light of this, your belief can be seen to amount to knowledge. Recently, however, a number of philosophers have challenged this 'belief-centred' analysis, and offered versions of an alternative view. On that view, the question of how we know what we know through perception is more basic than the question of what justifies or warrants perceptual beliefs, at least in cases of non-inferential perceptual knowledge. In such cases, we should approach the latter question in the light of our answer to the former. For example, the correct account of how you know the tile is blue may be that you can see (and thus know) that it's blue. That account makes no reference to any basis for your belief that it's blue. And we should be drawing on this explanation of your knowledge in understanding your entitlement, and perhaps your reason, for your belief.

There is no obvious single motivation from which the minority view springs. Three distinguished philosophers — Alan Millar, Barry Stroud and Timothy Williamson — have proposed versions of it in recent work, but it can look as if their adherence to it reflects quite different concerns. Williamson's interest seems to lie mainly in applying his general account of the nature of evidence (as provided by knowledge) to the case of perceptually grounded knowledge, and perhaps in developing his view of propositional knowledge as a determinable of which propositional seeing is a determinate. In Stroud's work, the importance of propositional perception emerges in the context of reflection on how we can resist what Stroud describes as a 'restricted' conception of perception that he argues leads to philosophical scepticism. Millar characterizes his account of perceptual knowledge as 'commonsensical'. One inspiration is Austin's discussion of ordinary discourse about knowledge and perception (esp. in his 'Other minds'). These different concerns may not be mutually exclusive, of course, and in any case I think there is substantial agreement on a significant point, that the majority view (which accords explanatory priority to 'perceptual warrant') distorts the way perception figures in our ordinary explanatory/dialectical practice. We can put the idea as follows:

Epistemic Perception (EP): (a) 'I can see that the tile is blue' would ordinarily be regarded as a satisfactory account of how you know it's blue, yet (b) the account makes no reference to any evidence on the basis of which you believe the tile to be blue.

Let me clarify three terms. First, I speak of 'epistemic' perception since that, according to Millar, Stroud and Williamson, is what propositional perception amounts to: seeing that p entails knowing that p; it is a 'way of knowing' that p.[1] Second, I use the term 'evidence' in a somewhat loose and liberal sense here. There is no presumption, for example, that evidence is propositional or that beliefs based on evidence are inferential or even that evidence must be accessible to the subject. What matters is that evidence provides grounds for belief that may underwrite a belief's 'status as knowledge' and in that way explain how one knows what one knows. Third, the term 'ordinarily' raises important and delicate issues about the nature of what might be called the commonsense psychology of perceptual knowledge. Should we think of this as a 'folk theory'? To what extent does it exhibit cultural variation? How can we discover (if that is what we have to do) its content and commitments? Without being able to address these questions adequately here, one thing I will assume is that some understanding of perception and its role in knowledge is essential for comprehending and negotiating the 'space of reasons'. Without some such understanding one would not be able fully to participate in the practice of raising and answering 'reason-seeking' questions such as 'Why do you believe this?', 'How do you know?' or 'Are you sure?' — practices that are closely linked to other central human practices, such as testimony, joint attention, or shared reminiscing.

In addition to its more or less obvious epistemological significance, EP also has an important bearing on a basic question in the philosophy of mind. Consider John Campbell's suggestion that '(o)rdinary common sense today still finds it compelling that there is a fundamental role for sensory experience in knowledge.' (Campbell 2014: 14) A 'fundamental role', I take it, would be a certain kind of explanatory role: it is *because* of the visual experience you enjoy of the tile there right in front of you that you are in position to know it's blue, or so, according to Campbell, ordinary common sense still maintains. Why should common sense be assumed to take this view? Campbell does not elaborate, but many would argue the answer is obvious: we ordinarily think of sensory experience as what justifies perceptual beliefs about objects and in that way yields knowledge of what objects are like. If EP is correct, that interpretation must be rejected. There will be a real question as to whether the 'fundamental role' for sensory experience is a commitment of ordinary explanatory practice or perhaps merely a tenacious piece of revisionary epistemology. At this point, an interesting internal disagreement emerges between two ways of developing EP. On what I will call an austere read-

---

[1] For dissent, see McDowell 2002. For support, see Millar 2011.

ing of EP (encouraged by some of Stroud's and Williamson's writings on perceptual knowledge), perceptual explanations of knowledge terminate in attributions of epistemic perception. While seeing that p may somehow *involve* visual experience, there is no sense in which visual knowledge is *based on* such experience. A richer reading of EP (encouraged by Austin and Millar) would be more hospitable to Campbell's suggestion. On it, perceptual experience of objects plays an indispensable role in making epistemic perception itself intelligible.

My discussion falls into three parts. I start by saying more about the very idea of a 'vindicatory role' for perception. (Section 1) On a popular view, 'How do you know that p?' just is a request for the evidence on the basis of which you believe that p. I raise doubts about that view and propose an alternative account: briefly, the question is a request for a 'vindicatory explanation' of your knowing that p. In the second part (sections 2–4), I ask whether appeal to epistemic perception can provide the required 'vindicatory' sort of explanation (I suggest the answer is 'yes'), and whether it can do so without acknowledging a 'fundamental role for sensory experience' (I make a case for thinking that the answer is 'no'). In the last part (section 5) I consider where the correctness of EP would leave the traditional philosophical project of explaining our knowledge of the world around us in terms of perception's role in warranting beliefs.

1 Vindicatory Explanations

There are two routes to the conclusion that 'How do you know that p?' (henceforth HK) must be a request for your evidence that p. One route argues that the question is asking for an explanation of your knowing that p, and that only the evidence on the basis of which you believe that p can deliver the required explanation. Advocates of EP, of course, reject that evidentialist assumption, so I set the first route to one side for the moment. The second route involves reflection on what is involved in using HK as a challenge or a 'pointed question'. It contends that the 'evidence-seeking' interpretation of HK is the only, or at least the best, way to understand the nature of the challenge.

An example of this second route is Daniel Stoljar's discussion of what he calls two 'versions' of HK, an 'evidence-seeking' and an 'explanation-seeking' version. He traces the distinction to Austin's discussion of two kinds of motivations for asking HK: as a 'pointed question' vs 'out of polite curiosity' (Stoljar 2012, see Austin 1961). Stoljar does not spell out why asking HK 'pointedly' is supposed to be a matter of using it as a request for evidence, but I take it the idea is this. To be used as a challenge, HK would need to bring into play some normative question, a question concerning your right or entitlement to hold some attitude. Now, in the case of 'Why do you believe that p?' (WB), it is obvious which normative question is in play: WB itself is naturally and routinely used to ask for your normative reason for believing that p. By doing so, it raises the possibility that you have no adequate reason; as Austin says, it 'suggests that perhaps you oughtn't to believe' that p (Austin 1961: 78). In the case of HK, things are more complicated. Knowledge is not a 'judgement-sensitive attitude'.[2] It makes no sense to request your normative reason for knowing that p. Then how should we understand the dialectical significance of the question? What it must be asking for, it might be said, is once again your reason and entitlement to believe that p.[3]

The proposal cannot be quite right as it stands, though. HK is not the same question as WB. Its subject matter is your knowing, not just believing, that p. One might accommodate this by saying that the question asks for a normative reason for belief that meets a further condition: it should explain your knowing that p. At this point, however, we should ask whether conceiving of HK as a request for an *explanation* may not be enough to account for its 'pointed' character. Suppose our interest is in whether your claim to knowledge that p is acceptable — whether there is good reason to think you do know that p. Asking for an explanation of your knowing that p would be a natural way to press that question. Note, first, that quite generally requesting an explanation of the fact that q can be a way to seek reassurance that it is true that q. There is a sense, of course, in which the request presupposes that q; there would be nothing to explain unless q were true. But that does not mean that the question makes no sense unless the questioner is convinced that q. 'Why would she do such a thing?' can ask for an explanation of an action that would simultaneously help to convince a sceptic that the act in question happened. Similarly, in requesting an explanation of your knowing something, we may, as Williamson puts it, 'politely grant' that you do know, 'and merely ask how, perhaps suspecting that there is no answer to the question.' (Williamson 2000: 253) The suggestion might be put by saying that HK demands a

---

2 See Scanlon 1998 for the notion of a judgement-sensitive attitude. Austin notes that '(w)e seem never to ask "*Why* do you know?"' (Austin 1961: 78) This may reflect our habit of hearing a second-person why-question relating to a propositional attitude as a reason-seeking question: a question for which knowledge is not an intelligible target.

3 Marie McGinn relies on this view in defending her unorthodox view that in the case of direct observational judgements HK is off-key (more precisely: inappropriate as a matter of principle, rather than just, usually, conversationally odd, perhaps because of the obviousness of the answer). She writes that 'it is [in such cases], for example, very unclear what I might offer as evidence for the things I assert.' (McGinn 2012: 2) One might agree with this, but question whether evidence is what HK must be asking for.

'vindicatory explanation' of your knowing that p: an explanation that would show that your attitude to p is indeed knowledge, not (say) mere belief or conjecture.[4] This, I think, is exactly in line with Austin's observation that HK, when used 'pointedly', 'suggests that perhaps you *don't* know it at all'. (Austin 1961: 78) A good answer is expected to dispel that suggestion.

There may be a case for imposing restrictions on the sorts of explanations that would properly engage with HK, but this provides no support for the 'evidence-seeking' interpretation. One such restriction seems to be implicit in the phrase 'vindicatory explanation'. Consider the explanatory role of interests. Your knowing the date of the battle of Montaperti may be explained by your passion for medieval history. It's because of your interest that you came to know this. That may be a perfectly satisfactory (partial) explanation, but it does not by itself give us much of a reason to think that what you have is knowledge. Conspiracy theories equally reflect the subject's keen interests. It is not implausible to think that it's because of this that appeal to interests would not be a fully satisfactory answer to HK. What the question is seeking is an explanation of your knowing that p in terms of factors that make it clear that your attitude to p is knowledge.[5] A further restriction we might consider is that HK asks for an explanation in terms of a means or method for finding out whether p. Compare Ayer's suggestion that '(n)ormally we do not say that people know things unless they have followed one of the accredited routes to knowledge.' (Ayer 1956: 33) Even if these restrictions can be corroborated, though, they lend no immediate support to the 'evidence-seeking' interpretation. You might argue that only evidence delivers vindicatory explanations of knowledge, or that only evidence amounts to an 'accredited route to knowledge'. But that would be to adopt the first route to the 'evidence-seeking'

---

[4] See Stroud's discussion of the sense in which a successful account of how we know what we know should be 'legitimating', insofar as it should enable us 'to understand that what we have got *is* knowledge of, or reasonable belief in, the world's being a certain way.' (Stroud 2000: 152) I borrow the term 'vindicatory explanation' from David Wiggins's use of the term in connection with explanations that account for someone's believing something in a way that implies the truth of their belief. (Wiggins 1996)

[5] If this is right, we would need to revisit the question whether there is after all a distinction to be drawn between two 'versions' of HK: a 'dialectical' version (requesting a vindicatory explanation) and a 'merely biographical' version (asking for any kind of explanation, perhaps equivalent to 'How come you know that p?' or 'What explains your knowing that p?'). I am inclined to think the answer is 'no' (HK quite generally expects a vindicatory explanation, even when the audience needs no convincing that you know that p) but I won't pursue the matter here.

interpretation I mentioned at the beginning. It would be to argue that only evidence can provide the thing HK is requesting, viz. a certain kind of explanation of your knowing that p.

The upshot is that HK is a 'reason-seeking' question in its own right (a request for a reason to think you know that p), not just a proxy for the reason-seeking question 'Why do you believe that p?' In the light of this, consider Sellars's well-known claim that knowledge is a position in the 'logical space of reasons, of justifying and being able to justify what one says' (Sellars 1956: 298–299). The passage is usually interpreted as expressing a commitment to epistemological internalism. If you know that p you should normally be able to cite what might be called a 'knowledge-providing' reason, viz. a reason for believing that p that would help to underwrite the status of your belief as knowledge and would in that way explain how you know that p. (See e.g. McDowell 2011 for that reading.) This may well be the intended reading, but it is significant that Sellars's formulation — 'justifying what one says' — is open to a perfectly natural alternative construal. If you tell us that p, and we pointedly ask 'How do you know?', a good answer to our question would corroborate the claim to knowledge that's implicit in your act of telling and would thus 'justify what you say'. The passage from Sellars, in other words, may be read as suggesting that possession of propositional knowledge requires the ability to offer vindicatory explanations of one's knowledge. One reason the difference matters is that on this latter reading, there is nothing in the slogan advocates of EP need to object to. What they will question is whether it takes a 'knowledge-providing' reason (or any sort of warrant-conferring basis for belief) to validate a claim to knowledge.

2 Epistemic Perception

It will be useful to have three responses to EP before us. First, here, again, is EP itself:

> *Epistemic Perception* (EP): (a) 'I can see that the tile is blue' would ordinarily be regarded as a satisfactory account of how you know it's blue, yet (b) the account makes no reference to any evidence on the basis of which you believe the tile to be blue.

And here are the three responses, from an 'evidentialist' opponent and from advocates of the austere vs the richer reading of EP, respectively:

(1) EP cannot be right: without some grasp of the epistemic basis in virtue of which perceptual beliefs qualify as knowledge we could have no reason to think that what we get from perception is knowledge. While (a) may be correct, (b)'s gloss on (a) must be rejected. One way to do so would be to insist that 'I can see that the tile is blue' is the self-ascription of a 'belief-independent' perceptual state that may be one's reason for believing that the tile is blue, such that one knows it's blue because one believes it's blue for that reason. (McDowell 2011) Another option would be to think of propositional perception as a sort of promissory note. To say that you can see the tile to be blue is to say that a more detailed perceptual explanation of your knowledge, in terms of some sort of perceptual evidence, is in the offing.

(2) EP is correct: we find our possession of knowledge about the world around us intelligible in terms of 'ways of knowing' provided by propositional perception in various modalities. Such explanations have (to borrow a term from Cassam 2007) a distinctive 'finality'. There is nothing to add to the statement that you know the tile to be blue because you can see that it's blue, except perhaps the negative point that you can see this without inference. (Occasionally we say that someone is able to see that p when she more or less automatically infers that p from visually manifest evidence, as when the milk bottles piling up in your neighbour's porch enable you to see that she is away, or the presence of her car that she is not. In such cases, of course, the subject's possession of knowledge is to be explained in terms of the evidence that constitutes her reason for the relevant belief.)

(3) EP is correct so far as it goes, but it leaves out an important dimension of our ordinary understanding of perceptual knowledge. That you can see the tile to be blue is not something we would ordinarily regard as the last word on how you know that it is blue. There are two kinds of factors that render epistemic perception itself intelligible: (i) our perceptual experience of objects and (ii) our exercising certain standing abilities, e.g. the ability to tell whether something is a tile, or whether it's blue, when you see it, under favourable conditions. There is a sense, then, in which epistemic perception *is* a sort of promissory note. The important thing is that it does not take a 'belief-centred' explanation to redeem the promise. We make sense of our ability non-inferentially to perceive what the world is like in terms of the exercise of certain perceptual-epistemic capacities, to tell the features of things or to recognize or identify things as falling under certain kinds or as certain individuals.

It is worth stressing that the disagreement here is not about the shape of a satisfactory philosophical theory of perceptual knowledge. It's about the correct analysis of ordinary explanatory practice, and about the nature of the reasons we ordinarily take ourselves to have for thinking that we know what perceived objects are like. It is not clear, therefore, that advocates of the explanatory priority of 'perceptual warrant' at the level of epistemological theorizing are committed to (1). Perhaps they have no interest in understanding our ordinary reasons for claims to perceptual knowledge, or perhaps they may even accept some version of EP, with the proviso that ultimately our entitlement to claims to perceptual knowledge can only be understood (and corroborated) by a philosophical theory of perceptual warrant. I will return to this idea in section 5. My immediate question is how we should understand the disagreement between (2) and (3).

I suggested that there are traces of (2) in some of Stroud's and Williamson's recent writings on perceptual knowledge. The textual evidence is not entirely clear-cut, but there are passages that encourage the suggestion that perceptual explanations of knowledge simply identify a *way in which we know* what we know, without adverting to any explanatory factors external to our knowledge. A significant part of the motivation for this, I think, has to do with what Stroud and Williamson see as the disastrous consequences of giving conscious perceptual experience any kind of 'external' explanatory or vindicatory role. Consider Stroud's discussion of what he calls 'objectual perception'. He argues that your perceiving an object is not sufficient for explaining how you know what the object is like: '(y)ou can perceive an object without knowing anything about it; without even having any beliefs about it.' That seems right, but it would be consistent with a view on which 'objectual perception' nevertheless plays an indispensable explanatory role, in tandem with other factors. This does not seem to be Stroud's view, however.[6] He moves directly from the insufficiency of 'objectual perception' to the conclusion that '(t)he kind of perception [that] is needed to account for knowledge of the world is therefore what might be called propositional perception.' (Stroud 2009: 565) That conclusion, I think, reflects Stroud's resistance to giving perceptual experience of objects (and thus 'objectual perception') what Campbell calls a 'fundamental role' in making perceptual knowledge intelligible. Elsewhere Stroud puts this as follows:

---

[6] 'Seeing that the cat is on the mat typically involves seeing that cat and seeing the mat. But when I see only that it is foggy everywhere, for instance I see and thereby know that that is how things are, but it could be that I do not see any objects at all.' (Stroud 2011a: 93) There are also passages, however, that point in the direction of (3). Consider Stroud's remark that 'the kind of perceptual knowledge I want to draw attention to requires a capacity to recognize, in the right circumstances, that an item now within your awareness falls, or does not fall, under a concept you are master of and understand.' (Stroud 2011a: 95).

> I think a person can sometimes *see*, for example, that there is a red tomato on a white plate right before him, and in that way he *knows* it is so. It is not that he knows it *on the basis of* some experience he is having. No experience serves as his *ground* or *reason* for claiming or judging as he does. (Stroud 2013: 4)

There are some indications that Williamson shares this view:

> what the speaker is reporting [when she explains how she knows that p by saying 'I can see that p'] is not an experience somehow prior to knowledge, but simply a particular kind of knowledge: visual knowledge. (Williamson 2009: 348)

Admittedly, Williamson observes that 'if required, a much fuller account could be given of *how one sees* that there is a red cube before one' (Williamson 2009: 359, my emphasis). Again, Stroud notes that epistemic perception 'typically *involve(s)* perceiving one or more objects.' (Stroud 2009: 565, my emphasis; but see footnote 7 above.) Both seem happy to acknowledge that there is more to our ordinary thinking about perception than can be captured by listing concepts of epistemic perception in the various modalities or by saying that perceiving is a way of knowing. What they appear to deny is that any of this further material is of much interest when it comes to understanding how you know that the tile is blue, or understanding our reasons for thinking that your attitude is knowledge. To avoid the blind alleys of classical foundationalism we need to discard the whole idea that our knowledge can be made intelligible by reference to sensory experience 'somehow prior to knowledge'.

The trouble is that this picture makes it hard to understand the 'vindicatory' character or function of perceptual explanations of knowledge. Consider first a general challenge to EP that advocates of (1) will wish to press. What makes perceptual explanations of knowledge 'vindicatory'? According to (1), there is a ready-made general model for understanding our reason for thinking that you know the tile is blue. The model also applies, for example, to our reason for thinking that the attitude you acquire by competent deductive inference from known premises is knowledge. In both cases, the attribution of knowledge is compelling in the light of our understanding of your grounds for belief. Call this a 'generalist' approach to the vindicatory role of perception. While 'internalist' and 'externalist' theories of warrant offer competing articulations of the general model, they are agreed that some such model is needed to make sense of our reasons for crediting ourselves and others with perceptual knowledge. It must be possible, in other words, to state and understand our reasons by the use of general epistemic concepts, for example by saying that perception provides us with 'justifying reasons for belief' or constitutes a 'reliable belief-forming process'.

The challenge facing EP is to formulate a 'particularist' alternative. (3) promises to meet that challenge by reference to 'specialized' perceptual-epistemic abilities. Our reason for thinking that your attitude is knowledge turns on our conception of the ability you exercise in acquiring the attitude, as an ability visually to recognize — that is, come to *know* — whether something is a tile. Whether such abilities can carry the explanatory weight (3) places on them is a good question, to which I will turn in a moment. (2), on the other hand, would suggest that 'She can see (or otherwise perceive) that p' is all the reassurance we can offer in response to 'How does she know that p?' (when she knows that p through perception). You might say that conversational patterns bear this out. As Paul Snowdon observes, 'we treat it as totally unproblematic that someone's knowledge that p can be explained by saying they saw that p.' (Snowdon 1998: 301) But note that Snowdon presumably means 'by *truly* saying (i.e. by invoking the fact that) they saw that p'. Arguably, the claim that they did see that p is not something we generally treat as totally unproblematic. There are familiar ways to probe claims to epistemic perception, such as 'How can you tell?' or 'Are you sure?' — unsurprisingly, given that there are familiar ways in which claims to epistemic perception can be mistaken. It seems, then, that commonsense psychology is not indifferent to the enabling conditions of epistemic perception, and that its concern with these conditions is linked to the practice of questioning and corroborating claims to knowledge.

Defenders of (2) might consider another way to understand the 'vindicatory' role of perception. To see that p, as Williamson says, is to know that p 'by sight'. (Williamson 2009: 348) This suggests that 'I can see that p' after all invokes an explanatory factor external to your knowing that p, and that our reason for thinking you do know that p turns on that factor. Roughly: it is because you acquired your attitude by sight that it can be seen to be knowledge. On this analysis, 'I saw that p' seems akin to 'by inference' or 'someone told me'. In all three cases, we make good our claim to knowledge by reference to the kind of source from which the knowledge flows. In many contexts, this would be seen as a perfectly adequate reply to HK, and your inability to recall any particulars would not surprise anyone. On the other hand, we would ordinarily take it for granted, in all three cases, that a more informative or fine-grained explanation could be given, or would have been available to you at the time you acquired your knowledge. Moreover, there are circumstances in which only a more detailed account could successfully corroborate your claim to knowledge. If we think there is good reason to doubt that p, it may not be sensible to accept your claim to knowledge that p without considering who told you that p, or which argument led you to conclude that p, or how you are supposed to have been able to see that p.[7]

In summary, an austere version of EP, along the lines of (2), does not seem to get to the bottom of the reasons we ordinarily have (or think we have) for crediting ourselves and others with perceptual knowledge. I now consider the prospects for a richer version of EP, along the lines of (3). In section 4, I return to the question whether perceptual knowledge depends on sensory experience 'somehow prior to knowledge'.

3 Perceptual Recognition

Consider Austin's list of statements that would ordinarily be regarded as good answers to the question 'How do you know there is a bittern at the end of the garden?':
(a) I was brought up in the fens.
(b) I heard it.

---

[7] Uncompromising defenders of (2) might at this point be tempted to reject the assumption that HK is a request for a vindicatory explanation of your knowing that p. Inspired by elements of Williamson's account of knowledge as the most general factive mental state, they might suggest that HK asks for the specific *way* in which you know (which need not be a way of 'coming to know'), and that the dialectical force of HK is to be understood in terms of the fact that ways of knowing that p are determinates of the determinable knowing that p. The idea would be that by identifying the way in which one knows that p one vindicates one's claim to knowledge that p in much the same way as the observation that an object is blue serves to corroborate the claim that it is coloured. (Williamson's remark that 'How do you know?' 'presupposes that *somehow* you do know' (2000: 152, my emphasis) might be read in this way.) I see two sorts of problems with this suggestion. First, there are problems with the notion of ways of knowing. For example, since 'I regret that p' is not a good answer to HK, not any kind of factive mental state would seem to qualify as a 'way of knowing', in the technical sense, and it is not obvious how that sense is to be regimented. (See Cassam 2009). Williamson counts 'remembering that p' as a way of knowing that p, but this is surely not straightforward. 'I remember that p' hardly provides a fully adequate answer to HK. (On my interpretation of HK this is unsurprising: that you were able to retain your knowledge sheds no light on how you were able to acquire it.) Second, the interpretation of HK as a request for a 'way of knowing', in the stipulated sense of a determinate of the determinable 'knowledge', looks less promising when we look at languages other than English. Questions that perform the dialectical role HK plays in English include '*Whence* do you know that p? (Woher weißt du das? Nereden biliyorsun?) and '*How do you manage* to know that p?' (Come fai a saperlo?) These questions seem straightforwardly to request a (certain kind of) *explanation* of your knowing that p.

(c) The keeper reported it.
(d) By its booming.
(e) From the booming noise.
(f) Because it is booming. (1961: 79)

Setting aside (c), these statements seem to presuppose that your knowledge can be explained in terms of an acquired skill (see a) of telling whether something is a bittern by its call (see d-f), the exercise of which requires the perceptual presence of the object (see b). Now, if reflection on examples like this is to help elaborate and defend (3), it needs to show that two conditions can be met (and reconciled):
(i) Knowledge gained by perceptual recognition is not (always) inferential. Telling that something is F 'from' (or 'by') some mark or characteristic set of features may occasionally be a matter of first acquiring perceptual knowledge that the thing shows the relevant mark or features, and then inferring that it is F, hence coming to believe it is F for the reason that it has the relevant mark. But this is not how perceptual recognition works in basic, paradigmatic cases. Note that what is being exercised, in the inferential case, is not a 'dedicated' perceptual-recognitional capacity but simply the 'general purpose' capacity to be appropriately responsive to one's epistemic reasons. Admittedly, it may not be straightforward, in any given case, to say whether the resulting knowledge depends on inference. In the case of the bittern, for example, the matter is complicated by the question whether, as Austin seems to suggest, you can hear *the bittern* itself, or merely the booming noise it makes. I'll skirt this issue by reverting to visual examples. What matters is that in basic cases, appeal to perceptual recognition explains how we are able to perceive what an object is like without invoking our belief and its epistemic basis.

(ii) Your capacity visually to tell whether something is a tile, or blue, is not a mere disposition or 'power' to acquire knowledge of whether it's a tile, or blue; it is the reason why you have that disposition. The problem with a dispositional interpretation is that the explanatory value of capacities for perceptual recognition would be extremely limited. As Alan Millar puts it, appeal to such capacities would look like 'explaining why people fall asleep in terms of their having taken a drug with the power to make someone fall asleep.' It would amount to invoking 'some power or other — *we know not what* — to acquire such knowledge'. (Millar 2008: 336) Invocations of occult powers of knowledge-acquisition, of course, would hardly provide a fully satisfactory way to corroborate claims to knowledge. On a dispositional analysis, perceptual-recognitional capacities would really just be another sort of promissory note, to be redeemed, presumably, by some kind of underlying belief-centred explanation. (Perhaps a reliabilist analysis of perceptual telling à la Goldman (1976).)

Millar's response to the 'virtus dormitiva' objection is that a perceptual-recognitional capacity, as ordinarily conceived, is not a disposition but an ability 'that has a certain structure'. Visually identifying a finch, for example, involves being 'responsive to the shape of the bird, its size, how it moves, and so on' (Millar 2008: 336) — to features that constitute the distinctive visual appearance of a finch.[8] The challenge is to explain what this 'responsiveness' comes to, if it is not a matter of inference. There is also another question: what sort of 'structure', if any, is supposed to be present in cases where there seems to be nothing 'from which' we tell what an object is like (for example, in the case of recognizing an object's shape or colour)? Progress with these questions can be made, I want to suggest, by comparing and contrasting perceptual recognition, as ordinarily conceived, with examples of what might be called 'implicit' or 'opaque' perceptual telling. I want to highlight three kinds of differences, corresponding to three elements of the (non-inferential) 'structure' that makes ordinary perceptual-recognitional capacities richly explanatory.

Perceptual attention. Compare a perceptual judgement — 'that tile is blue' — with a 'blindseer's' statement 'it's blue', said in response to the experimenter's request to guess whether an object placed in the patient's blind field is blue. A salient feature of the latter case is that while a blindseer is able reliably to guess what an object in her blind field is like, her ability strikes us, and her, as completely mysterious. Vision science tells us that the ability is underpinned by 'implicitly processed' visual information, but neither the subject herself nor commonsense psychology in general have any insight into the basis of her guesswork, not even into whether vision has anything to do with it. We experience no such puzzlement in the case of your judgment 'that tile is blue'. Unlike the blindseer you can see the thing you are talking about, and doing so enables you visually to attend to it. According to one tradition in philosophical writings on attention, attending to a perceptually presented object provides a means for answering questions about the object.[9] I think this captures precisely the difference we would ordinarily see between sight and blindsight. It's partly in the light

---

8 Or perhaps a determinate of the determinable 'the distinctive visual appearance of a finch.' See Price 1953, esp. p. 54, for discussion.

9 Cedric Evans defines 'interrogative attention' as the 'the attention we pay to an object in order to enlarge our knowledge'(1970: 100). Naomi Eilan suggests that perceptual attention is 'among other things, the means by which we answer (..) questions about the environment.'

of that 'means' that we find your judgement about the tile (and the knowledge it expresses) intelligible. Perceptual attention to an experienced object is not a 'means' blindseers have at their disposal.[10] That, plausibly, is why their ability delivers, at least most immediately, mere guesswork, not perceptual knowledge.

Sensory appearances. It's a time-honoured theme in the literature on perceptual recognition that it can be hard to articulate the appearances to which a perceptual judgement is responsive. Consider Leibniz's illustration of what he calls 'confused perception': 'we see that painters and other skilled craftsmen can accurately tell well-done work from what is poorly done, though often they can't explain their judgments, and when asked about them all they can say is that the works that displease them lack a certain *je-ne-sais-quoi.*'[11] And it is not just 'expert perception' that can seem intangible in this way. As Alan Millar observes, 'there is no a priori reason to suppose that facility at recognizing people goes with facility at registering the person's features at the level of judgement'. What's more, even if we were able to identify the relevant visible features, this would 'fall short of articulating that to which we respond' when recognizing Bill by sight, viz. the 'Gestalt of a face, or a distinctive gait.' (Millar 2010: 122).

In the light of this, the idea that perceptual-recognitional capacities provide for intelligible knowledge may begin to look dubious. Elusive appearances, you might say, can hardly be expected to render the ability to identify kinds and properties comprehensible. But on reflection that would be too quick. Consider a second case of 'implicit telling', viz. professional chicken-sexing, as described in the philosophical literature. The subject looks at the chick (unlike a blindseer she can actually see the relevant object) and finds herself guessing 'female'. While it's plausible for her to associate her (as it turns out, reliable) guesses with seeing the chick, she has no idea what makes her think 'female' rather than 'male'. Note that the cases described by Leibniz and Millar are not like *that*. The subjects are struggling to articulate the visual appearances that prompt their judgements, but neither of them seems to be in any doubt that there *is* a certain way the object looks

---

(1998, p. 194) According to John Campbell, 'conscious attention to an object (..) affects the functional role of your experience of the object. Having once consciously focused on the object, you are now in a position to keep track of it deliberately, to answer questions about it, and to act on it.' (2002: 10–11).
10 To be precise, they are unable to engage in the activity of perceptually attending to experienced objects. That point is not inconsistent with evidence that the processing underlying blindseers' conjectures may implicate attentional mechanisms (Kentridge et al 2004).
11 Leibniz 1989, p. 291. I've used Jonathan Bennett's translation, available here: http://www.earlymoderntexts.com/search?q=leibniz+knowledge

to which they are responsive. The sense in which they 'can't explain their judgements' is quite different from the utter darkness in which blindseers and even 'chicken-sexers' find themselves when reflecting on the origins of their thoughts. Furthermore, we should not overstate the point that we may not be able to 'register' recognition-enabling features 'at the level of judgement'. It is one thing to point out, as is frequently and plausibly done in the literature on perceptual recognition, that we are not in general good at *describing* the features by which we can tell kinds of things. (Austin 1961 [first published 1946], Price 1953, Urmson 1956) It is another to say, less plausibly, that we have no idea of what they are. For one thing, so long as we are in the presence of the object, we may be able to indicate the relevant appearance by the use of perceptual demonstratives ('that colour'). Sometimes we may only be able to gesture towards a higher-level property or Gestalt ('something about his gait'). Sometimes we may have to resort to identifying appearances comparatively ('he looks like Bill').[12] The point that matters is that recognition-enabling features don't have the status of a 'theoretical posit', something the existence of which we hypothesize though we have no real idea of its nature. There is a sense in which we take ourselves to be presented with such features, and we seem to be sufficiently articulate about their character to invoke them in making our perceptual judgements (in particular, the predicates we apply to an experienced object) intelligible.[13]

Standing knowledge. The etymology of 'recognition' suggests that prior cognition of a finch is required to count as re-cognizing something as a finch. It might

---

12 Compare Millar's reference to the 'gesturing character' of explanations of how we can perceptually tell things (Millar 2010: 123).
13 One complication arises from the fact that we often exercise, or try to exercise, perceptual-recognitional capacities in less than ideal circumstances. For example, when your attention is attracted by something at the periphery of your visual field for a split second and you find yourself thinking (correctly) it was a sparrow, you may not be able even to gesture at any visual appearance that gave rise to your judgement. In some such cases, the right thing to say may be that you were not in fact able to exercise your capacity for recognizing sparrows but, as a result of *trying* to do so, found yourself guessing it was a sparrow. (See Millar 2010 for an illuminating exposition and defence of the view that 'exercising a perceptual-recognitional capacity is a success notion': we may unsuccessfully attempt to exercise the capacity to recognize whether something is a sparrow, but when we do exercise it what we gain is knowledge.) Perhaps at least some cases of 'implicit telling' involve such attempts at recognition under extreme conditions (for example, conditions of extreme speed). Biederman and Shiffrar's investigation of (real) chicken sexing seems to be in keeping with that interpretation. The subjects they interviewed routinely sex 1000 chicks per hour, 'spending less than a half second viewing the cloacal region' where males and females display slightly different 'eminences.' (In males the eminences are 'convex', in females 'flat or concave.') (Biederman / Shiffrar 1987: 640–1).

be said that what this involves is simply the standing capacity to discover whether a perceived object is a finch from the features making up its sensory appearance. Arguably, though, we make sense of that capacity in terms of possession of a certain kind of standing *knowledge*. To bring this out, here is my final example of a case of 'implicit telling' (though the label is debatable). In 'Imagination and Perception', Strawson contrasts the following cases:

> Compare seeing a face you *think* you know, but cannot associate with any previous encounter with seeing a face you *know* you know and can very well so associate, even though there does not, as you see it, occur any particular *episode* of recalling any particular previous encounter. The comparison will show why I say that the past perceptions are, in the latter case, not merely causally operative, but alive in the present perception. (Strawson 1974: 59)

The first case might be described by saying that someone's face strikes you as familiar or even that you 'recognize' the face, in the feeble sense that you find yourself thinking 'I've met this person', and do so as a result of some previous encounter. In the second case, you come to know 'that's Bill', by exercising something you apparently lack in the first case: a recognitional capacity for Bill. But that is not all. In the second, but not in the first case, it is natural to say that you know how Bill looks, and that this knowledge is reflected — 'alive' in some sense — in your judging and seeing that it is Bill. It is partly in the light of that standing knowledge that we find your ability to recognize Bill intelligible. The same point applies to the perceptual recognition of kinds or basic features. It's because you *know* what tiles, and blue things, look like under standard conditions that it's unsurprising that you can tell 'this tile is blue' when you see it in good daylight right in front of you.

It might be said that all of these points are compatible with an inferentialist model, on which thoughts about appearances matter because they provide us with premises from which to draw conclusions about reality. The idea would be that what your standing knowledge of how blue things looks provides for, most immediately, is just the recognition that the tile looks blue, from which, absent conflicting evidence, you may infer that it is blue. One problem with this model is that it distorts the role thoughts about appearances ordinarily play in perceptual knowledge. Such thoughts enable us to make our knowledge intelligible, but it does not seem right to suggest that to find out what objects are like through perception we *first* have to form a view of their sensory appearances. The model also raises familiar epistemological concerns. How, if perception never enables us to know reality directly, are we supposed to know that appearances provide good evidence of the nature of reality? Perhaps the most telling line of objection to the inferential model is that the capacity to recognize appearances *presupposes* the capacity (directly) to recognize the corresponding reality. In any given case, of course, you may reflect that something looks blue while reserving judgment on whether it is blue. But would you be able to do so without ever being able to tell directly that an object is blue? Intuitively, your reflection is a matter of registering what you would take the thing's colour to be (by visually recognizing it) if you had no reason to suspect appearances to be misleading. As Strawson put it, you 'use' the perceptual claim you would ordinarily have made without endorsing it (Strawson 1988). This analysis is in keeping with a natural suggestion about the way perceptual-recognitional capacities are acquired. We are not *first* taught how to tell the look of tiles or of the colour blue. Rather, we learn visually to tell blue things or tiles, in doing which we also learn to recognize the distinctive visual appearance that makes such perceptual identifications possible. The capacity to think about these appearances would not be available independently of the capacity for non-inferential perceptual recognition.[14]

Earlier I suggested that EP demands a 'particularist' account of the way perception vindicates claims to knowledge, an account of the 'reassurance' provided by perceptual explanations of knowledge that is not couched in general epistemic terms. The obvious suggestion, from the point of view of (3), is that our reason for accepting that you know that the tile is blue turns on your 'specialized' ability to recognize (hence come to *know*) whether something is blue, or a tile. We are now in a position to see how that suggestion might be filled out. If my sketch of the commonsense psychology of perceptual recognition is on the right lines, your ability has a sufficiently rich 'structure' to distinguish it from a mere disposition, yet the 'structure' is *sui generis*, not reducible to general-purpose inferential ca-

---

[14] Compare Millar's claim that 'we have no independent conceptual grip' on the notion of 'sensory experiences such that it looks to us as if an F is there' (2010: 136) — independent, that is, from our understanding of what it is to see that an F is there. Millar also makes a further, stronger claim that, to my mind, is less plausible, that the human capacity for perceptual recognition is independent of the ability to 'think of appearances as such.' (p. 123). On Millar's account, *reflective* perceptual recognition involves a combination of not-essentially-reflective recognitional capacities (which are operative in reflective and non-reflective perceivers alike) with capacities for reflective awareness (see Millar 2011 for a detailed development of this view). I think partly as a result of his adherence to this view of the nature of reflective perception, Millar would be inclined to deny that what I called standing knowledge of the distinctive appearance of a kind or individual or feature is part of what makes perceptual recognition intelligible. Without being able to argue this here, I have two concerns about this picture: (a) it is not clear to me that we can offer a fully adequate response to the 'virtus dormitiva' objection without giving a central role to standing knowledge of appearances, and (b) there may be independent grounds for scepticism about 'additive' conceptions of reflective perception (see Boyle 2016 for relevant discussion).

pacities. A noteworthy feature of this 'structure' is that, contra Stroud and Williamson, sensory experience 'prior to knowledge' plays an essential epistemic role. It is because visual experience presents you with the tile that you are able visually to attend to the tile and thus intelligibly answer questions about it. On the other hand, the role of sensory experience is strictly limited: your experience helps to make your knowledge intelligible only in combination with your capacity for recognizing tiles and blue things, informed by your standing knowledge of their distinctive visual appearances. I want to suggest that this provides a way to adjudicate a fundamental disagreement between McDowell and Stroud, with McDowell affirming and Stroud denying that perceptual knowledge is 'based on experience'. My diagnosis will be that each of the two positions is importantly right about the shortcomings of the other.

4 The Epistemic Role of Perceptual Experience

Consider McDowell's objection to what he calls the Stroud-Davidson view. That view denies that perceptual experience has, as McDowell puts it, a 'reason-giving capacity'; it denies, specifically, that perceptual experience gives us what I earlier called 'knowledge-providing' reasons (reasons for beliefs such that the beliefs can be seen to amount to knowledge because they are held for those reasons). McDowell's objection is that the 'Stroud-Davidson' view cannot accommodate the distinction between ordinary perceptual judgements and a (legendary) chicken-sexer's taking a particular hatchling to be female. To mark the distinction, he maintains, we need the notion of a 'perceptual impression', a perceptual state that does not implicate either belief or knowledge but provides a rational basis — 'something like an invitation' — for belief. The notion would enable us to say this: the chicken-sexers 'cannot find in their perceptual experience impressions whose content is that a chick is male, or that it is female.' (McDowell 2002:. 279) As a consequence, they lack the sort of reasons that explain and warrant ordinary perceptual beliefs. On this analysis, the 'Stroud-Davidson' view is revisionary: it is incompatible with a distinction commonsense finds compelling and with the part 'perceptual impressions' play in ordinary explanatory practice.

Stroud is unmoved by this objection, and I suspect part of his diagnosis is that the objection rests on an assumption that is itself revisionary: it projects ideas that have their home in classical foundationalist epistemology into commonsense psychology. In slightly more detail: on Stroud's view, we need to distinguish sharply between the claim that perceptual knowledge is 'based on' experience and the claim that it involves experience. Stroud acknowledges that we have perceptual experiences such as the experience of 'seeing and knowing that there is a red tomato and a plate there'. What he denies is that when someone sees and knows that there is a tomato, there is a visual experience that serves as 'the ground or basis of his knowledge that there is a tomato.' The sort of experience we undoubtedly have is what he calls a 'thick experience'. It is 'thick' in the sense that it is 'too close' to what we know to be able to explain how we know it. (Stroud 2013: 3–4)[15] Stroud's main objection to a 'thin' notion of perceptual experience — such as the notion of a 'perceptual impression' in McDowell's sense — is this. A perceptual 'impression' would provide a 'basis' for our knowledge in a sense akin to that in which the known premises of a valid argument may be said to be the 'basis' of our knowledge of the truth of its conclusion. In both cases, we can be seen to know something because we believe it for a good reason. There is a crucial difference, however. The reason-giving capacity of a perceptual 'impression' is not supposed to depend on the subject's knowing, or even believing, what the impression represents to be so. The problem with this account is that it extends the scope of reason-giving explanations beyond the conditions that make such explanations intelligible. 'It is not simply the content of a person's experience that gives the reason to believe something', Stroud argues, 'it is the person's experiencing, or being aware of, or accepting, or somehow "taking in" that content.' (Stroud 2002: 89) Without your accepting that content, it could not be your reason to believe anything, nor could you take it to be a reason. The putative 'belief- (and knowledge-) independence' of McDowell's 'perceptual impressions' defeats their essential purpose, to enable us to understand perceptual experience's 'reason-giving capacity'.

I think a sensible verdict at this point is that the objections McDowell and Stroud are trading with each other are both quite powerful. Stroud might of course insist that the chicken-sexers lack the 'thick' experience of 'seeing and knowing' that a hatchling is female. But given that a thick experience is not thought to *explain* how we know what we 'see and know', the question remains why its absence should make perceptual knowledge unavailable or unintelligible in the ordinary way. On the other hand, it does seem hard to make sense of McDowell's conception of the 'reason-giving capacity' of perceptual experience,

---

15 Once again, there is a striking affinity between Stroud's and Williamson's views. Williamson suggests that 'I can see that p' 'reports an experience only in the anodyne sense in which "I met John Boorman" reports an experience'. One thing that makes the sense anodyne is that one does not 'describe what it is like to have the experience'. Another, I think, is that the experience does not serve as the ground or basis for one's knowledge. In the case of 'visual knowledge', the correct explanation of how one knows is: 'by sight' (2009: 348).

something that (for one thing) would be surprising if, as McDowell contends, the conception were so much commonsense.[16] Might both objections be correct? I think the reason this possibility tends to be overlooked lies in an assumption McDowell and Stroud share. The assumption can be put in the form of a conditional:

> if perceptual experience plays a distinctive explanatory role in ordinary explanations of how we know what we know through perception, commonsense conceives of perceptual experience as an epistemic basis for beliefs (in the light of which such beliefs can be seen to qualify as knowledge).

McDowell accepts the antecedent, and argues by modus ponens. Stroud rejects the consequent, and argues by modus tollens. Neither of them, however, offers any reason for accepting the conditional. Suppose we reject it. Then we can agree with McDowell that sensory experience plays an essential role in accounting for perceptual knowledge. Without experience of objects (as in blindsight) or recognition-enabling features (as in chicken-sexing) intelligible perceptual recognition is impossible. We can also agree with Stroud that when someone makes an observational judgement, 'no experience serves as his *ground* or *reason* for claiming or judging as he does' — at least if by 'ground or reason' we mean what McDowell means by it, viz. a reason responsiveness to which would explain how he knows what he knows. In another sense, though, experience does provide a 'ground or reason'. By contributing to a vindicatory explanation of his knowledge, it provides a reason to accept the claim that what he has is indeed knowledge. In *that* sense, McDowell is right to insist that sensory experience has a 'reason-giving capacity'.

5 Perceptual Warrant: the Manifest vs. the Philosophical Image

One question defenders of McDowell's account will press is how, if we abandon the idea of 'perceptual impressions' that provide us with reasons for belief, we are to explain the *rationality* of perceptual beliefs. Knowing entails believing, and, in rational subjects, believing for good reasons. How can EP respect this?

---

16 For critical discussion of this aspect of McDowell's account, see Travis 2004, Ginsborg 2006, Roessler 2009, Giananti 2019.

This is one complaint that might be made under the general heading of 'perceptual warrant'. Another is this. There is a sort of methodological disjunctivism built into EP. It approaches the relation between perceiving and believing by narrowly focusing on 'good' cases, in which perception yields knowledge, not just belief. But perception also causes and warrants 'mere' beliefs, as when odd lighting condition mislead you about the colour of a white tile. How is it that it can be perfectly reasonable, in such circumstances, to believe that the tile is blue?

I don't want to minimize the importance or difficulty of these issues, but I think so long as our interest is merely in articulating ordinary explanatory practice they pose no very serious challenge. Put in general terms, the obvious response is that questions about our warrant for perceptual beliefs should be approached in the light of our independent understanding of the 'vindicatory role' of perception. What makes your belief that the tile is blue rational, when the blue tile is right in front of you in good daylight, is that you have a conclusive reason for it: you can see it's blue. As Stroud remarks, '(t)here is no better reason for believing and claiming to know that p than seeing or otherwise perceiving that p.' (Stroud 2009: 566) True, the reason would not be available to you if you were not aware that you can see the tile to be blue. But arguably, it is no accident that if a rational subject visually recognizes an object she will ordinarily be in a position to know that she recognizes the object.[17] In turn, this account may help to understand the sense in which 'mere' perceptual beliefs can be reasonable. That you are unaware of the unusual lighting conditions explains (and excuses) your mistaken belief that you're in a situation in which you can visually tell the tile's colour. That the tile is looking bright blue to you explains (and excuses) your mistaken belief that you are able to tell it's blue, and hence your belief that it is blue. (See Millar 2011)

Both suggestions (even if properly elaborated) will raise a number of detailed concerns. But I think the reason they are bound to strike many as unsatisfactory is not a matter of detail but of principle. They violate a maxim almost universally acknowledged in epistemology, that if you know that p through perception it must be possible to give an independent account of how your perception warrants your belief that p. Let's call this the explanatory priority of perceptual warrant (PPW). There are different perspectives from which one may try to understand the popularity of PPW. From one point of view, it can seem as if there are

---

17 See Millar 2011 for a version of this idea, which appeals to the notion of a 'second-order perceptual-recognitional capacity.' An alternative version, I think, is implicit in the discussion of the previous section: roughly, the idea would be that perceptual recognition, in the case of rational subjects, is inherently intelligible and so inherently self-conscious.

simply a variety of quite heterogeneous traditions and concerns in epistemology that happen to converge on PPW. One of the sources of its appeal, for example, is surely the traditional view that knowledge can be reductively analyzed as warranted true belief. That view makes it utterly natural to assume that explaining how you know that p can only be a matter of explaining how your true belief comes to be warranted in the relevant sense. Another source may be a traditional, 'narrow' view of the nature of sensory experience. If, as the 'slightest philosophy' supposedly teaches us, 'nothing can ever be present to the mind but an image or perception' (Hume 1975: 152), sensory experience could not intelligibly put us in a position non-inferentially to tell what mind-independent objects are like. The only role it could conceivably play in making knowledge of objects possible would be that of contributing in some way to our justification for forming beliefs about objects.

The various traditions that may be responsible for PPW's popularity would all deserve detailed attention. But here I want to focus on an alternative perspective that can fruitfully be adopted in thinking about PPW. There may be a way of motivating PPW that does not rely on contentious doctrines about the nature of propositional knowledge or perceptual experience. A commitment to the principle, it may be argued, is inseparable from the project of achieving a philosophical understanding of perceptual knowledge, at least if epistemology is to be the 'critical' discipline it has traditionally aspired to be. The route to PPW I have in mind would involve two steps. The first step would insist that epistemology is not exhausted by what might be called 'descriptive epistemology'. The latter, to adapt Strawson's explication of 'descriptive metaphysics' (Strawson 1959: 9), aims to 'describe the actual structure of our thinking' about perceptual knowledge. Without diminishing the value of that exercise, it cannot, by itself, answer epistemology's question, which is: how does perception provide us with knowledge of (and justified beliefs about) mind-independent objects? This is not a question about the structure of our ordinary thinking about perceptual knowledge. It is, simply, a philosophical question about perceptual knowledge itself. The second step would add that not only is the question not *about* commonsense psychology, but it cannot satisfactorily be answered simply by rehearsing commonsense psychology. We may ordinarily take it that seeing the tile will enable a (suitably equipped) perceiver to tell that it's a blue tile. But epistemology should stand back and ask whether we are right about this. That enterprise would be greatly facilitated if we had a definition or reductive analysis of knowledge, ideally as a kind of belief that meets certain further conditions. We could then simply ask whether perception provides for the satisfaction of the necessary and sufficient conditions for knowledge.[18] But even if we lack a definition of knowledge, it is natural to think that the way to probe perceptual explanations of how we know what objects are like is to compare them with what we have independent reason to regard as the prototype of a vindicatory explanation of knowledge, in terms of conclusive reasons for belief. Whether perception can explain and vindicate our knowledge of the world around us, in the end, depends on whether it resembles the prototype in relevant ways. Internalists and externalists have different ideas about what counts as relevant similarity here, but they agree that what matters is that you come to believe something in a way that explains how you are warranted in believing it.

The suggestion, then, is that what I called a 'generalist' approach to perceptual knowledge (in section 2) is unavoidable if we are to take the philosophical question seriously. We need to be able to understand the epistemic role of perception in terms we have independent reason to think yield vindicatory explanations. In contrast, as I emphasized, ordinary explanatory practice, as represented by EP, is incorrigibly 'particularist'. It makes our knowledge of objects intelligible by reference to specialized perceptual-epistemic skills rather than general-purpose capacities, such as responsiveness to evidence or reliable belief-forming dispositions. The exercise of the specialized skill is seen as sufficient for knowledge, despite being, as Williamson puts it, highly unnecessary. (Williamson 2009: 359)

I think the two-step route to PPW captures something of the spirit in which work on perceptual warrant is commonly conducted. I will leave open whether a case for PPW along these lines is convincing, and whether it is free of contentious assumptions about the nature of perception or propositional knowledge.[19] But I want to conclude by indicating grounds for scepticism, not about the philosophical project itself but about its chances of corroborating our everyday thinking

---

[18] The attraction of simultaneously understanding the nature of knowledge and the way vindicatory explanations of knowledge work may be responsible for the tendency for 'what the press corps calls mission creep' that John Hyman discerns in contemporary work on the nature of knowledge: 'We start out wanting to say what knowledge is; but we quickly find ourselves embroiled in the question of how it can be acquired. And before long we have to evacuate by helicopter, leaving chaos behind us.' (Hyman 1999: 435).

[19] If so, this would be one way in which the two-step route to PPW differs from Stroud's suggestive discussion of the sources of what he describes as the philosophical project of giving a 'completely general' explanation of our knowledge of the world around us, despite similarities in other respects (Stroud 2000, esp. essays 8 and 10). At least some of his formulations suggest that according to Stroud, a central commitment of the philosophical project is a certain view of sense perception, one on which 'we could perceive exactly what we perceive now even if there were no material world at all' (2000: 102).

about perceptual knowledge. Philosophers differ in the degree to which they are interested in the latter. Sometimes commonsense merely figures in the guise of 'intuitions' used to prompt epistemological theorizing. But many theorists of perceptual warrant think of their work as something that will deepen and validate our ordinary practice of explaining knowledge by reference to perception. The problem is that if EP is correct, there seems to be a sufficiently profound dissonance between the perspective of commonsense and the perspective of the philosophical project to scupper the prospect of any such validation. There seems to be a 'gap or dislocation' here, akin to the one Bernard Williams identifies in the enterprise of justifying ordinary ethical thinking on the basis of utilitarian theory: a 'gap or dislocation between the spirit of the theory itself and the spirit it supposedly justifies.' (Williams 1985: 108). The spirit of commonsense psychology says that the best (though of course not the only) way to convince others that one knows that a certain tile is blue would be to invite them to look at the tile, something that will enable them to recognize both the tile's colour and the justice of one's claim to knowledge. The spirit of epistemology says that there cannot be any really good reason to think that one's attitude is knowledge without an independent account of how one's visual experience helps to warrant one's belief. On the face of it, there is a straightforward conflict here over the reasons we have for crediting ourselves and others with knowledge. In view of this 'dislocation', it is perhaps unsurprising that epistemologists have sought to domesticate commonsense, by analyzing everyday explanatory practice in terms of some sort of belief-centred schema, internalist or externalist. But the desire to avert the threat of 'dislocation' would not be a good reason for accepting any such analysis. There is an obvious risk here of surreptitiously retrojecting a revisionary philosophical theory into commonsense psychology.[20]

To say that pursuit of the philosophical question cannot succeed in validating our everyday thinking is not, of course, to say that it cannot succeed at all. It

---

[20] I borrow the term from Janet Broughton's suggestion that Descartes 'retrojects' some of the metaphysical and epistemological results reached in Meditation VI into the putatively commonsensical view the meditator finds himself holding at the beginning of Meditation I (Broughton 2003: 31). See also Stroud's discussion of the risk of 'metaphysical conviction' leading to 'distortion or misunderstanding' of our everyday ways of thinking (Stroud 2011b: 15). A nice example of the retrojection of a revisionary philosophical theory into commonsense is provided by William Kneale's gloss on Locke's theory of secondary qualities: 'When Locke said that the secondary qualities were powers in things to produce sensations in us, he stated the facts correctly, but he did not realize that his statement was only an analysis of the plain man's use of secondary quality adjectives.' (Kneale 1950: 123). I owe this quote to Keith Allen's illuminating discussion of what he calls the 'Oxford view of colour', in Allen 2007.

might succeed, for example, in *debunking* our everyday thinking. Colour provides an analogy here. On one analysis, we ordinarily take it that the colours of objects, which we conceive neither as dispositions nor as microphysical properties, explain the experience we enjoy when we perceive colours. The manifest image, thus described, might then be said to have been superseded by vision science. It may be said, similarly, that the commonsensical notion that we find out what objects are like by deploying capacities for perceptual recognition has been debunked by epistemology, which reveals that the explanation and vindication of our knowledge in fact turns on whether and how perception warrants our beliefs. This would obviously be to place a lot of confidence in PPW. One important question would be whether the case for PPW is strong enough to warrant that confidence. But a successful debunking manoeuvre would also depend on another condition. It would require that jettisoning the commonsense psychology of perceptual knowledge would not take with it too much — nothing, at least, that's indispensable for human thought and knowledge. That condition would also deserve careful scrutiny. As in other areas,[21] breaking away from the manifest image may turn out to be no straightforward matter.[22]

References

Allen, K. (2007): "The Mind-Independence of Colour". In: *European Journal of Philosophy* 15.2, pp. 137–158.
Austin, J.L. (1961): "Other Minds". In his *Philosophical Papers*. Oxford: Clarendon Press.
Ayer, A. (1956): *The Problem of Knowledge*. London: Penguin.
Biederman, I. and Shiffrar, M. (1987): "Sexing day-old chicks: A case study and expert systems analysis of a difficult perceptual-learning task". In: *Journal of Experimental Psychology: Learning, memory, and cognition* 13.4, p. 640.
Boyle, M. (2016): "Additive theories of rationality: A critique". In: *European Journal of Philosophy* 24.3, pp. 527–555.
Broughton, J. (2003): *Descartes's Method of Doubt*. Princeton: Princeton University Press.
Campbell, J. (2002): *Reference and Consciousness*. Oxford: Oxford University Press.

---

21 Compare Stroud's discussion of modal, causal and evaluative thinking in his 2011b.
22 For helpful comments on previous drafts of this paper I'm grateful to Lucy Campbell, Naomi Eilan, Andrea Giananti, Thor Grünbaum, David Hunter, Hemdat Lerman, Guy Longworth, Mike Martin, Krisztina Orban, Eylem Özaltun, Christoph Pfisterer, Stefan Riegelnik, Barney Walker and Hong-Yu Wong. Special thanks to the participants at a workshop at the University of Roma Tre (some time ago) who helped me to get started on this paper. I've presented versions of the paper at conferences or colloquia at Salzburg, Southampton, Warwick, Tübingen, Kirchberg am Wechsel and Zürich. I'm grateful to the audiences for suggestions and comments.

Campbell, J. (2014): *Berkeley's Puzzle*. (with Q. Cassam) Oxford: Oxford University Press.
Cassam. Q. (2007): "Ways of Knowing". In: *Proceedings of the Aristotelian Society* 107 (1), pp. 339–358).
Cassam, Q. (2009): "Can the Concept of Knowledge be Analysed?". In: P. Greenough & D. Prichard (Eds.): *Williamson on Knowledge*. Oxford: Oxford University Press.
Eilan, N. (1998): "Perceptual intentionality, attention and consciousness". In: *Royal Institute of Philosophy Supplements* 43, pp. 181–202.
Evans, C. (1970): *The Subject of Consciousness*. London: George Allen & Unwin.
Evans, G. (1982): *The Varieties of Reference*. Oxford: Oxford University Press.
Giananti, A. (2019): "The weight of facts: A puzzle about perception, reasons and deliberation". In: *Ratio* 32, pp. 1–10.
Ginsborg, H. (2006): "Reasons for belief". In: *Philosophy and Phenomenological Research* 72.2, pp. 286–318.
Goldman, A. (1976): "Discrimination and perceptual knowledge". In: *The Journal of philosophy* 73.20, pp. 771–791.
Hume, D. (1975): *Enquiries concerning Human Understanding and concerning the Principles of Morals*. Ed by L.A. Selby-Bigge. Oxford: Clarendon Press.
Hyman, J. (1999) "How knowledge works". In: *The Philosophical Quarterly* 49.197, pp. 433–451.
Kentridge, R., Heywood, C. and Weiskrantz, L. (2004): "Spatial attention speeds discrimination without awareness in blindsight". In: *Neuropsychologia* 42.6, pp. 831–835.
Kneale, W. (1950) "Sensation and the Physical World". In: *Philosophical Quarterly,* 1.2, *pp.* 109–126.
Leibniz, G. W. (1989): "Meditations on knowledge, truth, and ideas". In: *Philosophical Papers and Letters*. Springer, Dordrecht.
McDowell, J. (2002): "Responses". In: N. Smith (Ed.): *Reading McDowell*. London/New York: Routledge.
McDowell, J. (2011): *Perception as a Capacity for Knowledge*. Milwaukee: Marquette University Press.
McGinn, M. (2012): "Non-Inferential Knowledge". In: *Proceedings of the Aristotelian Society*. Vol. 112,1, pp. 1–28.
Millar, A. (2008): "Perceptual-recognitional abilities and perceptual knowledge". In: A. Haddock & F. E. Macpherson (Eds.): *Disjunctivism: Perception, Action, Knowledge*. Oxford: Clarendon Press.
Millar, A. (2010): "Knowledge and Recognition". In: D. Prichard, A. Millar & A. Haddock, *The Nature and Value of Knowledge*. Oxford: Oxford University Press.
Millar, A. (2011): "How visual perception yields reasons for belief". In: *Philosophical Issues*, 21(1), pp. 332–351.
Price, H. H. (1953): *Thinking and Experience*. London: Hutchinson.
Roessler, J. (2009): "Perceptual experience and perceptual knowledge". In: *Mind* 118 (472), pp. 1013–1041.
Scanlon, T. (1998): *What we owe to each other*. Cambridge, Mass.: Harvard University Press
Sellars, W. (1956): "Empiricism and the Philosophy of Mind". In: *Minnesota studies in the philosophy of science* 1.19, pp. 253–329.
Snowdon, P. (1998): "Strawson on the concept of perception". In L. Hahn (Ed.): *The Philosophy of P.F. Strawson*. Peru, Illinois: Open Court Publishing.
Stoljar, D. (2012): "Knowledge of Perception". In D. Smithies & D. Stoljar (Eds.): *Introspection and Consciousness*. Oxford: Oxford University Press.

Strawson, P.F. (1959): *Individuals,* London: Routledge.
Strawson, P. F. (1974): "Imagination and Perception". In his *Freedom and Resentment and Other Essays*. London: Methuen.
Strawson, P.F. (1988): "Perception and its Objects". In: J. Dancy (Ed.): *Perceptual Knowledge*. Oxford: Oxford University Press.
Stroud, B. (2000): *Understanding Human Knowledge*. Oxford: Oxford University Press.
Stroud, B. (2002): "Sense-experience and the grounding of thought". In: N. Smith (Ed.), *Reading McDowell*. London/New York: Routledge
Stroud, B. (2009): "Scepticism and the Senses". In: *European Journal of Philosophy* 17(4), pp. 559–570.
Stroud, B. (2011a): "Seeing what is so". In: J. Roessler, H. Lerman & N. Eilan (Eds.): *Perception, Causation, and Objectivity*. Oxford: Oxford University Press.
Stroud, B. (2011b): *Engagement and Metaphysical Dissatisfaction*. Oxford: Oxford University Press.
Stroud, B. (2013): "Doing something intentionally and knowing that you are doing it". In: *Canadian Journal of Philosophy* 43.1, pp. 1–12.
Travis, C. (2004): "The silence of the senses". In: *Mind* 113 (449), pp. 57–94.
Urmson, J.O. (1956): "Recognition". In: *Proceedings of the Aristotelian Society* 56, pp. 259–280.
Wiggins, D. (1996): "Objective and subjective in ethics, with two postscripts about truth". In B. Hooker (Ed.): *Truth in Ethics*. Oxford: Blackwell.
Williams, B. (1985): *Ethics and the Limits of Philosophy*. London: Fontana.
Williamson, T. (2000): *Knowledge and its Limits*. Oxford: Oxford University Press.
Williamson, T. (2009): "Replies to Critics". In: P. Greenough & D. Prichard (Eds.): *Williamson on Knowledge*. Oxford: Oxford University Press.

Philipp Berghofer & Harald A. Wiltsche
The Co-Presentational Character of Perception

Abstract: Phenomenologically, perception distinguishes itself from other modes of consciousness by presenting its objects and contents "in the flesh;" it has a presentive character. From the first person perspective, there is a clear difference between thinking about a laptop on the desk, imagining a laptop on the desk, believing or hoping that there is a laptop on the desk, and actually visually perceiving a laptop on the desk. Only perception has a presentive character with respect to physical objects. Epistemologically, perception distinguishes itself by being a source of immediate justification for beliefs about physical states of affairs. Believing, imagining, or hoping that there is a laptop on the desk does not justify a person in believing so. However, if the person sees that there is a laptop on the desk, it is plausible to assume that she is thereby justified in believing that there is a laptop on the desk. Only perception is a source of immediate justification with respect to such states of affairs. In the phenomenological as well as in the recent analytic tradition, there have been attempts to connect the phenomenological and the epistemological distinctiveness of perception: It has been argued that perception is a source of immediate justification precisely by virtue of its presentive phenomenal character. In the analytic tradition, however, it has been often overlooked that the phenomenal character of perception is not exhausted by its presentive character. Perception, essentially, also has a co-presenting character; it has a horizontal structure. The aim of this paper is to shed light on the epistemological significance of the horizontal structure of perception.

Keywords: Perception, Edmund Husserl, horizon, epistemic justification, phenomenology

1 The Presentive Character of Perception

Assume that you are enjoying a cup of coffee in the cafeteria when a colleague comes over and tells you that your office door is open. You are worried because there have been some burglaries at the department lately. Worse still, you have left your laptop in the office and the only version of the paper you are working on is saved on the laptop's hard drive. Thinking about your office door, you are worried that it is in fact open; you wish that it were closed; you try to remember

https://doi.org/10.1515/9783110657920-017

whether you have closed and locked the door; and you imagine it being open and thus inviting everyone to steal your laptop. After rushing back to your office, you find your door closed and locked. Your colleague was wrong. Just to be on the safe side, you enter your office and take a look at your desk. You see your laptop sitting on your desk and you breathe a sigh of relief.

It is beyond doubt that at least some mental states have a phenomenology, i.e., a phenomenal character. An experience's phenomenology or phenomenal character "is what it is like subjectively to undergo the experience" (Tye 2015: section 1). Having a phenomenal character is characteristic of experiences. "It is definitional of experience [...] that they have some phenomenal character, or more briefly, some phenomenology. The phenomenology of an experience is what it is like for the subject to have it." (Siegel 2016: section 1) Clearly, perceptual experiences have a distinctive phenomenology.[1] This is true in a threefold sense. 1) Different perceptual experiences of the same type, e.g., visual experiences, can differ phenomenologically. Seeing a closed door is phenomenologically different from seeing a laptop. 2) Perceptual experiences of different types differ phenomenologically. Seeing a door is phenomenologically different from touching it or from hearing the noise when it clicks shut. 3) Perceptual experiences differ phenomenologically from other mental states. Thinking about your office door, worrying or believing that it is open, hoping that it is closed, and imagining it being open are all mental states that are intentionally directed at your office door. Yet, having a perceptual experience of the office door is a mental state that is phenomenologically different from the aforementioned states.

So what does the phenomenal character of perceptual experiences look like? What does it mean, from a first-person perspective, to undergo a perceptual experience? In our opinion, it is a distinctive feature of perceptual experiences to have a *presentive* or *presentational* phenomenal character.[2] When you have a perceptual experience of your office door, then the door is presented to you within your experience, you seem to be perceptually aware of it. Experiences that give their objects in this way exhibit a special quality that is discussed in contemporary analytical philosophy under labels such as "presentational feel" (Foster

---

1 With respect to the term "perceptual experience", it has become common to distinguish between veridical perception, illusion, and hallucination. In the present paper, when we use the term "perception," we use it in the inclusive sense of perceptual experience.
2 To be sure, we do not want to suggest that only perceptual experiences have such a presentive character. Arguably, rational intuitions, introspective acts, and moral perceptions are candidates for having such a character too. However, only perceptual experiences have such a character with respect to physical objects. In this paper, our focus is on perceptual experiences.

2000: 112), "scene immediacy" (Sturgeon 2000: 24), "presentational phenomenology" (Chudnoff 2013), or "presentationality" (Bengson 2015). Susanna Siegel subscribes to these characterizations and points out that this idea has been expressed in many different terms (Siegel 2017: 45, fn. 13). We agree. Most important in the context of this paper, the idea has been systematically explored by philosophers with phenomenological leanings, and by Edmund Husserl in particular. For Husserl, perceptual experiences are originary presentive intuitions, which means that they present their objects "in the flesh," "as actually present," or "self-given" (Husserl 1997: 12).

The philosophical significance of perceptual experiences is largely due to their justificatory force. Consider again the earlier example: Neither thinking about your closed office door nor believing, hoping, or imagining that your office door is closed justifies you in believing that your office door is closed. However, seeing that your office door is closed clearly has some justificatory force with respect to the proposition that your office door is closed. It is often argued that perceptual experiences are justifying without being themselves in need of justification (cf., e.g., Husserl 2008: 9; 2001b: §22). If this is the case, then they are a source of immediate justification and thus lend support to some sort of foundationalism (cf. Huemer 2001: 97; Ghijsen 2016: 37 f.).

So far, we have distinguished between a phenomenological and an epistemological thesis: *Phenomenologically*, perception distinguishes itself from other modes of consciousness by presenting its objects and contents "in the flesh"; it has a *presentive* character. From the first person perspective, there is a clear difference between thinking about a laptop on the desk, believing or hoping that there is a laptop on the desk, and actually visually *perceiving* a laptop on the desk. *Phenomenological thesis*: Perceptual experiences, and only perceptual experiences, have a presentive character with respect to physical objects and states of affairs.

Epistemologically, perception is characterized by its being a source of *immediate justification*. Believing, imagining, or hoping that there is a laptop on the desk does not justify a person in believing so. However, if the person looks at the desk in front of her and sees that there is a laptop on the desk, then it is plausible to assume that the person is justified in believing that there is a laptop on the desk.[3]

---

[3] In the present paper, we are only concerned with propositional justification, not with doxastic justification.

Epistemological thesis: Perceptual experiences, and only perceptual experiences, are a source of immediate justification with respect to physical objects and states of affairs.

Some philosophers aim at connecting the phenomenological and the epistemological thesis, thus establishing an intimate relationship between epistemology and philosophy of mind. The claim is that perceptual experiences are a source of immediate justification precisely *because* they exhibit a distinctively presentive character. Let us call this the phenomenological conception of perceptual justification (PCPJ):

PCPJ: Perceptual experiences are a source of immediate justification by virtue of their distinctive, justification-conferring phenomenal character.

PCPJ is advocated, for instance, by James Pryor who argues "[...] that our perceptual experiences have the epistemic powers the dogmatist says they have because of what the phenomenology of perception is like. I think there's a distinctive phenomenology [...]" (Pryor 2004: 356 f.). Other analytic epistemologists who champion PCPJ are John Bengson (2015), Elijah Chudnoff (2013), Jennifer Church (2013), Ole Koksvik (2011), and Declan Smithies (2014). They all agree in their commitment to PCPJ but differ in their precise definition of the distinctive justification-conferring phenomenal character.

Interestingly, there are also passages in Husserl's works that suggest a commitment to PCPJ (Husserl 1982: 36; Husserl 2008: 343). As we have pointed out, Bengson, Chudnoff, Husserl, and others designate this distinctive, justification-conferring phenomenal character as a "presentive" character in the sense that perceptual experiences present their objects as bodily present. What is termed "presentational phenomenology" or "presentationality" by Chudnoff and Bengson is labeled "originary givenness" or "self-givenness" by Husserl. However, while we agree that perceptual experiences gain their justificatory force by virtue of this presentive character, there is one crucial fact that is investigated by Husserl in detail, but often ignored or overlooked in analytic circles.[4] What can be learned from Husserl's writings is that the phenomenal character of perceptual experiences is not exhausted by their presentive character. Perceptual experiences, essentially, also have a *co-presenting* character.

---

4 A notable exception is Church 2013, who explicitly refers to Husserl. For further contributions that exemplify the relevance of Husserl's conception of horizontal intentionality for current debates cf. Madary 2017 and Smith 2010.

2 The Co-Presenting Character of Perception

One of Husserl's main contributions to a phenomenological analysis of perceptual experience is the disclosure of what he calls the *horizontal structure* of experience. To make a long story short: As phenomenological descriptions reveal, perceptual experiences always and necessarily go beyond what is directly given.[5] Or, to be more precise: Perceptual experiences do not only have the above-discussed character of self-givenness, but also the character of co-givenness. What this means can be illustrated by means of an example: Assume that you have a veridical perception of a laptop. At first glance, what presents itself to you in experience is a three-dimensional object in space. But a more accurate description reveals that what is really sensuously given to you is not simply a laptop, but only *one single profile of the laptop*, its current frontside. To be sure, you could alter your position and make the current backside the new frontside, and vice versa. But this doesn't change the fact that the laptop is always given *in perspectives* and that, more generally, physical things always and necessarily have more parts, functions, and properties than can be actualized in one single intentional act. The laptop—as it is intended—is *transcendent*, not only in the sense that it can be seen from indefinitely more perspectives than you can take up at a given point in time. The laptop is also transcendent in the sense that it has, for instance, a momentarily hidden internal structure, a history, certain practical functions, or many properties that aren't in the center of attention right now.

So, a closer look at how physical things appear to us reveals that our intentions towards these things always "transcend" or "go beyond" the actual experiences that give rise to them. As the example of the laptop shows, there is a describable difference between what is meant through a particular perceptual act (the laptop in front of you) and what is sensuously given (the laptop's facing side with its momentarily visible features). Phenomenologically construed, this discrepancy does not represent a problem that must be somehow remedied, e.g. by proposing a theory that explains how a number of seemingly disconnected profiles add up to a homogeneous thing to which we then attribute these profiles. The fact that our perceptual intentions always transcend the sphere of direct givenness is rather to be treated as a phenomenologically discoverable feature of experience itself: Intending is, as Husserl puts it, always and necessarily an *"intending-beyond-itself"* (Husserl 1960: 46).

---

[5] Here many of Husserl's insights are in agreement with the findings of early experimental psychologists such as Gestalt psychologists and the members of the Graz school.

The important lesson to draw from these considerations is that perception is a composite of interwoven "fulfilled and unfulfilled intentions" (Husserl 2001c: 221) such that self-givenness could not be without co-givenness.[6] Or, to put it in an alternative terminology: Intentional experiences are always embedded in *horizons* of intentions that are momentarily unactualized, but that could be actualized in the course of further acts. Even though you can only see the laptop's facing side with its momentarily visible features, the laptop appears to you as something that could be explored more fully. You "know" that you could alter your vantage point and explore its currently concealed backside. You "know" that you could look more closely and explore its surface in more detail. You "know" that you could disassemble the laptop and study its inner workings. It is these and indefinitely many other potentialities that add up to the co-given horizon against the background of which intentions towards physical things always stand out.[7]

Phenomenological descriptions reveal that intentional acts towards things always point to co-given horizons of possible further experiences. Hence, on a phenomenological view, experience is never exhausted by what is actual; experience is always already saturated with implicit references to future experiences that are possible insofar as they could be actualized in the course of further acts. However, two things need to be emphasized at this point. The first thing to note is that an act's horizon is, as we have already indicated, *co-given* with the act itself. This is to say that the horizon is no theoretical construct that is *retrospectively* ascribed to the initial act. An act's horizon rather belongs to the perceptual experience even though we usually aren't aware of this. That the laptop in front of you has a backside isn't something that can only be asserted after you have changed your vantage point. It is also not something that is the product of some sort of inferential process. Rather, it is something that belongs to the very nature of being intentionally directed towards physical things.

The second important aspect is this: On the basis of what we have said so far, one could define horizons as sets of empty intentions against the background of

---

[6] Or, as Erhard puts it: "*No presence without absence*". (Erhard 2014: 179)
[7] Husserl distinguishes between *inner* and *outer* horizons: While the inner horizon comprises co-intended aspects of the thing itself (such as its backside), the outer horizon consists of the spatial field in which the intended object is embedded. Even if your attention is solely directed at the laptop in front of you, it is part of your experience that the laptop does not float around in nothingness. The laptop is rather sitting on a desk, which is standing in your office, which is located in a building on the university campus, and so on. In Husserl's terminology, these co-given objects (desk, office, campus, etc.) make up the *outer horizon* of your experience. The non-thematic, but co-intended aspects of the intended object itself, on the other hand, constitute the *inner horizon* (cf. Husserl 1973: §8).

which particular fulfilled intentions always and necessarily stand out. But this definition is somewhat misleading: Although it is correct to say that a horizon consists of empty intentions and thus can be described as a "halo of emptiness," it is crucial to stress that "this emptiness is not a nothingness," but rather that "the sense of this halo [...] is a *prefiguring* that *prescribes a rule* for the transition to new actualizing appearances" (Husserl 2001a: 42; our emphases). Hence, Husserl describes horizons in terms of "'predelineated' potentialities" (Husserl 1960: 45) and adds "that a hidden intentional 'if-then' relation is at work here: the exhibitings must occur in a certain systematic order; it is in this way that they are indicated in advance, in expectation, in the course of a harmonious perception." (Husserl 1970: 161 f.) Upon looking at your laptop, the horizontal structure of your experience is such that you have certain anticipations of how your laptop looks when you move or turn it around, of how it feels when you touch it, and of what will happen when you press a certain button. To be sure, anticipations of this kind are *motivated* by previous experiences with laptops and thus by your relevant background beliefs.[8] To a person who has never experienced a laptop before, a laptop would not look foldable. However, although background beliefs and horizontal anticipations are closely related, phenomenologists typically stress their distinctness: Rather than being identical with background beliefs, horizontal anticipations are *part of the phenomenal character of experience.* To say that you experience your laptop as foldable is to say that the laptop's disposition to be foldable is, in some sense, *visually* present. But is this view really tenable? One

---

[8] "Motivation" is a technical term that plays a prominent role in Husserl's understanding of the concept of possibility. Perhaps the best way to make this distinction clear is by way of an example (Husserl 1982: p. 337): Suppose that you enter an unfamiliar room with a desk in it. The desk is positioned such that its underside is currently out of view. Now, the question arises: How many legs does the table have? While the answer "Hundred!" corresponds to an *empty possibility*, the answer "Four!" corresponds to what Husserl calls a *motivated possibility*. How is this distinction to be understood? Well, first of all, neither answer refers to a scenario that is logically impossible. Although you may have never actually seen such a thing, it is easily conceivable that the table will indeed reveal an underside with exactly one hundred legs. But, apart from this, there is a fundamental difference nonetheless: The difference lies in the fact that the projected scenario of the table's four-leggedness is not only logically possible, but also probable in light of your previous encounters with tables and thus with your implicit background beliefs. It is, to put it differently, only in the latter case that "*something speaks on behalf of the positum*" (Husserl 1982: p. 334) and that, consequently, the respective possibility has considerable epistemic weight. This is what the distinction between empty and motivated possibility is designed to express (cf. Husserl 2001a: §§2-4; Husserl 1982: §140; Husserl 1989: §56). And, on Husserl's view, it is characteristic of perceptual horizons to be composed solely of motivated possibilities that regulate our expectations and anticipations concerning further perceptual experiences.

might, for instance, accept that the disposition to be foldable is part of what you experience when you see your laptop in front of you. One might deny, however, that the disposition to be foldable is *visually* present—that the laptop is foldable is rather something that you *believe* or are *disposed to judge* in addition to the originary givenness of the laptop's front side.

The reason why it might be tempting to think that perceptual horizons can be reduced to (a system of) background beliefs is that, as we have pointed out, an act's horizon is shaped by previous experiences, thus shaped by one's beliefs, and, as a consequence, usually in agreement with one's background beliefs. But this need not be the case. Consider two persons, P1 and P2, and suppose that P2 is afraid of spiders. P1 and P2 may both know that the spider in front of them is absolutely harmless, afraid of human beings, and not capable of feeling emotions such as anger. However, it may still be the case that P1 and P2 perceive the spider very differently. To P2 the spider may look angry and the horizon of P2's spider experience may include the anticipation that a spider attack is imminent. In short, P2's horizon does not match her background beliefs, which speaks against the reducibility of perceptual horizons to (systems of) background beliefs.

Furthermore, there are cases of "wrong" horizons in which somebody perceives an object O, has an experience that has a *presentive* character with respect to O, knows that she is perceiving O, has correct background beliefs about O, but nevertheless perceives O through a horizon h which is "wrong" in the sense that h includes elements that do not match O, but a different object G. Consider Matthew Ratcliffe's example of what he calls a "horizonal hallucination" (Ratcliffe 2016: 219):

> [S]uppose that one's perception of an entity, such as a chair, were associated with a horizonal structure more usually integral to the experience of a different entity or kind of entity, such as a hungry tiger. In one sense, the content of the experience would be unchanged. One would see a brown entity with four legs, a flat, horizontal surface, and a vertical back. At the same time, one would have the 'feeling' of encountering something different. [...] Thus, as one encounters the chair, one does not see something for sitting on, but something that offers threat, something to flee from, something menacing. (Ratcliffe 2016: 218)

The fact that there are recorded cases of people who suffer from horizonal hallucinations has obvious consequences for the question as to whether horizonal anticipations can be reduced to background beliefs: It is true that horizonal anticipations are usually in harmony with the background beliefs that give rise to them. In cases of horizonal hallucination, however, something goes wrong: The perceived chair is presented to you as a chair; you know it is a chair; and you know that chairs are not dangerous. Yet, you nevertheless experience the chair as a threat, as watching you, and as being about to attack. This is all part of your experience, not of your background beliefs. Of course, perceptual hallucinations occur only rarely, usually as a result of mental illness. But this is not important for our argument. That cases of mismatch between horizontal anticipations and background beliefs are possible at all makes the prospects of reducing the former to the latter dim.[9]

As Husserl repeatedly stresses, it is characteristic of the way in which physical things appear to us that perceptual experiences present these things *in perspectives* or, to use a distinctively Husserlian notion, *in adumbrations*. However, it is important to realize that we are not talking about empirical matters of fact here. As Husserl argues, "[i]t is neither an accident of the own peculiar sense of the physical thing nor a contingency of our 'human constitution,' that 'our' perception can arrive at physical things themselves only through mere adumbrations of them" (Husserl 1982: 90–91). On some occasions, Husserl even goes so far to declare that not even God could perceive physical things in a non-perspectival manner (Husserl 1982: 95). But this view has been met with criticism. Consider the following counterexample by Wayne Martin:

> Imagine some kind of conscious intelligence that is embodied in a kind of fog. We humans perceive an object from a single perspective, but the fogging consciousness simply fogs all around it, taking in all sides at once. Many animals manage to integrate sensory input from two sides of their body; why shouldn't the fogging being integrate views of an object from every side? (Martin 2005: 210)

Unlike humans, Martin's fogging being could perceive all aspects of a physical object at once, which seems to undermine Husserl's claim that perception is *essentially* perspectival. However, as Michael Madary has recently remarked, Martin's counterexample misses something important, namely that "the way that properties are given to us in adumbrations (perspectivally) is such that their appearances change in a way that is sensitive to self-generated movement" (Madary 2017: 183). The point of Madary's argument may be summarized as follows: While it is true that a fogging being would perceive physical objects in a way that is radically different from how human perception works, it does not follow from Martin's counterexample that a fogging being would not be subjected to perspectivity at all. It is, for instance, implausible to assume that an object would not appear differently to the fogging being if the object was located at different positions within the fog or if the object and the fogging being were in relative motion

---

[9] Cf. Smith 2010 for further arguments that "the phenomenology [of co-givenness] itself is belief-independent." (Smith 2010, 736)

to one another. So, all that Martin's counterexample shows is that perspectivity may take different forms, depending on certain contingencies in the physiological make-up of the perceiving subject. But this does not change the fact that even for a fogging being there is always more to a physical object than can be actualized in one single intentional act, and that perception is an open-ended process in which ever-changing appearances of objects are constantly projected against horizons through which we anticipate courses of possible further experiences.[10]

One final aspect of Husserl's conception of horizontal intentionality we would like to emphasize is its epistemological dimension. *Both* self-givenness and co-givenness determine the overall phenomenal character of any perceptual experience. But only what is self-given can be immediately justified, while what is co-given can only be inferentially justified. As Husserl puts it, "the *primal source of all legitimacy* lies in immediate evidence and, more narrowly delimited, in *originary evidence*, or in originary givenness motivating it" (Husserl 1982: 338). Imagine again perceiving a desk whose underside is currently out of view. By looking at the desk, you are immediately justified in believing that there is a desk, that its surface has a certain color, that there is a book on it, etc. All this is given to you originally and you are immediately justified in believing it *because* it is given originally. This is not true with respect to your belief that the desk has four legs. While the anticipation that you will see four legs when you change the perspective is part of the overall phenomenal character of the experience, this anticipation is not originally given but co-given as a motivated possibility. By looking at the surface of the desk, your belief that it has four legs may be *psychologically* immediate and the belief may be justified, but it is only *inferentially justified* since its justification depends on background beliefs concerning the four-leggedness of most other tables you have encountered so far. Thus, the difference between self-givenness and co-givenness is a phenomenological difference with crucial epistemological implications. But let us, before we discuss these implications in more detail, summarize the findings of this section by formulating eight hypotheses about perceptual experience.

H1: Perceptual experience is perspectival. You cannot perceive physical objects in their entirety, there are always aspects and features that are not in the center of attention right now. However, some of these aspects and features are co-given within experience. Experiences have an *inner horizon*.

---

[10] Cf., for a detailed phenomenological analysis of a similar thought experiment in which a sphere of eyeballs is wrapped around a physical object, Wiltsche 2013.

H2: Perceptual experiences do not present their objects as being isolated, objects are always given as being embedded in a surrounding world. Experiences have an *outer horizon*.

H3: Perceptual experience is never exhausted by what is actual. To perceive a physical object also means to anticipate courses of possible future experiences. Hence, perception is a composite of interwoven full and empty intentions such that certain aspects of the perceived object are presented and others are co-given. Self-givenness cannot be without co-givenness.

H4: Horizontal anticipations are usually grounded in motivated possibilities, i.e. in possibilities that are grounded in corresponding background beliefs.

H5: The horizontal nature of perceptual experience underscores the holistic structure of experience. The way you perceive is shaped by previous experiences and by your background beliefs. On this view then, experiencing is an open-ended process in which new appearances are constantly projected against horizons through which we anticipate courses of possible further experiences.[11]

H6: While it is true that perceptual horizons are shaped by previous experiences and background beliefs, the horizon must not be confused with or reduced to a set of beliefs or inclinations to believe. Co-givenness is part of your experience's phenomenology; it is belief-independent although horizontal anticipations are usually in accordance with your background beliefs.

H7: Both self-givenness and co-givenness determine the overall phenomenal character of any perceptual experience. But only what is self-given can be immediately justified, while what is co-given can only be inferentially justified.

H8: The perspectivity of perception is not a shortcoming of human beings but an essential property of perception.

3 Justification and Co-Givenness

Phenomenologists typically stress that epistemology must be preceded by phenomenological descriptions. If the aim is to determine the epistemic force of, say, beliefs, imaginings, or perceptual experiences, then the first step must be to clarify how these different types of mental states differ phenomenologically. The more precise the phenomenological description, the more accurate the resulting

---

[11] Importantly, the holistic character of horizontal intentionality tells us something about the structure of experience, not about the structure of experiential justification. Experiences can be a source of immediate justification despite their holistic structure (cf. Berghofer 2017: section 2.4).

conception of perceptual justification can be. What this means concretely shall be exemplified in the present section. In particular, we will show how the distinction between self-givenness and co-givenness helps to solve several pressing epistemological problems and leads to a conception of perceptual justification that is superior to a currently popular proposal, Michael Huemer's principle of phenomenal conservativism.

Let us begin by introducing a philosophically significant real-world example, the phenomenon of blindsight. Chris Tucker describes the phenomenon as follows:

> Subjects who have a damaged visual cortex often emphatically report that they cannot see anything within a certain region of their visual field. Nonetheless, such subjects often show remarkable sensitivity (though less than properly functioning humans) to such things as motion, the orientation of objects, and the wavelength of light within their reported 'blind spot'. These subjects are typically surprised to discover their success, thinking that they were making random guesses. (Tucker 2010: 530)

Assume an experiment in which a blindsighted person S is asked to look at a piece of paper with a circle in S's region of normal sight (region R1) and a triangle within S's blind spot (region R2). On the basis of what we know from similar experiments that were actually performed by psychologists, it is to be expected that S will judge that there is a circle in R1 and a triangle in R2. Now, the epistemologically relevant question is whether or not both judgments are equally justified. Building on the results of the previous sections, a phenomenological answer to this question goes as follows: The first step is to assume that her perceptual experiences make it seem to S that there is a circle in R1 and a triangle in R2. Without this assumption, S's judgment that there is a circle in R1 and a triangle in R2 would appear mysterious. However, the second step is to point to a crucial *phenomenological* difference between the ways in which the circle and the triangle appear to S. With respect to the circle, it seems safe to assume that S's perceptual experience has a presentive character. S is visually aware of the circle and the circle is presented to her in a "fleshed out" manner. But this is not true of the triangle. Phenomenologically construed, the most plausible view is that, although the triangle is somehow visually present to S, it is only *co-given* to S in the sense that S *anticipates* a triangle in R2. The triangle is in the horizon of S's attention, but it is not immediately present to her. Note that this *phenomenological* difference is in perfect harmony with the relevant *epistemological* difference. S's perceptual experience provides her with *immediate* justification for believing that there is a circle in R1. Since she sees that there is a circle, she is immediately justified in believing that there is one. Intuitively, however, S's perceptual experience does not provide her with immediate justification that there is a triangle in

R2. Of course, if S knows that her blindsight faculties are reliable in the sense that most of her previous blindsight seemings have turned out to be veridical, S may have mediate justification for the belief that there is a triangle in R2. But such a justification is not immediate. A plausible conception of perceptual justification should avoid the consequence that blindsight seemings can be a source of immediate justification (cf. Ghijsen 2016: 17–19 and Smithies 2014: 103 f.). And this is exactly what a phenomenological conception of perceptual justification is able to deliver: Although the triangle is, in some sense, visually present to S, she is not immediately justified in believing that there is a triangle in R2 because, unlike the circle in R1, the triangle is only co-given within S's perceptual horizon. In a similar sense in which seeing a laptop's frontside automatically comes with anticipations concerning its backside, S anticipates that, if she were to move her head accordingly, she would become directly aware of a triangle. Presumably, this horizonal anticipation is motivated by S's background belief that her blindsight faculties were reliable in the past.

As these considerations are supposed to show, phenomenology provides us with the means to offer a satisfying approach to the epistemological problem of blindsight. To be sure, one might want to object that our results are trivial because no one would disagree that S's seemings differ in their justificatory force. This, however, is not true. Michael Huemer's principle of phenomenal conservatism (PC) has it that *every* seeming is a source of prima facie justification.

PC: If it seems to *S* as if *P*, then *S* thereby has at least prima facie justification for believing that *P*. (Huemer 2001: 99)

It is a standard objection against PC that its proponents fail to provide a sufficiently detailed characterization of what seemings actually are (cf., e.g., Tooley 2013; Wiltsche 2015). This neglect has severe epistemological consequences, as the problem of blindsight shows: Proponents of PC accept that blindsighted subjects have seemings about what is going on in their blind spots. However, since the very point of PC is that *every* seeming is a source of immediate justification, proponents of PC are thereby also forced to hold that blindsight seemings are a source of immediate justification (Tucker 2010: 530 f.; Huemer 2013: 333). On our view, this consequence is implausible and could be avoided if proponents of PC paid closer attention to a phenomenological description of how co-given seemings (such as S's triangle seeming) differ from presentive seemings (such as S's circle seeming).

The point we are trying to make can also be emphasized by considering two other influential counterexamples against Huemer's PC. The first is Markie's example of *cognitive malfunction*:

> Suppose that I perceive the walnut tree in my yard, and, having learned to identify walnut trees visually, it seems to me that it is a walnut tree. The same phenomenological experience that makes it seem to me that the tree is a walnut also makes it seem to me that it was planted on April 24, 1914. Nothing in the phenomenological experience or my identification skills supports things seeming this way to me. There is no date-of-planting sign on the tree, for example. Cognitive malfunction is the cause of its seeming to me in perception that the tree was planted on that date. (Markie 2005: 357)

In this example, a visual experience is accompanied by two seemings with very different contents.

S1:[12] "This tree is a walnut."
S2: "This tree was planted on April 24, 1914."

Intuitively, one is only justified in believing S1, but not S2. However, if S2 is a seeming without being a justifier, then Huemer's PC is refuted. Like in the earlier case, however, there is an obvious and epistemologically significant phenomenological difference between the givenness of S1 and S2. In Markie's example, one's perceptual experience has a presentive phenomenal character with respect to the tree and its distinctive features. Thus, the experience provides immediate justification for believing that this is a (walnut) tree. But this is not true with respect to S2. The experience one has in this situation simply does not present a content that would specify the date of the tree's planting. Hence, S2 is just an empty seeming.

Considering Markie's example, we take the phenomenological difference between S1 and S2 to be fairly obvious. S1 and S2 are given differently, and the point of our proposal is that the way in which contents are given is of fundamental epistemological significance. But, of course, one could question whether the difference between S1 and S2 is really as obvious as we take it to be. What, precisely, is the difference between contents such as "there is a tree," "the leaves have a distinctive shape," and "the leaves are green" on the one hand and "this tree was planted on April 24, 1914" on the other? And how does this difference come about? Since a complete answer to this question would lead us too far afield, we shall restrict ourselves to one aspect that seems particularly relevant in the present context. Following the results of the previous sections, contents such as "there is a tree," "the leaves have a distinctive shape," and "the leaves are green" are given in perspectives and come with certain (pre-reflective) anticipations of how the tree will look from different angles or how the leaves will appear when

---

[12] In what follows, "S1" and "S2" refer either to the mental state—seeming 1—that has a specific content or to the content itself.

the sun sets, etc. But this is not the case with respect to the date of the tree's planting. That the tree was planted on April 24, 1914 is not given in perspectives. One does not have anticipations of how this content would look differently if one were to circle the tree. What this shows is that the content in question is not perceptual in any straightforward sense of the term. The perceptual experience one has may cause the belief that S2, but S2 is no content a perception could immediately justify. We may thus conclude that perceptual experiences can only justify contents that are perspectivally given and that come with horizontal anticipations.

Let us now turn to Markie's second counterexample, that of *wishful thinking*:

> Suppose that we are prospecting for gold. You have learned to identify a gold nugget on sight but I have no such knowledge. As the water washes out of my pan, we both look at a pebble, which is in fact a gold nugget. My desire to discover gold makes it seem to me as if the pebble is gold; your learned identification skills make it seem that way to you. According to (PC), the belief that it is gold has *prima facie* justification for both of us. Yet, certainly, my wishful thinking should not gain my belief the same positive epistemic status of defeasible justification as your learned identification skills. (Markie 2005: 357)

Cases of wishful thinking are often used to argue against internalist conceptions of justification.[13] Huemer responds to this challenge by, first, biting the bullet and by, second, pointing out that an experience's justificatory force is not affected by its etiology: "When the subject is unaware of an appearance's etiology, that etiology is irrelevant to what it is rational for the subject to believe." (Huemer 2013: 344) While we agree with Huemer that, in principle, the etiology of an experience cannot determine its justificatory force, Markie's example nevertheless poses a problem for Huemer. If the novice's perceptual experience has a presentive character only with respect to the content "this is a yellow pebble," but not with respect to "this is a gold nugget," then it is implausible that the novice is immediately justified in believing that she is in fact dealing with a gold nugget.

However, be that as it may, the problem with Markie's example is still that it is underspecified with respect to how the pebble is presented within experience. Do the novice's and the expert's experiences differ phenomenologically? Or does the difference only lie in their respective background knowledge? Does the nov-

---

13 However, as proponents of internalism have also pointed out, Huemer's PC seems particularly vulnerable to such objections. Audi, for instance, complains that Huemer cannot exclude cases "in which one already believes p wholly on the basis of a desire that it be true and lacks an intuition (or other basic ground) that it is true" (Audi 2013: 200). The problem to which Audi alludes to here is that such seemings lack the distinctive phenomenal character that is typically associated with justification-conferring experiences (Audi 2013: 189).

ice's wishful thinking result in an *illusion* of gold, similar to when one is desperately looking for a loved one and has the illusion that some stranger looks exactly like the person one is looking for? Or is the novice having an empty seeming like when it seems to a gambler that this specific slot machine will win?[14]

While we are in no position to provide an account of how it is for an expert to experience gold and how to distinguish a gold nugget from an ordinary yellow pebble, we believe that delving into the phenomenon of *perceptual learning* might provide us with the answers we are looking for. Perceptual learning "refers to an increase in the ability to extract information from the environment, as a result of experience and practice with stimulation coming from it" (Gibson 1969: 3). Assume that you are looking at a piece of paper with two lines that slightly differ in length. At time t_1 you are unable to spot the difference in length. It visually seems to you that both lines have the same length. Yet, after some practice, the content of your experience has changed in a way that allows you to spot the difference at time t_2. Now, it visually seems to you that the lines differ in length. It is plausible to assume that you are immediately justified in believing that the lines differ in length at t_2, simply because you can see it.

The point of this example is that perceptual learning can not only affect the horizon of experiences but even their presentive character. In philosophical debates, "cases of perceptual learning have often been used to show that through learning we come to represent new properties in perception, which we did not represent prior to learning" (Conolly 2017: section 3.1). In line with this, Siegel has argued "that being able to visually recognize things such as your own neighborhood, pine trees, or John Malkovich can influence how those things look to you when you see them" (Siegel 2017: xiii). Siegel adds that this insight has crucial epistemological consequences: "For instance, consider a tree expert and a non-expert who look at the same pine tree, and the expert gets more justification to believe it's a pine tree than the non-expert gets, because the expert's experience has the content *x is a pine tree*." (Siegel 2017: 75) Conolly comes to a similar conclusion: "The idea is that the best way to explain the change in perception is that perception *represents* [our emphasis] the property of *being a pine tree after*, but not before, learning takes place. That property becomes part of the content of perception: it comes to be *presented* [our emphasis] in perceptual experience." (Conolly 2017: section 3.1) Note, however, that Conolly oscillates between two different terms here, those of *representation* and *presentation*. On our view, this terminological ambiguity signifies an important difference. Is the property of being

---

[14] To be sure, the precise phenomenal character of the novice's seeming is irrelevant to Huemer because for him every seeming provides prima facie justification.

a pine tree merely *represented* in experience, like in the earlier examples of blindsight and cognitive malfunction, where the triangle in R2 and the tree's planting date were only emptily represented? Or is the property of being a pine tree more akin to a *presented* content such as "there is a circle in R1" or "the tree has green leaves"?

Let us consider one final episode that is analogous to Markie's example of *wishful thinking* (and based on a true event):

Philipp and Steven are looking for porcini. Philipp has been familiar with porcini for many years. He knows what they look like and he can distinguish them from other mushrooms by sight. Steven has just begun to become familiar with porcini. Theoretically, he knows what they look like but he is unable to distinguish them from other mushrooms by sight. Philipp and Steven are both looking at a mushroom, which, in fact, is a porcino. To both of them, the mushroom's cap looks brown and the stem looks white. However, Philipp's and Steven's perceptual experiences differ phenomenologically. To Philipp, the cap does not just look brown, it looks porcino-brown, and the stem does not just look white, it looks porcino-white. Steven's perceptual experience does not have such a distinctive phenomenology. However, due to wishful thinking it seems to him that the mushroom is a porcino.

In this example, it is safe to say that Philipp's and Steven's perceptual experiences differ phenomenologically, and that only Philipp is justified in believing that he has found a porcino. However, the question is whether Philipp is immediately or inferentially justified in holding this belief?[15] Similarly, in the case of *Wishful Thinking*, only the expert appears to be justified in believing that the pebble is gold. But is she immediately or inferentially justified?

It seems to us that a proper phenomenological analysis suggests that the respective experiences of Philipp, the tree-expert, and the gold-expert not only represent distinctive features, but also have a presentive character with respect to these properties. It does not just emptily seem to Philipp that the mushroom in front of him is a porcino. Since he underwent a process of perceptual learning, he has a presentive character with respect to distinctive porcino-characteristics. Likewise in the other examples discussed, where the experts' experiences are a source of immediate justification for the exact same reason. The novices' experiences, on the other hand, lack this distinctive phenomenal character, which is

---

15 Of, course, psychologically speaking, he is immediately justified. He does not need to make any conscious inferences. However, the question is whether his justification is epistemologically immediate, i.e., whether his experience is sufficient for providing immediate justification or whether he is in need of epistemic support from his background beliefs.

why they are not a source of immediate justification. Thus, phenomenological analyses have also proven to be fundamental for discussing the problem of *wishful thinking*.

References

Audi, Robert (2013): "Doxastic Innocence: Phenomenal Conservatism and Grounds of Justification". In: *Seemings and Justification. New Essays on Dogmatism and Phenomenal Conservatism*. Tucker, Chris (Ed.). Oxford & New York: Oxford University Press, pp. 181–201.
Bengson, John (2015): "The Intellectual Given". In: *Mind* 124 (495), 707–760.
Berghofer, Philipp (2017): "Why Husserl is a Moderate Foundationalist". In: *Husserl Studies*, https://doi.org/10.1007/s10743-017-9213-4.
Chudnoff, Elijah (2013): *Intuition*. Oxford: Oxford University Press.
Church, Jennifer (2013): *Possibilities of Perception*. Oxford: Oxford University Press.
Connolly, Kevin (2017): "Perceptual Learning". In: The Stanford Encyclopedia of Philosophy (Summer 2017 Edition), Zalta, Edward N. (Ed.). URL = <https://plato.stanford.edu/archives/sum2017/entries/perceptual-learning/>.
Erhard, Christopher (2014): *Denken über nichts – Intentionalität und Nicht-Existenz bei Husserl*. Berlin: De Gruyter.
Foster, John (2000): *The Nature of Perception*. Oxford: Oxford University Press.
Ghijsen, Harmen (2016): *The Puzzle of Perceptual Justification*. Dordrecht: Springer.
Huemer, Michael (2001): *Skepticism and the Veil of Perception*. Lanham, MD: Rowman & Littlefield Publishers.
Husserl, Edmund (1960): *Cartesian Meditations*. transl. by Dorion Cairns, The Hague: Martinus Nijhoff.
Husserl, Edmund (1970): *The Crisis of European Sciences and Transcendental Phenomenology*. transl. by David Carr, Evanston: Northwestern University Press.
Husserl, Edmund (1973): *Experience and Judgment*. transl. by James Churchill and Karl Ameriks, London: Routledge.
Husserl, Edmund (1982): *Ideas pertaining to a pure phenomenology and to a phenomenological philosophy, First book*. transl. by Fred Kersten, The Hague: Martinus Nijhoff.
Husserl, Edmund (1989): *Ideas Pertaining to a Pure Phenomenology and to a Phenomenological Philosophy, Second Book: Studies in the Phenomenology of Constitution*. transl. by Richard Rojcewicz and André Schuwer, Dordrecht: Kluwer.
Husserl, Edmund (1992): *Thing and Space. Lectures of 1907*. transl. by Richard Rojcewicz, Dordrecht: Springer.
Husserl, Edmund (2001a): *Analyses Concerning Active and Passive Synthesis*. transl. by Anthony Steinbock, Dordrecht: Kluwer Academic Publishers.
Husserl, Edmund (2001b): *Natur und Geist: Vorlesungen Sommersemester 1927*. The Hague: Martinus Nijhoff.
Husserl, Edmund (2001c): *Logical Investigations*, Vol. 2. transl. by J. N. Findlay, London: Routledge.

Husserl, Edmund (2002): *Logische Untersuchungen, Ergänzungsband, Erster Teil: Entwürfe zur Umarbeitung der VI. Untersuchung und zur Vorrede für die Neuauflage der Logischen Untersuchungen (Sommer 1913)*. Dordrecht: Kluwer Academic Publishers.

Husserl, Edmund (2008): *Introduction to Logic and Theory of Knowledge. Lectures 1906/1907*. transl. by C. O. Hill, Dordrecht: Springer.

Koksvik, Ole (2011): *Intuition*. Ph.D. Thesis, Australian National University.

Madary, Michael (2017): *Visual Phenomenology*. Cambridge: The MIT Press.

Markie, Peter (2005): "The Mystery of Direct Perceptual Justification". In: *Philosophical Studies* 126, pp. 347–373.

Martin, Wayne M. (2005): "Husserl and the Logic of Consciousness". In: *Phenomenology and Philosophy of Mind*, Woodruff Smith, David & Thomasson, Annie L. (Eds.). Oxford: Clarendon Press.

Pryor, James (2004): "What's wrong with Moore's Argument?". In: *Philosophical Issues* 14, pp. 349–378.

Ratcliffe, Matthew (2016): "The Integrity of Intentionality: Sketch for a Phenomenological Study". In: *Phenomenology for the Twenty-First Century*. Aaron Simmons and Edward Hackett (Eds.). London: Palgrave, pp. 207–230.

Siegel, Susanna (2017): *The Rationality of Perception*. Oxford: Oxford University Press.

Siegel, Susanna (2016): "The Contents of Perception". In: The Stanford Encyclopedia of Philosophy (Spring 2016 Edition), Zalta, Edward N. (Ed.). URL = <http://plato.stanford.edu/archives/spr2016/entries/perception-contents/>.

Smith, Joel (2010): "Seeing Other People". In: *Philosophy and Phenomenological Research* 81/3, pp. 731–748.

Smithies, Declan (2014): "The Phenomenal Basis of Epistemic Justification". In: *New Waves in Philosophy of Mind*. Sprevak, Mark & Kallestrup, Jesper (Eds.). New York: Palgrave Macmillan, pp. 98–124.

Sturgeon, Scott (2000): *Matters of Mind: Consciousness, reason and nature*. London: Routledge.

Tooley, Michael (2013): "Michael Huemer and the Principle of Phenomenal Conservatism". In: *Seemings and Justification. New Essays on Dogmatism and Phenomenal Conservatism*. Tucker, Chris (Ed.). Oxford: Oxford University Press, pp. 306–327.

Tucker, Chris (2010): "Why Open-Minded People Should Endorse Dogmatism". In: *Philosophical Perspectives* 24, pp. 529–545.

Tye, Michael (2015): "Qualia". In: The Stanford Encyclopedia of Philosophy (Fall 2015 Edition), Zalta, Edward N. (ed.). URL = <http://plato.stanford.edu/archives/fall2015/entries/qualia/>.

Wiltsche, Harald A. (2013): "How Essential Are Essential Laws? A Thought Experiment on the Perspectival Givenness of Physical Things". In: *Wahrnehmen, Fühlen, Handeln. Phänomenologie im Wettstreit der Methoden*, Mertens, Karl & Günzler, Ingo (Eds.). Paderborn: Mentis, pp. 421–436.

Wiltsche, Harald A. (2015): "Intuitions, Seemings, and Phenomenology". In: *teorema* XXXIV/3, pp. 57–77.

Frédérique de Vignemont
Knowledge Without Observation: Body Image or Body Schema?

Abstract: How do you know the posture of your limbs? Do I feel it or do I directly know it? In this paper I will describe Wittgenstein´s and Anscombe's theory, according to which bodily sensations play no epistemic role. They famously claimed that the sense of position – the ability to report how the limbs are located – does not depend on sensations of position. In this sense, bodily knowledge differs from perceptual knowledge. I know that the sky is blue in virtue of having a visual experience of the blueness of the sky but I know that my legs are crossed independently of the sensation I may have of them being that way. Why is there such a difference? What reasons do Wittgenstein and Anscombe have to deny that bodily sensations play an epistemic role? They claim that the kind of content that bodily sensations are endowed with cannot explain the beliefs that we form about our bodily posture. On their view, it is not fine-grained enough compared to the richness of our bodily knowledge. In addition, it would not be separately describable from the beliefs themselves. I will argue that these objections do not suffice to show that bodily sensations play no epistemic role.

Keywords: knowledge without observation, bodily sensation, bodily illusion, body schema, feeling

> Look up at the ceiling while your right arm is moved to the right. Attempt to recapture the original uninterpreted experience. Try to undo the lessons of time! Now somehow one cannot shake off the belief that the arm has gone to the right. Well, try again. Hard. Attempt to transfer all attention away from the limb and onto the feelings. Scrutinise them. Now tell us about them. Then you cannot in doing so help mentioning that they were in your arm, which was over to the right, poised like such and such, near to such and such a part of the body. (O'Shaughnessy 1980: 157)

Please obey O'Shaughnessy, focus on your body and undo the lessons of time. What can you say about the posture of your limbs? And how do you know it? O'Shaughnessy defends the view that our bodily knowledge is based in what we *feel*, in the spatial phenomenology of our bodily sensations. However, Wittgenstein, and later Anscombe, note that the use of the term "feeling" is misleading. It is not because we talk of sensations of a specific property *X* that we do have them. Instead, what we may really have is a kind of direct knowledge of *X*. The confusion arises because in some rare cases it seems to us that *X* whereas *X* is not true. Such errors do not show that we *feel* that X. On their view indeed, they only show that we are entitled to talk of knowledge when X is true. The problem is then to decide when our knowledge is really based on feelings and when it is not. Here I will focus exclusively on the case of bodily knowledge, and more specifically on its spatial dimension. Not only do I know where the various parts of my body are, but I also know where in these body parts I am touched and where I am in pain. The questions are: how do I have such knowledge? Do I feel it or do I directly know it? In this paper I will describe Wittgenstein and Anscombe's theory, according to which bodily sensations play no epistemic role. They famously claimed that the sense of position – the ability to report how the limbs are located – does not depend on sensations of position. In this sense, bodily knowledge differs from perceptual knowledge. I know that the sky is blue in virtue of having a visual experience of the blueness of the sky but I know that my legs are crossed independently of the sensation I may have of them being that way. Why is there such a difference? What reasons do Wittgenstein and Anscombe have to deny that bodily sensations play an epistemic role? They claim that the content that bodily sensations are endowed with cannot explain the beliefs that we form about our bodily posture. On their view, it is not fine-grained enough compared to the richness of our bodily knowledge. In addition, it is not separately describable from the beliefs themselves. I will argue that these objections do not suffice to show that bodily sensations play no epistemic role.

1 The Poverty of Stimulus

> I let my index finger make an easy pendulum movement of small amplitude. I either hardly feel it, or don't feel it at all. Perhaps a little in the tip of the finger, as a slight tension. (Not at all in the joint.) And this sensation advised me of the movement? — for I can describe the movement exactly. "But after all, you must feel it, otherwise you wouldn't know (without looking) how your finger was moving". But "knowing" it only means: being able to describe it. (Wittgenstein 1978)

According to Wittgenstein, the content of bodily sensations is too poor compared to the richness of bodily knowledge. Therefore, the former is insufficient to ground the latter. But is there really such a gap between what we feel and what we know? It is true that the phenomenology of bodily sensations is most of the time relatively limited, less detailed than the phenomenology of visual experiences, for instance, which can be analysed as full of fine-grained colour shades and well-individuated 3D shapes that move around. The crucial question is whether the relative poverty of our bodily sensations is a problem. One may indeed reply to Wittgenstein that bodily awareness is limited not only at the experiential level but also at the doxastic one. Although Wittgenstein pretends to be able to describe his finger movement exactly, it is not clear that it is the case. The knowledge that we have of our bodily movements is relatively sketchy. For instance, I doubt that Wittgenstein knows the amplitude of his finger movement. All he knows is that it is small. And there is a good reason why it is so rough-grained. There is indeed rarely any need to have fine-grained knowledge of our bodily position. Compare with vision. You need to know if this apple has a more reddish shade than this other apple in order to decide which one is ready to be eaten. There is no equivalent of this situation for bodily knowledge. When we need detailed and precise information about our body, it is only when we move it. Then indeed we cannot afford to have a sketchy representation of the position of our limbs because if it were the case the cost would be too high: we would simply fail to achieve our movements and reach our goal. What is important here is to clearly distinguish the declarative knowledge we have that supports the description we can make of our bodily position and the practical knowledge that we use to guide our bodily actions. Another way to put it is to draw a distinction between what is known in the literature as the body schema (sensorimotor representations that encode information necessary to guide action) and the body image (perceptual representations for recognition). The body schema must be fine-grained but the body image does not have to be. When we act, we need to have precise and detailed information about the posture of our limbs. But it does not matter whether we have precise and detailed beliefs about it. In other words, it is sufficient to know that our legs are crossed; we do not need to know in which specific angle. Consequently, the fact that the content of bodily sensations is poor is not an argument against its role for declarative bodily knowledge. It rather seems that they coincide.

Wittgenstein, however, does not only argue that the content of bodily sensations is insufficient. He also argues that we have bodily knowledge in the absence of bodily sensations. He acknowledges that when we are anaesthetized we are able neither to feel sensations nor to describe the posture of our body. But he claims this does not show that we normally can report that our arm is bent because of the corresponding sensation. On his view, there are some circumstances in which we can be aware of the position of our body and yet have no bodily sensation. This is the case when we simply do not pay attention to our body. Hence, he concludes, bodily awareness does not depend on bodily sensations.

The fact is that most of the time we do not pay attention to our body (with the exception of learning and painful situations). For instance, while typing on a laptop, we do not precisely experience the posture our fingers on the keyboard. Our awareness is primarily occupied by the content of what we are typing, by the external world, rather than by the bodily medium that allows us to perceive it and to move through it. The question then is dual: can we then describe the position of our body and do we really have no bodily sensation? Again, I believe that Wittgenstein confuses our practical and our declarative knowledge. When you do not pay attention at all to your body, you still have information about its bodily posture that you process unconsciously and that you can use for changing position for instance, but this is not the same as to say that you can describe the position of your limbs. It is only when you are asked to focus on your body that you suddenly realize that your legs are crossed. Before that, you simply had no idea. Hence, even if we experienced no bodily sensations, that would not be a problem since we would also have no beliefs about our body. Furthermore, one may challenge the idea that we feel nothing without attention. This seems indeed to assume a very tight connection between attention and sensations, a connection that might not be warranted. Take the example of vision: it is generally assumed that we have visual experiences not only about what we focus on but also about what is in the periphery. Why would that be different for bodily experiences?

We shall now turn to the problem that appears as the most fundamental for Wittgenstein and Anscombe, that is, the fact that the content of bodily sensations is not independent enough from the content of bodily knowledge.

2 Independent Sensations

> ... a man usually knows the position of his limbs without observation. It is without observation, because nothing shews him the position of his limbs; it is not as if he were going by a tingle in his knee, which is the sign that it is bent and not straight. Where we can speak of separately describable sensations, having which is in some sense our criterion for saying something, then we can speak of observing that thing. (Anscombe 1957: 13)

According to Anscombe, bodily knowledge cannot be grounded in sensations because only sensations whose content is "independently describable" can play an epistemic role. For example, there is a sensation of going down in a lift since one can provide an independent description of its internal content in terms of lightness and of one's stomach lurching upward. By contrast, it is not legitimate to talk of sensation of sitting cross-legged, Anscombe claims, because there is no

such independent description that can be given. Her argument can be summarized as follows:
(i) Only independent content can be used as the epistemic basis for judgments.
(ii) One cannot provide an independent description in the case of bodily position.
(iii) Thus, bodily knowledge is knowledge without observation.

The interpretation of the notion of knowledge without observation has given rise to many debates and I shall not go into them here. I just want to highlight three main issues. The first concerns Anscombe's epistemological theory. Why do contents have to be independent to ground judgments? The second problem is that the whole argument rests on the assumption (ii), according to which one cannot provide an independent description in the case of bodily position: "no question of any appearance of the position to me, of any sensations which give me the position" (Anscombe 1962: 58). But why is it so? Anscombe does not give any argument. She merely states that there cannot be independent descriptions. It then seems that the whole argument relies on phenomenological intuitions. But can one settle the debate by a direct use of our introspection in everyday life? As said earlier, most of the time bodily sensations are recessive and people have usually contradictory intuitions. This introspective quest is made even more difficult by the fact that we are not really sure of what we should look for. This is the third and most fundamental problem. The distinction between sensations whose content can be and sensations whose content cannot be separately describable is far from being clear and Anscombe's (1962: 57) own examples are not helpful. For instance, she claims that "the visual impression of a blue expanse" can ground the judgment that the sky is blue. Since she defends the view that sensations can be captured in intentional terms (Anscombe 1965), her point is not that there is a qualitative raw feel of blueness independently of the visual property of blue. But then it is not clear in what sense this qualifies as an independent description and it may sometimes be difficult to see why perceptual awareness does not fall into the same category as bodily awareness. It may then be helpful to go back to her own definition:

> When I say: 'the sensation (e.g. of giving a reflex kick) is not separable' I mean that the internal description of the 'sensation'—the description of the sensation-content—is *the very same as the description of the fact known*; when that is so, I should deny that we can speak of observing that fact by means of the alleged sensation. If we are considering an expression of the form 'sensation of X', we need to ask whether the words 'of X' are a description of the sensation content, or whether the sensation has some different content and X is *what produces or always goes with it*. (Anscombe 1962: 56, my emphasis)

Here we can reconstruct two criteria for a sensation of X to be independent: (i) the content should not coincide with the content that is believed, and (ii) the content should be about what is systematically associated with X. However, I believe these two criteria to be unsatisfactory because they are too liberal.

Consider the positive criterion ("X is what produces or always goes with it"). Imagine the following hypothetical scenario. Whenever I believe my legs to be crossed, I experience the taste of chocolate in my mouth. On the basis of such gustatory experiences, I can infer that my legs are crossed. Shall we then conclude that the chocolate taste is the independent description of my feeling of having my legs crossed? Such a conclusion does not seem right, at least if we take seriously Anscombe's original epistemic starting point. On her view, sensations must be able to ground knowledge. But if we describe the internal content of the sensation of X in terms of its side effects, then it can happen that the side effects occur for reasons other than X. It would be a logical fallacy to conclude that my legs are crossed on the only basis of their side effect. If now we describe the internal content of the sensation of X in terms of its causes, then this is also problematic because other factors can prevent X to be true. Consequently, it seems that mere causal connections, or even worse systematic association, cannot provide robust epistemic ground, and that they are not promising candidates for independent description.[1]

Let us now consider the negative criterion (not "the very same as the description of the fact known"). In response to this definition, Harcourt (2008) offers the following criterion for independent description: a sensation of bodily posture is independent if it can seem to one that one is in a specific bodily posture while one correctly judges that one is not. Anscombe's view can indeed accommodate the fact that one can be mistaken about one's bodily properties. However, what seems to be more problematic for her are cases in which the content of the alleged sensation is at odds not only with reality, but also with the content of the judgment. Harcourt then argues that there are bodily illusions, and concludes that bodily knowledge must thus be observational. The failure of Anscombe's argument would then simply come from the fact that she has overlooked the manifold of illusions that can happen even for bodily awareness. As Smith (2002: 24) noted:

---

[1] It is interesting to note that Bermúdez (2015) who appeals to Anscombe's argument for his own purpose requires the content of sensations to be not only independent, but also "focused". Their content must provide information that is precise and specific because if they are too vague, they fail to justify the specific judgment that one makes.

It is tempting to think that because our bodies are, as it were, so close to us, the scope for illusions here is minimal. In fact, however, recent research in this area has presented some of the most striking illusions in all the literature.

A well-known example is called the Pinocchio illusion (Lackner 1988). If the tendons of your arm muscles are vibrated at a certain frequency, you experience illusory arm movements. You feel, for instance, your arm moving away from you if your biceps tendon is vibrated. If you simultaneously grasp your nose, you experience your nose as elongating by as much as 30 cm. The Pinocchio illusion constitutes the solution of a sensorimotor conflict between erroneous proprioceptive information (i.e. your arm moving away from you) and accurate tactile information (i.e. contact of your nose and your fingers). Interestingly, this illusion can occur although you are fully aware that this is not true. Hence, it can seem to one that one's arm is stretched while one correctly judges that it is not. Another famous example is the rubber hand illusion (Botvinick and Cohen 1998). In the classic experimental set-up, one sits with one's arm hidden behind a screen, while fixating on a rubber hand presented in one's bodily alignment; the rubber hand can then be touched either in synchrony or in asynchrony with one's hand. After a couple of minutes, it has been repeatedly shown that there are significant differences between synchronous and asynchronous conditions. Participants report that they feel tactile sensations as being located not on their real hand that is stroked, but on the rubber hand. Furthermore, they mislocalize the finger that was touched in the direction of the location of the finger of the rubber hand. On Harcourt's view, such bodily illusions show that the sensation of bodily position is separately describable and thus, that Anscombe is wrong: bodily knowledge is observational.

The situation, however, is more complex. Harcourt is right that there are many bodily illusions that remain insensitive to beliefs in the same way as visual illusions. Yet this does not suffice to show that bodily knowledge is observational. McDowell (2011) rightly points out that attitudes other than feelings and sensations can be encapsulated and immune to the influence of beliefs and judgments. Consequently, one can dispense with sensations and provide a cognitive interpretation of bodily illusions. To refute Harcourt's argument, however, does not show that Anscombe is right. Instead, the discussion between McDowell and Harcourt merely reveals that Anscombe's criterion is too vague. Even if the content is not the very same as the description of the fact known, this does not show that it is the content of a sensation.

What this brief discussion reveals is that Anscombe does not provide a clear definition of independent sensations, which can be easily operationalized. In the absence of such a definition, we cannot determine whether there are bodily sensations whose content is independent and that can ground bodily knowledge, or not. Even more problematic for her, if we take her to her words and use the criteria that she gives, it seems that there are such sensations.

3 Knowledge Without Observation

I now want to focus on the notion of bodily knowledge without observation, which may be more helpful than the notion of independent content. According to Anscombe, knowledge without observation should be understood in motor terms. In a nutshell, knowing that your legs are crossed is not feeling them to be crossed; it is knowing how to uncross them. Her view shares some similarities with the more recent enactivist approach, which gives a central role to the procedural knowledge of how the way in which one moves affects the sensory signals that one receives (Noë 2004; O'Regan 2011).[2] Because of these similarities, however, she also shares the same difficulties (for more details on enactivism, see Vignemont 2011). Consider the following report given by a neurological patient:

> But, I don't understand that. You put something there; I do not feel anything and yet I got there with my finger. How does that happen? (Paillard et al. 1983: 550)

This patient, who was blindfolded, was amazed at her own ability to point to the site at which she was touched on her hand while she felt absolutely no sensation of having been touched. She suffered from what is called 'numbsense' in the neuropsychological literature (also called 'blind touch'). Following cortical or subcortical lesions, patients with numbsense become completely anaesthetized on their right side. Yet despite their apparent numbness, they are able to guide their opposite hand towards the approximate site at which they are touched when so instructed, and to their own surprise. Likewise, although they do not feel their arm location, they can accurately reach the position of their arm.

It may then seem that what Wittgenstein and Anscombe describe (knowing without feeling) can actually happen. One might indeed say that these patients have bodily knowledge without observation. But do they really have *knowledge*?

---

2 There are, however, two main differences. First, enactivists do not make a distinction between vision and touch or proprioception, while Anscombe does. On her view, visual knowledge is observational. Secondly, enactivists aim to account for bodily *experiences* while Anscombe is not interested in bodily experiences and instead aims to account for bodily *knowledge*.

The patients are not able to form beliefs about the tactile stimuli and their arm position, even in a forced choice condition (Rossetti et al. 1995). They cannot describe that they were touched nor where they were. What is preserved is only their bodily know-how, their practical knowledge of how to reach for their arm. Interestingly, they are no better in judging the location of their sensation when they are acting at the same time; instead they become equally bad in the verbal and in the motor tasks (Rossetti et al. 1995). Numerous findings actually show dissociation between body schema and body image, between how we act and what we know (Vignemont 2010). Another example concerns the rubber hand illusion. We saw earlier that participants mislocalize the location of their hand. If the motor interpretation of the notion of knowledge without observation were right, one could explain the effect as follows: participants localize their hand closer to the location of the rubber hand because they are misleadingly induced to expect that if they reach the location close to the rubber hand, they will touch their own hand. However, this explanation cannot account for the following facts. When asked, participants accurately direct their opposite hand to the real location of their own hand that was touched, and not to the illusory location that they report (Kammers et al. 2009). Their reaching movements are not sensitive to the spatial illusion. Interestingly, when participants are asked a second time to make a perceptual judgement about the location of their touched hand after having moved, they are still sensitive to the illusion, and they still localize their hand as being closer to the location of the rubber hand than it was (although less so). Hence, what they describe about their body cannot be explained by their bodily know-how.

What these findings show is that Anscombe's notion of knowledge without observation can be used to understand the body schema, that is, the bodily know-how that guides us in our movements. Clearly, action guidance and control, which constantly require information about the body, are not mediated by bodily sensations. If we were to wait for us to be aware of our bodily position before making any motor adjustment, our movements would be slow and inefficient. Hence, to use Anscombe's phrase, the motor system "usually knows the position of his limbs without observation". But this is not true of the subject himself. What he describes is not based on his practical knowledge without observation. In other words, the body image cannot be reduced to the body schema.

4 Conclusion

In this paper I did not show that bodily sensations ground bodily knowledge. Instead I merely argued that there is no good reason to prevent them for doing so. There is a further motivation to argue that they play an epistemic role. If indeed they played none, as suggested by Anscombe and Wittgenstein, then bodily sensations seem to have no role whatsoever. One may then be tempted by an eliminativist conception, according to which bodily sensations are merely "philosophical fictions": they do not exist (Bermúdez 2015). As far as I know, this is not what Anscombe or Wittgenstein wants to claim. But if indeed they reject such a conclusion, then they might simply grant that bodily sensations do play a role.

References

Anscombe, G. E. M. (1957): *Intention*. Ithaca: Cornell University Press.
Anscombe, G. E. M. (1962): "On sensations of position". In: *Analysis*, Vol. 22 (3), pp. 55–8.
Anscombe, G. E. M. (1965): "The intentionality of sensation: A grammatical feature". In Ronald J. Butler (ed.), *Analytic Philosophy*. Blackwell. pp. 158–80.
Bermúdez, J. L. (2015): "Bodily ownership, bodily awareness, and knowledge without observation". *Analysis*. Vol. 75 (1), pp. 37–45.
Botvinick, M. and Cohen, J. (1998): "Rubber hands 'feel' touch that eyes see". In: *Nature*, 391, p. 756.
Harcourt, E. (2008): "Wittgenstein and Bodily Self-Knowledge". In: *Philosophy and Phenomenological Research*, 77 (2), pp. 299–333.
Kammers, M. P., de Vignemont, F., Verhagen, L., and Dijkerman, H. C. (2009a): "The rubber hand illusion in action". In: *Neuropsychologia*, 47, pp. 204–211.
Lackner, J. R. (1988): "Some proprioceptive influences on the perceptual representation of body shape and orientation". In: *Brain*, 111, pp. 281–297.
McDowell, J. (2011): "Anscombe on bodily self-knowledge". In: *Essays on Anscombe's Intention*, edited by A. Ford, J. Hornsby, and F. Stoutland. Cambridge (MA): MIT Press.
Noë, A. (2004): *Action in perception*. Cambridge (MA): MIT Press.
O'Regan, K. (2011): *Why red doesn't sound like a bell*. Oxford: Oxford University Press.
O'Shaughnessy, B. (1980): *The will*. Vol. 1. Cambridge: Cambridge University Press.
Paillard, J., Michel, F., and Stelmach, G. (1983): "Localization without content. A tactile analogue of 'blind sight'". In: *Archives of Neurology*, 40, pp. 548–551.
Rossetti, Y., Rode, G., and Boisson, D. (1995): "Implicit processing of somaesthetic information: a dissociation between where and how?". In: *Neuroreport*. 6, pp. 506–510.
Smith, A. D. (2002). *The problem of perception*. Cambridge (MA): Harvard University Press.
de Vignemont, F. (2010), "Body schema and body image: pros and cons". In: *Neuropsychologia*, 48(3), pp. 669–680.
de Vignemont, F. (2011): "A mosquito bite against the enactive view to bodily experiences". In: *Journal of Philosophy*, CVIII, 4, pp. 188–204.

Wittgenstein, L. (1978): *Philosophical Investigations*. Tr. G.E.M. Anscombe. Oxford: Blackwell.

6 Perception and the Sciences

Romana K. Schuler
Scheinbewegungen. Wahrnehmung zwischen Wissensgeschichte und Gegenwartskunst

Zusammenfassung: Im vorliegenden Beitrag über die Wahrnehmung von Scheinbewegungen sollen zwei Aspekte in den Blick genommen werden: Erstens wird eine historische Skizze zur wissenschaftlichen Erforschung von Scheinbewegungen vorgelegt, und zweitens werden exemplarische Beispiele zur ästhetischen Realisierung von Scheinbewegungen in der Gegenwartskunst, insbesondere in der experimentellen Kunst vorgestellt.

Schlüsselwörter: experimentelle Physiologie, Scheinbewegung, Sinnestäuschungen, Virtualität, experimentelle Kunst

> When I write in the air, am I writing in my mind or in the air? (Wittgenstein, in: Brown 2007: 18)

Beobachtungen von Scheinbewegungen sind uns schon seit der Antike bekannt (Wade 1998: 207). Bis ins 19. Jahrhundert wurden derartige Phänomene vonseiten der Naturwissenschaftler und Philosophen als optischer „Betrug" (Roget 1825) erklärt. Noch bis weit ins 20. Jahrhundert wurde von „optischen Täuschungen" gesprochen. Aufgrund der so gut wie ständigen Konfrontation mit Scheinbewegungen durch neue moderne Bildtechnologien hat sich diese Auffassung radikal geändert. Diese – künstlich hervorgerufenen – Scheinbewegungen werden längst nicht mehr als „Betrug" an der menschlichen Wahrnehmung angesehen, sondern als schier unbegrenztes Potenzial zur Erweiterung der Realität, was dazu beigetragen hat, dass die Grenzen zwischen Illusion und Realität mehr und mehr verschwimmen. So stellt sich auch die Frage nach einer neuen Definition von Realität, welche die medialen visuellen Illusionen entsprechend impliziert und kommentiert. Das Engagement der Naturwissenschaften in der Erforschung von Sinneswahrnehmungen im 19. Jahrhundert drängte die klassischen Lehren der Naturphilosophie in den Hintergrund. Der bekannte Experimentalphysiker Ernst

Mach definierte diese wissenschaftlichen Forschungen als eine *ökonomisch* geordnete Erfahrung, deren Aufgabe es sei, die Vorgänge in der Natur möglichst nachvollziehbar zu beschreiben (Mach 1896, vgl. Jerusalem 1919).[1]

Eine Sichtung der Forschungsgeschichte zur Wahrnehmung der Scheinbewegung kann uns einen Zugang eröffnen, der diese Entwicklung vielleicht zu erklären vermag.

Neben Beobachtungen zum natürlichen Auftreten von Scheinbewegungen wie der Ufertäuschung (Oppel 1856) konnten Scheinbewegungen bald auch experimentell hervorgerufen werden. Die Versuche zielten darauf, die Logik der visuellen Sinnestäuschungen in ein mathematisches Formelwerk zu überführen. Die Vorgänge, die sich während des Sehens von Bewegung ereignen, sind bis heute – trotz Computertomografie – nicht restlos geklärt. Daher ist es nicht verwunderlich, wenn heute historische Studien wie beispielsweise zur Augenbewegung (Spering 2016) und zum Aufrechtsehen bei umgekehrten Netzhautbildern (vgl. Linden 1999) immer noch von Interesse sind.

Wann die ersten wissenschaftlichen Studien zur Scheinbewegung durchgeführt wurden, kann ebenfalls nicht eindeutig festgestellt werden. Es gibt dazu mehrere, sich überschneidende Eckdaten aus dem 18. und 19. Jahrhundert. Sehr frühe wissenschaftliche Untersuchungen über Scheinbewegungen finden sich um 1730, als der schottische Arzt William Porterfield das menschliche Schwindelgefühl als optische Auswirkung von Scheinbewegungen beschrieb. Er stellte fest, dass sich bei der Evozierung von Schwindelgefühl durch Körperdrehung Gegenstände immer gegensätzlich zur Drehungsrichtung des Körpers bewegten und sich noch weiter fortbewegten, obwohl die eigentliche Körperdrehung beendet war (Porterfield 1759, vgl. Ladewig 2001).

Fünfzig Jahre später verfasste der Berliner Philosoph und Arzt Marcus Herz bereits ein Buch zum Schwindel und zu Scheinbewegungen (Herz 1791: 180). Der Mediziner William Charles Wells erkannte, dass das Schwindelgefühl mit der Nachbildbewegung und der Augenbewegung in Zusammenhang steht (Wells 1792).[2] Wells bezog sich auch auf James Jurin, der 1738 erstmals seine grundlegenden Erkenntnisse zum Nachbild publizierte. Jurin experimentierte mit schwarzen Rechtecken, die die Versuchspersonen längere Zeit starr anblicken mussten, um ein Nachbild wahrzunehmen (Jurin 1738).

Die Phänomene der Nachbilder und der Scheinbewegungen standen bei Jan Evangelista Purkinje lange Zeit im Zentrum seiner Forschungstätigkeit. Er hatte – wie auch vor ihm bereits Erasmus Darwin – herausgefunden, dass mithilfe von

---

[1] Mach war mit Jerusalem eng befreundet.
[2] Wells stellt in dieser Schrift auch erstmals seine Theorie über das binokulare Sehen vor.

galvanischem Strom Scheinbewegungen erzeugt werden können. So schrieb er 1823:

> Die im Auge bei galvanischer Einwirkung entstehenden leuchtenden Phänomene können umso lebendiger und mit einem umso kleineren Aufwand hervorgerufen werden, je sensibler das dem Versuch unterworfene Nervensystem ist. (Purkinje 1823: 122)

Experimentelle Sinnespsychologie im 19. Jahrhundert wurde neben von Naturwissenschaftlern auch von gelehrten Persönlichkeiten wie J. W. Goethe betrieben, der mit Purkinje bekannt war.

Beide kamen zu der Ansicht, dass das Auge ein aktives Organ sei und kein reines Durchgangsmedium zum Gehirn, und sprachen vom „individuellen, subjektiven Sehen" (Goethe 1819 / 1950: 844–855).[3]

Um 1824 hielt der englische Arzt Peter Mark Roget eine interessante Beobachtung zu einer optischen Täuschung fest: Er erkannte eine Krümmung der Radspeichen bei fahrenden Wagenrädern, die bei schnellerer Umdrehungsgeschwindigkeit wieder verschwand. Er publizierte zu dieser Beobachtung 1825 in den *Annals of Philosophy* und bezeichnete sie als „optische[n] Betrug" (Roget 1825: 107).

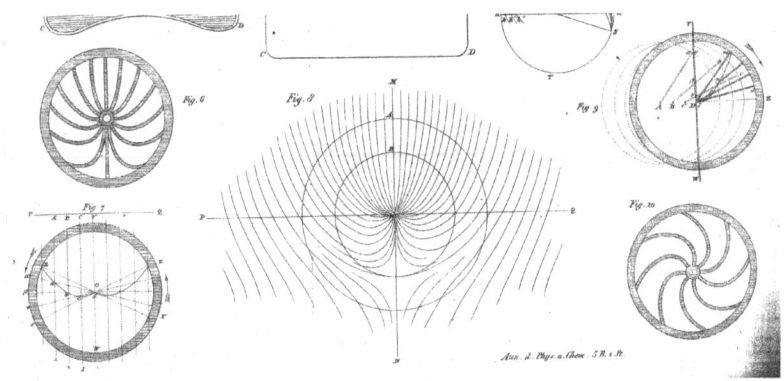

Abb. 1: Peter Mark Roget, Skizze der Radspeichen, (Foto: Archiv Autorin)

Ungefähr zur selben Zeit experimentierte William Henry Fox Talbot, der Erfinder des Negativbildes in der Fotografie, mit glühenden Kohlen, die in einem dunklen Raum in schnellem Tempo gedreht wurden, um einen Lichtring zu erzeugen. Der

---

3 Auf S. 893-904 geht Goethe auf Purkinjes Beobachtungen ein.

Versuch war für die Photometrie, die Lichtmessung, gedacht. Die Resultate waren zunächst nicht zufriedenstellend, Talbot setzte seine Experimente mit einer rotierenden Scheibe, auf der eine breite schwarze Spirale abgebildet war, fort. Damit erkannte er die Veränderung der Helligkeit der Farbe durch die Rotation der Spirale als grundlegendes photometrisches Prinzip. Talbot publizierte seine Erkenntnisse erst 1834, neun Jahre nach den Versuchen (Talbot 1834)

Plateau begriff Talbots Experiment als neuen Impuls für die Photometrie, da er selbst bereits mit rotierenden Scheiben dazu gearbeitet hatte. 1835 publizierte Plateau seine Versuchsergebnisse mit direktem Verweis auf Talbots Experimente, sodass diese Resultate schließlich als das Talbot/Plateau'sche Gesetz bekannt wurde (Plateau 1835).

Die Beobachtungen von partiell bemalten und in Rotation versetzten Scheiben waren bis ins 20. Jahrhundert ein sehr häufiges experimentelles Verfahren, um visuelle Wahrnehmungen zu studieren.

Im Jahr 1838 publizierte Theodor Gustav Fechner in den *Annalen für Physik und Chemie* seine Versuche mit einer Scheibe zur Erzeugung von subjektiven Farben (Fechner 1838)[4]. Er experimentierte mit einer Scheibe mit dem Durchmesser von 18 Zoll, die er in 18 Ringe unterteilte. Der innerste war völlig schwarz, der nächste erhielt 20 % Weißanteil, der nächste 30 % usw., bis zum letzten äußeren Ring mit 100 % Weiß. Das Verhältnis zwischen Schwarz und Weiß entsprach der Form einer archimedischen Spirale.

---

4 Ende des 19. Jahrhunderts griff Charles Benham Fechners Experimente auf und patentierte die rotierende Scheibe 1894 als Kinderspielzeug, wie im Übrigen viele der Gerätschaften zur Erzeugung von visuellen Erscheinungen als Kinderspielzeug recht populär wurden.

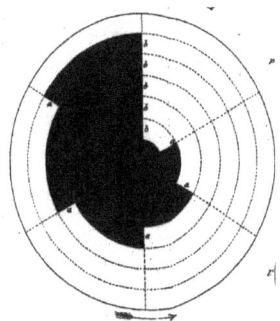

Abb. 2: Theodor Gustav Fechner, Scheibe zu subjektiven Farbenexperimenten, 1838 (Foto: Archiv Autorin)

> Als nun diese Scheibe gedreht wurde, war ich erstaunt, anstatt Abstufungen reines Grau's, vielmehr allerhand von der Mitte nach dem Umfang zu, so wie nach Beschaffenheit der Drehungsgeschwindigkeit sich ändernde Farben wahrzunehmen, die für mein Auge zwar nicht von starker Intensivität, aber doch nicht ohne Lebhaftigkeit waren. Ich habe dieses Phänomen vielen Personen gezeigt, und dabei gefunden, dass es von ihnen mit sehr ungleicher Deutlichkeit wahrgenommen wird, was auch in Betracht seines subjectiven Ursprungs nicht auffallend seyn kann. (Fechner 1838: 227)

Neben Fechners zentralem Hauptwerk *Die Elemente der Psychophysik* (1860) waren die experimentellen Forschungen über den Lichtreiz beim Nachbild mit rotierenden Scheiben von Ernst Brücke (1864) unter anderem für Ernst Mach inspirierend. Auch Mach experimentierte mit Scheiben und entdeckte in der Folge (1865) den Effekt, den wir als „Machbänder" kennen (Mach 1865).

Bei seinen vielen Experimenten zum Nachbild auf der Netzhaut beobachtete der Wiener Physiologe Siegmund Exner 1875 erstmals das Phänomen der Scheinbewegung bei zwei überspringenden Funken. Der Versuch fand in einem abgedunkelten Raum statt, wo mithilfe des Rotationsapparates eine horizontal liegende Scheibe in gleichmäßige Drehung versetzt wurde. An der unteren Seite der Scheibe waren zwei nadelförmige Metallteilchen bzw. Metallzeiger befestigt. Durch die Drehung der Scheibe kamen die Enden der Metalle regelmäßig mit einer Kuppe aus Quecksilber in Kontakt. Diese und die Spitze der Metallzeiger waren mit einer elektrischen Batterie verbunden, und so entstand ein Funke, der für die Beobachtung wesentlich war (Exner 1875). Auf Exners Experiment bezogen sich viele nachkommende Wissenschaftler bis weit ins 20. Jahrhundert, sodass Exner oft als der Entdeckung der eigentlichen Scheinbewegung genannt wird.

Als Sensation auf dem Forschungsgebiet der Sinneswahrnehmungen kann das Stroboskop angesehen werden, das 1832/33 von Joseph Plateau in Brüssel und von Simon Stampfer in Wien fast zeitgleich erfunden und zunächst als ‚Phaenakistikop' bezeichnet wurde. Mit dem Stroboskop war es endlich möglich, bewegte Bilder zu sehen. Dieser Apparat war eigentlich der erste Film und der erste Projektor in einem. Wie schnell das Stroboskop populär wurde, dokumentiert allein ein mehrseitiger Bericht von Johann C. Poggendorff, Herausgeber der *Annalen der Physik und Chemie*, von 1834 über das Stroboskop und dessen Variationen (Poggendorff 1834). Am Ende seiner Ausführungen bezeichnete er die neuen Apparate, die auf dem Prinzip des Stroboskops beruhten, als „Augentäuschungen" (Poggendorff 1834: 649).

Sechs Jahre später, 1838, hielt das Stereoskop, das in England von Charles Wheatstone erfunden worden war, Einzug in die Labors der Wissenschaftler. Entsprechend der physiologischen binokularen Voraussetzung konnte durch den Stereoskop-Apparat eine doppelte Darstellung einer Fotografie betrachtet werden, was eine räumliche Tiefenwahrnehmung der sonst flachen Bildebene ermöglichte.

Beide Apparate lösten eine wahre Revolution für die Erforschung des Sehens aus: Die Augenbewegung und auch das Nachbild wurden mittels des Stroboskops untersucht, das Stereoskop setzte neue Maßstäbe für Forschungen zum räumlichen Sehen. Darüber hinaus verdanken wir dem Stroboskop und dem Stereoskop den Film und die Möglichkeit der räumlichen Darstellung von Objekten auf einer zweidimensionalen Fläche, die heute in vielen Bereichen eingesetzt wird, u. a. in der Medizin. Ernst Mach war einer der Ersten, der stereoskopische Fotografien für Experimente einsetzte, sie also nicht bloß für dokumentarische Zwecke verwendete. Die Kombination von beweglichen Bildern und tiefenräumlichem Sehen mündete schließlich im 20. Jahrhundert in den 3-D-Film, der erstmals in den 1950er-Jahren in den Kinos gezeigt wurde. In den letzten zehn Jahren ist die Anwendung der 3-D-Darstellung im Bereich der VR-Entwicklung avancierter und immer beliebter geworden.

Interessant ist in diesem Zusammenhang, dass die Idee einer Kombination der beiden Apparate bereits von deren Erfindern Plateau und Wheatstone 1850 erläutert wurde:

> Allein kann man noch weiter gehen, wenn man eine Idee benutzt, die mir Hr. Wheatstone mitgetheilt hat, und darin besteht, das Princip des Stereoskops mit dem des Phaenakistikops zu vereinigen. [...] Gesetzt nun, es gelänge durch Combination beider Instrumente, diesen Effect dem des Phaenakistikops hinzuzufügen; alsdann werden Figuren, die einfach auf Papier gezeichnet sind, unwiderstehlich erhoben (en ronde bosse) und sich bewegend erscheinen, und somit das vollständige Ansehen von Leben erhalten. Dies heißt die Täuschung der Kunst auf die höchste Stufe tragen. (Plateau 1850: 156)

Plateau führte zwar sehr detaillierte theoretische Überlegungen aus, letztlich aber verfolgten die beiden Forscher ihre Idee nicht weiter.

Viele solcher Einzelerkenntnisse haben dazu beigetragen, dass zu Beginn des 20. Jahrhunderts eine noch intensivere Erforschung der Wahrnehmung von Scheinbewegung in die Gänge kam, die schließlich zur Neupositionierung der Experimentalpsychologie, nämlich zur Gestalttheorie führen sollte. So widmeten sich beispielsweise zwei maßgebliche Wissenschaftler unabhängig voneinander dem Phänomen der Scheinbewegung: einerseits Vittorio Benussi in Graz und andererseits Max Wertheimer in Frankfurt.

Der gebürtige Triester Vittorio Benussi war Student und später Mitarbeiter des Experimentalpsychologen Alexius Meinong, der 1894 in Graz das erste experimentalpsychologische Laboratorium in Österreich einrichtete. Benussi interessierte sich für Sinnestäuschungen wie die Zöllner Figur oder die Müller-Lyerschen Muster sowie für die Scheinkörperlichkeit bei umkehrbaren Zeichnungen. Daraus entwickelte er 1910/11 die Idee, Abbildungen wie die Zöllner'sche Figur und die Müller-Lyer-Täuschung zu animieren: 8 bzw. 12 Phasenbilder wurden aus Karton ausgeschnitten. Die einzelnen Phasenbilder wurden mittels eines Stroboskops in Bewegung versetzt und konnten so als Scheinbewegung beobachtet werden Benussi veröffentlichte seine Arbeiten im April 1912 (Benussi 1912).

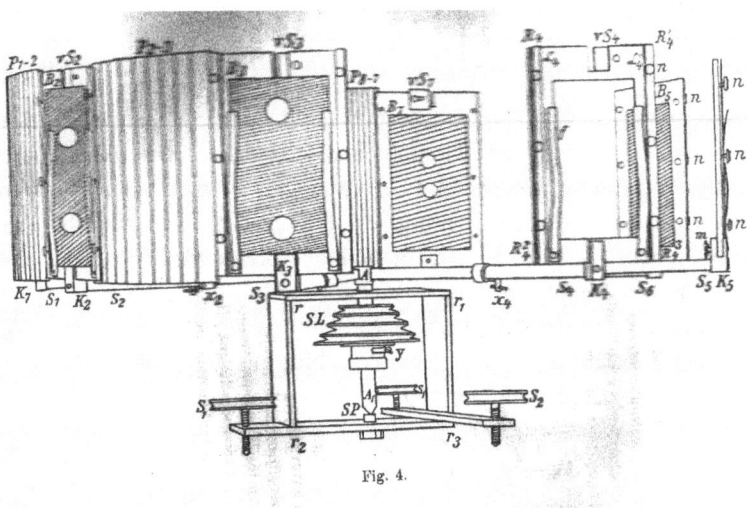

Abb. 3: Vittorio Benussi, Skizze adaptiertes Mikroskop, um 1911 (Foto: Archiv Autorin)

Später, um 1922 in Padua, beschäftigte er sich vor allem mit der sogenannten Stereokinese – einer der möglichen Kombinationen aus Scheinbewegung und Scheinräumlichkeit.

Abb. 4: Wertheimer / Schuman, Adaptiertes Rad-Tachistoskop, 1908/1912 (Foto: Adolf-Würth-Zentrum für Geschichte der Psychologie, Würzburg)

Zur selben Zeit, zwischen 1909 und 1911, entwickelte Max Wertheimer in Frankfurt im Labor von Friedrich Schumann eine andere Methode, um die Scheinbewegung zu untersuchen: Er verwendete ein sogenanntes modifiziertes Rad-Tachistoskop, welches er von Schumann übernommen hatte. Eigentlich handelte es sich dabei um ein Fahrrad-Rad, das für die Experimente zur Beobachtung von Scheinphänomenen adaptiert worden war.

Wertheimer entfernte den Radschlauch, über den Felgen waren Blechringe montiert. In diese Blechringe waren schmale Schlitze eingeschnitten, die mit einem Schieber geschlossen werden konnten.

Abb. 5: Max Wertheimer mit Rad-Tachistoskop, um 1912 (Foto: Archiv Autorin)

Das ganze Blechring-Fahrrad-Rad stand auf einem festen Podest und wurde mit einem Motor in gleichmäßige Bewegung versetzt. Mithilfe eines Fernglases wurde das zu beobachtende Objekt durch die Schlitze des sich drehenden Blechring-Rades betrachtet.

Wertheimer publizierte seine Arbeit über Scheinbewegungen ebenfalls erstmals 1912 und bezeichnete die Entdeckung aus seinen Beobachtungen der scheinbaren Bewegungen als „Phi-Phänomen" (Wertheimer 1912). Wie auch die Vertreter der Grazer Gestalttheorie definierte Wertheimer seine Theorie als Komplextheorie und war ebenso wie die Grazer Forscher von Christian von Ehrenfels' Untersuchungen zu Gestaltqualitäten (1890) beeinflusst.

Offensichtlich setzten Wertheimers Experimente über die Scheinbewegung Impulse für eine neue Gestalttheorie bzw. Gestaltschule. Wenig später gründete Wertheimer mit Kurt Koffka und Wolfgang Köhler die „Berliner Gestaltschule", die relativ schnell weit reichende wissenschaftliche Beachtung fand. Vor der Initiative, die zur Gründung dieses populären Instituts in Berlin geführt hatte, hatte es bereits vonseiten der Grazer Gestaltpsychologen (Meinong, Witasek, Benussi) und auch teilweise von der Würzburger Schule im Umkreis von Oswald Külpe eindeutige Anstrengungen gegeben, die innovativen Thesen von Ehrenfels und Mach nicht nur zu übernehmen, sondern auch weiterzuentwickeln.

Neben den Forschungen zur Wahrnehmung von Scheinbewegung rückte auch die Beobachtung der Scheinräumlichkeit mehr und mehr in den Fokus der Wissenschaftler.

Hier soll kurz an die Brillenexperimente von George Stratton (1896–98) und die Langzeitexperimente mit Umkehrbrillen erinnert werden, die an der Universität Innsbruck von Theodor Erismann und Ivo Kohler von 1929 bis in die 1950er-Jahre durchgeführt wurden. Schließlich haben all diese Experimente wesentlich dazu beigetragen, dass wir heute über Technologien wie die Virtual Reality verfügen – oder anders gesagt: über Entwicklungen, die uns eine erweiterte Realität offerieren. Denken wir nur an die VR-Brillen, die inzwischen schon überall angeboten werden.

Nun – was haben all diese historischen Experimente mit Kunst zu tun? Kunst sollte doch per se visionär sein? Der Kunstbegriff wird allgemein und traditionell mit „neuen Ideen" und „Vision" verbunden, tatsächlich aber reflektieren die Künstler sehr häufig Erkenntnisse aus der Grundlagenforschung, die im Kontext der Kunst innovativ erscheinen.

Seit der Antike war die visuelle Kunst oft mit dem Vorwurf, bloß ein Abbild oder ein Trugbild zu erzeugen, konfrontiert. Erst im 20. Jahrhundert wird der alltägliche Gegenstand, das Ready-made, als Material in die Kunst eingeführt. Diese ästhetische Erweiterung bzw. Innovation ist auf Marcel Duchamp zurückzuführen. Es gibt unzählige Vermutungen, wie der Künstler zu seinem ersten Ready-made, dem Fahrrad-Rad von 1913, gekommen sein mag. Allerdings wurde bisher in der Kunstgeschichte noch nie ein engerer Zusammenhang mit Wertheimer/Schumanns Laborapparat, dem Rad-Tachistoskop in Betracht gezogen.

So ist bekannt, dass der Künstler Marcel Duchamp ein begeisterter Anhänger der damaligen Erforschung der Bewegungswahrnehmung war. Es ist nachgewiesen, dass er die neuesten wissenschaftlichen Publikationen zum Thema studierte und dass er sich im Sommer 1912 für längere Zeit in Deutschland aufhielt, und zwar vorwiegend in München. Allerdings unternahm er auch Reisen nach Frankfurt und in andere deutsche Städte – er sprach fließend Deutsch. Über den wahren Grund für seinen damaligen ausgiebigen Deutschlandbesuch hat er sich kaum geäußert.

Tatsache ist aber, dass Duchamp ein paar Monate später, nämlich im Frühjahr 1913, in seinem Pariser Studio ein Fahrrad-Rad vor seinem Kamin aufstellte. Er betonte immer wieder, dass es sich bei diesem Fahrrad-Rad keineswegs um ein Kunstwerk handeln würde; er liebe es aber, das Fackeln des Kaminfeuers durch das sich bewegende Rad zu beobachten. Vielmehr sei das Fahrrad-Rad „ein privates Experiment, von dem ich niemals dachte, dass es öffentlich gezeigt werden wird." (Daniels 1992: 170)

Vergleichen wir dazu ein Foto von Max Wertheimer mit seinem Rad-Tachistoskop, ist die Ähnlichkeit zu Duchamps Fahrrad-Rad frappant. Daraus könnte man durchaus den Schluss ziehen, dass dieses Rad-Tachistoskop, welches u. a.

zur Erforschung der Scheinbewegung verwendet wurde, faktisch Pate für die Objektkunst stand.

Abb. 6: Marcel Duchamp mit Ready-made Fahrrad-Rad, 1913 (Foto © succession Marcel Duchamp)

Die Vertreter des „Bauhaus" und der abstrakten Malerei standen bis weit ins 20. Jahrhunderts unter dem Einfluss der Berliner Gestalttheorie (vgl. Boudewijnse 2012). Erst mit Aufkommen der Kybernetik sollte die Gestalttheorie ihre Vorreiterrolle verlieren. Die Konzepte der Kybernetik zielten auf die Vernetzung unterschiedlicher Bereiche wie Informatik, Technik, Naturwissenschaften, Soziologie und Kunst. Im Wesentlichen folgte dieser Gedanke dem Prinzip des Wiener Kreises. Neben Einflüssen aus den Neuen Medienwissenschaften (Marshall McLuhan) und vor allem aus den ästhetischen Ansprüchen der Informationstheorie (Abraham A. Molles, Max Bense), die maßgeblich die interdisziplinären Gepflogenheiten förderten, blieb das Interesse an der Erzeugung von Scheinbewegung aufrecht und wurde sogar weiter forciert.

Daraus gingen in den 1950er-Jahren die kinetische Kunst und bald darauf die OpArt hervor. Zu diesen neuen Kunstformen kamen in der Folge das Happening und aktionistische Performances hinzu. In den 1960er-Jahren definiert sich die mediale Kunst häufig über Expanded Art und Expanded Cinema, und auch Begriffe wie „intermedial", „transmedial" oder „Polymedialität", „Polyästhetik" oder eben „Polyartist"[5] sollten die neuen Kunstrichtungen beschreiben.

---

5 Der Begriff „Polyartist" (1968) geht auf Richard Kostelanetz zurück; vgl. Kostelanetz 1968.

Unter dem Einfluss der bewegten Bildobjekte der kinetischen Kunst begann der Schweizer Künstler Alfons Schilling 1962 in Paris kreisförmige, großflächige Bildträger aus Holz mit Motorenantrieb rotieren zu lassen und eimerweise Farbe darauf zu schütten. Schilling folgte der Idee der Entgrenzung aus dem statischen Bild und schuf mithilfe von Drehbewegung und Fliehkraft eine Malerei, die dem Prinzip der kinetischen Kunst entsprach (Schuler 2016: 208–209).

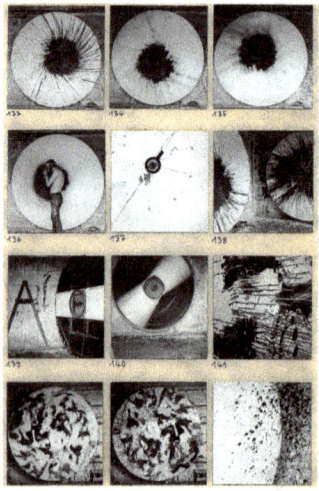

Abb. 7: Alfons Schilling, Drehbilder, 1962 (Foto: Alfons Schilling Nachlass, Wien)

Abb. 8: Jeffrey Shaw / Theo Botschuijver, Virtuelle Skulptur, 1981 (Archiv Jeffrey Shaw)

Schilling übersiedelte 1962 nach New York, wo er sich ab Mitte der 1960er-Jahre mit Holographie und Stereoskopie beschäftigte. Er freundete sich mit dem bekannten Wahrnehmungspsychologen Béla Julesz (1964) an, der auch als wichtiger Wegbereiter der digitalen Kunst angesehen werden kann. 1965 stellte der Wissenschaftler Béla Julesz gemeinsam mit dem Informatiker Michael Noll erstmals Computerzeichnungen in einer Galerie in New York aus.[6]

Gegenwärtig arbeiten Kunstschaffende mit raffinierten Apps und modernen Software-Technologien. Das Abspielen und/oder Interagieren geschieht über handliche Hardware wie Laptops, Tablets und Smartphones oder Kinect – oder VR-Brillen, die ein totales immersives Erlebnis erzeugen können. Von der Überzeugung, dass die Wahrnehmung der Scheinbewegung bloß ein „Betrug" oder „Augentäuschung" sei, hat man sich inzwischen fast gänzlich distanziert.

Der Künstler Jeffrey Shaw gilt als Pionier in der Umsetzung einer experimentellen Ästhetik. Seit den 1960er-Jahren ist er künstlerisch tätig. Zunächst dem Aktionismus verbunden, widmete er sich bald neuen Technologien, um neue Bilderfahrungen zu erzeugen.

In einer der Gemeinschaftsarbeiten mit Theo Botschuijver aus dem Jahre 1981, die sie als „Virtuelle Skulptur", die bezeichnet haben. Die Besucher beobachten den realen Raum mittels eines Stereoskops und sehen dort einen virtuellen schwebenden Würfel.

Für Shaw, der in seinem Werk höchst narrative Bildelemente verwendet, ist diese Überlagerung von Räumen hoch spannend. Er vertritt schon lange die Ansicht, zwischen realem und virtuellem Raum gäbe es überhaupt keinen Unterschied mehr, beide würden vom Betrachter als Wirklichkeit wahrgenommen. Die Scheinbewegung sei damit gleichwertig einer „realen" Bewegung (Vgl. Klotz 1997: 100 f.). Im Augenblick sieht er sich unter Verwendung von VR-Brillen fast schon imstande, perfekte immersive Räume zu erschaffen.

1986 produzierte Peter Weibel „Die Gesänge des Pluriversum", ein 60 Minuten langes Video ohne Ton, welches das Ziel hatte, das Potenzial der Digitalität vorzuführen. Weibel verstand dieses Video als eine Plastik, jedoch nicht mit den klassischen Materialien, sondern aus einem relativ substanzlosen Medium.

> Diese relative und veränderbare Größe der Dinge im Bild selbst, die ich Skalierung nenne, ermöglicht es, die Objekte der Welt beliebig zu verkleinern und zu vergrößern: als frei flottierende Zeichen des Raums kann ich sodann diese Objekte beliebig verschieben und in

---

6 Vgl. http://dada.compart-bremen.de/item/exhibition/172 (update: 10.12.2017)

eine neue Art von Mikro- bzw. Makro-Architektur verwandeln. Alle Objekte werden frei verfügbar, in ihrer Größe veränderbar und in jeder Position einsetzbar. Die Elemente der Landschaft und der Stadt werden zu Mikrochips des Raumes. (Weibel 1986: 73)

Weibel stellt hier die Frage nach Wirklichkeit in der Virtualität. Er wählt unter anderem das markante Motiv „The Truth Table" und führt in diesem Video eine rein mathematische Erscheinung vor, und doch erkennt unser Gesichtssinn die Abbildung eines Tisches, der aber einen höchst variablen Charakter aufweist.

Abb. 9: Peter Weibel, The Truth Table (Videostill aus *Gesänge des Pluriversums*), 1986 (Foto: Archiv Peter Weibel)

Abb. 10: Peter Weibel, Origin of Noise, Live-Multimediaperformance, 2013 (Foto: Archiv Peter Weibel)

In einer Szene des 3D-Rausch-Konzertt Live-Multimediaperformance „Origin of Noise" von 2013 zeigt Peter Weibel in Zusammenarbeit mit dem ZKM (Karlruhe) schließlich, wie er mithilfe eines realen, von der Decke hängenden Seils farbige Lichtgestalten und Töne (Rauschen) komponiert, die simultan auf der Bühne visualisiert und hörbar werden.[7]

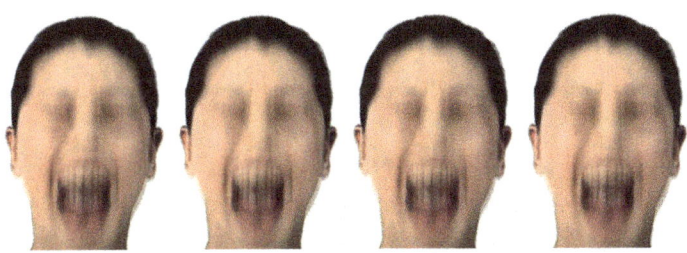

Abb. 11: Kurt Hentschläger / Ulf langheinrich, MODEL 5, 1994 (Foto: @ GRANULAR SYNTHESIS – Kurt Hentschläger & Ulf Langheinrich)

Die Arbeit Modell 5 der beiden Medienkünstlern Kurt Hentschläger und Ulf Langheinrich ist wohl ihre bekannteste gemeinsame multimediale Installation und zugleich Performance. Die Arbeit ist 1994 entstanden. Der menschliche Körper und die Sinneswahrnehmungen stehen im Vordergrund. Die Projektionen zeigen Verzerrungen und eine Unschärfe der Bilder, die bewusst durch optische Störungen erzeugt werden. Mit experimenteller Ästhetik wird hier die menschliche Wahrnehmungsfähigkeit an eine Grenze herangeführt. Der Betrachter wird damit faktisch seiner Sinne „beraubt".[8]

Hentschläger bezeichnet seine Installationen selbst als „viszeral und immersiv" (vgl. Hentschläger 2004).

Die Medienkünstlerin Ruth Schnell beschäftigt sich seit 2003 intensiv mit der Darstellung des Nachbildes.[9] In einen monochromen, mit mehreren transluzenten Epoxydharz-Schichten hergestellten Bildträger aus MDF-Platten ist vertikal ein Leuchtbalken, bestehend aus 32 Leuchtdioden, versenkt. Auf dem LED-Leuchtstab wurden Wortsammlungen oder Sätze zu einem bestimmten Thema,

---

7 Vgl. Die Uraufführung fand im Rahmen des Donaufestival Krems, am 25. April 2013 statt. https://www.youtube.com/watch?v=MIswE84Tk4o (update 10. 12. 2017)
8 Vgl. https://www.youtube.com/watch?v=micWnrTNNjo (update, 10. 12. 2017)
9 Vgl. http://www.ruthschnell.org/ (update, 10. 12. 2017)

beispielsweise über Wahrnehmungsmuster, Zeit, Arbeit oder Geschlechterdifferenzen programmiert. Das Werk entsteht erst dann, wenn der Beobachter beim Vorbeigehen durch das plötzliches Aufblitzen in der Luft schwebend einzelne Wörter oder kurze Sätze wahrnehmen kann.

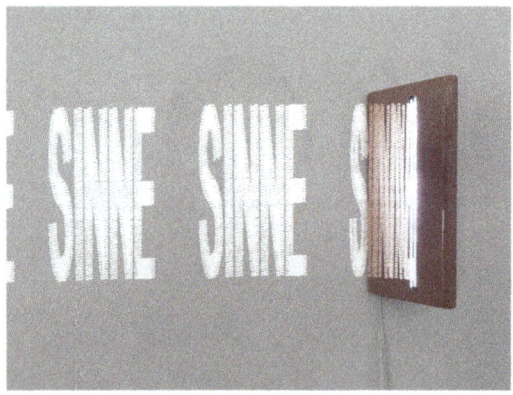

Abb. 12: Ruth Schnell, Floating Signs, 2005 (Archiv Ruth Schnell; Foto: Peter Kainz)

Mit dieser Arbeit wird uns das visuelle Nachbild, dessen wir uns ja an sich nie bewusst werden, eindrücklich erkenntlich gemacht.

Die Künstlerin Tamiko Thiel arbeitet seit einigen Jahren mit Augmented Reality im öffentlichen Raum. „Biomer Skelters – A bio-sensing crowd-sourced augmented reality public artwork" von 2013/14 hat sie gemeinsam mit dem New Yorker Künstler Willi Pappenheimer produziert. Über eine Smartphone-App wird der Herzschlag eines Besuchers gemessen, der durch die Stadt spaziert. Seine aktuellen Herzschlag-Daten werden auf ein elektronisches Tablet übertragen. Diese biometrischen Daten generieren eine exotische virtuelle Pflanzenwelt, die über das live übertragende Stadtbild erscheint.[10]

„Brush the Sky" von 2015/16 ist eine Gemeinschaftsarbeit mit der japanisch/amerikanischen Künstlerin Midori Kono Thiel, Tamikos Mutter. Hier verschmelzen die alten Schriftzeichen der Kunst der Kalligraphie (Midori Kono Thiel) mit der Technologie des 21. Jahrhunderts (Tamiko Thiel). Die aus Japan eingewanderte Familie der beiden Künstlerinnen lebt in vierter Generation in den USA. Die Familiengeschichte in Seattle wird mit Unterstützung von Augmented Reality in ein sinnliches Erlebnis transformiert.

---

10 Vgl. http://biomerskelters.com/video.html (update 10.12. 2017)

Abb. 13: Midori Kono Thiel / Tamiko Thiel, Brush the Sky, 2015/16 (Foto: Archiv Tamiko Thiel)

Das Beispiel „Brush the Sky" erinnert an die am Anfang zitierte Frage Wittgensteins. – Ich wüsste nur zu gerne, wie Wittgenstein diese Frage im Kontext der heutigen Technologie sehen würde.

Konklusion

Die weiterführende Forschung zu Scheinbewegungen, die im 19. Jahrhundert ihren Anfang nahm, prägt heute unseren Alltag. Virtuelle Environments – künstlich erzeugte bewegte Bilder – sind allgegenwärtig geworden.

Die Definitionen von Scheinbewegungen im 19. Jahrhundert bezeichneten solche Erscheinungen klar als optischen Betrug.

Diese vormals negative Einstellung gegenüber virtuellen Erscheinungen ist heute kaum mehr nachvollziehbar. Virtuelle Bilder bestimmen längst unsere Realität, und unsere heutigen Wirklichkeiten werden mittels Virtualität vermittelt. Die Grenzziehungen zwischen realen Bildern und dem sogenannten „Schein" gestalten sich zunehmend schwieriger.

Die Grundlagen für das Verständnis der sinnlichen Wahrnehmungen in unserer Welt bzw. unser Bewusstsein für die gegenwärtige Realität verdanken wir vor allem den Erkenntnissen der Wissensgeschichte.

Literatur

Benussi, Vittorio (1912): „Stroboskopische Scheinbewegung und geometrisch-optische Gestalttäuschungen". In: *Archiv für die gesamte Psychologie*, Bd. 24, pp. 31–62.
Boudewijnse, Geert-Jan (2012): „Gestalt theory and Bauhaus – A Correspondence". In: *Gestalt Theory*, No. 1, Vol. 34, pp. 81–98.
Brown, Jason W. (2007): *Time, Will, and Mental Process*, New York, Wien: Springer.
Brücke, Ernst W. (1864): „Über den Nutzeffect intermittierender Netzhautreizungen". In: *Sitzungsberichte der Kaiserlichen Akademie der Wissenschaften*, Math.-Naturwissenschaftliche Classe, Bd. 49, Abt.II., pp. 128–153.
Daniels, Dieter (1992): *Duchamp und die andern. Ein Modellfall einer künstlerischen Wirkungsgeschichte*, Köln.
Exner, Siegmund (1875): „Experimentelle Untersuchung der einfachsten psychischen Processe: III. Abhandlung, Der persönlichen Gleichung zweiter Theil". In: *Archiv für die gesammte Physiologie des Menschen und der Thiere*, pp. 403–432.
Fechner, Theodor G. (1838): „Ueber eine Scheibe zur Erzeugung subjectiver Farben". In: *Annalen der Physik und Chemie*, Bd. 45, pp. 227–232.
Goethe, Johann Wolfgang (1819): „Das Sehen in subjektiver Hinsicht". In: Beutler, Ernst (Ed.), *Briefe und Gespräche, Gedenkausgabe der Werke*, Bd. 16, Zürich, Artemis, pp. 844–856.
Hentschläger, Kurt, Langheinrich, Ulf (2004): *Immersive works, Granular Synthesis*. Ostfildern: Hatje Cantz.
Herz, Marcus (1791): *Versuch über den Schwindel*, Berlin, Voss.
Jerusalem, Wilhelm (1919): *Einleitung in die Philosophie*, Wien, Leipzig: Braunmüller
Julesz, Béla (1964): „Binocular Depth Perception without Familiarity Cues". In: *Science*, Vol. 145, No. 3630, pp. 356–362
Jurin, James (1738): „Essay upon distinct and indistinct vision". In: Smith, Robert (Eds..), *Compleat System of Opticks*, Cambridge (printed for the Author), Vol. 2, pp. 115–171.
Klotz, Heinrich (Hg.), Jeffrey Shaw (1997): *Eine Gebrauchsanweisung. Vom Expanded Chinema zur Virtuellen Realität*, Katalog, Ostfildern: Cantz.
Kostelanetz, Richard (1968): *The Theater of Mixed-Means. An Introduction to Happenings, Kinetic Environments and Other Mixed-Means Presentations*. New York: The Dial Press.
Ladewig, Rebekka (2011): „Augenschwindel. Nachbilder und die Experimentalisierung des Schwindels um 1800". In: Busch, Werner, Meister, Carolin (Eds..): *Nachbilder. Das Gedächtnis des Auges in Kunst und Wissenschaft*, Zürich: Diaphanes, pp. 107–126.
Linden, David (1999): *Spatial analysis in the human cerebral cortex: Behavioural and functional magnetic resonance studies of spatial transformations in visual perception and imagery* (= Dissertation Max Planck Institut), Frankfurt/M.
Mach, Ernst (1865): „Über die Wirkung der räumlichen Vertheilung des Lichtreizes auf die Netzhaut". In: *Sitzungsberichte der Kaiserlichen Akademie der Wissenschaften*, Math.-Naturwissenschaftliche Classe, Bd. 52, Abt. II., pp. 303–322.
Mach Ernst (1896): „Die ökonomische Natur der physikalischen Forschung". In: ders., *Populär wissenschaftliche Vorlesungen*, Leipzig, Bath 1896, pp. 203–230.
Oppel, Johann, J. (1856): „Neue Beobachtungen und Versuche über eine eigenthümliche, noch wenig bekannte Reactionsthätigkeit des menschlichen Auges". In: *Annalen der Physik und Chemie*, 1856, pp. 540–561.

Plateau, Joseph (1835): „Betrachtungen über ein von Hrn. Talbot vorgeschlagenes photometrisches Princip. In: *Annalen der Physik und Chemie*, Bd. 35, pp. 457–470.

Plateau, Joseph (1850): „Dritte Notiz über neue sonderbare Anwendungen des Verweilens der Eindrücke auf die Netzhaut". In: *Annalen der Physik und Chemie*, Bd. 80, pp. 150–157.

Poggendorff, Johann C. (1834): „Stroboskopische Scheiben, Phänakistikop, Phantasmaskop". In: *Annalen der Physik und Chemie*, Bd. 32, pp. 636–649.

Porterfield, William (1759): *A Treatise on the Eye, the Manner and Phenomena of Vision*. Vol. 2, Edinburgh: Hamilton and Balfour.

Purkinje, Jan E. (1823): *Abhandlung über die physiologische Untersuchung des Sehorgans und des Hautsystems*. Halle: Acta Historica Leopoldina.

Roget, Mark Peter (1825): „Explanation of an optical Deception in the Appeerance oft he Spokes of Wheel in seen through vertical Apertures". In: *Annals of Philosophy,* Vol. 10, pp. 107–112.

Schuler, Romana K. (2016): *Seeing Motion. A history of Visual Perception in Art and Science*. Berlin, Boston: De Gruyter.

Spering, Meriam (2016): „The Interaction between Seeing and Moving: Eye Movements as a Window to the Mind?". In: Gsöllpointer, K., Schnell, R., Schuler

Talbot, William H. F. (1834): „Experiments of Light". In: *The London and Edinburgh Philosophical Magazine and Journal of Science*, Third Series, Vol. 5, Nr. 29, pp. 321–334.

Wade, Nicholas J. (1998): *A Natural History of Vision*. Cambridge, London: MIT Press, 1998.

Weibel, Peter (1986): „Gesänge des Plurisversum". In: *Computerkulturtage Linz, ORF-Videonale 86*, Ars Electronica, Linz: Druck und Verlagsanstalt Gutenberg, pp. 73–77.

Wells, William Charles (1792): An Essay upon Single Vision with Two Eyes together with Experiments and Observations on Several Subjects in Optics. London: T. Cadell

Wertheimer, Max (1912): „Experimentelle Studien über das Sehen von Bewegung". In: *Zeitschrift für Psychologie*, pp. 161–265.

Ulrich Arnswald
Zur Analogie von Wittgensteins Konzept des Aspektwechsels und der wissenschaftlichen Metapher als Vehikel der Innovation

Zusammenfassung: Zwischen Wittgensteins Konzept des Aspektwechsels und innovativen Metaphern in den Naturwissenschaften gibt es eine erstaunliche Analogie, die das Selbstverständnis der Naturwissenschaften als „exakte Wissenschaften" partiell infrage stellt. „Innovative Metaphern" dienen nämlich den Naturwissenschaften als Vehikel der Innovation, denn ohne diese könnte kaum erfolgreich eine konzeptuelle Idee von einem wissenschaftlichen Paradigma auf ein anderes übertragen werden. Dabei eignet sich die Kombination von Bildfeld und Sprache besonders für die Erklärung und Übermittlung von Theorien. Die konzeptuelle Innovation, die letztlich Paradigmenwechsel auch in den Naturwissenschaften einleitet, ist durchaus das Verdienst der eingesetzten, konzeptuellerweiterten Metapher – auch wenn diese noch nicht zwangsläufig originäre, wissenschaftliche Innovationen nach sich ziehen muss. Der Beitrag zeichnet diesen Vorgang nach.

Schlüsselwörter: Metapher, Aspektwechsel, Innovation, Wittgenstein, Wissenschaft

Im 19. Jahrhundert kategorisierte man die Metapher als nicht-rationale und unwissenschaftliche Form der Rede (vgl. Goatly 1997: 1). Seit der Wissenschaftstheorie-Debatte der ausgehenden 1950er Jahre hat aber eine Neueinstufung des linguistischen Status von Metaphern und ihrer Leistungen im Rahmen wissenschaftlicher Denkmodelle eingesetzt,[1] die das Selbstverständnis der Naturwissen-

---

[1] Hierzu schreiben Lutz Danneberg, Andreas Graeser und Klaus Petrus affirmierend: „Ermuntert durch die in den sechziger Jahren von Thomas S. Kuhn und anderen unternommenen Versuche, Wissenschaftstheorie mit Wissenschaftsgeschichte zu verbinden, mehren sich die einschlägigen Untersuchungen: zum einen *historische* Fallstudien, die unter wissenschaftstheoretischen Fragestellungen die Genese von Theorien im Hinblick auf die Rolle untersuchen, die Metaphern, Analogien und Modelle hierbei spielen; zum anderen *theoretische* Studien, die systematische Aspekte ihrer Verwendung bei der Ausbildung, aber auch Weiterentwicklung wissenschaftlicher Theorien analysieren." (Danneberg/Graeser/Petrus 1995: 16).

schaften als „exakte Wissenschaften" insofern erschüttern, dass diese innovativen Metaphern einen eigenen Status sogar in der Theoriebildung ihrer Fächer einräumen müssen.[2]

Willard Van Orman Quine erklärt den Bedarf der Wissenschaften, insbesondere auch der Naturwissenschaften, an Veränderung mittels Metaphern aufgrund der Notwendigkeit dieser Wissenschaften nach Umgestaltung ihres eigenen Feldes:

> Die philosophischen Grenzen der Wissenschaft entlang können wir auf Gründe stoßen, grundlegende Begriffsstrukturen in Frage zu stellen und tastend nach Möglichkeiten ihrer Umgestaltung zu suchen. Alte Ausdrucksweisen können uns dabei nicht helfen, und zunächst kann nur die Metapher die neue Ordnung umreißen. (Quine 1991: 227)

Innovative Metaphern dienen nämlich den Naturwissenschaften als Vehikel der Innovation, denn ohne diese könnte kaum erfolgreich eine konzeptuelle Idee von einem wissenschaftlichen Paradigma auf ein anderes übertragen werden. Zugleich mussten die so genannten „exakten Wissenschaften" auch im Hinblick auf die Möglichkeit der Exaktheit ihrer Aussagen insoweit Defizite einräumen, dass auch ihr wissenschaftlicher Diskurs nicht jenseits jeglicher Alltagssprache vonstattengehen kann.[3] Der Physiker Carl Friedrich von Weizsäcker hat diese Einsicht wie folgt formuliert:

---

2 Manche Beispiele für Metaphern in den Naturwissenschaften basieren allerdings auf relativ einfachen Analogien. Z. B. wird die DNA oftmals mit einem Alphabet verglichen: „Der genetische Code entspricht einem Wörterbuch, das die Vier-Buchstaben-Sprache des Erbmaterials zu der Zwanzig-Buchstaben-Sprache des Proteins, der Vollzugssprache, in Verbindung setzt. Alle Lebewesen benutzen zur Beförderung der Erbinformation ein und dieselbe Vier-Buchstaben-Sprache. Alle benutzen ein und dieselbe Zwanzig-Buchstaben-Sprache für den Aufbau ihrer Proteine, der Werkzeugmaschinen der lebenden Zelle." (Göpfert 1997: 76) Gerne werden auch Metaphern wie z. B. der Treibhauseffekt herangezogen, die Prozesse in den Naturwissenschaften nur verständlich machen sollen: „Das Kohlendioxid in der Atmosphäre wirkt wie eine unsichtbare Folie, wie eine Glasscheibe bei einem Gewächshaus. Jeder kennt ja die Wirkung einer Glasscheibe sehr gut. Man braucht nur an das in der Sonne parkende Auto zu denken. Glas läßt die Sonnenstrahlung als Licht sehr gut durch, die im Innern des Autos oder eines Gewächshauses entstehende Wärme aber hält es gefangen. Der berühmte Treibhauseffekt." (ebd.) Solche Metaphern sind erklärend, aber nicht innovativ. Um eine innovative Metapher zu sein, bedarf es eines plötzlichen Zündens eines Funkens in Form eines Aspektwechsels, der eine gänzlich neue Sichtweise auf das Forschungsfeld begründet.

3 Vgl. hierzu Whorf 1997: 46: „Die langen heroischen Bemühungen der Naturwissenschaften, strenge Tatsachenwissenschaft zu sein, haben sie nun endlich mit den ganz unvermuteten Tatsachen der sprachlichen Struktur in Verwicklung gebracht. Die ältere klassische Naturwissenschaft hat diese Tatsachen niemals als solche anerkannt, untersucht oder gar verstanden. Eben

> Die sog. exakte Wissenschaft kann niemals und unter keinen Umständen die Anknüpfung an das, was man die natürliche Sprache oder die Umgangssprache nennt, entbehren. Es handelt sich stets nur um einen Prozeß, der vielleicht sehr weit getriebenen Umgestaltung derjenigen Sprache, die wir immer schon sprechen und verstehen. Und eben deshalb ist die Vorstellung einer vollkommen exakten Sprache zumindest für solche Wissenschaften, die sich, wie man sich ausdrückt, mit realen Dingen beschäftigen, eine reine Fiktion. (von Weizsäcker 1971: 65)

Bereits diese beiden zwischenzeitlich notwendig gewordenen Korrekturen – letztere Einsicht kann in ähnlicher Form auch vorlaufend dem *Tractatus Logico-philosophicus* des Philosophen Ludwig Wittgenstein zugeschrieben werden – stellen heutzutage das Selbstverständnis der Naturwissenschaften als „exakte Wissenschaften" partiell infrage und zwingen diese zu einer wesentlich stärkeren alltagsweltlichen Rückbindung ihrer Fächer an die Sprach- und Darstellungsformen der geisteswissenschaftlichen Fächer als vielen Naturwissenschaftler bewusst ist. Es führt nämlich kein Weg an der Einsicht vorbei, dass auch naturwissenschaftliche Paradigmenwechsel der Einführung von Metaphern bedürfen und in keiner Weise rationaler oder exakter als die Verwendung von Metaphern im Alltagsleben sind.[4]

---

deshalb kamen sie unbemerkt durch die Hintertür in ihr Gebäude und wurden für das Wesen der Vernunft selbst gehalten."
4 Eigentlich müsste den Naturwissenschaften diese Erkenntnis durchaus vertraut sein, da z. B. die Elektrizitätslehre schon immer umfänglich mit metaphorischen Konzepten wie dem „Fluss/Fließen" bzw. „Strom/Strömung" im Sinne Elektrizität = Flüssigkeit oder der „Entladung" bzw. dem „Widerstand" im Sinne Elektrizität = Körper operierte, die unmittelbar der Alltagssprache entlehnt waren. Selbst elektrische Phänomene wurden mit durchschlagenden metaphorischen Begriffen wie z. B. „Stromschlag" oder „Lichtbogen" ausgedrückt. Ähnlich stellt es sich mit den anderen Fachsprachen der „exakten Wissenschaften" dar, die man so gerne als „Wissenschaftssprachen" bezeichnet, obwohl die Beschreibung ihrer Phänomene auf die Alltagssprache rekurriert. Man schaue sich z. B. nur Charles Darwins' Metapher des „Kampfs um's Dasein" bzw. „Existenzkampf" in *On the Origin of Species* (1859); dtsch.: *Über die Entstehung der Arten* (1860), als ein weithin bekannten Klassiker des Faches der Biologie an. Für die Physik hat Hanna Pulaczewska umfangreich in ihrem Buch *Aspects of Metaphor in Physics* den weithin stattfindenden Rückgriff auf Metaphern im Fach Physik untersucht und dokumentiert (vgl. Pulaczewska 1999).

1 Wittgensteins Aspektwechsel als Beschreibung der konzeptuellen Wechselwirkung einer Metapherübertragung

In den Naturwissenschaften wird gerne übersehen, dass naturwissenschaftliche Paradigmenwechsel der Einführung von Metaphern benötigen. Die Metapher-Theorie der Innovation sieht in figurativen Vergleichen die eigentliche Quelle konzeptueller Innovationen. Für Karin Knorr-Cetina werden durch

> eine Metapher [...] zwei Phänomene, die normalerweise nicht miteinander assoziiert sind, plötzlich in irgendeiner Art von Übereinstimmung gesehen. Durch diese halberahnte Ähnlichkeit zwischen bisher nicht miteinander verbundenen Ideen können die mit jedem dieser Objekte verbundenen Wissens- und Glaubenssysteme wechselseitig zum Tragen gebracht werden und dadurch eine kreative Erweiterung des Wissens bewirken. (Knorr-Cetina 1991: 94)

Diese konzeptuelle Wechselwirkung macht den Kern der Metapher-Theorie der Innovation aus, denn der Vergleich bezieht sich nicht nur auf das verglichene Bild des neu zu beschreibenden Phänomens, sondern verändert auch das Bild des zum Vergleich hinzugezogenen Objekts. Im Falle des erstmaligen Erkennens können wir nicht zwischen zwei konzeptuellen Systemen unterscheiden, denn das erstmalige Erkennen umfasst immer das *Sehen als*, also das Sehen von etwas als etwas. Dieses *Sehen als* ist ein Konzept, das auf Wittgensteins Überlegungen im zweiten Teil der *Philosophischen Untersuchungen* zurückgeht. Dort führt er einen kategorischen Unterschied zwischen zwei Objekten des Sehens ein: Ersteres besteht aus dem Sehen auf die Frage „Was siehst du dort?", die man mit „Ich sehe *dies*" beantworten kann, während die letztere Art des Sehens mit der Antwort „Ich sehe eine Ähnlichkeit in diesen beiden Gesichtern" verbunden ist (PU 1984: xi 518).

Bei der zweiten Art des Sehens waren die beiden Gesichter zwar sowohl dem Fragenden als auch dem Antwortenden sichtbar, aber möglicherweise *sah* der eine etwas anderes in ihnen als der andere – nämlich besagte Ähnlichkeit in den Gesichtszügen. Diesen Vorgang benennt Wittgenstein als „das Bemerken eines Aspekts", den er so beschreibt:

> Ich betrachte ein Gesicht, auf einmal bemerke ich seine Ähnlichkeit mit einem anderen. Ich *sehe*, daß es sich nicht geändert hat; und sehe es doch anders. Diese Erfahrung nenne ich ‚das Bemerken eines Aspekts'. (PU 1984: xi 518)

Noch klarer wird dieser Vorgang am Beispiel des Wiedererkennens eines alten Bekannten. Plötzlich erkennt man im veränderten Gesicht die Züge des früheren Gesichts. Wittgenstein schildert dies:

> Ich treffe Einen, den ich jahrelang nicht gesehen habe; ich sehe ihn deutlich, erkenne ihn aber nicht. Plötzlich erkenne ich ihn, sehe in seinem veränderten Gesicht sein früheres. Ich glaube, ich würde ihn jetzt anders porträtieren, wenn ich malen könnte. (PU 1984: xi 525)

Was nun den Vorgang zu einem Aspektwechsel, zu einer Änderung der Wahrnehmung im Sinne Wittgensteins macht, lässt sich auf zwei Momente zurückführen: erstens die Plötzlichkeit des anderen Sehens, und zweitens die *Gleichzeitigkeit* des Sehens des betrachteten Objekts im Sinne unveränderter und zugleich veränderter Wahrnehmung. Für Wittgenstein gilt somit: „Der Ausdruck des Aspektwechsels ist der Ausdruck einer *neuen* Wahrnehmung, zugleich mit dem Ausdruck der unveränderten Wahrnehmung." (PU 1984: xi 522–523)

Im Aspektwechsel liegt ein „Aufleuchten eines Aspekts" im Gegensatz zum „stetigen Sehen" eines Aspekts bei dem kein Aspektwechsel erfolgt. Obwohl der Gegenstand derselbe ist, wird er nun anders wahrgenommen, so als hätte er sich verändert. Daraus resultiert auch das Gefühl, „jemanden jetzt anders porträtieren zu wollen", obwohl sich objektiv der Gegenstand für die Augen des Betrachters nicht geändert hat. Das bekannteste Beispiel für dieses Phänomen der Doppeldeutigkeit eines Gegenstandes (*optical illusion*) ist der „H-E-Kopf" von Joseph Jastrow, den man sowohl als Hasen- als auch als Entenkopf sehen kann, und den Wittgenstein aus Jastrows Buch *Fact and Fable in Psychology* entnommen und in zeichnerisch vereinfachter Form als Beispiel eingeführt hat (vgl. PU 1984: xi 519–524):

Abb. 1: Wittgensteins „Hasen-Entenkopf" (Ludwig Wittgenstein (1984) *Philosophische Untersuchungen*, Frankfurt am Main: Suhrkamp, S. 520)

Auch wenn uns bewusst sein mag, dass nie klar ist wie ein anderer ein Bild erkennt, macht es wenig Sinn, ihn zu fragen „Was siehst du da?" – zumindest nicht, wenn man davon ausgeht, dass der Gegenstand eindeutig ist. Wittgenstein verweist auf die grundsätzliche Unsinnigkeit einer mit „als" formulierten Antwort:

> Zu sagen ‚Ich sehe das jetzt als...', hätte für mich so wenig Sinn gehabt, als beim Anblick von Messer und Gabel zu sagen: ‚Ich sehe das jetzt als Messer und Gabel'. Man würde diese Äußerung nicht verstehen. – Ebensowenig wie diese: ‚Das ist jetzt für mich eine Gabel', oder ‚Das kann auch eine Gabel sein'. (PU 1984: xi 521)

Eine Verwendungsweise von „sehen" in Verbindung mit „als" für eindeutig eingeschätzte Gegenstände ist sinnlos. Nur wenn der Betrachter sich der Mehrdeutigkeit eines Gegenstandes bewusst wird, drückt er dies im „als" aus, um die mögliche oder tatsächliche Alternative eines anderen Sehens zu signalisieren. Das Sich-Bewusstmachen, der durch das „als" signalisierten Mehrdeutigkeit, erlaubt dem Dialogpartner den betreffenden Gegenstand sowie die Folgen einer solch mehrdeutigen Ausdrucksweise zu analysieren. Er kann sich daher mit Wittgenstein fragen: „Was teilt mir Einer mit, der sagt ‚Ich sehe es jetzt als...'? Welche Folgen hat diese Mitteilung? Was kann ich mit ihr anfangen?" (PU 1984: xi 533)

Die individuelle Einstellung zum Gesehenen teilt daher einen weiteren Aspekt des *Sehen als* mit – nämlich den der eigenen Perspektive. Im Sprachspiel des *Sehen als* kommt immer eine individuelle Sichtweise zum Ausdruck, die neben der Bewusstheit über die Deutbarkeit des Gegenstandes als mehrdeutigen, immer auch die andere alternative Sichtweise in Form der neutralen oder allgemeinen Redensweise „Man kann das so oder so sehen", „Das kann man als ..." und somit implizit „oder auch als..." sehen einbezieht. „Und darum", schreibt Wittgenstein, „erscheint das Aufleuchten des Aspekts halb Seherlebnis, halb ein Denken" (PU 1984: xi 525) und in einer späteren Stelle heißt es noch deutlicher: „Der Begriff des Aspekts ist dem Begriff der Vorstellung verwandt." (PU 1984: xi 551) Und so versucht nach Wittgenstein ein jeder Betrachter seinen gesehenen Aspekt, seine Vorstellung als eine Alternative des *Sehen als* zu manifestieren, indem er zugleich auf die Möglichkeit anderer Sichtweisen verweist.

Aus dem gemeinsamen Gegenstand lässt sich grundsätzlich keine Sichtweise deduktiv verbindlich ableiten. Die verschiedenen Sichtweisen sind sich vielmehr einander auf ungreifbare Weise ähnlich. Wittgenstein prägt für diese Ähnlichkeiten das charakteristische Wort der „Familienähnlichkeiten" (PU 1984: 67), denn die verschiedenen Ähnlichkeiten kreuzen und vermischen sich wie bei den Angehörigen einer Familie, ohne dass ein spezifisches Kriterium dieser Ähnlichkeit *a priori* definierbar ist.⁵ Wörtlich: „Und das Ergebnis dieser Betrachtung lautet nun: Wir sehen ein kompliziertes Netz von Ähnlichkeiten, die einander übergreifen und kreuzen. Ähnlichkeiten im Großen und Kleinen." (PU 1984: 66)

Dieses „lückenlose Übergreifen der Fasern" (PU 1984: 67) oder, wenn man so will, der „rote Faden", der die Familie zusammenhält, erfüllt eine wichtige Verbindungsrolle und Mittlerfunktion für das *Sehen als*, das sich in der Spannung zwischen dem wörtlichen und metaphorischen Sinn einer lebendigen Metapher widerspiegelt (vgl. Draaisma 1999: 24). Denn *x* als *y* zu sehen, bedeutet immer auch anzuerkennen, dass *x* nicht *y* ist. Das metaphorische „ist" bleibt zwangsläufig immer mehrdeutig, denn das „ist nicht" ist zugleich im „als" ausgedrückt. Gerade Wittgensteins *Sehen als* ist sich dieser Mehrdeutigkeit bewusst. Das *Sehen als* verbindet Bildlichkeit und Ähnlichkeit und verweist auf eine bestimmte Perspektive, die Zugang zur Sichtweise eines Anderen erlaubt.

2 Die neue Aspekte eröffnende Sichtweise der Metapher

Metaphern erlauben durch Abweichung und Regelverletzung eine ähnlich enthüllende und neue Aspekte eröffnende Sichtweise zu produzieren. Sie verweisen andere Menschen auf eine neue bzw. andere Sicht der Dinge:⁶

> Metaphern als kognitive Instrumente sind daher auch für neue epistemische Sichtweisen konstitutiv: Sie ermöglichen relevantes Wissen. Dabei handelt es sich immer um ein perspektivisches Wissen – vermittelt durch einen ganz bestimmten ‚Filter'. (Hänseler 2005: 7)

Durch Metaphern kann man etwas als etwas anderes sehen, kann ein Aspektwechsel stattfinden.⁷ Sie liefern nicht nur ihre Perspektive, sondern immer auch

---

5 Wittgenstein hebelt mit seinem Begriff der „Familienähnlichkeit" die Idee terminologischer Stringenz, die noch vom Mythos literaler Eigentlichkeit lebte, „metaphorisch" aus (vgl. Müller-Richter 1998).
6 Die Wortbedeutung im Sinne der Determinationsbestimmung wird dementsprechend gerne als „die eigentliche Rede" verstanden, während die Metapher „die uneigentliche Rede" genannt wird und gegen die Eigentlichkeit der ursprünglichen Wortbedeutung angeht.
7 Hier teile ich ausdrücklich die Meinung von Harald Weinrich, der zu Gunsten der Bildhaftigkeit festhält: „Für unser Sprachbewußtsein, insbesondere für das Evidenzerlebnis gegenüber einer Metapher, ist es sehr wesentlich, ob eine Metapher durch ein profiliertes Bildfeld gestützt wird oder nicht." (Weinrich 1967: 13)

eine Anleitung wie man etwas sehen soll. Die Metapher ist insofern eine Repräsentation einer individuellen Leitvorstellung, also Ausdruck der persönlichen Sichtweise des Sprechers. Fritz Mauthner weist hierauf explizit hin:

> Aus dem Weltbilde des Einzelnen ergibt sich die Möglichkeit, Ähnlichkeiten zu sehen und die Vergleichung kurz und schlagend durch eine Metapher auszudrücken. Der Hörer kann die Metapher des Redenden nur verstehen, wenn eine gleiche Seelensituation, ein gleiches Weltbild ihn befähigt, die angeregte Vergleichung ebenfalls vorzunehmen. (Mauthner 1913: 240)

Wittgensteins Interesse am Aspektwechsel ist in seiner Plötzlichkeit begründet. Wir nehmen etwas wahr, und plötzlich nehmen wir etwas ganz anders wahr, obwohl sich im Wahrgenommenen grundsätzlich nichts geändert hat. Die Bedeutung ist urplötzlich eine andere. Da Aspektwechsel aber nicht ständig anstehen, empfinden wir sie als überraschend und erstaunlich. Würden permanent Aspektwechsel stattfinden, könnten wir uns im Übrigen nicht miteinander sprachlich austauschen, da wir in diesem Fall ständig damit beschäftigt wären, die Bedeutungen unserer Wahrnehmungen festzulegen.

Metaphern überraschen uns deshalb, weil sie mit dem Wechselspiel von Normalität und Abweichung verbunden sind. Harald Weinrich beschreibt den Vorgang wie folgt:

> Auch für die Metapher erhalten wir zwei Werte, den Bedeutungswert und einen von ihm abweichenden Meinungswert, der durch den Kontext bestimmt ist. Dieser weicht freilich, das haben wir schon unter dem Gesichtspunkt der Konterdetermination besprochen, in überraschender Weise vom Bedeutungswert ab. Das gibt der Metapher ein Plus an Spannung und ein *nescio quid* an Witz. Darum lieben wir die Metapher. (Weinrich 1967: 10)

Die innovative Metapher fasziniert, da sie mit Hilfe eines bewussten Regelverstoßes aus dem Gewohnten ausbricht. Der Vorgang der widerstreitenden Metaphernübertragung lässt folglich Aufmerksamkeit entstehen, denn der Wechsel von Normalität zur Abweichung bzw. von der Regel zum Regelverstoß wird als ein plötzlicher wahrgenommen. Daher stellt Wittgenstein treffend fest: „Aber der Wechsel ruft ein Staunen hervor, den das Erkennen nicht hervorrief." (PU 1984: xi 528)

Das Unerwartete ist Bestandteil der Wirkung und Lebendigkeit der innovativen Metapher. Die Überraschung der Metapher liegt in der „plötzlichen Einsicht" der neuen Erkenntnis.[8] Wittgenstein nennt dies das „Aufleuchten einer Perspektive", die uns überrascht und erstaunt. In jedem Aspektwechsel liegt immer ein unkontrolliertes, irrationales Moment, denn erst „[i]m Aspektwechsel wird man sich des Aspekts *bewußt.*" (LSPP 169)

Der Aspektwechsel ist ein deutender Vorgang (vgl. Baltzer 2002), der die ursprüngliche Bedeutung der Metapher nachträglich mit verändert. Die metaphorische Aussage betont nur die Ähnlichkeit mit einem anderen Vorgang. Die dadurch entstehende Wahrnehmung schafft Verbindungen, die als besondere Fähigkeit des Sprechers, Anderen einen Aspekt *sichtbar machen zu können,* gelten kann. Daraus resultiert eine Unterscheidung zwischen dem metaphorischen Sprechen und den konzeptuellen Metaphern. Während das Sprechen wörtlich ist, ist bei der innovativen oder konzeptuellen Metapher das evozierte Konzept im Denken angesiedelt.[9] Dies deckt sich auch mit dem Fazit der Untersuchung von Lakoff und Johnson:

---

8 Der oft gemachte Vorwurf, dass Beispiele, die Metaphern „Kippfiguren" gleichsetzen, immer schon dual strukturiert seien und damit nicht hinreichend berücksichtigen würden, dass durch das Zusammenspiel von Wort und Kontext eine Vielzahl von Metaphern entstehen können, ist m. E. nicht berechtigt. Denn es ist doch immer gerade nur ein Vergleich zum „Sehen als" eines Kippbildes denkbar, da ein Individuum beim „Sehen als" nur seine individuelle Sichtweise darlegen kann, die nun mal darin besteht, dass man etwas nun plötzlich anders als zuvor sieht, aber nur in *einer anderen,* neuen Weise und nicht zugleich in *mehrfach anderer* Weise. Daher kann die neue Sichtweise nur im Singular eine neue individuelle Leitvorstellung repräsentieren, was uns überhaupt erst erlaubt, uns sprachlich hierüber miteinander zu verständigen. Insoweit erscheint mir die Bipolarität der metaphorischen Übertragung unabdingbar zu sein. Einer erneut kontextuell begründeten, asynchron stattfindenden Verschiebung der besagten Metapher tut dies keinen Abbruch.
Bezüglich der innovativen Metapher ist hierbei ebenso zu bedenken, dass eine Polyphonie der Sichtweisen jegliche Innovation *ad absurdum* führen würde, da in der Vielfalt selbige nicht länger wahrnehmbar wäre: „Denn wenn das Innovative, d.h. die modifizierte semantische oder syntaktische Regel von dem Gesamt der überschrittenen Regeln aus in endlich vielen semantischen Vergleichsoperationen erreichbar wäre, verlöre der Gedanke der Innovation jeden Witz." (Müller-Richter 1998: 14)
9 Gottfried Gabriel beschreibt einen solchen Vorgang exemplarisch: „Als Beispiel anderer Art möchte ich die Entdeckung des Benzolrings durch August Kekulé anführen. Den entscheidenden Anstoß erhielt Kekulé (nach eigener Aussage), als er sich nach angespanntem Nachdenken über die chemische Struktur des Benzols, ohne einer Lösung näher zu kommen, ermüdet vor sein flackerndes Kaminfeuer zur Ruhe setzte. Bei entspannter Kontemplation der Bewegungen der Flammen fielen Kekulé langsam die Augen zu; aber nicht ganz – auf der Schwelle zum Schlaf sah er Flammen, die züngelnd in sich selbst zurückschlugen – wie die mythische (und alchemistische!) Figur der Uroborus-Schlange, der Schlange, die sich selbst in den Schwanz beißt. Das war die Lösung: der Atombau des Benzols stellte sich ihm als ‚geschlossene Kette' dar. In der

> Wir haben dagegen festgestellt, daß die Metapher unser Alltagsleben durchdringt, und zwar nicht nur unsere Sprache, sondern auch unser Denken und Handeln. Unser alltägliches Konzeptsystem, nach dem wir sowohl denken als auch handeln, ist im Kern und grundsätzlich metaphorisch. (Lakoff/Johnson 1998: 11)

Eine Metapher ist immer wörtlich, und – falls innovativ – zugleich konzeptuell, denn eine Metapher ist naturgemäß grundlegend und somit nicht weiter reduzier- bzw. erklärbar. Metaphern sind daher bereits mit Beginn des Spracherwerbs Grundelemente unserer Sprachspiele. Im engeren Sinn kann man mit Fritz Mauthner jedem Wort eine metaphorische Bedeutung zumessen, da uns heute die Urbedeutung nicht mehr bekannt ist (vgl. Mauthner 1912: 451). Die Fähigkeit der Übertragung sprachlichen Sinns von einer Ausgangsbedeutung zu einer deduktiven, wenn auch nicht verbindlichen Verwendung ist also in gewöhnlichen Worten schon angelegt.[10]

Beschreibung dieses Erlebnisses spricht Kekulé davon, dass ihn diese Einsicht wie ein ‚Blitzstrahl' getroffen habe. Er vergisst aber nicht hinzuzufügen, dass er den ‚Rest der Nacht' damit verbrachte, ‚die Konsequenzen der *Hypothese* auszuarbeiten'. Diesen Zustand gilt es zu betonen: Analogien sind noch keine Erkenntnis, sie müssen erst auf ihre Angemessenheit überprüft werden." (Gabriel 2009: 20) Letzterer Punkt wird auch von Donald Davidson in *Was Metaphern bedeuten* (1978) hervorgehoben, wenn dieser davon spricht, dass „Sehen-als [...] nicht dasselbe wie Sehen-daß" ist (Davidson 1990: 370). Gabriel ist zumal zuzustimmen, wenn er betont, dass grenzüberschreitende Metaphernübertragungen „nicht nur zwischen den Wissenschaften, sondern auch unter Rückgriff auf Vorstellungen der Einbildungskraft erfolgen können, die uns durch Kunst oder gar Mythos vermittelt worden sind (Ebd.: 20–21).
Einen ähnlichen Hinweis auf die Bedeutung der Kunst als Inspirationsquelle für innovative Metaphern verdanke ich im Rahmen meines Vortrags auf dem 40. Internationalen Ludwig Wittgenstein Symposium in Kirchberg am Wechsel, der diesem Beitrag zugrunde liegt, der Wiener Kollegin Romana Schuler. Es scheint offenkundig irrelevant zu sein, wer – ob Philosoph, Wissenschaftler oder Künstler – es ist, der die Mitwelt zu einer neuen Metaphorik anregt.
10 Harald Weinrich betont nicht von ungefähr: „Der Kontext determiniert nämlich das Wort [...] in einer besonderen Weise, und eben dadurch entsteht die Metapher. Wort und Kontext machen zusammen die Metapher." (Weinrich 1967: 5) Der Gedanke der Simultaneität verschiedener denkbarer Aspekte, die durch eine Metapher übertragen werden, ergibt sich auch aus der Tatsache, dass die Metapher durch Wort und Kontext entsteht und somit in verschiedenen Kontexten dementsprechend verschieden aufleuchtet. Hierbei findet zwangsläufig eine Art Übertragung der Metapher in den neuen Kontext statt, die dem bildhaften plötzlichen Sehens eines Aspektwechsels – wenn auch nicht bildförmig im Sinne eines „Anschaulich-Visuellen" – „bildanalog" nahe kommen kann, wenn auch nicht muss. In diesem Sinne kann die Metapher in einem neuen Kontext zugleich den Bruch mit dem Normalverstehen des Wortes bewirken, indem sie eine bestimmte Determinationserwartung nicht länger erfüllt, so dass der Widerspruch als Konterdetermination wahrgenommen wird, was zugleich die bereits erwähnt Zweipolarität einer Metaphernübertragung begründet.

Innovative Metaphern sind dazu da, den Horizont der Sprachgemeinschaft über das Alltägliche hinaus zu vergrößern.[11] Durch ihr Verstoßen gegen konventionelle Sprachregeln sind sie regelinnovativ, wobei es zu den besonderen Befähigungen von Menschen gehört, Metaphern zu kreieren.

Inwieweit sich Wissenschaftler auf solche Regelverstöße einlassen, hängt stark von ihrem Naturell ab. Sie nehmen für die Innovation durch die Metapher in Form des „Aufleuchtens einer Perspektive" durchaus auch Verluste in Kauf, da die empirische Beschreibung zumindest dem wahrgenommenen Aspektwechsel hinterherhinkt. Quine hat dies folgendermaßen zusammengefasst:

> Das, womit wir uns begnügen, ist – wenn ich von einer dynamischen zu einer ökonomischen Metapher übergehen darf – ein Tauschhandel. Wir gewinnen, in gebührendem Rahmen, Einfachheit der Theorie, indem wir unsere Zuflucht zu Termini nehmen, die sich nur indirekt, hin und wieder und recht dürftig auf Beobachtung beziehen. Die Werte, die wir so gegeneinander austauschen – Belegwert und systematischer Wert – sind inkommensurabel. Wissenschaftler mit verschiedenen philosophischen Temperament werden unterschiedliche Bereitschaft an den Tag legen, wieviel Verwässerung des Belegmaterials für einen gegebenen systematischen Vorteil in Kauf zu nehmen ist (und umgekehrt). (Quine 1991: 47)

Das Entstehen des Neuen mittels von Metaphern ist die eigentliche Faszination, die sich im Werke Wittgensteins sowohl durch seine philosophischen Auseinandersetzungen mit dem Aspektwechsel als auch der großzügigen Verwendung von Metaphern als Ausdrucksmittel seiner Philosophie niederschlägt.

3 Innovation durch Übertragen einer konzeptuellen Idee mittels einer Metapher

Unter einer „Begriffserweiterung" versteht man dann die Bedeutungsverschiebung einer Metapher, wenn der neue Begriff zum alten in einer engen Relation

---

[11] In einer gewissen Weise ist die nicht besonders neu und überraschend, wenn man zurate zieht, dass es ausgerechnet in der Theologie sprichwörtlich überhaupt nie einen anderen Weg gab, um über den Inhalt des Faches einen Diskurs zu führen: „Das Erschließen *per analogiam*, das übertragende Sprechen über einen Gegenstand, der aus prinzipiellen Gründen selber als der (direkten) Darstellung nicht zugänglich gilt, ist seit alters Thema der Gotteserkenntnis in der Theologie oder – wie es auch heißt – des Redens über Gott." (Danneberg/Graeser/Petrus 1995: 16)

der semantischen Einbettung steht. Es entsteht eine Art *Ko-Referentialität* zwischen dem alten und dem neuen Begriff. Die ursprüngliche Metapher dient als eine Art von Paradigma, die auf die neue, gegenwärtige Situation angewendet wird. Die gegenwärtige Situation soll mit derjenigen analog sein, von der wir die Interpretation der gegenwärtigen Situation ableiten.[12] Die neue Situation mit der erweiterten Metapher wird in Bezug zur alten Metapher gesetzt, bevor die Begriffserweiterung sichtbar werden kann. Der erweiterte Begriff umfasst über die alten Anwendungsbedingungen hinaus neue, veränderte Bedingungen. Diesen neuen Anwendungsbedingungen liegt ein modifiziertes, meistens umfangreicheres Wissen über die involvierten Bezugsgegenstände zugrunde als der alte Begriff umfassen konnte. Insofern erlaubt uns der paradigmatische Fall der ursprünglichen Metapher, auf neue, unbeobachtete Aspekte der gegenwärtigen Situation schließen zu können (vgl. Bartels 1994: 328).

Der Preis, der hierfür bezahlt werden muss, liegt in der partiellen Destruktion der vorlaufenden ursprünglichen Metapher. Ein Stück weit wird diese durch die Schaffung der neuen, bedeutungsverschiebenden Metapher entwertet. Klaus Müller-Richter beschreibt dies so:

> Schafft also die Metapher einerseits die Bedingung sinnvoller Weltinterpretation, so sprengt sie andererseits zugleich als unkontrollierbares Prinzip permanenter Verschiebung und semantischer Neuerung den Untergrund, aus dem sie sich speist, und fällt so dem mit ihrer Hilfe allererst Konstituierten destruktiv in den Rücken. (Müller-Richter 1998: 5)

Im Prinzip können sich die ursprüngliche paradigmatische und die erweiterte Metapher gegenseitig beeinflussen. Die erweiterte Metapher führt dann zu einer Modifikation der ursprünglichen Metapher und wird somit selbst paradigmatisch. Dies ist insbesondere dann der Fall, wenn die involvierten Ähnlichkeitsklassifikationen *wörtlich* gebraucht werden. Ursprüngliche Metaphern können aber trotz dieser Modifikationstendenz unabhängig bleiben, nämlich dann, wenn sie unabhängig beschreibbar bleiben. In diesem Fall wird die Interpretation der erweiterten Metapher so abgeändert, dass diese sich situativ so deutlich von der ursprünglichen Metapher des erstmaligen Erkennens absetzt, dass Verwechselungen weitestgehend ausgeschlossen sind (vgl. Zymner 1991: 58). Da Metaphern Ereignisse unter dem Gesichtspunkt der Ähnlichkeit betrachten, ist das durch die Metapher *sichtbar Gemachte* nicht wirklich der Fall eines anderen Geschehens.

---

12 Vgl. hierzu Engerer 2013: 23: „Metapher gilt in diesem Bereich als wissenstransferierendes Verfahren der Übertragung von Konzepten einer Disziplin auf eine andere."

Allerdings ist es möglich, dass Metaphern mit der Zeit als wörtliche Interpretationen Einzug in den Sprachgebrauch halten können und dann mehr Worten oder fixierten Konzepten ähneln (vgl. Knorr-Cetina 1991: 95–96).

Zwangsläufig können erweiterte Metaphern einerseits in Richtung der ursprünglichen, paradigmatischen Metapher angepasst werden, damit man den erweiterten Begriff in der Tradition des ursprünglichen Paradigmas darstellt. Andererseits ist es ebenso möglich, die Überzeugungs- und Entscheidungsaspekte eines Wissenschaftlers bei der Entdeckung der Analogie zwischen der paradigmatischen und der erweiterten Metapher so zu verändern, dass die plötzlich auftretende Ähnlichkeit nicht mehr akzidentell, sondern evolutorisch wahrgenommen wird. Nichtsdestoweniger liegt das eigentlich Interessante bei Metaphern in ihrer konzeptuellen Wechselwirkung und der daraus resultierenden Wissenserweiterung. Dabei werden metaphorisch gefasste Konzepte über den ursprünglichen Anwendungsbereich hinaus übertragen. Sie werden für Ereignisse importiert und in Kontexte migriert, die sich von der ursprünglichen Situation ihres Entstehens unterscheiden. Die Metapher wird in Problembereichen appliziert, für die sie ursprünglich nicht zuständig war und für deren Problemlösung sie nun überraschenderweise durch die „Übertragung einer Idee" beitragen soll (vgl. ebd.: 96–98).

Ziel ist es, die Erfahrungen in einer Problemsituation von einem Bereich auf einen anderen zu transferieren und damit zu dessen Problemlösung beizutragen. Daran ist aber nur zu denken, wenn zwei Problemsituationen ähnlich erscheinen, wobei „es keine genau definierbare Ähnlichkeit zwischen zwei Entitäten gibt, die perspektivenunabhängig angegeben werden könnte." (Strub 1995: 106) Letzteres wäre auch nicht die Aufgabe der Metapher, denn die Interaktion hat die Transformation eines Forschungsbereichs im Auge, um die wissenschaftlichen Gegenstandsobjekte in einem neuen Kontext, also in Form von neuen Rahmenbedingungen für die Forschung zirkulieren zu lassen. Die Metapher ist dabei als wahrgenommene Analogie einer möglichen Problemlösung das Vehikel der Innovation (vgl. Black 1983).

Max Black spitzt den Charakter der innovativen Metapher in einem mittlerweile berühmten Satz noch weiter zu, indem er schreibt:

> Es wäre in einigen dieser Fälle [in denen Menschen Ähnlichkeiten zu erkennen meinen, die sonst nur schwer erkennbar wären] aufschlussreicher zu sagen, die Metapher schafft die Ähnlichkeit, statt zu sagen, sie formuliert eine bereits vorher existierende Ähnlichkeit. (Ebd.: 68)

Dieser Aspekt, der die bisherige alltagssprachliche Verwendung der ursprünglichen paradigmatischen Metapher von der erweiterten deutlich abgrenzt, greift in seiner semantischen Verallgemeinerung auf Freges Begriffspaar „Sinn" und „Bedeutung" zurück (vgl. Frege 1967). In der erweiterten Metapher kommt also ein anderer „Sinn" zum Ausdruck. Dies erklärt, warum für Forscher die Konstruktion semantischer Verallgemeinerungen in Form von Metaphern ein nützlicher Bestandteil beim Aufbau des begrifflichen Gerüstes neuer Theorien ist.

4 Fazit

Das Postulieren einer möglicherweise erfolgreichen Lösung eines Problems in Form einer erweiterten Metapher steht am Anfang dessen, was wir als „Innovation" bei Paradigmenwechseln in den Naturwissenschaften begreifen. Dass auch Naturwissenschaftler Metaphern nicht nur zum Nachvollziehen historischer Begriffsentwicklungen verwenden, zeigt sich am Beispiel der Entdeckung des Benzolrings (siehe Fußnote 8). Ebenso muss beispielsweise die Metapher des „Drehmoments" in der Elektronentheorie Bohrs bereits begriffen sein, um die Theorie überhaupt erst erlernen zu können (vgl. Bartels 1994: 56). Der Vorgang beginnt folglich mit dem vermeintlichen Endprodukt, das metaphorisch ausgedrückt wird und somit den Innovationscharakter einer Forschung bereits als gegeben für sich verbuchen kann.

Die vorab antizipierte Lösung stellt den normalen Forschungsprozess auf den Kopf, indem sie die Suchprozesse anleitet und durch ihre *a priori* suggerierte Lösungsmöglichkeit dem gesamten Forschungsvorgang sowohl mit einer Art Lösungsglauben als auch einer Realisationskraft bestückt, die ihn nachhaltig vorantreibt. Der gesamte Forschungsvorgang beinhaltet eine *a priori* gegebene Ostension, also eine Stoßrichtung, die die noch stattfindenden Lösungsnachweise und Suchprozesse organisiert und selektiert. Das „Aufleuchten des Aspektwechsels" proklamiert, dass in dieser Richtung auch ganz selbstverständlich die größten Realisierungsmöglichkeiten liegen. Die Ostension der Forschung kann auch als falsche Fortschrittsgläubigkeit verstanden werden, denn es ist nicht gesagt, dass sich die Problemlösung wirklich in diese Richtung entwickelt. Die Richtung kann wechseln, dennoch wird es als innovativ betrachtet, das Forschungsfeld im Sinne der Stoßrichtung zu untersuchen, da die neue Perspektive neue Entscheidungsparameter einführt, alte Wertigkeiten revidiert, Entscheidungen fast automatisch nahelegt bzw. andere degradiert.

Die Innovation der Metapher liegt im plötzlichen Zünden des Funkens, der die Forschung durch den erstaunlichen Aspektwechsel – der bereits Wittgenstein faszinierte – antreibt, ja sogar auch dann, wenn sich der Anfangsverdacht einer möglichen Problemlösung in der durch die Metapher vermuteten Weise als falsch herausstellt. Dabei orientieren sich die Selektionen des Forschungsprozesses gar nicht am Abstrakten, wie es die Naturwissenschaftler so gerne für sich in Anspruch nehmen. Vielmehr stehen die praktischen Probleme im Vordergrund. Die nicht realisierte Lösung und die aus ihr wachsenden potentiellen Möglichkeiten mobilisieren den Forschungsprozess der Naturwissenschaftler, der durchaus spekulative Züge trägt (vgl. Knorr-Cetina 1991: 108–110).

Die „Innovation der Metapher in den Naturwissenschaften" resultiert aus dem erfolgreichen Übertragen einer konzeptuellen Idee. Wir gehen dabei oft fälschlicherweise davon aus, dass innovative Metaphern automatisch zu erfolgreichen wissenschaftlichen Innovationen führen, da die wissenschaftliche als auch wissenschaftshistorische Literatur primär erfolgreiche Innovationen dokumentiert. Die Rolle der Metapher im Forschungsprozess liegt hingegen vor allem in der Mobilisierung von Realisierungsressourcen für Probleme durch Erweiterung des Wissens um mögliche Problemlösungsalternativen. Diese erlauben dem Wissenschaftler, die „gefühlten" situativen Beschränkungen zu transzendieren und neue Lösungswege bis hin zu spekulativen Überlegungen anzupeilen (vgl. ebd.: 124–125).

Literatur

Baltzer, Ulrich (2002): „Konstitutive Regeln". In: Baltzer, Ulrich/Schönreich, Gerhard (Hrsg.). *Institutionen und Regelfolgen*. Paderborn: Mentis, S. 193–206.
Bartels, Andreas (1994): *Bedeutung und Begriffsgeschichte. Die Erzeugung wissenschaftlichen Verstehens*. Paderborn: Schöningh.
Black, Max (1983): „Die Metapher". In: *Theorie der Metapher*. Haverkamp, Anselm (Hrsg.). Darmstadt: Wissenschaftliche Buchgesellschaft, S. 55–79.
Danneberg/Lutz/Graeser, Andres/Petrus, Klaus (1995): „Metapher und Innovation". In: Danneberg/Lutz/Graeser, Andres/Petrus, Klaus (Hrsg.): *Metapher und Innovation. Die Rolle der Metapher im Wandel von Sprache und Wissenschaft*. Berner Reihe philosophischer Studien. Bd. 16. Bern, Stuttgart, Wien: Paul Haupt, S. 9–21.
Darwin, Charles (1859): *On the Origin of Species by Means of Natural Selection, or the Preservation of Favoured Races in the Struggle for Life*. London: John Murray. [Deutsch: 1860: *Über die Entstehung der Arten im Thier- und Pflanzen-Reich durch natürliche Züchtung, oder Erhaltung der vervollkommneten Rassen im Kampfe um's Daseyn*. Übersetzt von Heinrich Georg Bronn. Stuttgart: E. Schweizerbart'sche Verlagsbuchhandlung und Druckerei].
Davidson, Donald (1978 / 1990): „Was Metaphern bedeuten". In: Davidson, Donald, *Wahrheit und Interpretation*. Frankfurt am Main: Suhrkamp.
Draaisma, Douwe (1999): *Die Metaphernmaschine. Eine Geschichte des Gedächtnisses*. Darmstadt: Wissenschaftliche Buchgesellschaft.

Engerer, Volkmar (2013): „Metapher und Wissenstransfers im informationsbezogenen Diskurs". In: *Information. Wissenschaft & Praxis*. Bd. 64. Heft 1, S. 23–33.
Frege, Gottlob (1967): „Über Sinn und Bedeutung". In: Frege, Gottlob: *Kleine Schriften*. Darmstadt: Wissenschaftliche Buchgesellschaft, S. 143–162.
Gabriel, Gottfried (2009): „Begriff – Metapher – Katachrese. Zum Abschluss des *Historischen Wörterbuchs der Philosophie*". In: Danneberg, Lutz/Spoerhase, Carlos/Werle, Dirk (Hrsg.): *Begriffe, Metaphern und Imaginationen in Philosophie und Wissenschaftsgeschichte*. Wolfenbütteler Forschungen. Bd. 120. Hrsg. von der Herzog August Bibliothek. Wiesbaden: Harrassowitz, S. 11–22.
Goatly, Andrew (1997): *The Language of Metaphors*. London, New York: Routledge.
Göpfert, Winfried (1997): „Verständigungskonflikte zwischen Wissenschaftlern und Wissenschaftsjournalisten". In: Biere, Bernd Ulrich/Liebert, Wolf-Andreas (Hrsg.): *Metaphern, Medien, Wissenschaft. Zur Vermittlung der AIDS-Forschung in Presse und Rundfunk*. Opladen: Westdeutscher Verlag , S. 70–80.
Hänseler, Marianne (2005): „Die Metapher in den Wissenschaften. Die Assimilierung eines Fremdkörpers in den epistemologischen Konzepten der Science Studies". In: *Österreichische Zeitschrift für Geschichtswissenschaften*, 16. Jhrg., Heft 3, S. 123–132.
Knorr-Cetina, Karin (1991): *Die Fabrikation von Erkenntnis. Zur Anthropologie von Naturwissenschaft*. Mit einem Vorwort von Rom Harré. Frankfurt/M.: Suhrkamp.
Lakoff, George / Johnson, Mark (1998): *Leben in Metaphern. Konstruktion und Gebrauch von Sprachbildern*, Heidelberg: Carl-Auer-Systeme.
Mauthner, Fritz (1901): *Beiträge zu einer Kritik der Sprache*. Bd. 2: *Zur Sprachwissenschaft*. 2. Auflage. Stuttgart: J.G. Cotta'sche Buchhandlung Nachfolger.
Mauthner, Fritz (1913): *Beiträge zu einer Kritik der Sprache*. Bd. 3: *Zur Grammatik und zur Logik*. 2. Auflage. Stuttgart: J.G. Cotta'sche Buchhandlung Nachfolger.
Müller-Richter, Klaus (1998): „Einleitung". In: Müller-Richter, Klaus/Larcati, Arturo (Hrsg.): *Der Streit um die Metapher. Poetologische Texte von Nietzsche bis Handke*, Darmstadt: Wissenschaftliche Buchgesellschaft, S. 4–30.
Pulaczewska, Hanna (1999): *Aspects of Metaphor in Physics. Examples and Case Studies*. Tübingen: Max Niemeyer.
Quine, Willard Van Orman (1991): „Zweiwertigkeit – um welchen Preis?". In: Quine, Willard Van Orman, *Theorien und Dinge*. Übersetzt von Joachim Schulte. Frankfurt a.m. 1985, S. 47–54.
Quine, Willard Van Orman (1991): „Metaphern – ein Postskriptum". In: Quine, Willard Van Orman, *Theorien und Dinge*. Übersetzt von Joachim Schulte. Frankfurt a.m. 1985, S. 227–229.
Strub, Christian (1995): „Abbilden und Schaffen von Ähnlichkeiten. Systematische und historische Thesen zum Zusammenhang von Metaphorik und Ontologie". In: Danneberg, Lutz / Graeser, Andreas / Petrus, Klaus (Hrsg.): *Metapher und Innovation. Die Rolle der Metapher im Wandel von Sprache und Wissenschaft*. Berner Reihe philosophischer Studien. Bd. 16. Bern, Stuttgart, Wien: Paul Haupt, S. 105–125.
Weinrich, Harald (1967): „Semantik der Metapher". In: *Folia Linguistica*. Bd. 1. Heft 1–2, S. 3–17.
Weizsäcker, Carl Friedrich von (1971): „Die Sprache der Physik". In: Weizsäcker, Carl Friedrich von, *Die Einheit der Natur. Studien*. München: Hanser, S. 61–83.
Whorf, Benjamin Lee (1963 / 1997): *Sprache – Denken – Wirklichkeit. Beiträge zur Metalinguistik und Sprachphilosophie*. 21. Auflage. Reinbek bei Hamburg: Rowohlt.

Wittgenstein, Ludwig (1989): „Philosophische Untersuchungen". In: Wittgenstein, Ludwig: *Werkausgabe*. Bd. 4. Frankfurt/M.: Suhrkamp. [PU]
Wittgenstein, Ludwig (1989): „Letzte Schriften über die Philosophie der Psychologie". In: Wittgenstein, Ludwig: *Werkausgabe*. Bd. 7. Frankfurt/M.: Suhrkamp. [LSSP]
Zymner, Rüdiger (1991): *Uneigentlichkeit. Studien zur Semantik und Geschichte der Parabel*. Paderborn: Schöningh.

7 **Wittgenstein**

David G. Stern
The Structure of *Tractatus* and the *Tractatus* Numbering System

Abstract: An introduction to the University of Iowa *Tractatus* Map, including a brief history, a rationale, and a discussion of plans for future development. That project builds on a pair of subway-style maps of the numbering system used in the *Tractatus* and the *Prototractatus* that display those books' structures. The online map tool is available at: http://tractatus.lib.uiowa.edu/ I will argue that our *Tractatus* map's visually compelling presentation of the numbering system of that book delivers on Wittgenstein's cryptic claim in a letter to his publisher that it is the numbers that "make the book surveyable and clear". It also has far-reaching implications for the interpretation of that text, and its relationship to earlier drafts.

Keywords: Tractatus, numbering system, logical tree, hypertext

This essay began its life as a PowerPoint presentation of over 100 slides on "Mapping the *Tractatus*", created for the closing plenary lecture of the 2017 Kirchberg Wittgenstein conference. About half of that set of slides—the ones containing one or more whole sentences—provided an outline for this essay on the *Tractatus* numbering system. The rest of the slides were images, and most of the images were of two sorts of maps: maps of transit systems, and especially those of the London Underground and the New York City subway system, and maps of the structure of the numbering system of Wittgenstein's *Tractatus*. As it was not possible to include that visual dimension of the lecture here, the focus of this essay is on the numbering system itself.

For a large part of the presentation, the audience looked at about twenty five maps of transit systems and *Tractatus* gathered from around the web, and a similar number of maps of various parts of *Tractatus* and *Prototractatus* from the University of Iowa *Tractatus* map site. I made use of these maps both as graphic backdrop and as "*objects of comparison*", meant to throw light on features of *Tractatus* by looking at "similarities and dissimilarities" (PI 130) between those maps and that book. In addition to the PowerPoint presentation, I also hung up two large wall maps of *Tractatus* and *Prototractatus*, each roughly four feet high and nine feet wide, reproducing the two main pages of the University of Iowa *Tractatus* map site.[1] This visual dimension to the lecture made it possible to introduce some key ideas that are more easily accessible when they are initially presented visually. By means of looking carefully at some graphically striking illustrations of structural similarities and dissimilarities between subway system route maps and maps of the *Tractatus* numbering system, I introduced the ideas (1) that *Tractatus* is a logical tree whose structure is determined by its numbering system, and (2) that the best way of visualizing this tree structure is to see the remarks that make up the book as having a structure very similar to the relationship between stations and lines on a subway map. To be specific, Harry Beck's classic London Underground tube map, and the many maps of transit systems inspired by it, are topological maps of a network of lines, not a geographical map of the city's topography. Such maps make it easy to take in the connections between stations, and the relations between the various lines. Likewise, a map of the *Tractatus* numbering system makes it easy to take in the tree structure that connects the remarks, along lines that will be set out in greater detail in due course. But this unillustrated paper can only arrive at that destination later on.

I began my talk by highlighting a fundamental issue, or difficulty, that arises for most readers and teachers of *Tractatus*: it is unusually difficult to know how to approach Wittgenstein's *Tractatus*. Wittgenstein's *Tractatus*, first published in 1922, has not only given rise to an enormous, and extraordinarily diverse, philosophical literature, but has also inspired and influenced readers and artists of every kind as a work of art in its own right. Nevertheless, there is an almost complete lack of scholarly agreement about even the most elementary exegetical matters. *Tractatus* is a canonical work of early analytic philosophy and a modernist masterpiece, yet there is so little agreement about how to approach it that it can be difficult to know where to start. The book has generated an extraordinarily wide-ranging debate that is approaching its centennial and already has an extraordinarily complex history (see Stern 2003 and Biletzki 2003 for complementary histories of the first eighty years of *Tractatus* interpretation).

Nevertheless, it is safe to say that the opening and the closing words have generally been regarded as crucial points of departure, not only by philosophers, but also by the artists, poets, writers, cinematographers, and musicians who have responded to it. The book begins with remark 1, "1* The world is all that is the case", eight short words that seem to promise a metaphysics of a world of facts. The rest of the book does at first sight appear to be an extraordinarily concise,

---

1 Readers with a browser handy can find these images by following the links to maps of *Tractatus* and *Prototractatus* at http://tractatus.lib.uiowa.edu. For further information about those maps, see Stern 2016.

compressed, and systematic treatise in the philosophy of logic, language, mind, mathematics, probability, science, aesthetics, ethics and religion. It was not until quite late in the process of assembling the book that Wittgenstein added an ending telling the reader that anyone who understands him must recognize that the propositions it contains are nonsensical:

> My propositions serve as elucidations in the following way: anyone who understand me eventually recognizes them as nonsensical, when he has used them as steps—to climb up beyond them. (He must, so to speak, throw away the ladder after he has climbed up it.) He must overcome these propositions, and then he will see the world aright.
> Whereof one cannot speak, thereof one must be silent. (TLP: 6.54–7. My own translation)

So a central question for any reader of the book is this: How are we to relate the apparently confident assertions of the opening sentences, and the closing explanation that if the reader understands the author, then the reader will see that the very words of the book we have just read are themselves nonsensical, a ladder that must be thrown away once we've climbed up it?[2]

One reason that there has been so little agreement about how to approach *Tractatus*, or how to understand the relationship between the opening words and the conclusion, is that very few readers have grasped the crucial structural role of the numbering system, a numbering system that Wittgenstein regarded as indispensable, and that is the topic of the footnote to the first remark. Whether or not one ultimately accepts some form of traditional reading of the book, on which its words are to be taken at face value, as systematically clarifying the logic of our language, or a resolute reading, on which we ultimately recognize them as nonsensical, we still face the task of identifying the book's structure: how the remarks that make up the book are arranged, or in other words, how the Tractarian ladder is constructed.

Furthermore, so much has already been written about *Tractatus* that many readers take it for granted that there must be little left to learn. Nothing could be further from the truth. For one hundred years after Wittgenstein wrote that book, and as we approach the centennial of its publication, we have only just begun to appreciate the role of the decimal numbering system in its construction and structure, largely thanks to pioneering research by Brian McGuinness (1989, 1996, 2002) on the genesis of *Tractatus*, and those who have made good use of those results, including Verena Mayer (1993), Andreas Geschkowski, (2001), Jinho Kang

---

[2] For some further discussion of the relationship between the beginning and end of *Tractatus*, and the philosophical implications of Wittgenstein's unusual way of writing, see Stern 2004, ch. 2, and 2017.

(2005), Luciano Bazzocchi (2005, 2007, 2010, 2014, 2014a, 2015), Michael Potter (2013), Peter Hacker (2015), Oskari Kuusela (2015), and Martin Pilch (2015, 2016). All of these authors have made a significant contribution to our understanding of the numbering system, but three of them stand out. Mayer (1993) was the first person to publish an interpretation of the numbering system that showed how to make use of McGuinness's work on the composition history of the book to see how the numbering system works in *Tractatus*, and Pilch is currently at work on his "*Prototractatus* Tools" (2016), an extraordinarily thorough and detailed edition that reconstructs the various stages of its construction, but it is Bazzocchi who has been the foremost advocate of the tree-structure reading of the numbering system of *Tractatus*.

Recently, Bazzocchi (2010a, 2014) and Hacker (2015) have argued that the tree-structure construal of the numbering system decisively supports a traditional reading of the book as systematically clarifying the logic of our language. Kuusela (2015) has responded that a resolute reading is entirely compatible with a tree-structure construal, while Kraft (2016) has provided a detailed response that criticizes their reading of the text as a logical tree, and defending a sequential reading on which the remarks that make up *Tractatus* are to be read in the order in which they were printed. While I am unpersuaded by some of the more far-reaching methodological conclusions that Bazzocchi (2010a, 333–340) and Hacker (2015, 661–668) draw from their construal of the logical tree reading of *Tractatus*, such as the claim that it decisively undermines New Wittgensteinian interpretations, which supposedly presuppose that the remarks which make up the book are a single sequence, it would be difficult to overstate the importance of his insights into the structure of *Tractatus*, and the extraordinary contribution that he has made to developing this new reading of the book.

My own view is that *both* of these approaches—a sequential reading, and a tree reading—are legitimate and appropriate interpretive strategies, and that to hold that either one of them is the *only* correct way to read the text is a mistake. In other words, we need to pay attention not only to the final sequential order in which the book was published, but also to the tree-structure arrangement determined by the book's numbering system. At first sight Hacker (2015) and Kraft (2016) seem to be on diametrically opposed sides in this debate, and both entirely opposed to a middle of the road starting point on which one follows both readings and sees where they lead. Hacker tells us that we must read the book as a logical tree; Kraft writes a rejoinder to Hacker in which he tells us that we must read it sequentially. But both of them are equivocal on this very issue. Kraft begins his discussion of this question carefully, observing that

> it is useful to distinguish between the thesis that the *Tractatus* can be read and interpreted as a tree and the thesis that it must be read and interpreted that way. (Kraft 2016: 98)

But he then goes on to dismiss the former option, saying that "the weaker thesis is too non-committal" and so construes the tree reading as defending the stronger thesis. Next, Kraft points out that in the first full paragraph of his paper, Hacker states what is clearly a version of the weaker thesis, recommending that one "avoids reading the work only consecutively, and also reads it tree-wise" (2015, 649). Indeed, if one takes the very next sentence of Hacker's paper out of context, it reads like an extremely insistent statement of the strong thesis:

> The *Tractatus* must be read *in accordance with the numbering system*, and that *demands* that the reader follow the text after the manner of a logical tree... (Hacker 2015: 649)

In view of its setting, on the other hand, it seems to be doing no more than insisting and demanding that one must not only read the work consecutively, but also read it as a logical tree. Nevertheless, shortly after making his observation about Hacker, Kraft makes a strikingly similar move. After expressing his conviction that where the tree reading and his own reading conflict, his own reading is clearly superior, he observes that it is not a bad idea "to keep in mind that both interpretations of the numbering system exist and can both be applied whenever discussing specific (series of) remarks." (Kraft 2016: 103) That, on the other hand, is something that we can all agree on.

Here, I will argue for a somewhat different reason for taking the numbering system, and its role in the construction of the book, very seriously, one that ought to be capable of commanding a very broad consensus. Whether or not looking at *Tractatus* as tree ultimately settles the methodological debates that divide Wittgenstein interpreters, it offers *any* reader of *Tractatus* an excellent way of reading and approaching the book, one that is particularly accessible and attractive. It is not only an important resource for the expert interpreter, but also to the beginner looking for an accessible way of seeing the connections between the various parts. The book was originally written as a logical tree, and when read in that way, is often much easier to follow. Properly understood, the numbering system lets the reader see two crucial ways in which the book was put together, or assembled from the various parts of which it is composed: the *structure* of the published book, as cryptically summarized in the opening footnote, and the *genesis* of the book, for the numbering system was used to assemble and rearrange it.

The first is *structural*: the decimal numbering system, and the way in which he used that numbering system to organize his remarks gives the book a quite specific kind of hierarchical structure, one that can be represented by a subway map of a certain kind. In other words, the book has the structure of a logical tree.

The second is *genetic*: the book was gradually assembled in its current order over the course of several years, and tracing this trajectory can help us to uncover a number of earlier, rather different, versions, and visions, of the book as a whole. In this paper, largely building on work by McGuinness, Mayer, and Bazzocchi, I will lay out some of the main reasons for looking at the book in this way. Once we acknowledge the crucial role that the intricate and complex decimal numbering system plays in the genesis and structure of the book, this naturally leads to the question as to how best to map that structure, how best to represent that system so that we can fully appreciate its significance.

In his first published article on *Tractatus*, McGuinness drew attention to a fact about its numbering system that has rarely received the attention it deserves: the unusual complexity and intricacy of the numbering system is evidence of a great deal of hard work and careful planning on the author's part, and so one should expect that there would be much to be learned from paying closer attention to that system:

> That a system of numeration so troublesome for an author to devise will give many useful indications to the interpreter, is a truth that has only to be stated to be acknowledged. (McGuinness 1956: 202; Copi and Beard 1966: 137)

Despite the prominent role that the numbering system plays in the arrangement of the book, and despite many attempts to explain precisely how it works, in practice very few interpreters have identified any of the "useful indications" McGuinness predicted. Forty years later, Kevin Gibson published one of the few twentieth century defenses of the view that the numbering is not only systematic and coherent, but also can significantly advance our understanding of the book by identifying sequences of remarks that form what he called "hubs" and "spokes", such as 2 and 2.1–2.2, or 2.1 and 2.11–2.19, or 2.2 and 2.21–2.22 (McGuinness 1996: 143). In his conclusion, immediately after recommending that we follow McGuinness's advice in the passage quoted above, Gibson rightly observed that "the truth that the apparently baroque system of numbering may help in understanding the work has not only rarely been stated, it has often been denied" (McGuinness 1996: 147). Indeed, although McGuinness saw from the start that the very complexity and intricacy of the numbering system ought to be a valuable source of information for an interpreter, it was not until the late 1980s, long after he had edited *Prototractatus* (PT 1971), an early version of the book, that he began to see how Wittgenstein had used the numbering system to put it together as a logical tree.

The principal reason we have only recently been in a position to appreciate the full nature of the numbering system is that Wittgenstein's explanation of the system at the beginning of the book is very short and cryptic, and there he has nothing to say about the role of the numbering system in the book's genesis. Nevertheless, it has always been clear that Wittgenstein took the numbering system of *Tractatus* very seriously. When an editor asked him if it could be published without the numbers, Wittgenstein replied in the strongest possible terms that the decimal numbers were absolutely indispensable, and must be printed next to his remarks: without them the book would be an "incomprehensible jumble", for "they alone make the book surveyable and clear" (letter to von Ficker, 6 December 1919, translation from Hacker 2015: 652). "Surveyable" ("übersichtlich", literally, overview-able) is a key term of art for Wittgenstein, and carries the sense of making it possible to take in a complex structure at a glance, in the way that one can grasp the lay of the land by looking at a landscape from a well-placed hill or tower.

However, Wittgenstein's only official explanation of how the decimal numbers are supposed to enable the reader to take in the structure of the book is to be found on the first page of the book, in the form of footnote number one, attached to remark 1. It consists of just two lapidary sentences:

> The decimal numbers assigned to the separate remarks indicate the logical weight of the remarks, the stress laid on them in my exposition. The remarks $n.1$, $n.2$, $n.3$, etc., are comments on remark No. n; the propositions $n.m1$, $n.m2$, etc., are comments on the remark No. $n.m$; and so on. (TLP, footnote to 1. My translation)

More than a few *Tractatus* interpreters have found the footnote, and the numbering system, not only unhelpful but positively misleading. For present purposes, we need only consider three representative examples of this kind of response. In a review of the book published in the *Philosophical Review* in 1924, Theodor de Laguna contended that the numbering made the book less clear and less comprehensible, asserting that "to follow the numbers is a constant distraction from sense" and that "the writer himself sometimes get mixed up" (Copi and Beard 1966, 25). However, de Laguna's assessment of the value of the numbering system, like any other such evaluation, is only worth as much as his account of what is involved in following the numbers, which in his case is disappointingly meagre: he appears to consider that its only function is to show which remarks are comments on others. Likewise, Erik Stenius's book, *Wittgenstein's* Tractatus, subtitled "A Critical Exposition of its Main Lines of Thought", begins with a chapter on the structure of the book. He opens his discussion on "The Formulated Principle of the Numbering" (Stenius 1964: 3) by observing that Wittgenstein is "speaking like a mathematician" in his footnote, using the letter 'n' to express an arbitrary number" (Stenius 1964: 3), but after a very brief discussion of some questions about how it is supposed to work, Stenius soon concludes that "(thank heaven!) he does not keep consistently to any rule." (Stenius 1964: 4) Max Black's discussion of the decimal numbering system in *A Companion to Wittgenstein's Tractatus* is even more dismissive, winding up by entertaining the possibility that the whole thing could have been a surreptitious prank:

> The book is arranged as a series of remarks, identified by decimal numbers purporting to indicate their 'logical importance' and the 'stress' they should receive. ...the device is so misleading here as to suggest a private joke at the reader's expense. (Black 1964: 2)

Most readers who have taken the decimal numbers seriously have taken it to do no more than indicate the order in which the remarks are to be read. Those who have reflected more carefully on the wording of the footnote have taken it to tell us that remarks with fewer decimal numbers are in some sense more important than those with more decimal numbers, that the numbers with no decimals are the most important. Furthermore, there is some kind of hierarchical structure connecting any number with another number that is just like it, but has more, or less decimal numbers at the end, so that 3.001, 3.01, 3.02, 3.1, 3.2, among others, are all comments on 3, and 3.201, 3.202, 3.21, 3.22, among others, are all comments on 3.2, for instance. But this is to get ahead of our story, for it is not immediately clear from the introductory footnote how to handle the numbers containing zeros, as the footnote appears to be saying that 3.001 is a comment on 3.00. On the one hand, there is no remark numbered 3.00 in the book for 3.001 to comment on, on the other 3.001 is surely a comment on 3. Putting that problem aside, we can put these fairly widely accepted ideas about the *Tractatus* numbering system in terms that more closely follow the wording of the footnote. In other words, the decimal numbering system is taken to matter because it does the following three things:

[1] It provides the *numerical order* in which the remarks are to be read (1, 1.1, 1.11, etc.)

[2] It gives greater weight to shorter numbered remarks (e.g., n over $n.1$, $n.1$ over $n.m1$, etc.)

[3] It indicates which remarks are *comments on others* ($n.1$ on n, $n.m1$ on $n.1$, etc.)

While all three are true, they are not the whole truth. If we take [1] + [2] + [3] to be all that Wittgenstein is saying in the footnote, then we arrive at roughly the position Grayling extracts from it:

> The system is one which anyone familiar with business or official reports can quickly grasp; chief points are marked with whole numbers (1, 2, etc.), comments subordinate to those with a single decimal (1.1, 2.1, etc.) and so on in the standard way. The *Tractatus* is rather elaborate structurally, yielding remark-numbers with as many as five decimals, for example 2.02331; but the principle of the arrangement is straightforward, as described. (Grayling 1988: 28)

But the arrangement is not as simple and straightforward as Grayling, and others like him, have thought. To begin with, if we take [3] at face value, it does not do full justice to what Wittgenstein actually has to say about the nature of the commenting relation in the second sentence of his footnote. He does not characterize the relationship of commenting as a binary hierarchical parent-child relation between pairs of remarks, one of which comments on the other. Instead, he introduces it as a multiple-member relationship between one remark and a sequence of remarks that jointly comment on it. (While his explanation of the commenting relation surely is not supposed to rule out cases such as 1.21 and 1.2, in which the former remark is the only comment on the latter, such cases are fairly rare.) What Wittgenstein actually says is that "*n.1, n.2, n.3, etc.*" are comments on n, not just that n.1 is a comment on n:

> The remarks *n*.1, *n*.2, *n*.3, etc., are comments on remark No. *n*; the propositions *n.m*1, *n.m*2, etc., are comments on the remark No. *n.m*; and so on. (TLP, footnote 1. My translation)

Wittgenstein draws our attention to the *sibling* relations between remarks at the same level on the tree with a common parent, such as *n*.1, *n*.2, *n*.3 etc., and *n.m*1, *n.m*2, etc. It is these *sequences* of sibling remarks that he calls comments on the remark at the next level up.

In other words, the relationship between the remarks created by the numbering system is not reducible to the hierarchical, vertical, parent-child relation, constituting a set of binary relations between pairs of remarks, one commenting on the other. In addition to those two-level relations between parent and child remarks, such as the relationship between *n.m* and *n.m*1, or between *n.m* and *n.m*2, the same-level horizontal sibling relations, between *n.m*1, *n.m*2 (and *n.m*3...) are equally important. In addition to reading it sequentially, as we would an official report, we also have to pay attention to each series of remarks that makes up one of these sibling sequences, jointly commenting on the same remark at the next level up. Taking this relationship seriously involves not only reading the 2s in *Tractatus* as starting at 2 and ending at 2.225, but also as a tree-structured family of series of siblings: 2.1–2.2, 2.11–2.19, 2.21–2.22, 2.01–2.06, and so on.

So it would be more accurate to say of the numbering system that:

[3´] It indicates which remarks are *sequences of remarks that comment on others* (*n*.1, *n*.2, *n*.3, etc., on *n*; *n.m*1, *n.m*2, etc., on *n.m*, etc.)

Once we see these sequences of remarks are working in this joint way as going to make up an ordered set of paragraphs that are on the same level and belong together as a comment on a remark at the next level up, then it is a natural next step to read those remarks in that order, even if they are printed on separate pages. So we should also note that the numbering system also does the following

[1´] It provides an alternative reading order: arranging the sequences of sibling remarks that comment on their parent remarks as a *tree structure* (1, 2, 3, 4, 5, 6, 7; 1.1, 1.2; 1.11, 1.12, 1.13; …)

[1] amounts to a statement of an assumption usually regarded so obvious that it was very rarely explicitly articulated, and had seemed to need no defense, namely that the book should be read *sequentially*, from beginning to end. The new alternative, as stated in [1´], is to *read the book as a tree-structure* defined by the author's numbering system, or in other words, as a *hypertext*.

At first sight, the proposal that *Tractatus* should be read as a hypertext may appear anachronistic, for hypertext is often specified in terms that presuppose the existence of a computer or something similar that is capable of making the appropriate connections, or hyperlinks, that connect the parts in question. For instance, according to Wikipedia, hypertext is "text displayed on a computer display or other electronic devices with references (hyperlinks) to other text which the reader can immediately access, or where text can be revealed progressively at multiple levels of detail".[3] On that definition, there cannot have been hypertexts before there were electronic devices.

However, there is also a broader, and equally well-established, understanding of hypertext on which that term is applicable to any non-linear text, any text "which contains links to other texts"[4], and in that sense, *Tractatus* is a dense network of such links between its parts. The decimal numbering systems of both *Tractatus* and *Prototractatus* are non-linear and linked: each remark begins with a number which indicates its relationship to those remarks above, below, or neighboring it in the tree structure which connects those remarks. And so their structure can be represented using hyperlinks on a computer, in the more narrow Wikipedian sense of a hypertext.

---

3 https://en.wikipedia.org/wiki/Hypertext
4 https://www.w3.org/WhatIs.html

It is very difficult to read the remarks in the order defined by the hypertextual numbering system while working with the traditional printed text. So one rationale for a *Tractatus* hypertext is to bring out these connections between sequences remarks that form part of a single branch of the logical tree. But the connections are complex, and not easy to survey.

This tree structure was already represented in Jonathan Laventhol's online hypertext of *Tractatus*, which is also the structuring principle for Bazzocchi's web hypertext of his edition of *Tractatus*. Laventhol (1996), the oldest surviving *Tractatus* map, includes a link to an extraordinarily long, narrow, and unperspicuous map which serves as a good illustration of the problems faced by any such attempt to map the *Tractatus* as a whole along these lines.[5] From a purely logical perspective, Laventhol and Bazzocchi's tree-structure maps are an almost entirely satisfactory representation of each of the many relationships between remarks that we have just discussed, for they include lines connecting each parent with each of its offspring, and each sibling with its other siblings.[6] However, this dense network of connections becomes increasingly intricate once one attempts to chart the relationship of more than a few remarks, and makes it impossible to legibly represent more than a small fraction of the whole structure on an ordinary sheet of paper or the usual sized browser window. Given the complexity of the connections between remarks, one way around the challenge of representing them all on a single page is to focus on smaller parts, and enable the reader to navigate between them. Michele Pasin, who has designed several imaginative *Tractatus* sites (Pasin 2013), provides a more compressed rendition of the whole as a logical tree by using polar co-ordinates and a shifting center, but despite this ingenuity, one can only look at a small fraction of the whole at any one time.[7] Most previous approaches to the basic design problem either take this way out, or focus on the new terrain—the text of sequences of siblings—not the map.

The motivation that led to the design of the University of Iowa *Tractatus* Map was to find a way of representing the structure of the *Tractatus* numbering system in a more compact and simple way. The solution to this problem, originally developed by Phillip Ricks while taking part in my graduate seminar, turned out to be surprisingly simple. In a standard tree structure, every node stands in at least

---

5 See: http://www.kfs.org/jonathan/witt/mapen.html A very similar map is included on Bazzocchi's *Tractatus* site: http://www.bazzocchi.net/wittgenstein/tractatus/eng/mappa.html

6 I say "almost" because they make use of intermediate "dummy" nodes, using non-existent remark numbers, in order to connect remarks containing a zero to their parents. For instance, Bazzocchi includes a node named "2.(00)" in between remarks 2 and 2.01.

7 See http://hacks.michelepasin.org/witt/spacetree#.WC4P5Mk-KX8_.

one parent-child relationship, and many nodes are related to both a parent and a child. The *Tractatus* also makes use of the sibling relationship, and does so in a way that cannot be eliminated or analysed away as a product of those parent-child relationships, because zeros are used to create more than one set of sibling offspring from a single remark. For instance, 2.01 and 2.02 are siblings, as are 2.1 and 2.2, and both have 2 as a parent, but 2.01 and 2.1 are not siblings. Consequently, the Laventhol and Bazzocchi maps not only include lines representing vertical parent-child relations between 2 and 2.01, 2 and 2.02, 2 and 2.1, and 2 and 2.2, but also horizontal lines representing sibling relations between 2.01 and 2.02, and between 2.1 and 2.2, and so on. Ricks saw that most of these lines are quite unnecessary. If we structure our map around the sibling relationship, we do not need to show each parent-child relationship individually: we only need one line connecting the series of siblings, a line which can then be extended so that it terminates at the remark which is the parent of the whole series of remarks. In other words, we can replace the filigree of lines connecting each of the remarks making up the branches of a logical tree with each part of each sub-branch, with a subway-map style network made up of many fewer lines, that is not only much easier to take in, but without any loss of information.

On the approach taken in the University of Iowa *Tractatus* map, we start with a horizontal "main line" at the top of the page, the series of whole-numbered remarks, (1, 2...7), each of which is represented by a station on that line. Each series of remarks which comment on one of those top-level remarks is a single vertical line on the map, branching off one of the first six junction stations. One line branches off remark 1 (1.1–1.2); two lines branch off remark 2 (2.01–2.06 and 2.1–2.2); three lines branch off remark 3 (3.1–3.5, 3.01–3.05, and 3.001), and so on. Likewise, each series of remarks which comments on one of those next level remarks branches off horizontally from those remarks, each of which is thus another junction station. And so on. While there is no need to use color, as the nature of these relations is fully represented by the use of numbers as names for the stations, and the lines that connect them, we have found it helpful to follow the convention of using a spectrum of colors to systematically indicate the different kinds of line, starting with purple for the top line, followed by red, orange, green, aqua and blue for the five decimal levels used in the *Tractatus* numbering system. As remarks containing a single or double zero are not comments on a non-existent remark ending in zero but rather the number preceding the zero—for instance, 4.001 and 4.01 each begin a series of remarks on 4, they are equipollent to the series beginning with 4.1, and so the three are colored in increasingly pale shades of the same red, making the 4.01 line a dark pink, and the 4.001 line a light pink.

At this point, sceptical readers are likely to ask, if they haven't already done so, whether this really matters. The quick answer to this question is that it leads to a new, and rather different way of reading *Tractatus*. On a numerical order reading, remark 2 comes between 1.21 and 2.01. But the hypertext consists of a series of branching and interconnected groupings of remarks. So approaching *Tractatus* as a logical tree, or a hypertext, involves taking seriously an alternative way of arranging, or ordering the text, on which it is not only true that (a) 2 comes after 1, and before 3, 4, 5, 6 and 7 but it is also the case both that (b) 2 is commented on by the series of remarks 2.1, 2.2, 2.3, and that (c) 2 is commented on by the series of remarks 2.01, 2.02, 2.03... 2.07. Hacker lucidly sums up this approach as follows

> the seven cardinal propositions, which are the basis of the logical tree, should be read in sequence—otherwise the structure of the tree cannot be understood. More clearly, the *Bemerkungen* (comments, remarks) *n*.1, *n*.2, *n*.3 are *sequentially* (not severally) comments or remarks on proposition *n* and meant to be read as such. Each such sequence develops a specific line of thought to its end. And so too for propositions *n.m*1, *n.m*2, etc. They too are to be read sequentially, being a continuous line of elucidation of proposition *n.m*. (Hacker 2015: 650)

Taken seriously, this amounts to a new way of reading the book, one that challenges a basic assumption that has been just about universally presupposed: that the book was meant to be read sequentially, from beginning to end. In other words, until very recently almost everyone took for granted not only that one should start at the first sentence on the first page and end at the last sentence of the last page, but that each numbered remark should be seen as following the remark before it on the page when reconstructing the argumentative structure of the book.

But the quick answer comes at a price, for it is at best what Wilfrid Sellars used to call a "promissory note", a promise to deliver in more detail on such a far-reaching and programmatic claim about the tree structure of the book. For that tree structure, as determined by [3′], has far-reaching consequences. These include the claim that the book has a structure that few readers have fully appreciated, which in turn leads to new ways of reading the book. Such strong claims call for stronger and more far-reaching support than can be provided by a careful reading of Wittgenstein's footnote about the numbering system. However, as Bazzocchi has shown, we can find such support by looking at how *Tractatus* was first assembled. For it turns out that the key to appreciating why the decimal numbering system mattered as it did to Wittgenstein, is to see the absolutely indispensable role that it played in putting the book together in the first place. That was a matter of gradually organizing short passages culled from his notebooks, writing down short series of such passages in another notebook as he decided to include them in the book, but indicating their intended order by use of the decimal numbering system.

Crucially, the numbering system served as a tool by which Wittgenstein could work out how best to arrange his remarks over the course of several years. In this way, he gradually assembled the final arrangement of the hundreds of numbered remarks that make up the book. When Wittgenstein began to assemble his book, almost certainly some time in 1915, he had not yet finished writing it, yet he had clearly arrived at a point where he needed to work out how to arrange the parts that he had written. So it could not simply be written up in the ultimate numerical publication order. If he had not been serving in the Austrian army during the first world war, he would undoubtedly have had a typist produce a typescript of the material for his book, and he would then have put them together in the order he thought best. Instead, Wittgenstein wrote them down in a large notebook, starting with the first six top level, whole numbered remarks.[8] The next page repeats the first six whole-numbered remarks, but intersperses single-decimal remarks through 4.4 in numerical order, which provided the initial tree-trunk and most of the first four main branches for the growing book draft. The first double decimal remarks occur on the page that follows this sequence. Most of the rest of the manuscript is a record of adding progressively finer branches to the trunk and its branches.

Throughout this process of constructing and assembling the first draft of the book, Wittgenstein gradually added remarks as he decided to make use of them, each remark prefaced by a decimal number indicating its ultimate location in the sequence. Progressively higher-numbered remarks soon make an appearance, but throughout the process of construction recorded in MS 104, remarks are added to the tree-structure, not to a numerical sequence, by using the numbering system to indicate where they belonged, and were written down in the form of a log of new sequences of remarks. His numbering system enabled him to organize, review, and repeatedly reorganize his work in progress, despite the very limited resources available to him while serving as a soldier. From each of the first six whole-numbered remarks, numerical sequences branch, starting with one-decimal series such as 1.1, 1.2; from these nodes, further branches stem. The notebook, MS 104 (also known as "Bodleianus", as it is owned by the Bodleian library) provided the basis for *Prototractatus* (1971), edited by von Wright and McGuinness.

---

8 This page was later torn out, but traces of the first six remarks that were written there survive in the form of impressions on the next page (see Pilch 2015 for details).

For well over twenty years after MS 104 was first discovered by von Wright in 1965, who took charge of preparing the text for publication over the next few years, the full significance of the order in which the remarks were written down was not yet appreciated. As a result, the focus of that book and of von Wright's introductory essay, is on the path to the *Tractatus*, not the composition of MS 104. This is already made clear in the wording of the book's subtitle: "an early version of *Tractatus Logico-Philosophicus*". Consequently, the text of the first 103 pages was rearranged in the familiar numerical order, while the last fifteen pages of "corrections" were left out, as they belonged to a later stage of revision that could not be fully reconstructed from the available evidence. The immediate result of this enormous amount of careful and conscientious scholarly work was very disappointing: it was hard for the first generation of readers of the *Prototractatus* to see what, if anything, there was to be gained or learned from this edition.[9] The edited text looked too much like the familiar text of the *Tractatus* to be instructively different, while the set of photographic facsimiles of each page of the original manuscript that preceded that text seemed quite opaque. In other words, while the published *Prototractatus* looks very similar to the final *Tractatus*, the source manuscript on which that book was based was put together in a very different way. Indeed, while von Wright did not himself provide any further discussion of the "the most interesting differences between the two works", (Wittgenstein 1971, 4) his work made those materials available in a form which provoked others to identify those differences, and this may well have been one of his most important contributions to our understanding of the complex relationship between MS 104, *Prototractatus* and *Tractatus*. If we can see so much further than the previous generation, it is because we are standing on their shoulders, or building on their accomplishments, when we do so.

In October 1915, Wittgenstein wrote to Russell that he had recently done a great deal of work, and that he was "in the process of summarizing it all and writing it down in the form of a treatise [Abhandlung]. ...If I don't survive [the war], get my people to send you all my manuscripts: among them you'll find the final summary [letzte Zusammenfassung] written in pencil on loose sheets of paper." (Wittgenstein 2012, 84-85) That loose-leaf "final summary" has not survived, but it is likely that it consisted of some kind of a tree-structure arrangement of his book in progress, as a sequentially-ordered arrangement would have involved constant and extensive additions to what had already been composed, while inserting material into sheets containing remarks arranged in a tree structure

---

9 For further discussion of the early reception of *Prototractatus*, see Stern 2016, parts 4–5. Part of this discussion is based on that material.

would have been simple. Certainly, it would have been impracticable to take in either the hypertextual structure or the sequential arrangement of the projected treatise by reviewing MS 104, the bound ledger containing a chronological ordered record of his additions to the book draft.

In this essay I have appealed to two different, but related, reasons for reading *Tractatus* as a logical tree. The first is an argument "from above": we should take the author's instructions at the beginning of the book about the relations between the remarks seriously, and respect his insistence that without the numbers the book would not be surveyable or clear. The second is an argument "from below": we know that the author relied on the numbering system to organize his successive drafts of the book when he wrote it down in MS 104, and looking at a map of the various stages makes it possible to survey that process.

However, none of this shows that it should only be read as a logical tree, or that the numerical order of the remarks on the printed page can be disregarded. In the end, the question of how best to read those remarks is one that can only be settled, passage by passage, by means of a close reading and evaluation of *all* the relevant texts. Both *Tractatus* and *Prototractatus* deserve to be read equally carefully in tree order as well as sequentially. Print readers can only consult Bazzocchi's tree-structured edition of the Ramsey and Ogden translation of *Tractatus* (2014a). But there are a number of online editions in both English and German, such as Laventhol's, Bazzocchi's, and Klement's *Tractatus* sites, and the University of Iowa maps of *Tractatus* and *Prototractatus*. In the end, the strongest case for a tree-structure reading is simply to read such an edition for oneself, and to see how each series of remarks both amounts to a complete and distinct unit, and at the same time functions as a comment on the connected remark at the next level up.[10]

---

10 The University of Iowa *Tractatus* Map is the result of a great deal of collaborative teamwork, and I would like to take this opportunity to acknowledge the crucial contributions made by the other members of the group that have worked on this project from the earliest stages. As previously mentioned, Phillip Ricks drafted the first version of the *Tractatus* map, using a pencil and graph paper while taking part in my graduate seminar on Wittgenstein's philosophy. I turned it into an Excel spreadsheet, and suggested that we use it as the basis for an online map of both the *Tractatus* and the *Prototractatus*. Landon D. C. Elkind, another seminar participant, joined us in working on the design of the online map, and took the lead on the *Prototractatus* part of the project. Matthew Butler, Senior Developer in the Digital Scholarship & Publishing Studio at the University of Iowa Libraries, expertly transformed our initial ideas into a state-of-the-art digital resource. Nikki J. D. White, Digital Humanities Librarian in the University of Iowa Libraries Digital Scholarship and Publishing Studio, gave us valuable advice on the design of the map and interface. We are grateful to Kevin Klement for his careful editorial work on the public domain English and German editions of the *Tractatus* used on the site (Wittgenstein 2016). I would also like to thank Tom Keegan, Head of the Digital Scholarship and Publishing Studio, for his support and guidance. Finally, a recent grant from the University of Iowa's Arts and Humanities Initiative enabled us to upgrade the Map's display technology, so that it can be used on touchscreen devices. This involved a complete redesign of the site, in order to develop a new version that can not only be accessed by conventional web browsers, but also on small mobile devices, tablets, and large displays suitable for a classroom or a public exhibition.

Earlier versions of parts of this paper were presented in 2016 at the "Von Wright and Wittgenstein in Cambridge: von Wright Centenary Symposium", held at Strathaird, Cambridge, UK, at a session on early analytic philosophy organized by the Society for the Study of the History of Analytic Philosophy at the American Philosophical Association's Central Division, held in Kansas City, via videolink at the 9th Summer School on Mind and Language, organized by Luciano Bazzocchi at the University of Siena, Italy, the 2017 Kirchberg Wittgenstein Symposium, and a Russell Society meeting at the American Philosophical Association's Central Division, held in Chicago, in 2018. I learned a great deal from the discussion at all these events, and also for my Fall 2015 graduate seminar at the University of Iowa, and want to express my gratitude to everyone who took part. For further discussions of these topics and related matters, see Stern 2016, which includes earlier versions of much of the material in this paper.

394 — David G. Stern

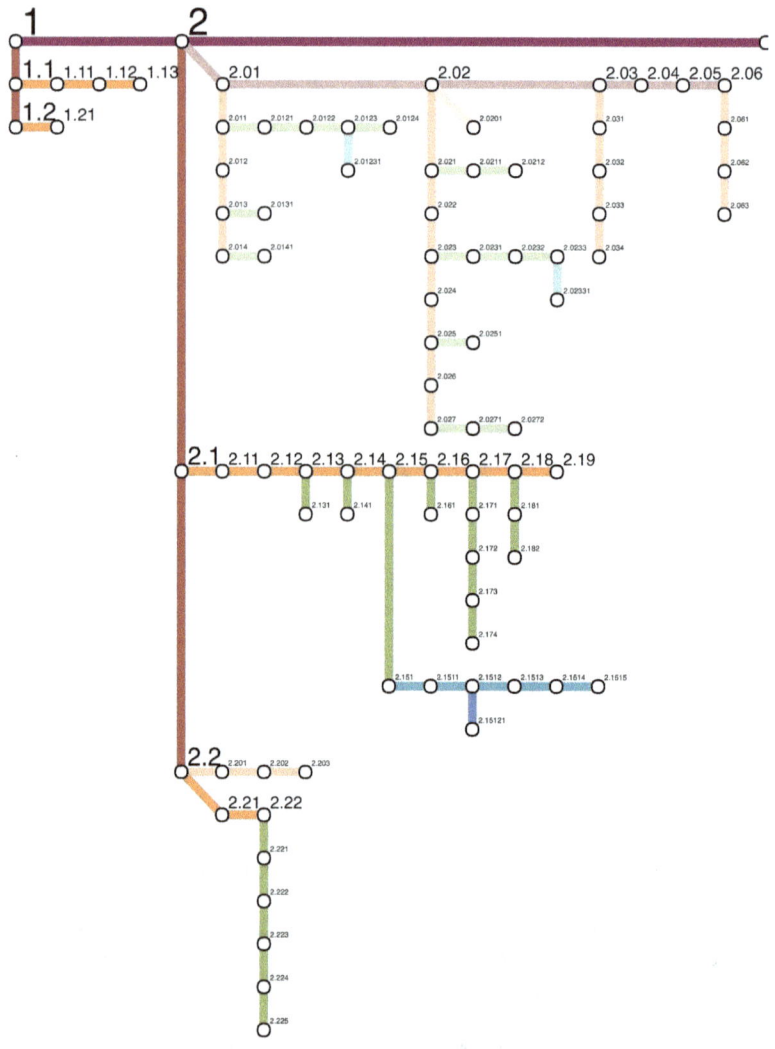

Fig. 1

References

Bazzocchi, Luciano (2005): "The strange case of the *Prototractatus* note". In: Friedrich Stadler and Michael Stöltzner (eds.) *Time and History,* Papers of the 28th International Wittgenstein Symposium, Kirchberg am Wechsel, pp. 24–26.
Bazzocchi, Luciano (2007): "A database for a *Prototractatus* Structural Analysis and the Hypertext Version of Wittgenstein's *Tractatus*". In: H. Hrachovec, A. Pichler, J. Wang (eds.): *Philosophy of the Information Society*, Papers of the 30th International Wittgenstein Symposium. Kirchberg am Wechsel, pp. 18–20.
Bazzocchi, Luciano (2010): "The *Prototractatus* Manuscript and its Corrections". In: N. Venturinha (ed.), *Wittgenstein after his Nachlass,* New York: Palgrave-Macmillan, pp. 11–29.
Bazzocchi, Luciano (2010a): "Trees, Levels and Ladders". In: V. Munz, K. Puhl, J. Wang (eds.): *Language and World. Part One. Essays on the Philosophy of Wittgenstein*, Heusenstamm: ontos verlag, pp. 329–341.
Bazzocchi, Luciano (2014): *L'arbre du Tractatus.* Peterborough: College Publications.
Bazzocchi, Luciano (Ed) (2014a): *The* Tractatus *According to Its Own Form*, ed. Luciano Bazzocchi. Raleigh, NC: Lulu. See also
http://www.bazzocchi.com/wittgenstein/tractatus/index.htm
Bazzocchi, Luciano (2015): "A Better Appraisal of Wittgenstein's *Tractatus* Manuscript". In: *Philosophical Investigations* 38.4, pp. 333–359.
Biletzki, Anat (2003): *(Over)Interpreting Wittgenstein*. Dordrecht: Kluwer.
Black, Max (1964): *A Companion to Wittgenstein's* Tractatus, Cambridge MA: Cambridge University Press.
Copi, Irving M. and Robert W. Beard (Eds.) (1966): *Essays on Wittgenstein's* Tractatus. London: Routledge and Kegan Paul.
Geschkowski, Andreas (2001): *Die Entstehung von Wittgensteins* Prototractatus. Bern: Books on Demand. Bern Studies in the History and Philosophy of Science.
Gibson, Kevin (1996) "Is the Numbering System in Wittgenstein's *Tractatus* a Joke?". In: *Journal of Philosophical Research,* 21, pp. 139–148.
Grayling, A. C. (1988): *Wittgenstein*. Oxford University Press.
Hacker, P. M. S. (2015): "How the *Tractatus* was Meant to be Read". In: *The Philosophical Quarterly,* 65, pp. 648–668.
Hart, W. D. (1973): "Prototractatus: An Early Version of Tractatus Logico-Philosophicus". In: *The Journal of Philosophy*, 70.1, pp. 19–24.
Kang, Jinho (2005): "On the Composition of the *Prototractatus*". In: *The Philosophical Quarterly,* 55.218, pp. 1–20.
Kraft, Tim (2016): "How to Read the *Tractatus* Sequentially". In: *Nordic Wittgenstein Review,* 5 (2), pp. 91–124.
Kuusela, Oskari (2015): "The Tree And The Net: Reading The *Tractatus* Two-Dimensionally". In: *Rivista di storia della filosofi,* 1, pp. 229–232.
de Laguna, Theodore (1924) "Review of 'Tractatus'". In: *Philosophical Review,* 23, pp. 103–109. Reprinted in Copi and Beard (1966), pp. 25–30.
Laventhol, Jonathan (1996): Hypertext of the *Tractatus Logico-Philosophicus.* See:
http://www.kfs.org/jonathan/witt/tlph.html and
http://tractatus-online.appspot.com/Tractatus_en.html
Mayer, Verena (1993): "The numbering system of the *Tractatus*". In: *Ratio* 6.2, pp. 108–120.

McGuinness, Brian (1956): "Pictures and form in Wittgenstein's *Tractatus*". In: *Filosofia e Simbolismo, Archivio di Filosofia*, pp. 207–228. Rome: Fratelli Bocca Editori. Quoted from the reprint in Copi and Beard (1966), pp. 137–161.
McGuinness, Brian (1989): "Wittgenstein's Pre-*Tractatus* Manuscripts". In: *Grazer Philosophische Studien*, 33, pp. 35–47. Reprinted with revisions in McGuinness (2002a).
McGuinness, Brian (1996): Preface to the second edition of Wittgenstein 1971.
McGuinness, Brian (2002): "Wittgenstein's 1916 'Abhandlung'". In: Rudolf Haller and Klaus Puhl (Eds.): *Wittgenstein and the Future of Philosophy: A Reassessment After 50 Years*, Proceedings of the 24th International Wittgenstein-Symposium, Vienna: Hölder-Pichler-Tempsky, pp. 272–282.
McGuinness, Brian (2002a): *Approaches to Wittgenstein: Collected Papers*. London: Routledge.
Pasin, Michele (2013): *Wittgensteiniana* website. Links to multiple hypertext editions of the *Tractatus*. See: http://hacks.michelepasin.org/witt/
Pilch, Martin (2015): "A Missing Folio at the Beginning of Wittgenstein's MS 104". In: *Nordic Wittgenstein Review*, 4:2, pp. 65–97.
Pilch, Martin (Ed.) (2016): Wittgenstein Source Prototractatus Tools. See: http://www.wittgensteinsource.org
Potter, Michael (2013): "Wittgenstein's pre-*Tractatus* manuscripts: a new appraisal". In: Sullivan, Peter and Potter, Michael (Eds.): *Wittgenstein's Tractatus: history and interpretation*, Oxford University Press, pp. 13–39.
Schmidt, Alfred (Ed.) (2016): Wittgenstein Source Facsimile Edition of *Tractatus* Publication Materials. See: http://www.wittgensteinsource.org
Stenius, Erik (1964): *Wittgenstein's* Tractatus. Ithaca, NY: Cornell University Press.
Stern, David G. (2003): "The Methods of the *Tractatus*: beyond positivism and metaphysics?". In: Parrini, Paolo, Salmon, Wes and Salmon, Merrilee (Eds.): *Logical Empiricism: Historical and Contemporary Perspectives*, part of the Pittsburgh-Konstanz Studies in the Philosophy and History of Science series, Pittsburgh University Press, pp. 125–156.
Stern, David G. (2004): *Wittgenstein's* Philosophical Investigations: *An Introduction*. Cambridge University Press.
Stern, David G. (2016): "The University of Iowa Tractatus Map". In: *Nordic Wittgenstein Review*, 5(2), pp. 203–220. See: http://tractatus.lib.uiowa.edu/
Stern, David G. (2017): „Wittgenstein's Texts and Style". In: Glock, Hans-Johann and Hyman, John (Eds.), *A Companion to Wittgenstein*, Blackwell, pp. 41–55.
von Wright, G. H. (1971): "The Origin of Wittgenstein's *Tractatus*". In: *Historical introduction to Wittgenstein*, pp. 1–34. A revised and expanded version, "The Origin of the *Tractatus*" was published in von Wright (1982), pp. 63–109.
von Wright, G. H. (1982) *Wittgenstein*. Oxford: Blackwell.
Wittgenstein, Ludwig (1922): *Tractatus Logico-Philosophicus*. Translated by C. K. Ogden (& F. P. Ramsey). London: Routledge and Kegan Paul.
Wittgenstein, Ludwig (1961): *Tractatus Logico-Philosophicus*. Translated by D. Pears & B. McGuinness. London: Routledge and Kegan Paul.
Wittgenstein, Ludwig (1971): *Prototractatus: an Early Version of Tractatus Logico-Philosophicus*. Edited by BF McGuinness, T. Nyberg [and] GH Von Wright, with a translation by D. F. Pears [and] B. F. McGuinness, and historical introduction by G. H. von Wright and a facsimile of the author's manuscript. Cornell University Press.
Wittgenstein, Ludwig (1996): *Prototractatus: an Early Version of Tractatus Logico-Philosophicus*. Second edition, with a new preface by McGuinness.

Wittgenstein, Ludwig (1989): *Logische-philosophische Abhandlung: kritische Edition*. Ed. B. F. McGuinness and J. Schulte. Frankfurt am Main: Suhrkamp.
Wittgenstein, Ludwig (2012): *Wittgenstein in Cambridge: Letters and Documents 1911-1951*. Edited by BF McGuinness. Malden, MA: Wiley-Blackwell.
Wittgenstein, Ludwig (2016): Side-by-side-by-side edition, version 0.43 (November 16, 2016), of *Tractatus Logico-Philosophicus*, containing the original German, alongside both the Ogden/Ramsey, and Pears/McGuinness English translations.
From http://people.umass.edu/klement/tlp/

Hans Sluga
Wittgensteins Welt

Zusammenfassung: Die Welt ist ein zentrales Anliegen der Frühphilosophie Wittgensteins. In seinen Notizbüchern von 1914-18, im *Tractatus Logico-Philosophicus*, und in seiner „Vorlesung zur Ethik" kommt Wittgenstein immer wieder auf den Begriff der Welt zurück. Dann wird es vergleichsmäßig still zu diesem Thema. Aber auch in Wittgensteins späteren Denken spielt der Begriff der Welt eine Rolle, insbesondere in Über Gewissheit, wo von anderen Welten und Weltbildern die Rede ist. „Die Welt ist alles, was der Fall ist." Was bedeutet der erste Satz des Tractatus? Was heißt es, dass die Welt meine Welt ist? Warum kommt das Subjekt nicht in der Welt vor? Warum kann es in der Welt keine Werte geben? Was sind die ethischen Implikationen dieser Weltauffassung? Was heißt es, wie Wittgenstein zum Abschluss des Tractatus schreibt, die Welt richtig zu sehen? Und wieso muss man dazu erst einmal die philosophischen Sätze aufgeben?

Schlüsselwörter: Welt, Schopenhauer, Ethik, Zufall, logische Notwendigkeit, Erfahrungswelt

Welt ist ein zentraler Begriff in Wittgensteins *Tractatus* vom ersten Satz mit seiner summarischen Kennzeichnung der Welt als all dem, was der Fall ist, bis zur abschließenden Aufforderung, die Welt richtig zu sehen. Der *Tractatus* macht insgesamt 43 explizite Aussagen über die Welt. Dazu kommen noch zahlreiche Bemerkungen über die Welt in Wittgensteins Kriegstagebüchern und weitere Bemerkungen noch einmal in seinem „Vortrag zur Ethik." Dennoch hat sich die Wittgenstein-Literatur bisher kaum mit Wittgensteins Weltverständnis und seinem Weltbegriff auseinandergesetzt.

Das liegt auch daran, dass Wittgenstein selbst schon von den frühen dreißiger Jahren an, dem Weltbegriff jegliche philosophische Bedeutung abgesprochen hat. So sagt er zum *Tractatus*-Begriff der Sprache im Februar 1933 in den Vorlesungen, die Moore aufgezeichnet hat:

> This idea of *one* calculus is connected with [the] consequence that certain words are on a different level from others, e.g., 'proposition', 'world', 'word', 'grammar, 'Logic'. I had the idea ... that certain words were *essentially* philosophical words ... But it's not the case that those words have a different position from the others. E.g., I could now just as well start [the] *Tractatus* with a sentence in which 'lamp' occurs, instead of 'world'. (Stern 2016: 259, 260)

Seinen Gedanken noch einmal unterstreichend, fügt er ein paar Monate später hinzu: "The words 'meaning', 'proposition', ‚world' have no special place in our investigation." (Stern 2016: 259, 260) Diese Bemerkungen nehmen wiederum eine Aussage in den *Philosophischen Untersuchungen* vorweg, in der wir lesen, dass die *Tractatus*-Konzeption des Denkens von einem „Nimbus" – also von einem trügerischen Schein – umgeben ist: „Sein Wesen, die Logik, stellt [dem *Tractatus* gemäß] eine Ordnung dar, und zwar die Ordnung *a priori* der Welt, d.i. die Ordnung der Möglichkeiten, die Welt und Denken gemeinsam sein muß." (PU: 97) Wittgenstein fährt fort:

> Der besonderen Täuschung, die hier gemeint ist, schließen sich, von verschiedenen Seiten, andere an. Das Denken, die Sprache erscheint uns nun als das einzigartige Korrelat, Bild der Welt. Wir sind in der Täuschung, das Besondere, Tiefe, das uns Wesentliche unserer Untersuchung liege darin, dass sie das unvergleichliche Wesen der Sprache zu ergreifen trachtet. Während doch die Worte "Sprache", "Erfahrung", "Welt", wenn sie eine Bedeutung haben, eine so niedrige haben müssen, wie die Worte "Tisch", "Lampe", "Tür". (PU: 97)

Und im Abschnitt 125 sagt er noch, dass man bei logisch-mathematischen Widersprüchen ihre „Stellung in der bürgerlichen Welt" betrachten solle. Und hier bedeutet „bürgerliche Welt" vermutlich soviel wie die „Alltagswelt" der mathematischen Praxis und die hat, im Gegensatz zur Welt, von der im *Tractatus* die Rede ist, wiederum keinen spezifisch philosophischen Status. Die wiederholten Aussagen erweisen, wie wichtig es Wittgenstein in dieser Periode war, dem Weltbegriff jede philosophische Bedeutung abzustreiten.

Aber der Bruch zwischen dem *Tractatus* und den *Philosophischen Untersuchungen* ist weniger scharf, als er zunächst aussehen mag. Während die Welt in den *Philosophischen Untersuchungen* aus dem Blick gerät, bleibt nämlich die Weltanschauung. Wittgenstein fragt in den *Philosophischen Untersuchungen*, ob die Idee der übersichtlichen Darstellung zu einer bestimmten, modernen „Weltanschauung" gehört. (PU: 122) Und diese Bemerkung stellt ein Band her zwischen Wittgensteins früherem und seinem späteren Denken. Sie bezieht sich zunächst auf eine Notiz von 1931 zu Frazers *Golden Bow*, wo wir lesen:

> The concept of perspicuous representation is of fundamental importance for us [d.h., für uns als charakteristisch moderne Menschen]. It denotes the form of representation, the way we see things. (A similar kind of 'Weltanschauung' is apparently typical of our time. Spengler.) (Luckhardt 1979: 69)

Und dieser Gedanke bezüglich unserer „Form der Darstellung" (*the form of representation*) bezieht sich wiederum direkt auf die *Tractatus* Bemerkung über die Mechanik als einer bestimmten „Form der Weltbeschreibung" und der Ausdruck

„unsere Art die Dinge zu sehen" (*the way we see things*) bezieht sich gewiss – wenn vielleicht auch nur als Gegensatz – auf das richtige Sehen der Welt, auf das der *Tractatus* am Ende abzielt.

Aus der Weltanschauung in den *Philosophischen Untersuchungen* wird dann etwas später in *Über Gewissheit* das Weltbild. Wittgenstein schreibt dort: „Mein Weltbild habe ich nicht, weil ich mich von seiner Richtigkeit überzeugt habe; auch nicht weil ich von seiner Richtigkeit überzeugt bin. Die Sätze, die dieses Weltbild beschreiben, könnten zu einer Art Mythologie gehören." (ÜG: 94–95) Dieses Weltbild „ist vor allem das Substrat alles meines Forschens und Behauptens." (ÜG: 162) Von Lavoisier, der aus seinen Experimenten bestimmte Schlüsse zieht, schreibt Wittgenstein noch: „Er ergreift ein bestimmtes Weltbild, ja er hat es natürlich nicht erfunden, sondern als Kind gelernt. Ich sage Weltbild und nicht Hypothese, weil es die selbstverständliche Grundlage seiner Forschung ist und als solche auch nicht ausgesprochen wird." (ÜG: 167) Neben diesen Bemerkungen zum Weltbild, spricht Wittgenstein im Zusammenhang mit Moores Aufsatz „Proof of an External World" auch von der „äußeren Welt" (ÜG: 20) und der „Außenwelt" (ÜG: 90) Und er fragt in diesem Zusammenhang auch noch: „Warum sollte ein König nicht in dem Glauben erzogen werden, mit ihm habe die Welt begonnen?" Moore könnten diesen König vielleicht bekehren. „Aber es wäre eine Bekehrung besonderer Art: der König würde dazu gebracht, die Welt anders zu betrachten." (ÜG: 92)

Es zeigt sich also, dass Wittgenstein von früh bis spät mit einem Netz von Begriffen gearbeitet hat, das sich in einer oder der anderen Weise auf die Welt bezieht: Welt, Weltbeschreibung, Welt sehen, bürgerliche Welt, Weltanschauung, Außenwelt, Weltbild, Weltbetrachtung. Meine Frage ist: was bedeuten diese Begriffe für Wittgenstein und wie hängen sie miteinander zusammen?

1 Die Welt als philosophisches Thema

Meine Überlegungen gehen vom ersten Satz des *Tractatus* aus. „Die Welt ist alles, was der Fall ist." Wir lesen gewöhnlich schnell über ihn weg. Sagt er nicht dasselbe, wie Wittgensteins zweiter Satz: „Die Welt ist die Gesamtheit der Tatsachen, nicht der Dinge" – aber in weniger präziser Form? Und sind diese beiden Sätze nicht nur eine Einführung in die Darstellung des logischen Atomismus, die auf sie folgt? Ich werde versuchen zu zeigen, dass sie viel mehr sind als vorbereitende Einführungssätze: dass sie für Wittgenstein in der Tat von grundlegender philosophischer und programmatischer Bedeutung sind. Und ich werde auch versuchen zu zeigen, dass diese beiden ersten Sätze verschiedenes zu sagen haben.

Aber bevor ich mich mit dem Inhalt dieser beiden Sätze befasse, müssen wir unsere Aufmerksamkeit auf ihre Stellung im Text richten. Der Anfang des *Tractatus* ist uns inzwischen so geläufig, dass wir nicht länger die Herausforderung erkennen, die in diesen zwei Sätzen liegt und die Wittgenstein zweifellos mit ihnen beabsichtigt hat. Um dies richtig in den Blick zu bekommen, müssen wir uns drei Fragen stellen: (1) Wie kann ein philosophischer Text überhaupt mit einer apodiktischen Behauptung über die Welt als Ganzes beginnen? Muss die Philosophie nicht mit einer Frage, einem Zweifel, oder einer Kritik anfangen? Das ist jedenfalls die Annahme der gesamten modernen Philosophie von Descartes über Kant bis in die Gegenwart und Wittgenstein selbst ist in dieser Weise im *Blauen Buch* und in den *Philosophischen Untersuchungen* auch so vorgegangen. Sein *Tractatus* beginnt aber anders und radikaler, nämlich mit einer Herausforderung an die moderne Tradition. (2) Zweite Frage: Kann die Philosophie überhaupt etwas über die Welt als Ganzes sagen? Ist Metaphysik überhaupt möglich? Der *Tractatus* erklärt es am Ende als seine philosophische Aufgabe, „wenn ein anderer etwas Metaphysisches sagen wollte, ihm nachzuweisen, dass er gewissen Zeichen in seinen Sätzen keine Bedeutung gegeben hat." (TLP: 6.53) Aber das Problem des *Tractatus* ist doch, dass es nicht ein anderer ist, der etwas Metaphysisches sagen will, sondern, wie es scheint, Wittgenstein selbst zu Beginn seines Buches. Geht es nur darum zu zeigen, dass solche metaphysischen Sätze auf einem „Missverständnis der Logik unserer Sprache" beruhen? (TLP: Vorwort) Wenn so, warum setzt Wittgenstein diese Sätze nicht von Anfang an in Anführungszeichen um sie als fraglich zu kennzeichnen? Warum gibt er den Anschein, dass er selbst diese Behauptungen unterschreibt? (3) Wir sollten drittens auch fragen: Wenn die Philosophie etwas über die Welt als Ganzes zu sagen hat, wird sie das nicht erst am Ende einer langen Reihe von Überlegungen tun können? So sieht es, zum Beispiel, in Descartes' *Meditationen* aus. Die beginnen mit einem Zweifel und arbeiten sich von dort aus vor, bis sie am Ende die Welt als Ganzes theoretisch erfasst haben. Der *Tractatus* verkehrt aber genau diese Reihenfolge. Er beginnt mit einer anscheinend apodiktischen Aussage über die Welt als Ganzes und endet mit einem Zweifel, ob diese Aussage einen Sinn hat. Es heißt in ihm am Ende, die Welt richtig zu sehen, nicht sie theoretisch zu erfassen.

Man muss sich lange umsehen, um noch einen anderen philosophischen Text zu finden, der mit dergleichen Ansprüchen beginnt und mit ähnlichen Zweifeln endet. Es findet sich, in der Tat, nur ein einziger, nämlich Arthur Schopenhauers Werk *Die Welt als Wille und Vorstellung*. Dessen erster Satz lautet bekanntlich: „Die Welt ist meine Vorstellung." (Schopenhauer 1960: 31)[1] Strukturell, wenn auch nicht inhaltlich, entspricht diese Aussagen dem ersten Satz des *Tractatus*. Und auch die rhetorische Absicht, die sich in ihr ausdrückt, ist dieselbe wie Wittgensteins. Es geht in beiden Fällen darum, die philosophische Tradition mit einer herausfordernden Feststellung zu konfrontieren. Auch der letzte Satz von Schopenhauers Werk spricht noch einmal, genau wie der letzte Satz des *Tractatus*, von der Welt. Und auch in diesen beiden korrespondierenden letzten Sätzen geht es noch einmal um eine Herausforderung an die philosophische Tradition. In ihren letzten Sätzen sprechen Schopenhauer und Wittgenstein beide davon, wie man die Welt richtig sehen soll. Für diejenigen, „in welchen der Wille sich gewendet und verneint hat," schreibt Schopenhauer, ist „diese unsere so sehr reale Welt mit all ihren Sonnen und Milchstraßen – nichts." (Schopenhauer 1960: 558) Nach Schopenhauer löst sich die Welt für den, der sie richtig zu sehen gelernt hat, in ein Nichts auf. Das scheint zunächst weit von Wittgenstein entfernt zu sein. Aber was meint Schopenhauer eigentlich, wenn er sagt, dass die Welt zu einem Nichts wird. Ist dies als eine ontologische oder metaphysische Aussage zu verstehen? Er sagt aber doch nur, dass die Welt *für denjenigen* zum Nichts wird, in dem der Wille sich verneint hat, nicht dass sie als solche zu einem Nichts wird. Wir sollten Schopenhauers Aussage daher vielleicht als eine epistemologische auffassen, die besagt, dass für den Einsichtigen die Faktizität der Welt unbedeutend und also zu einer Nichtigkeit wird. So verstanden ist Schopenhauer vielleicht nicht so weit von Wittgenstein entfernt.

Wittgensteins Beziehungen zu Schopenhauer sind jedenfalls komplex, selbst wenn er ihn später einmal als „oberflächlich" bezeichnet hat. Wir dürfen sicher nicht von einer Übereinstimmung der beiden sprechen. Aber Schopenhauer gibt Wittgenstein, sowohl früh bis spät, immer wieder wesentliche Gedankenanstöße. Es geht mir aber nicht darum, bloße Ähnlichkeiten zwischen Wittgenstein und Schopenhauer festzustellen. Der Hinweis auf die Beziehung zwischen den beiden soll uns vielmehr helfen, Wittgensteins Weltverständnis zu erklären. Dabei ist wesentlich, dass der *Tractatus* demselben Gedankengang folgt wie *Die Welt als Wille und Vorstellung*.

---

[1] Schopenhauer fügt noch hinzu, dass man auch sagen könnte: „Die Welt ist mein Wille." (S. 33)

2 Die Sorge um die Welt

Allerdings müssen wir Schopenhauer erst einmal in der richtigen Weise lesen lernen. Philosophiegeschichtlich zählen wir ihn gewöhnlich zu den Idealisten. Aber das ist ganz unzureichend und erklärt nicht die Distanz, die Schopenhauer von der gesamten westlichen Denktradition sucht. Die idealistische Interpretation von Schopenhauer kann auch nicht erklären, warum er sich oft auf materialistische, evolutionäre, und biologische Begriffe und Erklärungen beruft. Man kann ihn sowohl als Realisten als auch als Idealisten lesen. Er klingt oft mehr wie Hobbes als wie Kant oder Hegel. Es geht ihm aber am Ende darum, die gesamte metaphysische Tradition zu überwinden.

Schopenhauer entwickelt seinen Gedankengang in den vier „Büchern" von *Die Welt als Wille und Vorstellung*, die der Reihe nach von Epistemologie, Metaphysik, Ästhetik, und Ethik handeln. Man beachte, dass das, was man als Schopenhauers Metaphysik ansieht, nicht am Ende seines Werks steht, sondern im zweiten Buch und so nur als Zwischenstation dient zwischen der alltäglichen Welterkenntnis, die im ersten Buch abgehandelt ist, und den dritten und vierten Büchern, die von Ästhetik und Ethik handeln. Schopenhauer geht es letztlich gar nicht um die Formulierung einer metaphysischen Theorie, sondern um das Verfolgen eines Denkprozesses, der von der Alltagserfahrung zu der Erkenntnis der Nichtigkeit der Welt führt. Jeder Schritt in diesem Prozess soll uns in dieser Beziehung weiterbringen; jeder Schritt geht zugleich über die vorgehenden hinaus, in dem er das, was zuvor gesagt ist, zugleich wieder aufhebt. Am Ende dieses Prozesses steht nicht die philosophische Theorie, sondern das richtige Verhältnis zur Welt. Der Ausgangspunkt der Überlegung ist die Welt, wie sie uns in der Erfahrung vorgestellt ist. „In diesem ersten Buch," so schreibt Schopenhauer,

> ist es nötig, unverwandt diejenige Seite der Welt zu betrachten, von welcher wir ausgehen, die Seite der Erkennbarkeit, und demnach ohne Widerstreben alle irgend vorhandenen Objekte, ja sogar den eigenen Leib, ... nur als Vorstellung zu betrachten. (Schopenhauer 1960: 33)

Durch Metaphysik und Kunst, so Schopenhauer, lernen wir dann über diese begrenzte Weltansicht hinauszugehen. Dabei ist die Metaphysik allerdings nur eine Durchgangsstufe zu einer besseren, endgültigen Sicht der Welt. Theoretisches Verständnis reicht nicht aus, um die Welt richtig zu sehen; sowohl Realismus wie Idealismus müssen überwunden werden. Zu der richtigen Weltsicht nähern wir uns nur auf der Ebene des Ethischen. Schopenhauers Ethik formuliert allerdings keine Theorie der Pflicht oder des Guten. Viel weniger noch befasst sie sich mit moralischen Regeln und Imperativen. „In diesem ethischen Buche," schreibt Schopenhauer, finden sich

> keine Vorschriften, keine Pflichtenlehre...; noch weniger soll ein allgemeines Moralprinzip, gleichsam ein Universalrezept zur Hervorbringung aller Tugenden angegeben werden. (Schopenhauer 1960: 376)

Philosophie, die Ethik eingeschlossen, ist vielmehr

> stets rein betrachtend... Hingegen praktisch zu werden, das Handeln zu leiten, den Charakter umzuschaffen sind alte Ansprüche, die sie [die Philosophie] bei gereifter Einsicht endlich aufgeben sollte. Denn hier, wo es den Wert oder Unwert eines Daseins, wo es Heil oder Verdammnis gilt, geben nicht ihre toten Begriffe den Ausschlag, sondern das innerste Wesen des Menschen selbst. (Schopenhauer 1960: 375)

Schopenhauer fügt hinzu:

> Die Philosophie kann nirgends mehr tun als das Vorhandene deuten und erklären, das Wesen der Welt, welches *in concreto*, d.h. als Gefühl, jedem verständlich sich ausspricht, zu deutlichen. (Schopenhauer 1960: 376)

Derjenige, der gelernt hat, die Welt richtig zu deuten, so fährt Schopenhauer fort,

> erkennt das Ganze, fasst das Wesen desselben auf und findet es in einem steten Vergehen, nichtigem Streben, innerm Widerstreit, und beständigem Leiden ergriffen, sieht, wohin er auch blickt, die leidende Menschheit und die leidende Tierheit und eine hinschwindende Welt. (Schopenhauer 1960: 515)

Die Folge dieser Einsicht ist:

> Der Wille wendet sich nunmehr vom Leben ab: ihm schaudert jetzt vor dessen Genüssen, in denen er die Bejahung desselben erkennt. Der Mensch gelangt zum Zustande der freiwilligen Entsagung, der Resignation, der wahren Gelassenheit und gänzlichen Willenslosigkeit. (Schopenhauer 1960: 515)

Und in diesem Zustand wird ihm die Welt dann zugleich ein Nichts.

Ethische Ausrichtungen können, wie sich zeigt, verschiedene Objektive haben. Ich unterscheide (1) eine Ethik der Sorge um das Selbst (*epimeleia heautou*), die Michel Foucault als zentrales Element der antiken Ethik identifiziert hat. In ihr geht es, zum Beispiel, darum, die eigenen Tugenden zu entwickeln und so in sich selbst eine Persönlichkeitsideal zu verwirklichen. (2) Eine interpersonale Ethik, in der die Beziehungen zwischen einzelnen Menschen reguliert sind. Was wir „Moral" nennen gehört typisch zu dieser Form von Ethik. Man denke hier an die zehn Gebote oder auch den kategorischen Imperativ. (3) Eine Gesellschaftsethik, die sich mit menschlichem Verhalten in Gemeinschaft befasst und die von Platon in seinem *Politikós* eine *epimeleia koinonias* genannt wird. Von diesen müssen wir aber noch eine weitere Form unterscheiden, nämlich (4) eine Ethik, in der die menschliche Beziehung zur Welt als Ganzer thematisiert ist. Wir kennen verschiedene Formen einer solchen Ethik. In einer erscheint sie als Sorge um die Welt, als ein *epimeleia tou kosmou*. Eine solche Ethik kann sich als Hinwendung auf die Welt verstehen oder auch als Überwindung der Welt – oder, genauer gesagt, als Überwindung eines falschen, begrenzten oder vorläufigen Verständnisses der Welt und dem Erreichen einer tieferen und richtigeren Sicht. Bei Schopenhauer und Wittgenstein ist sie die letztere, und zwar bei Schopenhauer in einer mehr buddhistischen Form und bei Wittgenstein in einer Form, die wesentlich von der christlichen Tradition geprägt ist. Das wird in Wittgensteins Vorlesung über Ethik einsichtlich, wo die drei paradigmatischen ethischen Erfahrungen, von denen er spricht, (1) der Schöpfungsmythos, (2) die Erbsünde, und (3) die Heilserwartung sind. Alle drei Erfahrungen beziehen sich auf die Welt als Ganzes. Schopenhauers und Wittgensteins Erkenntnis der Möglichkeit und, in der Tat, der Notwendigkeit einer Weltethik ist uns insofern von Interesse als eine radikal-ökologische Ethik eigentlich nur als Weltethik möglich ist. Es ist daher auch nicht Zufall, dass Ansätze einer ökologischen Ethik bei Schopenhauer klar zu erkennen sind.

Sowohl bei Wittgenstein wie bei Schopenhauer ist diese ethische Haltung mit einer bestimmten Einstellung zu philosophischen Theorien verbunden. Theorien sind danach nur Wegsteine auf dem Pfad zum richtigen Sehen der Welt, aber als solche auch unabdingbar. Wir können Schopenhauers Vorgehen mit einem neueren Wort als „dekonstruktiv" bezeichnen, denn sein Werk geht durch die Konstruktion philosophischer Wahrheit hindurch und schreitet so zu deren Destruktion fort. Und insofern wir Schopenhauers Werk als Modell des *Tractatus* verstehen, können wir dieses Werk gleichermaßen als die Beschreibung eines dekonstruktiven Denkprozesses charakterisieren. Es geht danach im *Tractatus* darum, eine Reihe philosophischer Sätze aufzustellen, die am Ende überwunden werden, indem man sie als unsinnig erkennt. Die philosophischen Aussagen des *Tractatus* dürfen also nicht als endgültig betrachtet werden, sie sind für Wittgenstein vielmehr ein Durchgang zu der Frage, wie wir uns zur Welt als Ganzer stellen sollen. Und mit dieser Schlussfolgerung können wir endlich zum ersten Satz des *Tractatus* zurückkehren.

3 Was ist das „ist"?

Jeder Teil des ersten Satzes des *Tractatus* erfordert unsere Aufmerksamkeit. Beginnen wir mit dem Ausdruck „die Welt." Nach seinen Vorlesungen im Jahre 1933, war dieser Terminus für den Wittgenstein des Tractatus ein „wesentlich philosophisches Wort." Aber was für ein Wort ist es? Ist es ein Name? Wir können die Bedeutung des Ausdrucks „die Welt" sicher nicht mit einer hinweisenden Geste bestimmen. Wir können uns nicht außerhalb der Welt stellen, auf sie zeigen und sagen: das ist die Welt. Man ist versucht, das Wort mit einer umschließenden Geste zu erklären, in dem man mit ausgebreiteten Armen einen Kreis zieht und sagt: All das ist die Welt. Aber der spätere Wittgenstein hat uns auf die Hilflosigkeit solcher Gesten im philosophischen Diskurs hingewiesen. Sie kann uns jedenfalls nicht über das Faktum hinweghelfen, dass die Welt kein Gegenstand im Sinne des *Tractatus* ist. Denn Gegenstände sind einfach. Aber die Welt als alles, was der Fall ist, oder, wie Wittgenstein in seinem zweiten Satz sagt, eine Gesamtheit von Tatsachen und kann als solche nicht einfach und daher auch kein benennbarer Gegenstand sein.

Es hilft vielleicht weiter, die Aufmerksamkeit auf das Wort „ist" zu richten, das gleich zweimal in ersten Satz vorkommt. Mir geht es hier um sein Vorkommen als Hauptverbum des Satzes und ich mache dabei drei Beobachtungen. Erstens, dieses „ist" ist nicht das prädikative „ist", sondern das der Identität. Wittgensteins Satz besagt, dass die Welt identisch ist mit all dem, was der Fall ist. Die Welt ist nichts anderes als all das, was der Fall ist. Meine zweite Beobachtung ist, dass diese „ist" ein zeitloses „ist" ist wie etwa in „zwei und zwei ist vier". Wenn Wittgenstein sagt: „Die Welt ist alles, was der Fall ist" dann meint er nicht, dass die Welt jetzt, gegenwärtig, im Augenblick mit dem, was der Fall ist, identisch ist. Sondern er meint, dass die Welt immer, unvergänglich, oder zeitlos identisch ist mit all dem, was der Fall ist. Und das bringt mich unmittelbar zur dritten Beobachtung: nämlich, dass Wittgenstein die Welt als etwas charakterisiert, dass in einem zeitlosen Zustand ist. Die Welt „besteht" in derselben Weise wie die Tatsachen, deren Gesamtheit sie ist. Aber worin besteht dieses Bestehen? Der Tractatus weiß von zwei Arten von Existenz. Er spricht von der Existenz von Dingen und vom Bestehen von Tatsachen. Aber *besteht* die Welt je? Ist sie jemals in einem *Zustand*? Sollten wir nicht anstatt von einem Welt*verlauf* sprechen, in dem jeweils nur einiges aber nicht alles der Fall ist. Heidegger hat vorgeschlagen, dass wir hier vom Welten der Welt sprechen sollten. Aber diese verbale Neubildung führt uns leider auch nicht weiter.

Wenn der erste Satz des *Tractatus* ein Identitätssatz ist, dann bedeutet der Ausdruck „die Welt" jedenfalls soviel wie der Ausdruck „alles, was der Fall ist" oder auch, wie der nächste Satz sagt „die Gesamtheit der Tatsachen." Aber kann man von diesem allen, dieser Gesamtheit, überhaupt sinnvoll sprechen? Wittgenstein sagt uns, dass sich eine solche Gesamtheit nur darin zeigt, dass wir Variablen haben, die über alle Tatsachen reichen. Das heißt dann aber auch, dass der Terminus „die Welt" eigentlich keinen Sinn hat und damit verliert natürlich auch der erste Satz des *Tractatus* seinen Sinn. Wittgenstein schreibt am Ende das *Tractatus*, wie wir wissen:

> Die richtige Methode der Philosophie wäre eigentlich die: Nichts zu sagen, als was sich sagen lässt, also Sätze der Naturwissenschaft – also etwas, was mit Philosophie nichts zu tun hat – und dann immer, wenn ein anderer etwas Metaphysisches sagen wollte, ihm nachzuweisen, dass, er gewissen Zeichen in seinen Sätzen keine Bedeutung gegeben hat. (TLP: 6.53)

Der erste Satz des *Tractatus* ist allerdings sicher kein Satz der Naturwissenschaft. Er ist, wenn er überhaupt etwas ist, ein philosophischer und metaphysischer Satz. Und nun stellt sich heraus, dass er zumindest ein Zeichen enthält – den Terminus „die Welt" – dem wir keine Bedeutung gegeben haben. Der erste Satz des *Tractatus* ist also genau einer dieser Sätze, die wir als unsinnig überwinden müssen. Der *Tractatus* beginnt, so müssen wir folgern, mit einem unsinnigen Satz.

Aber wozu dann dieser Anfang? Wohl um zu helfen, am Ende „die Welt richtig zu sehen". Denn so sagt Wittgenstein von den unsinnigen philosophischen Sätzen: „Man muss diese Sätze überwinden, dann sieht man die Welt richtig." Man braucht diese unsinnigen Sätze als eine Leiter, auf der man hinaufsteigt. Aber es bleibt zu fragen, wieso man Unsinn braucht um eine sinnvolle Einsicht zu erreichen. Im Augenblick weise ich nur auf ein Dilemma hin, das sich am Ende des *Tractatus* offenbart. Denn was soll das Ergebnis des ganzen Gedankengangs sein? Wittgenstein sagt: die Welt richtig zu sehen. Aber was kann es heißen, *die Welt* richtig zu sehen, wenn der Ausdruck „die Welt" keine Bedeutung hat?

Aber wir sind noch nicht am Ende mit dem ersten Satz des Tractatus. Wir müssen noch fragen, was bedeutet der Ausdruck „alles, was der Fall ist"? Was ist ein Fall? Man könnte die Antwort natürlich abkürzen und einfach sagen, dass ein Fall zu sein heißt eine Tatsache zu sein. Das hieße dann, dass der zweite Satz, zum Teil jedenfalls, eine Wiederholung und vielleicht eine Erklärung des ersten ist. Aber damit ist es nicht getan. Das Wort „Fall," das Wittgenstein hier gebraucht, ist eine Lehnübersetzung des Lateinischen „casus." Im Englischen übersetzt man „was der Fall ist" daher auch mit „what is the case." Aber das Lateinische meint etwas, das auch im Deutschen noch mitklingt. „Casus" bedeutet eigentlich das Fallen eines Würfels. Die Würfel sind gefallen und jetzt ist etwas der Fall. Tatsachen sind geschaffen worden. Man nennt dieses Fallen des Würfels auch zufällig, weil es sich durch das anscheinend willkürliche Rollen des Würfels ergeben hat. Und das alles muss man in Wittgensteins erstem Satz mithören. Der Satz besagt: Die Welt besteht aus Tatsachen und diese sind insgesamt zufällig. Ist diese Interpretation des Satzes ein willkürlicher Einfall? Keineswegs, denn Wittgenstein selbst bringt die Sache genau auf diesen Punkt, wenn er später im *Tractatus* schreibt: „Alles Geschehen und So-Sein ist zufällig." (TLP: 6.41) Das heißt, dass alles, was der Fall ist, die Gesamtheit der Tatsachen, ohne Ausnahme zufällig ist. Und so sagt der erste Satz des *Tractatus* nicht nur, dass die Welt aus Tatsachen besteht, die als einzelne zufällig sind, sondern auch, dass die Welt selbst in ihrer Gesamtheit zufällig ist. Und damit wird auch verständlich, warum Wittgenstein in seiner Vorlesung über Ethik vom Erstaunen spricht, dass es überhaupt etwas gibt und nicht nichts, dass es die Welt gibt. Und dieses Erstaunen hat natürlich in der Tradition seinen Ausdruck in der Idee gefunden, dass Gott die Welt aus Nichts erschaffen hat.

Aber warum muss uns Wittgenstein die Zufälligkeit der Welt gleich im ersten Satz des Tractatus mitteilen? Warum ist ihm diese Sache so wichtig? Wir müssen verstehen: die ausdrückliche Feststellung, dass alles Geschehen und So-Sein zufällig ist, kommt erst später aber sie steht an einer entscheidenden Stelle In Wittgensteins Buch. Sie begründet nämlich für Wittgenstein die Erkenntnis, dass „der Sinn der Welt außerhalb ihr liegen" muss. Wittgenstein fügt hinzu: „In der Welt ist alles, wie es ist und geschieht alles, wie es geschieht." (TLP: 6.41) Und diese Zufälligkeit der Welt erweist ihm, dass es in der Welt keine Werte geben kann. Zufällige Werte, so glaubt er, wären nicht Werte. Er schreibt: „Wenn es einen Wert gibt, der Wert hat, so muss er außerhalb alles Geschehens und So-Seins liegen." Was nicht zufällig ist, kann nicht ein Bestandteil der Welt sein, „denn sonst wäre dies wieder zufällig." Und daraus folgt für Wittgenstein, dass es keine „Sätze der Ethik", keine ethische Theorie, und keine ethischen Vorschriften geben kann. (TLP: 6.42) Und weiterhin folgt daraus auch, „dass sich die Ethik nicht aussprechen lässt." (TLP: 6.421)

Es scheint mir, dass Wittgenstein an diesem Punkt etwas Wesentliches über den ethischen Naturalismus wie auch über den ethischen Rationalismus gesagt hat. Zum letzteren etwa, wenn man fragt: wie kann es apriorisches Gesetze in der Moral geben – etwa Kants kategorischer Imperativ oder John Rawls' Prinzipien der Gerechtigkeit – wenn die Existenz der Welt, die Existenz des Menschen und die der menschlichen Rationalität rein zufällig sind? Und der ethische Naturalismus wird von Wittgenstein wiederum mit der Frage konfrontiert, warum rein zufällige Umstände moralischen Sinn und Bedeutung haben sollen. Das ist mehr als eine Feststellung der Unabhängigkeit von Sein und Sollen. Es geht vielmehr, wie man sagen möchte, um eine Sicht der Welt als einer Gesamtheit zufälliger, sinnloser Umstände; einem Bild, das Wittgenstein sicher von Schopenhauer herkommend und durch seine Kriegserfahrung bestätigt sah. Man könnte es eine existenzielle Sicht der Welt nennen.

Viel hängt aber davon ab, was Wittgenstein mit dem Wort „zufällig" meint. Wir sagen manchmal, dass etwas zufällig ist, wenn es zu *einer* Zeit existiert aber nicht zu einer anderen. Zufällig fällt ein Meteor vom Himmel. Aber Wittgensteins Tatsachen sind nicht von dieser Art. Tatsachen sind nicht zeitgebunden. Es ist wahr, dass Donald Trump im Jahre 2017 Präsident ist und möglich, dass er es 2018 nicht mehr ist. Aber die Tatsache, dass Trump im Jahr 2017 Präsident ist, ist dem *Tractatus* nach zeitlos wahr und in diesem Sinne zumindest nicht zufällig. Zufällig ist ein Modalbegriff wie notwendig und möglich. Es ist wichtig zu sehen, dass Wittgenstein von früh bis spät ein deflationistisches Verständnis der Modalität pflegt. Im *Tractatus* heißt es, dass „notwendig" so viel wie tautologisch bedeutet und „unmöglich" kontradiktorisch. Möglich ist das, was dazwischenliegt und zufällig das, was möglich und dazu noch der Fall ist. Dass alles So-Sein zufällig ist, bedeutet dann zunächst, dass es keine logisch notwendigen Tatsachen gibt. Und das Bestehen *einer* Tatsache bestimmt in keiner Weise logisch das Bestehen irgendeiner anderen. Tatsachen sind daher auch logisch unabhängig voneinander. In Wittgensteins Wahrheitswerttafeln sind also alle genannten Kombinationen wirklich gleich möglich.

p	q	p & q
T	T	T
T	F	F
F	F	F
F	F	F

Es gibt allerdings logische Notwendigkeit. In der Welt ist zwar alles zufällig, aber „in der Logik ist nichts zufällig." (TLP: 2.012) Auch das sagt Wittgenstein gleich zu Anfang des *Tractatus*, weil es für sein Bild der Welt entscheidend ist. Die logische Notwendigkeit ergibt sich aber nicht aus dem, was wirklich besteht, sondern daraus, dass Sachverhalte entweder bestehen oder nicht bestehen. Die Logik beruht somit auf der Bipolarität der Sachverhalte, der Möglichkeit des Bestehens oder Nichtbestehens von Sachverhalten, nicht auf dem, was der Fall ist. Weiterhin ist wesentlich, dass Sachverhalte „Verbindungen von Gegenständen" sind. Und daraus ergibt sich ein zweites Merkmal der logischen Notwendigkeit. „Wenn die Dinge in Sachverhalten vorkommen können, so muss dies schon in ihnen liegen." (TLP: 2.0121). Es gilt hier, in diesem Satz auf den Übergang von einer Modalität zur anderen – von der Möglichkeit zur Notwendigkeit, aufzupassen. Logische Notwendigkeit ergibt sich nämlich solcher Maßen aus der *Möglichkeit* des Bestehens von Sachverhalten und der *Möglichkeit* des Vorkommens von Dingen in Sachverhalten. Aber diese Möglichkeiten sind natürlich unabhängig vom wirklichen Bestehen der Welt. Die Zufälligkeit der Welt und die Notwendigkeit der Logik sollen so miteinander versöhnt werden.

Aber damit nicht genug. Es gibt nämlich auch keine kausale Notwendigkeit in der Welt. Keine Tatsache bedingt notwendigerweise kausal irgendeine andere Tatsache. Wir lesen: „Einen Zwang nach dem Eines geschehen müsste, weil etwas anderes geschehen ist, gibt es nicht." (TLP: 6.37) Die einzige Sorte von Notwendigkeit ist die logische und die weiß von keiner Abhängigkeit einer Tatsache von einer anderen. „Die Erforschung der Logik bedeutet die Erforschung aller Gesetzmäßigkeit. Und außerhalb der Logik ist alles Zufall." (TLP: 6.3) Die Idee eines Kausalnexus ist also ein Mythos. „Einen Kausalnexus ... gibt es nicht." (TLP: 5. 136) Der Glaube an ihn ist ein Aberglaube. Es gibt insbesondere keine kausale Verbindung zwischen meinem Willen und dem, was in der Welt geschieht. Wittgenstein sagt daher auch, dass die Welt von meinem Willen unabhängig ist. (TLP: 6. 373) Das ist eine weitere Art in der die die Dinge und die Welt insgesamt zufällig sind. Sie fallen uns zu und wir haben keine Gewalt über sie. Sie sind ein Geschick. Und schließlich ist die Welt zufällig, in dem sie für sich genommen belanglos ist, weil es in ihr keine Werte geben kann. Um es zusammenzufassen: Tatsachen sind zufällig, weil sie logisch kontingent, nicht voneinander abhängig, nicht kausal bedingt, kein Ergebnis unseres Wollens, und in sich belanglos sind.

All das muss erkannt werden, wenn wir die Welt richtig sehen wollen. Aber wir müssen hinzufügen, dass diese Erkenntnis noch nicht selbst das richtige Sehen der Welt darstellt. Sie ist nur einer ihrer Vorbedingungen.

4 Die Welt des *Tractatus*

Was heißt es, die Welt richtig zu sehen? Es heißt natürlich zunächst einmal, die Dinge zu sehen, wie sie sind. Aber wie sind die Dinge? Wir können vier Grundthemen im Tractatus ausmachen:
(1) Die Welt als eine Gesamtheit von (objektiven) Tatsachen
(2) Das Subjekt in Bezug auf die Welt: die Welt als meine Welt
(3) Die Welt und ihre Beschreibung in der Physik
(4) Die Welt als ethisches Problem und dessen Auflösung durch richtiges Sehen

Es fällt dabei auf, dass Wittgenstein vieles von dem, was uns als wesentlich für die Welt erscheinen mag, überhaupt nicht anspricht oder nur beiläufig erwähnt. Ich nenne fünf bemerkenswerte Auslassungen:
(1) Zeit und Zeitlichkeit (werden angesprochen aber nur gestreift)
(2) Geschichte (bleibt ungenannt)
(3) Ereignisse, Vorgänge, Prozesse, Entwicklungen
(4) Die menschliche Gesellschaft und ihre Kultur

Und schließlich, mit all diesen Dingen verbunden:
(5) Krieg, Kriegserfahrung, menschliche Beziehungen, persönliche Gefühle, Sexualität, Tagesarbeit und die Schwierigkeit des (philosophisches) Denkens

Ich habe diese letzten Dinge aufgezählt, weil sie alle in Wittgensteins sogenannten *Geheimen Tagebüchern* von 1914–1916 abgehandelt werden. Wir können uns also fragen: was ist für Wittgenstein eigentlich die Beziehung zwischen der philosophischen Welt des *Tractatus* und seiner Alltags- oder Erfahrungswelt von der er in den *Geheimen Tagebüchern* schreibt?

5 Wittgensteins Erfahrungswelt

Schopenhauers Denkweg, so haben wir gesehen, beginnt mit der Erfahrungswelt und schreitet von dort zu einem philosophischen Bild der Welt fort, das uns am Ende zur Erkenntnis der Nichtigkeit der Welt bringt: einer Nichtigkeit, die sowohl die Erfahrungswelt wie unser philosophisches Denken über sie betrifft. In der Erfahrungswelt befinden wir uns nicht nur als erkennende, sondern auch als wollende Wesen; Erkennen ist in der Tat selbst eine Funktion des Wollens. Wollen ist aber zugleich der Grund, warum wir fortwährend leiden. Die philosophische Erkenntnis begründet damit einerseits eine Ethik des Mitleids; sie zeigt uns aber zugleich auch, warum selbst die philosophische Einsicht überkommen werden muss.

Wittgenstein folgt Schopenhauers Denkweg. Wir müssen uns daher fragen, wie sieht die Erfahrungswelt nach Wittgenstein aus. Ein Bild von ihr bekommen wir aus seinen *Geheimen Tagebüchern*. Diese sind in Wirklichkeit ein Teil der Kriegstagebücher aus denen Wittgenstein den *Tractatus* exzerpiert hat. Die *Geheimen Tagebücher* bestehen aus Notizen, die Wittgensteins Kriegserfahrung in der Zeit von 1914 bis 1916 betreffen. Die Notizen sind in den gleichen Heften enthalten, wie die philosophischen Bemerkungen, die Georg Henrik von Wright und Elizabeth Anscombe 1961 unter dem Titel *Notebooks 1914–1916* herausgegeben haben. In Wittgenstein Notizbüchern sind die persönlichen Bemerkungen aber gewöhnlich auf der linken Blattseite notiert, oft in chiffrierter aber leicht zu entziffernder Form, während die philosophischen Bemerkungen auf der rechten Blattseite stehen. Und in dieser Unterteilung wird vielleicht schon Wittgensteins Trennung zwischen Erfahrungswelt und der im *Tractatus* beschriebenen „philosophischen" Welt deutlich.

In Wittgensteins *Geheimen Tagebüchern* ist von der Erfahrungswelt die Rede, in der die philosophischen Gedanken des *Tractatus* entstanden sind. Im dritten Band seiner Romantrilogie *Die Schlafwandler* hat Hermann Broch seine Erfahrung des ersten Weltkriegs in dem Satz zusammengefasst: „Die Welt hat keine Logik." Wittgensteins Erfahrungswelt, wie sie sich in seinen *Geheimen Tagebüchern* manifestiert, hat auch keine Logik; aber in ihr, in Wittgensteins Denken, erscheint zugleich eine Welt, die Logik hat. Diese Logik erweist uns aber auch, warum wir über unsere philosophischen Einsichten hinausgehen müssen, um die Welt, die Erfahrungswelt, richtig zu sehen.

Wittgenstein ging als idealistisch motivierter Freiwilliger in den Weltkrieg. Aber die Kriegserfahrung erwies sich bald als viel härter, als er erwartet hatte. Schon innerhalb weniger Wochen fand er sich mitten in der Materialschlacht. Seine Erwartung, dass seine Mitsoldaten von denselben Idealen bewegt seien, die ihn selbst motivierten, wurde bald enttäuscht. Gewohnt an Menschen von hoher und akademischer Kultur, entdeckte er, in seinen Mitstreiten nichts als „Gemeinheit." Der Fortgang des Krieges und der Umgang mit seinen Mitstreitern erweckten in Wittgenstein so die stärksten Gefühle. Seine Aufzeichnungen dazu sind besonders bemerkenswert, weil nur ein einziger Satz im *Tractatus* auf menschliche Gefühle hindeutet: „Die Welt des Glücklichen ist eine andere als die des Unglücklichen." (TLP: 6.43) Wir dürfen fragen: Ist die Welt des Unglücklichen für Wittgenstein vielleicht die normale Erfahrungswelt und die des Glücklichen, die richtig gesehene Welt? Zu den Gefühlen, die Wittgenstein bewegen sind auch die sexuellen. Sie beunruhigen ihn, weil sie keine Erfüllung zulassen. Wir werden hier noch einmal an Schopenhauer erinnert, für den der Sexualtrieb der stärkste Ausdruck des Willens zum Leben ist und so auch der stärkste Motor des menschlichen Leidens. Schopenhauer schreibt: „Das eigene Bewusstsein, die Heftigkeit des Triebes lehrt uns, dass in diesem Akt sich die entschiedene Bejahung des Willens zum Leben rein und ohne weitern Zusatz ... ausspricht.... Die Erkenntnis dagegen gibt die Möglichkeit der Aufhebung des Wollens, der Erlösung durch Freiheit der Überwindung und Vernichtung der Welt." (WWV: 449, 453) Wittgenstein entkommt den Bedrängnissen der Erfahrungswelt, dem Druck der Gefühle, und dem Drang der Triebe durch „Arbeit." Das Wort bezeichnet in seinem Munde nicht die Soldatenarbeit oder irgendeine andere physische Beschäftigung sondern die Denkarbeit. Diese Arbeit soll dabei zu einem bestimmten Ziel führen: und das ist eine besondere Art des Sehens, der er den Namen „Übersicht" gibt. Das Ziel des Denkens ist ihm nicht die Formulierung einer Reihe theoretischer Erkenntnissen, sondern das Erhalten eines Überblicks. Ich zitiere einige Notizen aus den *Geheimen Tagebüchern:*

> 25. 9. 14: Ziemlich viel gearbeitet, aber ohne rechte Zuversicht. Es fehlt mir immer noch der Überblick, und dadurch erscheint das Problem unübersehbar. (GT 1991: 25)
> 12. 11. 14: Ziemlich viel gearbeitet, *aber ohne rechte Klarheit des Sehens.* (GT 1991: 41)
> 13. 11. 14: Das klare Sehen will sich nicht einstellen. (GT 1991: 42)
> 15. 11. 14: Wieder keine Klarheit des Sehens, obwohl ich ganz offenbar vor der Lösung der tiefsten Fragen stehe, daß ich mir fast die Nase daran stoße!!! Mein Geist ist eben jetzt dafür einfach blind! Ich fühle, daß ich *an dem Tor* DARAN stehe, kann es aber nicht klar genug sehen, um es öffnen zu können. (GT 1991: 43)
> 13. 1. 15: Ich sehe die Sachen nicht frisch, sondern alltäglich ohne Leben. Es ist als ob eine Flamme erloschen wäre und ich muß warten, bis sie von selbst wieder zu brennen anfängt. Mein Geist aber ist rege. Ich denke. (GT 1991: 54)

Im Verfolgen dieses klaren Sehens, sucht er nach ähnlichen Geistern. Tolstoy, Emerson, aber auch Nietzsche kommen ihm zur Hilfe.

> 2. 9. 14: „Gestern fing ich an in Tolstois "Erläuterungen zu den Evangelien" zu lesen. Ein herrliches Werk. Es ist mir aber noch nicht das, was ich davon erwarte." 15. 11. 14: „Lese jetzt in Emersons ‚Essays'. Vielleicht werden sie einen guten Einfluß auf mich haben." 8. 12. 14: „Nietzsches Band 8 gekauft und darin gelesen. Bin stark berührt von seiner Feindschaft gegen das Christentum. Denn auch in seinen Schriften ist etwas Wahres." (GT 1991: 20, 42, 49)

In diesen Überlegungen geht es Wittgenstein um eine Reihe von Einsichten. Erstens, im Geiste von Tolstoy: "Der Mensch ist *ohnmächtig* im Fleische aber *frei* durch den Geist." (GT 1991: 21) Der Einzelwille kann die Welt nicht verändern, genau wie Schopenhauer es ihn gelehrt hat. Wittgenstein notiert: „Ich kann in einer Stunde sterben, ich kann in einem Monat sterben oder erst in ein paar Jahren. Ich kann es nicht wissen und nicht dafür oder dagegen tun. *So ist dies Leben.*" Und so fragt er sich: „Wie muß ich also leben, um in jedem Augenblick zu bestehen?" (GT 1991: 28) Und darauf hat er sich bereits kurz zuvor eine Antwort gegeben: „Der Mensch darf nicht vom Zufall abhängen. Weder vom günstigen noch vom ungünstigen." (GT 1991: 27) Das heißt auch, nicht mehr von der Welt abzuhängen, insofern alles Geschehen und So-Sein in ihr zufällig ist. Und damit sind wir beim ersten Satz des *Tractatus* angekommen.

Die letzten, kurzen Eintragungen in Wittgensteins *Geheimen Tagebüchern* vom 6. Juli bis zum 19. August 1916 werfen noch einmal ein wesentliches Licht auf den Ausgang des *Tractatus* und damit auch auf dessen philosophische Bedeutung. Am 4. Juni 1916 hatte der Russische General Brusilov eine erfolgreiche Offensive gegen die österreichische Ostfront begonnen. Wittgenstein war von Anfang an in die heftigen Kämpfe verwickelt, die über drei Monate dauerten und den Österreichern heftigste Verluste brachte. Wittgensteins eigene Einheit verlor 12,5000 von 16,000 Mann und mehr als 300,000 österreichische Soldaten gerieten in russische Gefangenschaft. Wittgenstein selbst erhielt in diesen Kämpfen mehrere Tapferkeitsmedaillen und wurde in dieser Zeit mehrmals befördert. Von den wenigen Notizen in den *Geheimen Tagebüchern* ist klar, dass Wittgenstein nicht erwartete die Offensive zu überleben. Diese Ereignisse stehen in direktem Zusammenhang mit Wittgensteins philosophischen Gedankengängen in dieser Periode. Im dritten der erhaltenen *Notebooks* ändert sich der Ton seiner philosophischen Überlegungen radikal. Während sich Wittgenstein vom Kriegsanfang bis zum Juni 1916 fast ausschließlich mit logischen und metaphysischen Fragen befasst hatte, schreibt er am 11. Juni, also eine Woche nach Beginn der Brusilov Offensive, überraschend: „Was weiss ich über Gott?" (GT 1991: 72) Von diesem Augenblick an beschäftigt sich das philosophische Tagebuch mit Fragen nach dem Sinn des Lebens, der Natur des Ichs, mit Welt und Wille, mit Sünde und Vergebung, mit Leben, Tod und Selbstmord – Themen, die sich auch auf den letzten Seiten des *Tractatus* widerspiegeln. Wenn man all dies ins Auge fasst, ist man zu sagen geneigt, dass der *Tractatus* schließlich und vor allem (auch) ein Kriegsbuch ist. Die Erfahrungswelt, die der Text hinter sich zu lassen strebt, ist hier in ihrer Abwesenheit doch wieder präsent. Die Zufälligkeit der Welt, was es heißt, diese richtig zu sehen, und was die ethischen Folgerungen sind, die sich daraus ergeben, formen die Grundstruktur des gesamten Werkes.

Literatur

Baum, Wilhelm et al. (1991): *Geheime Tagebücher*, Wien: Turia & Kant.
Luckhardt, C. G. (1979): *Wittgenstein. Sources and Perspectives*. Ithaca, N. Y.: Cornell University Press.
Schopenhauer, Arthur (1960): *Die Welt als Wille und Vorstellung* I, Stuttgart/Frankfurt: Cotta-Insel.
Stern, David G. et al. (2016): *Wittgenstein Lectures, Cambridge 1930–1933. From the Notes of G.E. Moore*. Cambridge: Cambridge University Press.

Index of Names

Allais, Lucy 44, 55
Anscombe, Gertrude Elizabeth Margaret 57, 412, 323f., 326ff.
Aristotle 166, 190, 193, 195
Audi, Robert 317, 320
Ayer, Alfred 24, 38
Azevedo, Ruben T. 237, 245

Baillargeon, Renée 185, 187f.
Bain, Alexander 49, 55
Baldwin, Thomas 49, 55
Banaji, Mahzarin R. 236, 238, 240, 243, 246
Baron Cohen, Simon 185
Baz, Avner 135f., 140, 142ff.
Bazzocchi, Luciano 380, 382, 387ff., 392f., 395
Beard, Robert W. 382f., 395f.
Beck, Harry 378
Beck, Jacob 164, 169
Bengson, John 305f., 320
Bense, Max 347
Benussi, Vittorio 343, 345
Berghofer, Philipp 303, 313, 320
Berkeley, George 39ff., 48f., 51, 55f., 123
Bermúdez, José Luis 328, 332
Biletzki, Anat 378, 395
Black, Max 384, 395
Block, Ned 227, 232
BonJour, Laurence 96, 103, 110f., 117f.
Boswell, James 39, 41, 50, 55f.
Botschuijver, Theo 349
Botvinick, Matthew 329, 332
Brandl, Johannes 113, 117f.
Breckenridge, Wylie 77
Brentano, Franz 96, 113, 118ff.
Brewer, Bill 23, 38, 78, 94, 116, 118
Broad, C. D. 192ff.
Broch, Hermann 413
Brogaard, Berit 199, 203ff., 207, 210f., 214f.
Bronfman, Zohar 227, 232
Brücke, Ernst 341
Burge, Tyler 23ff., 69, 71, 73, 87

Campbell, John 23, 38, 60f., 73

https://doi.org/10.1515/9783110657920-023

Carrasco, Marisa 225f., 232f.
Carruthers, Peter 217, 233
Cassam, Quassim 24, 38
Cecchi, Ariel S. 217, 232
Chalmers, David John 158, 169, 200, 215
Chaplin, George 236, 246
Chelazzi, L. 225, 232f.
Chisholm, Roderick Milton 111, 120, 133, 204, 208, 215
Chomanski, Bartek 199f., 214f.
Chomsky, Noam 179, 187
Chudnoff, Elijah 305f., 320, 200ff., 215
Church, Jennifer 306, 320
Churchland, Patricia 220, 232
Clark, Andy 241, 245
Cohen, Jonathan 329, 332
Condillac, Etienne Bonnot de 49, 55
Connolly, Kevin 320
Copi, Irving M. 382f., 395f.
Corbetta, Maurizio 203, 215
Correia, Fabrice 46f., 55
Correll, Joshua 236, 245
Crane, Tim 44, 55, 116, 118, 120, 122, 124, 133, 158, 169

Darwin, Erasmus 338
Davidson, Donald 59, 73, 103, 112f., 118
Davies, Martin 78, 94
Dawkins, Richard 175, 187
Deroy, Ophelia 235, 237, 239, 243, 245, 247
Descartes, René 59
Destutt de Tracy, Antoine 48f., 55
Dorsch, Fabian 63, 73
Dretske, Fred I. 88, 94, 156, 169
Drewes, J. 218, 232
Duchamp, Marcel 346

Erhard, Christopher 308, 320
Erismann, Theodor 346
Exner, Siegmund 341
Fales, Evan 110, 118
Farkas, Katalin 24, 38
Fechner, Theodor Gustav 340
Fine, Kit 46, 55

Fiocco, Marcello-Oreste 95, 99, 114, 118
Firestone, Chaz 199, 206, 215, 237, 239, 245, 228, 230, 232
Fish, William 61, 73
Fodor, Jerry A. 150, 169
Føllesdal, Dagfinn 122, 133
Foster, John 304, 320
Foucault, Michel 405
Frassle, S. 227, 232
Frazer, James George 400
Fréchette, Guillaume 119, 125, 133
Frege, Gottlob 155, 251f., 254, 256ff., 260, 263, 265, 267, 271, 273
French, Craig 120, 122, 128, 133
Friston, Karl J. 241f., 245f.
Fumerton, Richard 103, 110, 118

Geschkowski, Andreas 379, 395
Ghijsen, Harmen 305, 315, 320
Gibson, James J. 48, 55
Gibson, Kevin 382, 395
Gilbert, Charles D. 227, 232
Goethe, Johann Wolfgang 339
Goldman, Alvin 199, 215
Goldstone, Robert L. 217, 232
Grayling, Anthony C. 384f., 395
Greenwald, A. G. 238, 246
Gregory, Richard 129, 133
Grice, H. Paul 172, 187
Grzankowski, Alex 114, 118

Hacker, Peter 380f., 383, 389, 395
Haladjian, Harry 227, 233
Hallett, H. F. 39f., 49, 55
Hanson, Norwood Russell 220, 232
Harcourt, Edward 328f., 332
Harman, Gilbert 152, 169
Hartley, David 49, 55
Heck, Richard G. 156, 169
Heeger, David J. 225, 232
Hegde, Jay 227, 232
Heidegger, Martin 122, 133, 136, 146
Heinen, K. 218, 233
Helmholtz, Hermann 125ff., 133
Hempel, Carl 102, 118
Hentschläger, Kurt 351
Hering, Ewald 126f.

Herz, Marcus 338
Hickerson, Ryan 122, 134
Hohwy, Jakob 241, 246
Holyrod, Jules 238
Hopfinger, J. B. 225, 233
Howe, Catherine 207, 215
Huemer, Michael 222, 233, 305, 314ff., 320f.
Hugenberg, Kurt 236, 246
Hume, David 23f., 34ff., 43ff., 48, 55, 120, 134
Husserl, Edmund 122, 133f., 152, 303, 305ff., 311f., 320f.
Hutto, Daniel 66, 73

Itti, Laurent 227, 233

Jablonski, Nina G. 236, 246
Jackson, Frank 83, 94
Jacob, Pierre 171, 174f., 187
Jacquette, Dale 122, 134
Jenkins, Carrie 46, 55
Johnson, Samuel 39ff., 48ff., 55f.
Johnston, Mark 84, 94
Julesz, Béla 349
Jurin, James 338

Kammers, Marjolein P. M. 331f.
Kang, Jinho 379, 395
Kant, Immanuel 144
Kastner, Sabine 225ff., 230f., 233
Kemp, Gary 135, 140, 146
Kentridge, Bob 203, 215
Kersten, Daniel 227, 232
Koch, Christof 227, 233
Koffka, Kurt 345
Kohler, Ivo 346
Köhler, Wolfgang 345
Koksvik, Ole 306, 321
Kosslyn, Stephen 84, 94
Kovács, Ágnes Melinda 184, 187
Kraft, Tim 380f., 395
Kriegel, Uriah 149, 153, 157, 159, 163, 169
Kripke, Saul 67, 73
Kuhn, Thomas 220, 233
Külpe, Oswald 345
Kulvicki, John 190ff., 194
Kuusela, Oskari 380, 395

Lackner, James R. 329, 332
Lamme, V. A. F. 218, 233f.
Langheinrich, Ulf 351
Laventhol, Jonathan 387f., 392, 395
Lavoisier, Antoine Laurent de 401
Leddington, Jason 190, 194
Levin, Daniel T. 236, 238, 240, 243, 246
Li, Jun 227, 232
Ling, S. 225f., 233
Locke, John 25, 30, 38, 123
Logue, Heather 117f.
Lowe, Edward Jonathan 46, 55
Luckhardt, Charles Grant 400, 415
Lupyan, Gary 217, 233, 241, 246
Lyons, Jack 199, 201, 214f.

Mach, Ernst 123, 338, 341f., 345
Mackie, John Leslie 25
MacPherson, Fiona 199, 214f., 237
Madary, Michael 306, 311, 321
Malebranche, Nicolas 49, 56
Malone, Edmund 41, 55
Markie, Peter 199, 215f., 315ff., 319, 321
Martin, Michael G. F. 78, 94, 116, 118
Marty, Anton 130, 134
Massin, Olivier 39, 47, 49ff., 56
Mayer, Verena 379f., 382, 395
McDowell, John 23, 35f., 38, 63, 67ff., 73, 96, 102, 104ff., 118, 122, 134, 252ff., 257, 265ff., 329, 332
McGrath, Matthew 199, 208, 209, 216, 222, 233
McGuinness, Brian 379f., 382, 390, 396f.
McLuhan, Marshall 347
Meinong, Alexius 343, 345
Merleau-Ponty, Maurice 143ff.
Mill, John Stuart 123
Millikan, Ruth G. 171ff.
Molles, Abraham A. 347
Montemayor, Carlos 227, 233
Moore, George Edward 399, 401, 415
Mras, Gabriele 135, 140, 146
Mulhall, Stephen 136, 140, 146
Müller, Johannes 126ff., 134
Myin, Erik 66, 73

Neander, Karen 174, 188

Newen, Albert 217, 234, 235, 237, 246
Nobre, A. C. 229f., 234
Noë, Alva 330, 332

O'Regan, Kevin 330, 332
O'Shaughnessy, Brian 323, 332
O'Shea, Jacinta 229, 233
Ofan, Renana H. 236, 246
Ogilivie, Ryan 217, 233
Onishi, Kristine H. 185, 188
Oppel, Johann J. 338

Paillard, Jacques 330, 332
Pappenheimer, Willi 352
Pasin, Michele 387, 396
Pasnau, Robert 190, 195
Patey, Douglas Lane 39f., 49, 56
Payne, B. Keith 236, 246
Perner, Josef 185, 188
Phillips, Ben 153, 164, 169
Pietroski, Paul 174, 188
Pilch, Martin 380, 390, 396
Pitt, David 151, 169
Plateau, Joseph 340ff.
Poggendorff, Johann C. 342, 355
Porterfield, William 338
Potter, Michael 380, 396
Price, Henry Habberley 123, 134
Proust, Joëlle 243, 246
Pryor, James 103, 107, 118, 306, 321
Purkinje, Jan Evangelista 338f.
Purves, Dale 207, 215
Putnam, Hilary 59, 61, 65, 67, 73
Pylyshyn, Zenon 207, 216, 220, 230, 233, 237, 246

Raftopoulos, Athanassios 217, 219, 221ff., 227, 233f., 237, 247
Ratcliffe, Matthew 310, 321
Rawls, John 409
Recanati, François 164f., 169
Reid, Thomas 41, 43f., 48, 56
Ress, David 225, 232
Reynolds, J. H. 225, 233
Rigoli, Francesco 239, 246
Robinson, Howard 23f., 34, 37f., 131, 134
Roget, Peter Mark 339

Rorty, Richard 103, 118
Russell, Bertrand 30, 32, 86

Sainsbury, Mark 81, 93f.
Scheler, Max 48f., 56
Schellenberg, Susanna 60, 63f., 72f. 87, 117ff.
Schilling, Alfons 348f.
Schlick, Moritz 102, 118
Schmitz, Michael 57, 70, 73
Scholl, Brian J. 199, 206, 215, 228, 230, 232, 237, 239, 245,
Schopenhauer, Arthur 403ff., 410, 413ff.
Schulte, Joachim 135ff., 140, 146
Scott-Philipps, Tom 173, 188
Searle, John R. 60, 65, 67, 70, 72f., 79, 94, 135ff., 137ff., 163ff.
Sellars, Wilfrid 68, 103, 118, 220, 234, 389
Shaw, Jeffrey 349
Shea, Nicholas 243, 246
Shulman, Gordon L. 203, 215
Siegel, Susanna 43, 56, 199f., 202f., 206, 216, 219f., 222, 230, 234, 237, 246, 304f., 318, 321
Siewert, Charles 151, 169
Silins, Nicholas 216
Silver, Bruce 39, 56
Simons, Peter 46, 56
Smith, Barry 120, 134
Smith, Joel 306, 311, 321
Smithies, Declan 306, 315, 321
Sorabji, Richard 193, 195
Sperber, Dan 172, 188
Sporer, Siegfried Ludwig 236, 246
Stalnaker, Robert 156, 170
Stampe, Dennis 158, 170
Stenius, Erik 383f., 396
Stepanova, Elena V. 236, 247
Stern, David 415, 377ff., 391, 393, 396, 399f.
Steup, Matthias 199, 216
Stokes, Dustin 221, 234
Stratton, George 346
Strawson, Peter F. 44, 56, 86f., 94
Strube, Michael J. 236, 247
Stumpf, Carl 130, 134
Sturgeon, Scott 305, 321

Sweetman, Joseph 238, 246

Talbot, William Henry Fox 339f.
Taylor, P. C. J. 229f., 234
Tenenbaum, Sergio 158, 170
Textor, Mark 119, 133f.
Thiel, Midori Kono 352
Thiel, Tamiko 352
Tooley, Michael 315, 321
Travis, Charles 66, 72f., 116, 118, 135f., 138ff., 142f., 145f.
Trump, Donald 410
Tucker, Chris 199, 203, 208, 214ff., 222, 233f., 314f., 320f.
Tye, Michael 77, 81, 85, 88, 93f., 304, 321

Ungerleider, Leslie G. 225, 233

Vandenbroucke, A. R. F. 227, 234
Vetter, Petra 217, 234, 237, 246
Vignemont, Frédérique de 323, 330ff.

Watzl, Sebastian 203, 214, 216
Weibel, Peter 349ff.
Wellman, Henry 185, 188
Wells, William Charles 338
Wertheimer, Max 343ff.
Wheatstone, Charles 342
Williams, Bernard 49, 56
Williamson, Timothy 89, 94
Wilson, Deirdre 172, 188
Wiltsche, Harald A. 303, 312, 315, 321
Wimmer, Heinz 185, 188
Winkler, Kenneth P. 54, 56
Witasek, Stephan 345
Wittgenstein, Ludwig 57, 62, 71, 73, 135ff., 140ff., 251f., 269, 273, 323ff., 330, 332f., 359ff., 370, 373, 377ff., 381ff., 389ff., 395ff., 399ff., 406ff.
Wollheim, Richard 141, 143, 146
Wright, Georg Henrik von 390f., 393, 396
Wu, Wayne 202, 216

Yablo, Stephen 200, 216

Zeimbekis, John 237, 247

www.ingramcontent.com/pod-product-compliance
Lightning Source LLC
Chambersburg PA
CBHW051554230426
43668CB00013B/1842